A GUIDE BRITAIN'S CONSERVATION HERITAGE

A GUIDE TO BRITAIN'S CONSERVATION HERITAGE

Franklyn Perring

Published in association with

R · S · N · C
The Wildlife Trusts
PARTNERSHIP

Thorsons
An Imprint of HarperCollins*Publishers*

Thorsons
An Imprint of GraftonBooks
A Division of HarperCollins*Publishers*
77-85 Fulham Palace Road,
Hammersmith, London W6 8JB

Published by Thorsons 1991
10 9 8 7 6 5 4 3 2 1

A CIP catalogue record for this book
is available from the British Library

ISBN 0-7225-2138-3

Typeset by Harper Phototypesetters Limited,
Northampton, England

Printed in Great Britain by
Mackays of Chatham, Kent

CONTENTS

FOREWORD

For anyone who has an interest in the British countryside and its wildlife, this book is an essential companion. With your binoculars and field guides, it will find a permanent place in your car or knapsack. In the past, the location of many of Britain's nature reserves run by the 46 Wildlife and Conservation Trusts have been a well-kept secret, their charms known only to a handful of Trust members and dedicated enthusiasts. This was not a deliberate policy but a consequence of the low profile of the Trusts, of their lack of funds to pay for publicity and educational material.

Now, thanks partly to the British Wildlife Appeal, the work of the RSNC and the Trusts is more widely known. Frank Perring's book provides the key that will unlock the door to many of their priceless treasures. He has packed it with practical information on when to go to the reserves, how to reach them, what to look for and on other places of interest you may like to visit on your tour. It is an ideal gift for anyone who cares about our countryside. This book deserves to be successful not only because a percentage of royalties go to the RSNC but because it may make people realize what an excellent job their Trusts are doing.

Julian Pettifer

ABBREVIATIONS

AONB = Area of Outstanding Natural Beauty
ASI = Area of Scientific Importance (Northern Ireland)
A/V = Audio-visual
AYR = Open all year round
BHs = Bank Holidays
CP   = Car park
[D] = Toilet for disabled
FC   = Forestry Commission
FNR = Forest Nature Reserve
ha   = Hectare (1 ha = 2.47 acres)
LNR = Local Nature Reserve
NCC = Nature Conservancy Council
NNR = National Nature Reserve
NT   = National Trust
NTS = National Trust for Scotland
PNNR = Proposed National Nature Reserve
RSNC = Royal Society for Nature Conservation
RSPB = Royal Society for the Protection of Birds
SSSI = Site of Special Scientific Interest
T   = Toilet
TI   = Tourist Information (Office)
W/Es = Week-ends

INTRODUCTION

The RSNC Wildlife Trusts Partnership is the largest voluntary organization in the UK concerned with all aspects of wildlife protection. It is a partnership of 47 Wildlife Trusts, 50 Urban Wildlife Groups and WATCH, the junior wing, joining forces for nature both locally and nationally.

There are over 3000 nature reserves and similar places in Britain, managed with the primary aim of protecting wildlife. They vary in size from 63,000 acres, nearly 100 square miles, in the Cairngorms, to 800 square yards on a Northamptonshire farm where a rare hellebore is safeguarded. Two out of every three reserves in Britain are owned or cared for by one of the Wildlife Trusts.

The book sets out to locate and describe 325 reserves in England, Wales, Scotland and Northern Ireland. They have been carefully chosen so that they are fairly evenly spread and representative of the range of wildlife habitats which occur in that part of the country. In addition, and most importantly, they have been selected because they are places which are not difficult to find, have reasonable parking space and provide information on site, or nearby, which will help you to enjoy and understand the reserve when you visit it.

The typical reserve described is a place in the countryside where you drive along a lane to a small car park, collect a leaflet from a dispenser or an Information Centre, read a descriptive notice board and set off on a well-marked, easily walked, path on a round trip of 1-2 hours with perhaps a hide or a viewpoint on the way—ideal for a family half-day outing.

Because this is the RSNC Guide and a proportion of the royalties go towards the work of the Wildlife and Conservation Trusts, priority in choosing the six or so reserves that illustrate each county or region has been given to Trust reserves—but it is by no means an exclusive account of their properties. Not all Trusts have enough reserves which meet the criteria for selection or have reserves which cover the range of habitats adequately—so reserves of all the other major conservation organizations have also been included: Nature Conservancy Council, National Trust, National Trust for Scotland, Royal Society for the Protection of Birds, Wildfowl and Wetlands Trust, Woodland Trust, Forestry Commission and several Local Authorities.

The Trusts have offices and staff in every county and have an intimate knowledge of their area, so they are the best people to turn to for advice, and nearly all have guides and leaflets about all the reserves which are open to the public. Their addresses and telephone numbers have been given within each section.

Though I have sought advice in deciding what to include and what to leave out, the final selection has been mine—a personal choice based on experience gained during my eight years as General Secretary of RSNC.

My most difficult decision has been deciding to omit reserves in or near big cities, notably London and Birmingham, though both have vigorous and effective Trusts with many urban reserves. Their addresses and telephone numbers are included in the list of other organizations. However, this is essentially a book for those who want to get out into the countryside.

I am grateful to all the Trusts and their staff who found time in their over-busy days to stop and help me when I called, who provided so many books and leaflets, and who read and commented, often at great length, on my first drafts on their area. Ultimately any mistakes which remain are my responsibility but will not, I hope, diminish your enjoyment of the wonderful places for wildlife which are open to you in every corner of the kingdom.

Oundle,
1991

HOW TO USE THIS GUIDE

Sites marked on the regional maps at the beginning of each section in this book are numbered to correspond with the sites described in the text. They are intended as a rough regional guide. Locating the reserves more precisely is most easily done using the appropriate 1:50,000 map in the Landranger Series published by Ordnance Survey. These are referred to at the beginning of each site description. Each map shows a grid, the smallest unit of which is a 1 km square. Except for a very few large reserves, where the reference is to a 10 km square, the letters and numbers after the map number are a reference to the 1 km square in which the reserve occurs.

The letters identify the 100 km square. The first pair of numbers after the letters refers to those along the bottom and top of the map, the second pair to those along both sides of the map: the lines joining these numbers cross at the bottom left hand corner of the 1 km square in which the reserve occurs. That the square is the correct one can be checked by the first part of the description of the location which is, with few exceptions, a straight line (not by road) measurement of the distance of the reserve from a nearby town or village—in miles. The information which then follows is to help visitors reach the entrance or entrances to the reserve. A more exact reference is given to the car park or parking space under **Access,** and to the Visitor Centre, if there is one, under **Information**.

E N G L A N D

SOUTH-WEST

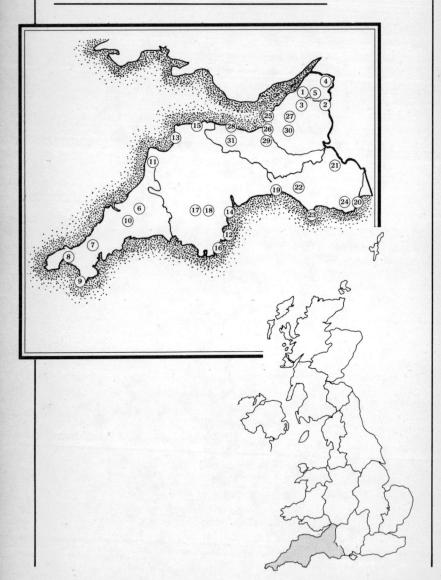

Avon

Although Avon is a small county embracing the two large cities of Bristol and Bath, it is remarkably endowed with areas of wilderness and wildlife. This is partly because of the diverse and complex geology and partly because of the extensive urbanization which covers so much of it.

The most important and, in many ways, most natural site is in the heart of the city of Bristol—*the Avon Gorge*, which cuts a cleft 245 ft deep through the Carboniferous limestone below the famous Clifton Suspension Bridge. There are few places in Britain with so many rare and local species of wild plants in such a small area, here including two trees found nowhere else in the world. For Bristol botanists, Mecca is to the West.

A much smaller wildlife area, almost engulfed by buildings, is tucked away behind the Avon Wildlife Trust headquarters within 300 yds of the University where the Trust has turned 5 acres of municipal parkland on Brandon Hill into a Nature Park. It contains a flower-rich meadow, woodland, a pond and a butterfly garden.

This creative approach to wildlife habitats is again superbly demonstrated by the Avon Trust at its *Willsbridge Mill* Centre, 4 miles south-east of Bristol. On a small site beside a swiftly flowing stream, adaptation, restoration and re-creation have turned 20 acres of derelict landscape and ruined buildings into a delightful area for studying plants and animals, or for just enjoying a woodland walk. It is also a good place to go to find out what is happening to wildlife in Avon as a whole.

Other sites in Avon owe less to direct creative activity and more to accident. To create the beauty of Bath the stonemasons obtained their materials from the surrounding hills, in particular from the great bluff of oolitic limestone above Bathford to the east, surmounted today by the Victorian *Brown's Folly*, which now has a reserve named after it. The mining of the stone left a 'bench' and 'crag' type of landscape now partially hidden by trees, and a haven for lime-loving flowers.

Avon has no natural lakes but it does have an ever-growing population demanding water. A series of reservoirs has been developed in low-lying valleys between the River Avon and the Mendips south of Bristol round the base of the 765 ft Dundry Hill. The largest and most recent of these is the *Chew Valley Lake* which, together with Blagdon close by, forms one of the most important refuges for wildfowl in the south-west. These lakes are so large that they can be used for sailing and angling and other countryside pursuits without materially affecting their value for birds.

On the other side of the county near the Gloucestershire border quiet enjoyment of the countryside is *de rigueur*—in Wellington boots. Here in the clay vale, on the Lias clays between the Carboniferous and Jurassic limestones, formerly lay the Royal Forest of Kingswood. An impression of that dark, dank, woodland wilderness can be gained from a walk through Lower Woods and into the Gloucestershire Trust reserve of *Wetmoor* and along its 'trenches', or hollow rides, beneath its ancient oaks—a time warp only 10 miles from the bustle and brusqueness of Bristol and Bath.

- Avon Wildlife Trust (AWT), The Old Police Station, 32 Jacob's Wells Road, Bristol BS8 1DR. 0272 268018.
- Gloucestershire Trust for Nature Conservation (GTNC), Church House, Standish, Stonehouse, Gloucester GL10 3EU. 0453 822761.

Avon Gorge

1

Map 172 ST55-74- 260 acres (105 ha)
West bank of River Avon north of Clifton Suspension Bridge in Bristol. NNR Mixed plateau oak/ash woods, wooded limestone gorge.

Access AYR on foot from two CPs to a network of paths.

1. off A369 Bristol to Portishead road 3 miles east of Exit 19 off M5: turn left at Gatehouse towards Gorge to FC CP at ST553740.
2. on east side of Suspension Bridge on Clifton Downs at ST564741 then walk across bridge and turn right down to the Avon Walkway.

Information Nothing on site: *Avon Gorge* ed. A.E.Frey from bookshops in Bristol.

History The River Avon has cut a deep gorge through the Carboniferous limestone. Above the cliffs, on the plateau where the soils are mainly marl and clay, mixed woods of pedunculate oak, ash, small-leaved lime and wych-elm have developed with occasional yew, and sessile oak on occasional bands of sandstone. On the limestone of the steep gorge slopes the open woodland carries a large number of endemic or local whitebeams, notably *Sorbus bristoliensis* and *S. willmottiana*, known nowhere else in the world.

In clearings between the trees, often on inaccessible rocks, a large number of wild flowers of very limited distribution in Britain are to be found.

What to See Flowers of particular interest on the cliffs include spiked speedwell, hutchinsia, Bristol rock-cress, spring cinquefoil, honewort and dwarf sedge, whilst the woods have columbine, fingered sedge, bird's-nest orchid, wild madder, ivy broomrape, toothwort and green hellebore.

Amongst a long list of butterflies silver-washed fritillary, marbled white, ringlet, speckled wood, purple hairstreak and chalkhill blue are most noteworthy. Woodland birds include sparrowhawk, lesser spotted woodpecker, willow, wood and garden warblers and hawfinch.

Picnic site at FC CP.

Wheelchairs have some access, with assistance, from FC CP.

Brown's Folly

2

Map 172 ST79-66- 95 acres (38 ha)
3 miles north-east of Bath above Bathford via A4 east from Bath: turn onto A363

and, immediately after passing under a railway bridge, take left turn onto minor road to Kingsdown: after ½ mile turn right towards Monkton Farleigh for reserve on right at top of very steep hill. SSSI. Geology: limestone woods, scrub and grassland.

Access   AYR on foot from CP at ST799661 to two way-marked trails on good paths (muddy in winter).

Information   Nothing on site.

History   The hill on which the Folly stands is famous as the origin of Bath stone from which so much of that fair city was built. High above the River Avon it was cut into terraces and cliffs whose scars have since been covered in a mixture of wood, scrub and grassland. Mines were driven into the hillside which now house an important colony of greater horseshoe bats. (Please do not enter old mine shafts.)

What to See   Limestone grassland plants include woolly thistle, common rock-rose, wild thyme and harebell whilst the open woodland holds fly orchid, broad-leaved and white helleborines. Of particular interest here is spiked star-of-Bethlehem, locally known as Bath asparagus, formerly gathered locally and sold in Bath market as an acceptable substitute for the real thing. There are many butterflies including marbled white and green hairstreak and the green tiger beetle also occurs.

Chew Valley Lake   3

Map 172 ST56-60-1200 acres (485 ha)
7 miles south of Bristol east of B3114 at Chew Stoke. SSSI. Waders and waterfowl.

Access   AYR from numerous CPs and parking places round periphery of lake. The most important are at the Visitor Centre on the east side of the dam at the north end at ST571606, on the road at the south end at Herriott's Bridge at ST570581 and on Heron's Green Bay at ST555591.

Information   Water and Wildlife exhibition at the Visitor Centre which also sells leaflets and a book *The Natural History of the Chew Valley* ed. Rowland Jones : open daily 10 a.m.–sunset.

History   This reservoir, created in 1953, has since become one of the most ornithologically important in Britain, especially for wildfowl in winter, but it also attracts large numbers of migrating waders to its muddy margins and warblers and other small birds to extensive areas of reed-bed, scrub and woodland along the shoreline.

What to See   In winter Bewick's swan regularly visit along with gadwall, pintail, smew, goldeneye and goosander. A feature is the ruddy duck which first bred in Britain here. Migrating waders, mainly in the autumn, include knot, golden plover, curlew sandpiper, dunlin, ruff, snipe, black-tailed godwit, greenshank and common sandpiper.

T[D] Refreshments at Visitor Centre: picnic sites.
Wheelchairs have access to good paths and to a hide at Chew.

Wetmoor 4

Map 172 ST74-87- 55 acres (22 ha)
1¼ miles east of Wickwar off B4060 road to Wotton under Edge, forking right
for Inglestone Common. Opposite Inglestone Farm take track to Lower Woods
Lodge where there is limited parking. SSSI. Wet woods of pedunculate and sessile
oak.

Access AYR on foot from parking space 400 yds south to Shepherd's Knap at
ST745877 which is the entrance to the reserve. Paths are very muddy, even in
summer.

Information Nothing on site: booklet from GTNC. Included in *Wildlife
Walkabouts: South Cotswold and North Avon* by Rosemary Teverson from local
bookshops.

History Ancient oakwood overlies mainly heavy, poorly drained clay with
dominant pedunculate oak but, in more acid better-drained, patches, sessile oak
occurs. It once formed part of a much larger Royal Hunting Forest which
extended through the Vale of Berkeley to Bristol. The understorey of hazel, ash
and field maple was coppiced from about the thirteenth century whilst suitable
ash and oak were left as standards. Blocks of woodland were separated by banks
and ditches, and parallel banks, known as 'trenches', are a feature. Many of the
trenches were named after woodsmen and are still in use today.

What to See Interesting trees and shrubs include Midland hawthorn, wild
service, spindle and buckthorn whilst moschatel, agrimony, pendulous sedge,
thin-spiked wood-sedge, violet helleborine, archangel, bird's-nest orchid and
herb-Paris are some of the notable woodland flowers.

Badger and fox visit the wood and, amongst the smaller mammals, dormouse,
short-tailed vole, wood mouse and yellow-necked mouse have all been recorded.
Nearly 40 species of birds breed in, or close to, the reserve including blackcap,
chiffchaff, all three woodpeckers, cuckoo, garden and wood warblers, goldcrest,
nightingale, nuthatch, treecreeper and tawny owl. There are almost as many
(35) butterflies on the list such as brown, green and purple hairstreak, five
species of fritillary, four skippers and white admiral.

Willsbridge Mill 5

Map 172 ST66-70-20 acres (8 ha)
4 miles south-east of Bristol off A431 road to Bath in Long Beach Road, a turning
to left 400 yds beyond Longwell Green Church Woods. Scrub, meadows, pond
and stream: wildlife garden.

Access AYR on foot from CP at ST665710 on good way-marked trail of over
1 mile.

Information   Trail guide and historical leaflet from Visitor Centre at Mill building 400 yds through woods: open daily (except Mon other than BHs) April–October 10 a.m.–5 p.m. Visitor Centre has wildlife and historical exhibition.

History   The Willsbridge Valley lies at the south end of the former Kingswood Forest, most of which was cleared in the seventeenth century and from which coal was mined as early as 1228 and continued until 1904. The first Mill was built about 1716 and the water from the dammed Siston Brook used to drive machinery to manufacture iron roofing sheets and iron bars using raw iron imported from Russia. The present Mill was built to grind corn in 1820 and continued, with a turbine which eventually replaced the water-wheel, until the early 1970s. The derelict building was leased to AWT in 1981 and, after extensive building and restoration, was opened to the public in 1985.

What to See   The wooded stream attracts kingfisher and grey wagtail and occasional dipper, whilst the bramble-covered banks have food for migrating fieldfare and redwing. In dense scrub blackcap, chiffchaff and nightingale may be heard. Butterflies include comma, gatekeeper and speckled wood whilst two ponds, created on the site of the former mill-pond, provide excellent breeding grounds for dragonflies and caddis flies. Many of the trees have been introduced but there are still native woodland flowers—bluebell, red campion, archangel and, on steep unshaded slopes of the brook, pignut, lousewort, betony, bugle and quaking-grass flourish.

T [D]. Refreshments, shop.

Wheelchairs have limited access to trail by contacting Mill in advance via Trust HQ.

Cornwall

Cornwall is the most westerly county in England, pointing like an arrow-head into the Atlantic and lashed by ferocious winds and storm-tossed seas. The sea dominates—no part is more than 15 miles from its 400 mile length of coast—and salt-laden winds stunt and bend the trees so that, even in the mists, which are frequent in this damp atmosphere, the lost traveller is provided with a sense of direction. But there are no trees to help on the granite heights of Bodmin Moor, which reaches 1377 ft on the summit of Brown Willy, just a wilderness of bare, open moorland with rocky tors, bogs, and infant streams. Bodmin is the highest and most easterly of the granite intrusions which form the spine of the county terminating, at the arrow head, in the great cliffs of Land's End. Sources of china-clay, tin and copper which have been exploited for centuries, these naturally bleak hills have been made more desolate by the wounds and scars of abandoned mines. However, leading from them, especially on their southern, sheltered sides, are bright streams in wooded valleys running into muddy estuaries where frost is rare and smoke rises vertically into a clear blue sky—the picture postcard Cornwall.

Coasts, moors and wooded streams are the setting for enjoying the wildlife of a county which has many sites of national and international importance, particularly on the coast. For botanists one place sticks out literally and metaphorically—*The Lizard* peninsula—one of half-a-dozen places like the Avon Gorge, Teesdale, Ben Lawers, and Breckland which have a high concentration of rare species because of an unusual combination of circumstances. At the Lizard it is the highly alkaline pre-Cambrian serpentine rocks, found elsewhere only in Anglesey and Scotland on exposed west-facing cliffs, which are so special: they reach their most exciting expression in Kynance Cove which, as Revd C.E.Johns wrote in 1848 in *A Week at The Lizard*, 'combines more objects of interest than any other part of the coast'.

Ornithologists too have a special place which attracts almost as many birdwatchers as birds. At *Hayle Estuary*, tucked in behind St Ives on the north coast, many American birds which have flown in off-course during their autumn migration, many of them carrying names of peculiar charm; long-billed dowitcher, semi-palmated sandpiper and laughing gull.

Hayle provides shelter for birds and men. There is a hide in the car park of a comfortable inn. Those who visit the moors must be more hardy. High up on Bodmin Moor at nearly 1000 ft lies a mysterious, isolated, unsheltered lake, *Dozmary Pool*, which gives refuge to wildfowl and waders in winter whilst dipper flash in the upper Fowey nearby. Birds have increased on the Moor since the construction of *Colliford Lake* reservoir where now some shelter is provided.

The granite intrusions become less formidable going westward, and the next, Hensbarrow, scarcely reaches 1000 ft. On its eastern flank nestle two fascinating reserves of the Cornwall Trust, *Red Moor* and *Breney Common*. Although scarred by mining in the past, colonization by willows and waterside plants has turned them into havens for all forms of wildlife, especially for butterflies and dragonflies. However, rich as these are, they cannot compete with the valley woodland. The shelter of their, often stunted, trees provides a luxuriance, especially of ferns and mosses, which is only found on this western fringe of Britain. Nowhere can this green haven be better enjoyed than along the paths which lead through the *Welcombe and Marsland Valleys* on the coast north of Bude. If that is too remote then there is much easier access to valley woods from the National Trust Centre at Lanhydrock, only a mile south of the A30 near Bodmin from which walks lead off into woods along the River Fowey.

Lanhydrock is an excellent place to gather information about the National Trust properties open to the public in Cornwall, many along that superb coastline. But for enjoyment of other wildlife areas inland also visit the headquarters of the Cornwall Trust for Nature Conservation at *Five Acres, Allet*, a mile south of the A30 near Truro.

- Cornwall Trust for Nature Conservation (CTNC) Five Acres, Allet, Truro TR4 9DJ. 0872 73939.

Colliford Lake and Dozmary Pool   6

Map 201 SX17-74- circa 600 acres (240 ha)
8 miles north-east of Bodmin, south of A30 near Bolventor. SSSI. Reservoir, natural pool, moorland.

Access   AYR on foot:

1. to Dozmary Pool: turn south in Bolventor just before dual carriageway begins, signposted to Dozmary Pool. The pool is on the east of the road after 2 miles; parking space on road.
2. to Colliford Lake: turn south off dual carriageway 1½ miles west of Bolventor to several CPs on south and west shores, e.g. SX165731 and SX176708.

Information   Leaflets on walks from Colliford Lake Park Centre on west side at SX166739.

History   Dozmary Pool was once an isolated lake on the heights of Bodmin Moor where it lies at almost 900 ft. But now it sits beside Colliford Lake—the largest reservoir in Cornwall which, with the surrounding moorland, has become a good site for watching ducks and waders especially in autumn and winter. The best views are from roads on the east and west sides.

What to See   The moorland flora over the granite is poor but has 'Atlantic' species such as western gorse, bristle bent, pale butterwort and, on rocks, English stonecrop: spring quillwort occurs on the shore of the Pool. Ducks include garganey, smew, goosander and the occasional scaup and ruddy duck whilst pectoral sandpiper and spotted crake are amongst the rarer waders. Dipper occur in the Fowey valley to the east whilst merlin, short-eared owl and hen harrier may occur in small numbers. Buzzard and raven are frequently seen over the moor whilst meadow pipit, skylark and stonechat are never far away.

   T. Refreshments are available at Colliford Lake Park. Wheelchairs have access to good paths at Colliford.

Five Acres, Allet   7

Map 204 SW79-48- 5 acres (2 ha)
3 miles north-west of Truro on B3284. Woodland, arboretum, hedges, pond, butterfly garden.

Access   AYR on foot from CP beside headquarters along well-marked paths.

Information   Nature trail leaflets from Visitor Centre in CP: open weekdays 9 a.m.–5 p.m.

History   This reserve was left to CTNC by two members, Dr and Mrs Allsop, with a bequest which helped towards the building of the Trust HQ at the south end.

What to See   The triangular site has been developed to demonstrate 10 different kinds of woodland with ponds, thickets, hedges and glades. Fallen trees have been left, a 'fungal alley' created, and a badger mound built. An arboretum has been planted which includes all the trees native to Cornwall. The woods are being managed to demonstrate traditional practices such as coppicing. A butterfly garden has been planted near the building.

T in Visitor Centre. Picnic site. Wheelchairs have access to the trail.

Hayle Estuary 8

Map 203 SW54-36- 220 acres (90 ha)
At the southern end of Hayle Estuary on B3074 to St Ives just after it leaves A30. SSSI. Sand and mud flats, salt marsh, pools for birds.

Access   AYR from CP of Old Quarry House Inn at SW545364; 50yds to hide at edge of estuary (free parking for RSPB members 10 a.m.–noon, 2–6 p.m.).

Information   *Guide to Wildlife of Hayle Estuary* from bar of Inn. From Easter–end October guided walks every Weds 10 a.m.–noon.

History   Hayle is the most south-westerly estuary in Britain: the first, or last, resting place for migrant wildfowl, waders or gulls. This has resulted in an impressive list of nearly 240 species of birds recorded here. The estuary has two arms, of which the western is more important, with large areas of sand and mud flats and a fringing saltmarsh. There is also an area of scrub and woodland beside the railway where the Hayle river enters the estuary which gives extra shelter.

What to See   Winter wildfowl include teal, wigeon, gadwall and shelduck with occasional goldeneye and red-breasted merganser. Amongst the waders knot, spotted redshank, greenshank and common sandpiper may be seen with whimbrel, little ringed plover, dunlin, sanderling and turnstone coming with the spring migration. Autumn brings even greater variety when little stint, curlew sandpiper and a number of American vagrants such as the pectoral sandpiper arrive. Little and Mediterranean gulls are regularly seen.

T [D]. Refreshments at the Old Quay House Inn (good crab sandwiches). Wheelchairs have access to shore and hide.

The Lizard 9

Maps 203 & 204 SW6-1- circa 3400 acres (1376 ha)
10 miles south of Helston on either side of A3083. NNR in part, cliff, heath, pools.

Access   AYR on foot from numerous points on roads, also from NT CP 1 mile west of Lizard Town at Kynance Cove SW685133.

Information   Leaflets, books and map from Lizard Centre on A3083 north of Ruan Pool at SW698161 or from NT Centre at Lanhydrock.

History   This flat-topped peninsula combines its unique geographical position of exposure to the highest incidence of gales in Britain with the large expanse of serpentine rocks, both of which strongly affect the plant communities present. Cornish heath, found only in Cornwall, is dominant over large areas inland together with much western gorse and a large number of unusual species, particularly in wet hollows. The coastline is especially important where the very stunted vegetation holds a large number of spring annuals and other early flowering species. The cliffs have many nesting sea-birds whilst Ruan Pool attracts a large number of dragonflies.

What to See Unusual plants on a very long list include, on the heath, dwarf rush, pygmy rush, chives, Dorset heath, bristle bent and pale butterwort, with pillwort around pools and, on the cliffs, wild asparagus, juniper, western, twin-headed, long-headed and upright clovers, hairy bird's-foot trefoil, hairy greenweed, fringed rupturewort, spring sandwort and thyme broomrape. Spring squill make a fine display in April, autumn squill in August and September. Sea-birds to be seen include gannet, fulmar, kittiwake, guillemot, razorbill, cormorant and shag. Adders are frequent on the heath where small copper and speckled wood butterflies also occur.

T. Refreshments (in summer) in Kynance Cove CP, and in Lizard Town.

Red Moor
10

Map 200 SX07-62- 60 acres (24 ha)

2½ miles north-west of Lostwithiel via B3268 Bodmin road to junction with B3269 at Sweetshouse. Take unsigned lane, by village pump, for 1 mile to small triangle of land with parking space at SX075622. SSSI. Heath, bog, ponds, willow carr.

Access AYR on foot along track going to left at triangle to entrance on right after 200 yds. Then on good paths along way-marked trail for about 1 mile.

Information Nature trail guide from CTNC.

History Until about 1900 open-cast mining for gravel from the granite here was carried out leaving a landscape of heaps and holes. The holes filled with water creating nine ponds whilst the heaps became covered in heathland. The ponds have a varied vegetation from open water to dense willow 'carr' whilst the heath ranges from heather moor to dense gorse. The Trust is managing the site to maintain the delicate balance needed to support a wide range of species.

What to See Interesting wild flowers include royal fern, bog asphodel, devil's-bit scabious, marsh cinquefoil, round-leaved sundew, southern marsh-orchid and gipsywort. Among resident and summer visiting birds are buzzard, sparrowhawk, willow tit, reed bunting, sedge and grasshopper warblers, tree pipit, coot, moorhen, mallard, yellowhammer and linnet. The pools have newts, frogs and toads whilst adder and grass-snake are frequent on the heath. The most unusual butterfly is the marsh fritillary on the wing in June: other butterflies and many different dragonflies also occur.

Wheelchairs have access to the trail at Red Moor.

Welcombe and Marsland Valleys
11

Map 190 SS21-18- 520 acres (208 ha)

7 miles to the north of Bude via A39 to Bideford turning west at Welcombe Cross

on minor road through Welcombe to parking area on clifftop ½ mile beyond village. SSSI. Sea shore, cliffs, grassland, heath, scrub, woodland.

Access   AYR on foot from CP at SS213180 along coastal footpath to Marsland Mouth and then, on public footpath, up the Marsland Valley.

Information   Notice boards in CP.

History   The reserve consists of two adjacent, steep-sided valleys running to the sea in tiny bays or mouths between impressive 400 ft cliffs in the wonderfully folded Culm Measures. The whole is an intimate mixture of small meadows, clearings in the, often scrubby, woods and high forest leading to a rich shoreline of rock-pools, cliffs and maritime grassland. The woods are a mixture of oak and ash with an understorey of hazel and holly with spindle and privet where the soils are deeper.

What to See   Amongst more than 320 flowering plants and ferns there are, in the woodland, primrose, bilberry, common cow-wheat and sanicle, and in the damper areas wild daffodil, yellow pimpernel, marsh marigold and meadowsweet. The coastal turf has early-purple orchid and spring squill at Easter with sea campion, thrift and kidney vetch later in the spring. Breeding birds include buzzard, kestrel, sparrowhawk, raven, dipper, grey wagtail, rock pipit, wheatear and stonechat whilst wood white, marbled white and five species of fritillary feature amongst the butterflies. There are several badger setts.

Devon

Devon is a large county, dominated by its coastline. Measuring over 70 miles from Ilfracombe in the north to Start Point in the south, and 60 from the outskirts of Lyme Regis in Dorset to the Cornish border near Launceston, it is the only English county to boast coasts facing all points of the compass, north, south, east and west. The journey through by road or rail is deflected towards the coast by the great granite mass of Dartmoor so that the Cornish Riviera Express, so loved by both jig-saw puzzle and calendar, is normally shown steaming along the coast between Exeter and Torquay. Devon's major rivers end in long, muddy estuaries which bring salt water and the evocative smell of rotting seaweed up to a dozen miles inland from the roar of the breakers—the Taw at Barnstaple, the Tamar above Plymouth, the Kingsbridge estuary, the Dart to Totnes, Teign to Newton Abbott, and Exe to Exeter.

Wildlife, too, shows to best advantage on the coast of Devon—uncultivatable coombes and cliffs lead down through woods to hidden coves; sand dunes, salt marsh, mud flat and shingle bar are all protected and represent some of the finest examples in Britain. Inland it is the moors which beckon—Exmoor in the north and the incomparable mysterious, misty, Dartmoor in the south. Woods descending to the sea are features of short valleys with swift streams which rush down from Exmoor to the north coast about Lynton—where there is access to

National Trust estates at Woody Bay and the *Heddon Valley*. This pattern is repeated, though from a lower altitude, in the streams which flow west or north round Hartland Point. Two of these near the Cornwall/Devon border north of Bude run through the mild, damp *Welcombe and Marsland Valleys* reserve of the Royal Society for Nature Conservation, and where autumn gives way to spring at the turn of every year.

Between Lynton and Hartland, facing the full force of the westerlies beating up the Bristol Channel, one of the finest sand dune systems in the kingdom rears its 100 ft front at *Braunton Burrows* by Barnstaple. Here the ground-up shells of millions of molluscs produces a sward of lime-loving flowers as rich as, or richer than, the white sands of the Outer Hebrides.

Nearly 50 years ago Braunton was the setting for the training of American troops for D-day landings in Normandy. On the east coast it was Slapton which they used—not dunes here but a firm, curving sweep of shingle for over 3 miles backed by the natural freshwater lake of *Slapton Ley*. Then a refuge for tired men coming over the sea, today its reed-beds offer a refuge to birds sheltering from storms at sea or frost and snow inland.

Food, and shelter, is provided for birds in the Exe estuary further north. This attracts the largest concentration of wildfowl in the region—indeed it is one of the most important wintering grounds in the northern half of Europe, regularly being host to 1500 dark-bellied Brent Geese, 5000 wigeon, 350 teal, 900 mallard and 10 other species. Many of these can be watched, in the season, from a hide on the north side of the sandy spit of *Dawlish Warren*, where in spring the major attraction is the tiny sand crocus.

Elsewhere it is the cliffs which fascinate. *Berry Head* is one of the only breeding sites for auks in southern England and has great importance for plants. There are a small number of sites in Britain which hold large concentrations of rare lime-loving species on cliffs which may never have been densely covered by trees: in the south-west Avon Gorge was one, Brean Down another, and Berry Head is a third—it shares honewort with the former and white rock-rose with the latter. Any rare plants on the cliffs along the *Axmouth to Lyme Regis Undercliffs* would have dropped into the Channel thousands of years ago but this geological phenomenon, with its tangled terrain and sub-tropical flora provides another example of the variety of the Devon coastline.

The contrast between the luxuriance of Axmouth and the bleakness of Dartmoor could hardly be greater. Much of Dartmoor is species-poor moorland which is not a botanist's delight for long. Thankfully Dartmoor is not *all* like that and, at over 1200 ft in the centre, there is the sudden relief of *Wistman's Wood*, the gnarled woodland whose trees shelter large numbers of epiphytes: plants—such as moss and lichen—growing on other plants. This occurs even on the exposed west-wind facing hillside. But, on the east side, a few hundred feet lower, the woods feel quite different, mild and balmy; you can wander through *Yarner Wood*, full of bird-song in the spring and carpeted with primroses even before February is out.

Away from the tors, Devon wildlife can be enjoyed at all seasons—but especially along that wondrous coast.

Devon Wildlife Trust (DWT) 35 New Bridge Street, Exeter EX4 3AH. 0392 79244.

Axmouth to Lyme Regis Undercliffs

See under Dorset

Berry Head Country Park   12

Map 202 SX94-56- 108 acres (43 ha)
1 mile east of Brixham. LNR, SSSI. Limestone cliffs, grassland, heath, scrub.

Access   AYR on foot from CP at SX943564 on good paths.

Information   Leaflet and nature trail guide from CP or Torbay Borough Council.

History   The largest exposure of Devonian limestone visible in Britain. The cliffs are not all sheer but, in the 200 ft fall to the sea, there is a series of ledges and slopes which support a rich, lime-loving flora, including several rare or local species. The flat, plateau top has some areas with acid soils covered in gorse, heather, bell heather and bracken. Old quarries, with restricted access, provide an additional habitat.

What to See   The plant list includes white rock-rose, honewort, goldilocks aster, small mouse-ear, small restharrow, rock stonecrop and autumn squill with considerable amounts of ivy broomrape and wild madder. There are colonies of sea-birds on the cliffs, one of the few in south England, with razorbill, fulmar and kittiwake. Linnet and stonechat breed in the heathy areas whilst buzzard and kestrel take to the air over the plateau which itself provides a vantage point for watching birds at sea. The quarry is an important roost for several kinds of bat.

Braunton Burrows   13

Map 180 SS45-35- 1490 acres (603 ha)
2½ miles south-west of Braunton at the end of Sandy Lane which leaves the B3231 Braunton to Saunton road ½ mile west of Braunton. NNR, UNESCO International Biosphere Reserve. Sand dunes, slacks, scrub, ponds.

Access   AYR on foot from CPs at the south end of Sandy Lane at SS462350 or at Broadsands at end of rough track, American Road, which continues from Sandy Lane to SS466327.

Information   Leaflet and plant list from Countryside Centre in Broadsands CP, open daily, or from Warden, Broadford Farm, Heddon Mill, near Braunton. 0271 812552.

History   One of the largest sand dune systems in Britain covering a total of nearly 2300 acres. Owned by the Christie Estate the south portion is leased to the Ministry of Defence which sub-lets to the NCC to manage as a nature reserve. The MOD retains some training rights and may close some areas to the public: at such time red flags are flown and sentries posted. The sand is wind-blown and of marine origin—much of it crushed shells. The fore dunes are built up by marram grass to a height of 100 ft which occasionally break down to form blow-outs. These dunes are colonized by lime-loving species and 'slacks', hollows which are flooded in the winter, hold marshland plants. Ponds have been dug to create permanent water. It is one of the few dune systems showing the complete succession to blackthorn/hawthorn scrub.

What to See   On a list of over 400 flowering plants the following are noteworthy: round-leaved wintergreen, first seen here in 1958 but now widespread, round-headed club-rush, sharp rush, water germander and sea stock, but the outstanding wildflower experience is the thousands of marsh-orchid and marsh helleborine in the slacks. Common birds are magpie, kestrel, buzzard, meadow pipit and skylark. Butterflies are superb in the flower-rich dunes and include holly blue, marbled white, green hairstreak, grayling, dark green fritillary, painted lady and clouded yellow, whilst amongst a dozen different dragonflies are emperor and golden-ringed dragonfly.

Dawlish Warren   14

Map 192 SX98-78- 505 acres (241 ha)
On the west side of Exe Estuary opposite Exmouth. SSSI. LNR. Dunes, mudflats, saltmarsh, reed-beds, pools.

Access   AYR on foot from CP at the end of the tunnel under the railway south of Dawlish Warren Station at SX980786. There is no access to the area within the golf course but there is access to a hide beyond the course overlooking the estuary. The sand and mudflats at the north end can be viewed from an area reached via the BR crossing point at SX978803.

Information   Leaflet and trail guide from Visitor Centre 200 yds beyond the far end of CP.

History   The Warren lies on fragments of New Red sandstone derived from cliffs to the west and moved here by the tide. Wind-blown sand has been deposited on top but the shape has altered over the centuries and Warren Point at the east end has been cut off to form a separate island at times. During the 7000 years since it first existed the Warren has developed a range of habitats from mobile and fixed dunes to extensive areas of saltmarsh and mudflats. This variety has resulted in a plant list of over 450 and in an annual list of birds of about 180 species.

What to See   The most celebrated plant is the sand crocus which grows nowhere else in mainland Britain. Perhaps the most obvious are the yellow-flowered evening-primroses introduced from North America, and the most spectacular the thousands of marsh-orchids in damp grassland in late May and early June to be replaced by that rather more modest orchid, autumn lady's-tresses, in August. Amongst the birds regularly seen on the mudflats are Brent goose, merganser, goldeneye, goosander, shelduck, wigeon, common, arctic and sandwich terns, curlew, greenshank, redshank, knot, sanderling, turnstone, dunlin, oystercatcher, ringed plover, bar-tailed and black-tailed godwits and, amongst the predators, peregrine and short-eared owl.

Heddon Valley   `15`

Map 180 SS65-48- 940 acres (381 ha)
4½ miles west of Lynton. Best route is via A39 to Blackmoor Gate, then A399 as far as Slade Lane Cross 2 miles west of Blackmoor, then turn right to Heddon Valley CP by Hunter's Inn. SSSI. Oak woods, damp meadows, coastal sand, grassland.

Access   AYR on foot from CP at SS655480 to a network of footpaths, particularly the mile to and from the coast at Heddon's Mouth on the east and west side of the river. The west side is easier on the legs and there are occasional seats.

Information   Leaflet to area from NT shop by CP, and notice boards in CP and at beginning of the path on the east side of valley.

History   The valley of the Heddon River cuts through the Old Red sandstone rocks on its path to the sea. Starting in a dense sessile oak wood the route gradually opens out passing steep scree slopes covered in a jumble of broken rock called Hangman Grits. The soils are so acid that limestone had to be brought across the Bristol Channel from Wales to be burnt in a kiln by the shore at Heddon's Mouth: the ships returned with timber from the woods as pit props for the mines of South Wales.

What to See   In addition to sessile oak the woods have ash, spindle and holly with pendulous sedge, common cow-wheat, wood sage, bilberry, shining crane's-bill and ferns such as hart's-tongue and soft shield-fern. Most prominent now are three introduced plants, Himalayan knotweed, Indian balsam, and montbretia which threaten to swamp the native vegetation. The river attracts dipper, kingfisher and grey wagtail whilst on the coast kittiwake and fulmar may be seen in the air.

  T[D]. Refreshments, shop.

Slapton Ley   `16`

Map 202 SX82-43- 460 acres (184 ha)
To the west of A379 road from Kingsbridge to Dartmouth between Torcross and Strete. SSSI. Shingle bank, lake, reed-beds, woodland.

Access   AYR on foot from car parking space at intervals along the road between Slapton Sands and the lake.

Information   Nature trail guide from Slapton Ley Field Centre at SX823449, the first house on the right on the road from the beach to the village.

History   The Ley is a shallow-water lake at the mouth of a small stream which is dammed by a shingle ridge formed at the end of the last Ice Age by a rise in the sea-level which pushed the shingle on shore between the headlands at Torcross and at Strete. The north end, above the bridge, has an extensive reed-bed, which is now regularly cut for thatching, with willow carr along the margin. The Ley gives shelter to birds from south-westerly gales and from cold weather inland.

What to See   The shingle beach carries many local plants such as shore dock, Ray's knotgrass, sea radish and yellow horned-poppy, whilst the Ley has masses of marsh-marigold, lesser bulrush, both grey and common club-rush, with shoreweed at the water's edge and pondweeds beneath the surface. Breeding birds include mute swan, great crested grebe, Cetti's, grasshopper, reed and sedge warblers and reed bunting with a few water rail. Buzzard, sparrowhawk and raven are resident whilst as many as 10,000 gulls roost on the reserve in winter. In autumn there is a spectacular gathering of swallows and martins, peaking at numbers of around 250,000. Mink and a few otter occur in the quiet shelter of the reed-bed.

T. Refreshments in Torcross at the south end.

Wheelchairs have excellent views over the Ley from the road.

Welcombe and Marsland Valleys

See under Cornwall

Wistman's Wood   `17`

Map 191 SX61-77- 60 acres (24 ha)
In the centre of Dartmoor 1½ miles north of Two Bridges up the east side of the West Dart River. FNR. Ancient oak wood, moorland.

Access   AYR on foot from CP opposite Two Bridges Hotel at SX609750 on difficult paths. There is a way-marked trail round the wood.

Information   Nothing on site: leaflet from NCC.

History   A wood of gnarled and stunted oaks, 8–15 ft tall, which lies at over 1200 ft on a steep rocky slope in a very exposed situation amongst angular masses of granite, known as clitter which make the floor of the wood extremely irregular, with deep crevasses between the blocks often hidden by bracken and bramble. The trees are festooned with epiphytes, particularly ferns, mosses, liverworts and lichens but with flowering plants and other trees as well. Grazing by ponies, sheep and cattle may have prevented the spread of the wood in the past but there is evidence that the wood is now growing again.

What to See   Other woody plants include rowan, holly, rusty willow, ivy and honeysuckle whilst bilberry, tormentil, English stonecrop, wood sage, heath bedstraw, wood-sorrel and climbing corydalis are the most prominent wild flowers. Like many oaks the trees are extensively attacked by leaf-eating caterpillars of the winter moth and numerous gall-forming flies.

Yarner Wood   18

Map 191 SX78-78- 370 acres (150 ha)
2 miles west of Bovey Tracey on B3344 road to Manaton: entrance is on left on sharp right-hand bend at Reddaford Water. NNR. Oak/birch wood, heather moor.

Access   AYR from dawn to dusk on foot from CP in wood at SX785788 on good way-marked paths.

Information   Nature trail guide and other information from dispenser and notice board in CP. Exhibition in museum in the middle of the wood, open April–end October. Warden lives on site. 0626 832330.

History   One of the first NNRs, established in 1952 because it is one of the finest oak woods which flank Dartmoor. It extends over an altitudinal range of 800 ft and has a wide variety of woodland including high forest, oak scrub with holly, rowan and honeysuckle, as well as a few areas of bog and heath and flushed areas under a canopy of ash and alder. The wood has been much used for experimental purposes: introduction of suitable nest-boxes was followed by immediate colonization by pied flycatcher nesting further south in Britain than ever before.

What to See   Wild flowers of the drier areas include bilberry, heather and common cow-wheat, with primrose and sanicle on deeper soils. In flushes opposite-leaved golden-saxifrage is abundant with occasional clumps of royal fern. Buzzard, sparrowhawk, raven, all three types of woodpecker, wren, spotted and pied flycatchers, redstart, wood warbler, treecreeper and nuthatch are amongst the nesting birds whilst siskin feed on birch seed in winter and redwing on holly. Holly blue and white admiral are on the butterfly list whilst the mounds of wood ants are common on the woodland floor.

Wheelchairs have access to a viewing hide by vehicle.

Dorset

Dorset, despite its modest size, has within its borders some of the largest and most memorable landscapes anywhere in England. This is based on a geological framework which embraces all the major formations which occur in south-east England from the Lower Lias clays at the beginning of the Jurassic period around Lyme Regis in the west to the Bagshot Beds of the Tertiary period at Bournemouth in the east, with a reprise of them all, except the Lias, in what is arguably the single most exciting geological open air study area anywhere in Britain—the Isle of Purbeck.

Chalk is the dominant feature of the centre of the county and, until after the Second World War, the Downs, which sweep in from Wiltshire through Cranborne Chase and Blandford to Dorchester before turning east to end in Ballard Down and Old Harry north of Swanage, were an almost continuous carpet of chalk grassland with yew woods on steep, south slopes and ash in damper coombes. Sadly the demise of the rabbits, lack of sheep or cattle grazing and modern agriculture changed most of that splendour into scrub, arable or species-poor leys. Only fragments have survived as reserves or around ancient monuments such as Neolithic long barrows, Bronze Age round barrows or Iron Age and Roman hill forts. One of the finest of these fragments lies on *Fontmell Down* on the west edge of Cranborne Chase commanding views over the clay vales and the infant Stour meandering through Sturminster Newton.

The east of Dorset is equally remarkable for its geology. It has a great wedge of Tertiary sands and gravels in the Poole Basin on which heath, bog and birch wood once extended from Christchurch to the outskirts of Dorchester. These are known as the Dorset heaths—a name for the area and for one of its rarest plants, *Erica ciliaris*. These heaths, which extend westwards from the New Forest should have been recognized as being of international importance and treated as such. But, just like the chalk, it has been broken up into smaller and smaller units until today, when only about 15 per cent of the heathland which occurred in the eighteenth century remains, it is in 800 fragments instead of the eight large blocks which were separated only by river valleys. Some notion of the wildness, which so moved the writer Thomas Hardy, can still be seen today in north Purbeck on *Studland Heath* and the Arne Peninsula.

To the west of the chalky areas lie valleys where bands of impermeable clay alternate with greensand resulting in areas with many springs and wet hollows difficult to cultivate and left as woodland or rough grazing. *Powerstock Common* was preserved in this way and, though it once suffered from an over-population of conifers, it is now being restored to a more natural state as the Dorset Trust progressively removes conifer plantations. Nearby another piece of landscape has been magically saved at Lower Kingcombe, one of the largest concentrations of old meadows to be protected in Britain and the single most important purchase ever made by the Dorset Trust.

Powerstock and Lower Kingcombe are hidden landscapes tucked into the fabric of Dorset: the coast is brazen in comparison, with three spectacular sections of contrasting character. In the far west the six miles of the *Axmouth to Lyme Regis Undercliffs*, which start in Dorset, are a testimony to the gigantic earth movements which continue to make man seem such a puny opponent of nature. In the centre is the finest example of a stony beach in Britain—the 18 mile length of Chesil Beach from Bridport (West Bay) to Weymouth—with the fascinating freshwater Fleet behind it, Abbotsbury swannery in the north and the RSPB reserves at *Radipole Lake* and Lodmoor near the south end: the whole forming an intricate and inter-dependent group of wildlife habitats for birds. Finally, in the east, is the gigantic natural harbour of Poole—a haven for boats and wildlife alike. Around its south shores there are still many isolated creeks and islands which are home to over-wintering waders, ducks and geese and five islands, including *Brownsea Island*, which harbours red squirrels, a large heronry and colonies of nesting Sandwich and common terns.

Dorset also offers the coast of the Isle of Purbeck—Lulworth, Kimmeridge, Tilly Whim, Durdle Door, and Dancing Ledge—the names alone suggest a land of much charm and interest.

- Dorset Trust for Nature Conservation (DTNC), 39 Christchurch Road, Bournemouth BH1 3NS. 0202 24241.
- Conservation Office, 15 North Square, Dorchester DT1 1HY. 0305 64620.

Axmouth to Lyme Regis Undercliffs   19

Map 193 794 acres (320 ha)
6 miles of the coastline from Devon and ½ mile south-east of Axmouth at SY25-89- to Ware on the western outskirts of Lyme Regis at SY32-91-. NNR. Wooded cliffs, grassy slopes, geology.

Access   AYR on foot from either end:

1. from Lyme Regis—from CP on A3052 immediately west of turning to the Cobb at SY330917: leave CP at far end following trail which leads to sign saying 'Footpath to Ware'.
2. from Axmouth—on footpath which starts at top of steep hill on minor road at SY263904 leaving car in village.

   An energetic walk on paths which are often steep and sometimes slippery.

Information   Leaflet from NCC. Mentioned in *Walks in West Dorset* by R.Legg from local bookshops.

History   Unstable cliffs of chalk and upper greensand are continually sliding over the underlying clays of the Gault and Lias beds and collapsing into the sea carrying mature woodland and gardens full of exotic plants such as pampas-grass with them. An enormous chasm was created on 25 December 1839—it is ½ mile long and 200 ft deep in places and up to 400 ft wide.

What to See   One of the wildest woodland walks in Britain through tall tangled trees of ash and field maple and shrubs including such lime-loving species as dogwood, privet, wayfaring-tree, spindle and traveller's-joy whilst the ground cover has wood spurge, pendulous sedge, purple gromwell and wild madder. The ferns, especially hart's-tongue, grow to an enormous size in the shady gulleys left by the landslides. Birds include such woodland species as goldcrest, nightingale and nuthatch with cliff-breeding buzzard and raven: hoopoe are occasional visitors.

   Butterflies include the rare wood white, on the wing in June, whilst sunny slopes have adder and common lizard: there are palmate newts in pools.

   T. Refreshments in Axmouth and Lyme Regis.

Brownsea Island 20

Map 195 SZ02-88- about 250 acres (100 ha)
5 miles south-west of Bournemouth at the east end of Poole Harbour. SSSI.
Saltmarsh, reed-beds, woodland, lakes, lagoon.

Access   April–September by boat from Poole Quay and Sandbanks: open daily
from 10 a.m.–8 p.m. (or dusk if earlier). Landing fee for non-NT members. The
way-marked trail of 1½ miles has hide with views over the lagoon.

Information   Nature trail leaflet from NT shop on island. There is daily access
to nature reserve in the north half of island either by trail or tour, but parties
only by arrangement with DTNC warden at Brownsea. (Tel. 02902 709445.)
There is also an Information Centre in the reserve.

History   A sandy 500 acre island at the mouth of Poole Harbour with heath
on the south side and a ridge to the north which is wooded with Scots and
maritime pines and occasional understorey of rhododendron. The central valley
has two large lakes which attract tufted duck, little grebe, roosting heron and
many species of dragonfly. The 70 acre brackish lagoon in the north-east corner
is the most important habitat and provides views of waders such as avocets in
the winter and nesting terns in the summer.

What to See   Breeding birds around the marsh include reed warbler, reed
bunting, little grebe, water rail and teal whilst common and Sandwich tern nest
on islands in the lagoon. Brownsea is one of the few places in South England
with native red squirrels: sika deer have been introduced. Several hundred
cormorants roost on the lagoon mud-flats.
   T[D]. Refreshments, shop.
   Wheelchairs have access to good paths once ashore.

Fontmell Down 21

Map 183 ST88-18- 145 acres (57 ha)
4 miles south of Shaftesbury and 1 mile east of Fontmell Magna off A350 via
minor road to Ashmore, turning left at crossroads at the top of the hill. Part SSSI.
Chalk grassland, scrub, woodland.

Access   AYR on foot from limited parking space by the triangle of roads at the
north end of the reserve at ST887185 over a series of public footpaths and other
passable paths.

Information   Leaflet from DTNC.

History   69 acres are owned by DTNC, the remainder is leased from NT. It is
one of the best remaining areas of chalk grassland in Dorset running down into
a dry valley with a well-developed woodland on the NW facing slope. This was
originally planted with conifers but these are gradually being overtaken by
native hardwoods such as ash, beech and whitebeam. Grazing by Dorset Trust
sheep and local cattle maintain a rich sward which includes some superb
ant-hills.

What to See   The rich turf has such local plants as early gentian, clustered bellflower and bastard toadflax and a number of orchids including frog and autumn lady's-tresses. Some of the following butterflies may be seen: adonis and chalkhill blues, marbled white, ringlet, large skipper, brown argus and dark green fritillary. Buzzard fly overhead: nightingale sing in the wood.

Powerstock Common   22

Map 194 SY54-97- 285 acres (116 ha)
5 miles north-east of Bridport below Eggardon Hill and 1 mile west-south-west of Toller Porcorum on the south side of an old railway line. SSSI. Ancient woodland, scrub, grass heath, ponds.

Access   AYR on foot from CP at SY547974 to a series of forestry paths and on the old railway line, a circular walk of about 1¾ miles.

Information   Notice board near entrance. Leaflet from DTNC or TI Office in Bridport.

History   The reserve lies on fuller's earth clay beneath outcrops of greensand and gault clay giving rise to landslips and many wet flushes. The Common was once part of the much larger Powerstock Forest, a hunting ground of King John.

What to See   Although much reduced by conifer planting, a large area of oak woodland with hazel coppice remains sheltering a woodland flora of bluebell, wood anemone, primrose, yellow archangel and stinking iris. Herb-Paris, bird's-nest and greater butterfly-orchid also occur. In wet springs surrounded by alder and sallow pendulous sedge and yellow iris abound. Thirty-seven species of butterfly have been listed including silver-washed fritillary and purple hairstreak, and all three varieties of British newts are in the several ponds.

Wheelchairs have reasonable access.

Radipole Lake   23

Map 194 SY67-79- 192 acres (78 ha)
In Weymouth opposite the bus station. SSSI. Freshwater lake, reed-beds, water meadows.

Access   AYR on foot from Swannery CP opposite bus station (small charge) at SY677796 to good paths leading to three hides.

Information   Guide and other information from Visitor Centre in CP: open W/Es all year and weekdays April–September 10 a.m.–5 p.m.

History   The lake was once the estuary of the River Wey but, after the building of the Westham Bridge just south of the CP in 1924, this has gradually changed into a freshwater lake. Reed-beds now cover much of the area whilst dense scrub has grown up round the perimeter.

What to See   In winter resident mute swan, grebes, coot and moorhen are joined on the lake by pochard, tufted duck, teal and shoveler with occasional gadwall, pintail and shelduck whilst Mediterranean, glaucous and Iceland gulls

are regularly present. In spring and summer there are hundreds of reed and sedge warblers and smaller numbers of bearded tit, Cetti's and grasshopper warblers, kingfisher and water rail. In autumn thousands of swallows, martins and swifts roost in the reeds before setting out on migration, their places to be taken by pied wagtails in the winter. Nearly 30 species of butterfly have been recorded here including marbled white and migrating painted lady and clouded yellow.
T[D].

Wheelchairs have excellent access on good paths.

Studland Heath

`24`

Map 195 SZO2-83- 425 acres (172 ha)
North-east corner of the Isle of Purbeck on south side of entrance to Poole Harbour. NNR. Sand dunes, heath, bog, freshwater lake, pools, woodland.

Access   AYR on foot from CP on the east side of toll road to ferry between road and sea 100 yds after Knoll House Hotel at SZ033835. The nature trail begins 300 yds up beach to the north and leads to observation hut overlooking Little Sea.

Information   Leaflet from NCC warden, 33 Priest's Road, Swanage BH19 2RQ. 09294 23453.

History   The lake of Little Sea has been formed by two arms of sand dunes from the north and south encircling a bay over a period of 400 years. Streams running into it have converted it into a freshwater lake around which a fringe of reed-beds and willow carr have grown up. On the east side old dunes have developed gorse, heather and birch scrub and, in one area, an open woodland of pine, oak and holly occurs.

What to See   Little Sea has bogbean and yellow iris with royal fern on the margins and shoreweed and spring quillwort below the surface. Small bogs have great sundew, Dorset heath and bog-myrtle whilst marsh gentian occurs in wet places on the heath, with greater bladderwort in some of the pools. Pipits, stonechat and willow warbler are amongst the heathland birds in summer whilst grebes, shelduck, water rail, reed and sedge warblers breed around Little Sea. Nightjar and Dartford warbler may be seen at the north end of the reserve. All six British reptiles occur including smooth snake and sand lizard and there are several rare dragonflies—notably the small red damselfly and the ruddy darter.
T[D] at CP. Refreshments.

Wheelchairs have access along part of beach.

Somerset

Somerset is a county of distinct and contrasting regions. Since much of the northern end was lost to Avon in 1974 the present day county begins, for most visitors, at the great Carboniferous limestone wall of the Mendip Hills. On its south side lies the vast, flat expanse of the Somerset Levels, covering over 150 square miles and separating the giant Mendips from the more modest ridges of the Quantocks, Blackdown and Brendon Hills, and the Vale of Taunton Deane which these hills surround on its north, south and western sides. Further west, beyond Brendon, lies the greatest contrast of all—the wide-open, heathery wilderness of Exmoor rising to over 1700 ft on Dunkery Beacon.

The landscape of the Mendips is celebrated nationally and the west end is rightly an Area of Outstanding Natural Beauty. The area attracts millions annually to places like the Cheddar Gorge and the caves of Wookey Hole. However, the limestone cliffs, grassland and woodland are also of national importance for their wildlife with a series of National Nature reserves, Trust reserves and SSSIs stretching from Asham Wood near Frome in the east to the spectacular 'whale' of *Brean Down* basking in the sea south of Weston-super-Mare. The easiest place to enjoy the complete range of these wildlife habitats is at the head of the *Cheddar Gorge*. Passing through Black Rock Gate gives access to a 5-mile round walk linking three Somerset Trust reserves.

The Somerset Levels, too, have many designated areas and reserves. This has been a response to the devastating changes which have been brought about by drainage followed by ploughing and reseeding of what, until only 40 years ago were marshy meadows and raised bogs separated by stagnant ditches or rhynes full of wetland plants: the whole area attracting waders and wildfowl in winter, or during autumn and spring migrations. The channelling of the main rivers, the Parrett, the Axe and the Brue, into 'canals' means that it is now difficult to maintain a high water-level in areas which have been acquired as reserves and some are in danger of drying out. This is not true of *Greater Westhay*, which is being developed by the Somerset Trust as a centre for visitors to the Levels at the very heart of the northern peat extraction section under the Polden Hills.

Visitors to the Quantocks already have access to a wildlife visitor centre—the Somerset Trust's headquarters at *Fyne Court* is 5 miles north of Taunton. It not only interprets the wildlife of the hills around but provides the best possible introduction to the county as a whole and to other attractions within easy reach in all directions. To the north the muddy shores of *Bridgwater Bay* at the mouth of the River Parrett provide one of the most important sites for birds in the county. To the west, in the Brendon Hills above Dulverton, the reservoirs of Clatworthy and Wimbleball have created sites for watching waterfowl in an area where open water is otherwise scarce. Walking and watching can be happily combined by visiting *Hurscombe* at the north end of Wimbleball Lake with ducks on the water, buzzards and ravens in the air and whinchat in the gorse.

From here the heights of Exmoor are close and the pastoral landscape of the Brendon Hills soon gives way to the windswept, rolling, summit of Exmoor but, on the north side the descent to the sea is swift and dramatic—plunging down from heather moors into wet valleys full of luxuriant oak woods where the trees drip with ferns and lichens. This change is best demonstrated on Dunkery Hill, taking in the view over *Cloutsham Woods* from Webber's Post. It seems very much further than 30 miles as the crow flies to the dry white limestone flanks of the Mendips or the trippers amongst the sand dunes of Burnham-on-Sea.

● Somerset Trust for Nature Conservation (STNC), Fyne Court, Broomfield, Bridgwater TA5 2EQ. 0823 451587.

Brean Down

25

Map 182 ST28-54- 158 acres (64 ha)
2 miles south-west of Weston-super-Mare: signposted to Brean off A370 at Bleadon. In Brean turn right and continue until road ends in CP. SSSI. Ancient Monument. Limestone grassland, cliffs.

Access AYR on foot from CP at ST296587 up some steep steps.

Information Notice board at bottom of steps. Booklet from Bird Garden at foot of Down or from STNC.

History The Carboniferous limestone mass of Brean Down was an island before the Bleadon Levels, which have to be crossed to reach it, were drained for farming in medieval times. It was farmed itself during the Iron Age—the terraces are visible on the top—but most of the Down remains a remarkable area for limestone-loving plants which require the treeless, unshaded conditions which have persisted on this exposed site since the last glaciation. The best limestone grassland is found on the south slopes: on the north there are deeper, more acid, soils with bracken and bell-heather. At the foot of the cliffs near the sea a maritime flora survives.

What to See Plants of particular interest are white rock-rose, dwarf sedge, dwarf mouse-ear and Somerset hair-grass with many other characteristic species such as wild thyme, small scabious and sheep's fescue. The maritime species include rock samphire, Danish scurvygrass, least soft-brome, sea spleenwort and sea carrot. Amongst resident birds are skylark, meadow and rock pipits and stonechat: stock dove and kestrel nest in the cliffs. The shoreline attracts shelduck and mallard and regular visitors are scaup, redshank, dunlin and oystercatcher with curlew, golden plover and lapwing feeding in nearby meadows in winter. Summer brings wheatear, whitethroats, blackcap and chiffchaff. The area is important for insects: marbled white and chalkhill blue butterflies and a number of rare weevils and grasshoppers are noteworthy.

Bridgwater Bay

26

Map 182 ST2-4- 6000 acres (2400 ha)
Estuary of the River Parrett 5 miles north of Bridgwater. NNR. Saltmarsh, shingle, mudflats with winter and migrating birds.

Access AYR on foot from CP in Steart village at ST270459 with direct access to the shore with views over the bay from hides. Steart Island may not be visited from 1 November to 31 March and then only with a permit.

Information Leaflet from Warden, Dowell's Farm, Steart 0278 652456.

History The reserve includes all the mudflats on the south side of the Parrett estuary which are exposed at low water. These attract enormous numbers of sea-birds, waterfowl and waders which are driven into the mouth of the estuary as the tide rises. Many ducks spend the winter here, particularly mallard, wigeon and shelduck. The latter also gather here to moult in midsummer—the only known site of its kind in Britain. There is also a considerable area of saltmarsh dominated by cord-grass and one of the largest, large-pebble beaches in Britain with species like henbane and knotted clover.

What to See   In winter there are 2500 each of mallard, shelduck and wigeon with smaller numbers of pintail, shoveler and teal accompanied by large flocks of dunlin, lapwing and curlew and occasional white-fronted geese. Spring and autumn bring large numbers of migrants—black-tailed godwit, oystercatcher and redshank—with smaller flocks of bar-tailed godwit, knot, grey plover and turnstone. Whimbrel are especially frequent in spring.

Cheddar Gorge Reserves

27

(Black Rock, Long Wood, Velvet Bottom)
Map 182 ST48-54- 264 acres (107 ha)
2 miles north-east of Cheddar above the gorge on B3135 to Priddy: the road makes 180° right-hand bend; immediately after bend look for Black Rock Gate on left and find parking space on roadside. SSSI. Limestone woodland, scrub, grassland cliffs, dry stone walls.

Access   AYR on foot from Black Rock Gate at ST482546 on good, way-marked paths.

Information   Leaflets from dispenser 50 yds inside Black Rock Gate with other information on display boards.

History   These three areas on the Carboniferous limestone of the Mendips are contiguous and occupy the bottom and sides of a summer-dry valley at the head of the Cheddar Gorge. Quarrying has cut into the hillsides and there is a good exposure in Black Rock whilst, in Velvet Bottom in particular, lead-mining, which began in pre-Roman times and continued until the 1880s, has left a landscape of pits and hummocks much of it so contaminated that only a few unusual plants can grow. Long Wood is mainly an ash wood with an understorey of hazel and hawthorn: the Somerset Trust has been restoring a coppice-with-standards management regime here since 1974.

What to See   Woodland flowers, best in spring, include herb-Paris and toothwort along with abundant wood anemone, red campion and bluebell. Some species are restricted to the lead spoil such as spring sandwort and alpine penny-cress but elsewhere the limestone rocks and grassland have lesser meadow-rue, rock stonecrop, spring cinquefoil and common rock-rose. Woodland birds such as willow and grasshopper warblers, redstart, whitethroat and buzzard are frequent. This is a very good butterfly area with dark green fritillary, marbled white, brown argus and Essex skipper on a list of nearly 30 species.
   T. Refreshments in Cheddar.

Cloutsham Woodland

`28`

Map 181 SS90-43- 16,000 acres (6600 ha)
4 miles south-east of Porlock at Webber's Post on minor road signposted to Dunkery. Part SSSI. Acid oak woodland, upland grassland.

Access   AYR on foot from CP at Webber's Post at SS902439 on way-marked trail of 3¼ miles.

Information   Nature trail leaflet from Exmoor National Park Centre, Exeter House, Dulverton. Notice boards in CP.

History   The land over which the trail passes was formerly part of the Holnicote Estate. It had belonged to the Acland family for 200 years before it was given to the NT by Sir Richard Acland in 1944. The trail enters a corner of Horner Wood SSSI, an ancient high forest of sessile oak with hazel, holly and rowan beneath the canopy with bilberry and bracken on the ground below. The soils, derived from rocks of the Devonian period, are mainly acid and stony. The rainfall is high (over 60 ins) and many of the trees are covered in large numbers of different lichens.

What to See   Unusual plants in the area include ivy-leaved bellflower, Cornish moneywort, lesser skullcap, and bitter-vetch. The stream in the valley bottom attracts dipper and grey wagtail whilst the woodland has wood warbler, redstart and pied flycatcher and, in the conifers planted near the CP, goldcrests are frequently seen. Red deer use the wood for shelter in winter and during the rut in autumn.

Fyne Court

`29`

Map 182 ST22-32- 23 acres (9 ha)
In the Quantock Hills 5 miles north of Taunton. Follow signs for Broomfield from North Petherton on A38. Arboretum, lake, beech woodland, old quarry, pond.

Access   AYR on foot from CP at ST221321 along several way-marked paths. Reserve open daily 9 a.m.–6 p.m.: other facilities—a Visitor Centre and a shop—available from Easter to the end of October 9 a.m.–5 p.m.

Information   Visitor Centre with exhibition on Somerset wildlife and reserves. Leaflets for STNC reserves and nature trails starting at Fyne Court in shop.

History   Fyne Court (now demolished) was the home of a pioneer electrician, Andrew Crosse. The Visitor Centre is in the stables and workshops and the walks go through the former pleasure grounds. These are now being managed to recreate the habitats which formerly existed. Sycamore and laurel are being removed from woodland whilst oak and beech are encouraged and hazel introduced into the understorey. The face of an old quarry has been cleared so that the section through the Devonian sandstone, here at the south end of the Quantocks known as Morte slates, can be studied.

What to See Woodland flowers include bluebell, willowherbs, foxglove, snowdrop and primrose. Woodland birds are represented by treecreeper, nuthatch, green and great spotted woodpeckers, four species of tits, chiffchaff and blackcap. A small lake attracts mallard and moorhen where they are found amongst the marsh-marigold, yellow iris, wild angelica and meadowsweet around the margin. Mammals are abundant from foxes and badgers to rabbits, squirrels and moles: toads breed in the lake, frogs and newts in a small pond.

T [D]. Refreshments on Sun and BHs in summer, shop, picnic site.

Wheelchairs have access to trail near Centre.

Greater Westhay `30`

Map 182 ST45-44- 100 acres (40 ha)
4 miles north-west of Glastonbury: follow B3151 through Meare and Westhay. Approximately ½ mile north of Westhay, where the road turns left, turn right into the lane to Godney and, after 1 mile, turn left down London Drove, a track with peat workings almost immediately on the right. SSSI. Raised bog, open water, reed-beds.

Access AYR on foot from car parking space in Drove at ST456440 to hide and well-marked paths.

Information Nothing on site: leaflet from STNC.

History In historic times the Somerset Levels were a series of raised peat bogs separated by areas of marsh and fen. Most have been drained and the peat has been removed. Though peat has also been dug here, Westhay is one of the best examples of the former vegetation which remains and, with the control of the water-level, the Trust hopes to restore the habitat as far as it is possible whilst at the same time welcoming visitors. The reserve also includes an ornithologically important 10-acre lake, and areas of reed-bed have been planted to provide an additional bird habitat.

What to See The raised bog has cottongrass, deergrass, heather, cross-leaved heath, bog asphodel and many species of *Sphagnum* moss. Birds which breed in and around the reserve include curlew, lapwing, redshank and snipe whilst in winter the lake attracts mallard, teal,large numbers of mute and occasional Bewick's swan.

T in Willows Garden Centre, Shapwick, 2 miles south-west.

Hurscombe `31`

Map 181 SS97-31- 46 acres (19 ha)
6 miles north-east of Dulverton at the north end of Wimbleball Lake. Follow signs to Water Park through the village of Brompton Regis to the bridge over the north end of the lake. The reserve lies north of the bridge, the entrance is at its west end. Woodland, scrub, rough grassland, marsh and water.

Access AYR on foot from the place where cars can park along the roadside at SS972318 and up a prominent bridleway which leads to the reserve entrance: then follow the way-marked trail for 2 miles.

Information Trail leaflet from small Visitor Centre on the west side of the lake at SS964310 or from STNC.

History The flooded north arm of Wimbleball Lake with the land round its margins, which was formerly farmland with beech hedges and a larch plantation, has been turned by the Somerset Trust into a wildlife refuge. Scrub and marshland have been allowed to develop and some trees, like crab and wild service, have been introduced, whilst the beech wood has been underplanted with oak, of which only three mature specimens grow on the reserve today.

What to See The trail gives excellent viewing over the reservoir which has resident heron and great crested grebe joined in winter by coot, wigeon, teal, pochard and tufted duck and a few goldeneye. Overhead buzzards wheel and kestrels hover whilst underfoot are the tunnels of small mammals—shrews, mice and voles. The butterflies are especially notewothy with holly blue, small and large skippers, speckled wood, green hairstreak, comma, marbled white and five species of fritillary are present amongst a long list of others.

T [D]. Refreshments, picnic site, shop at Visitor Centre.

Wheelchairs have good views over lake from bridge 100 yds east of the reserve entrance.

SOUTH

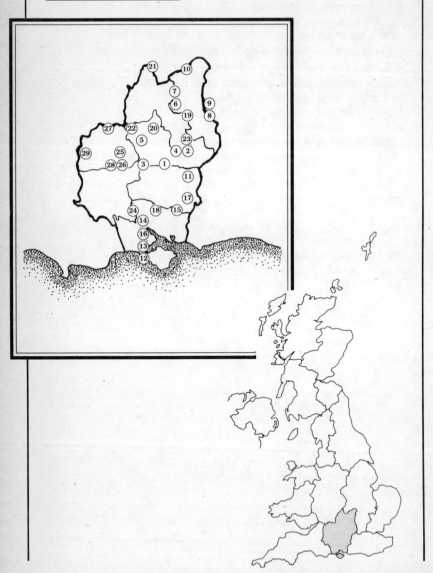

Berkshire

Berkshire is dominated by the broad band of chalk which crosses the county from the River Thames at Goring and Pangbourne in the east through East Ilsley and Lambourn into Wiltshire in the west—there is no way south from Oxford which does not take you across this lofty open landscape where the ancient Ridgeway along the crest almost reaches 800 ft near Wantage. A century ago most of these downs were open sheep-walk, covered in herb-rich, thyme-scented turf. Today that has been turned into a monoculture of barley or wheat and only fractured fragments of chalk grassland are left. The best are often found in association with archaeological remains where the humps and hollows of burial mounds have made ploughing impossible: such a site is *Seven Barrows*, 2½ miles north of Lambourn.

South of the chalk a wedge of younger, Eocene, deposits pushes westwards from the broad end near Windsor to a narrow point on the county boundary west of Newbury. Here a mixture of acid sands and gravels and heavy London clay has left a number of small wildlife areas which were too difficult or infertile to cultivate. A typical example of the heaths and bogs which arise when acid gravel overlies impervious clay can still be seen at *Inkpen Common*. Half a mile away, where the clay is on the surface, an old, herb-rich meadow has also survived, the Inkpen Crocus Field, famous for the display of crocuses in spring, but a reminder of what has been lost elsewhere with its list of 150 wild flowers in only 8 acres.

The richness of habitats where gravels and clays are intimately mixed is also demonstrated to the east of Newbury—this time in the woods which clothe the north-facing escarpment which overlooks the River Kennet running west to east below. There can be few other woods in the county to compare for such variety in a relatively small area as *Bowdown Woods* and *Baynes Reserve* which lie within a mile of each other—a pleasant and peaceful surprise so close to the recently notorious, and far from peaceful, Greenham Common.

The River Kennet, along with the Lambourn and the Pang, are still clear streams covered in sheets of water-crowfoot in summer where mayflies thrive and brown trout and grayling rise. A most delightful walk beside one of these, the Pang, can be enjoyed from *Moor Copse*. Equally delightful, and with its own special plants as an additional attraction, is the walk along the Loddon which can be conveniently started from *Dinton Pastures Country Park*, where the Loddon lily or summer snowflake can be seen in damp meadows and the Loddon pondweed may be spotted waving beneath the waters of the stream. Sadly it is hard to get away from the constant drone of the motorways—M4 and A329(M)—converging nearby.

For real peaceful enjoyment of wildlife the west of Berkshire is still the best—you can have Inkpen Common all to yourself in the spring sunshine amidst the golden gorse.

● Berkshire, Buckinghamshire and Oxfordshire Naturalists' Trust (BBONT), 3
Church Cowley Road, Rose Hill, Oxford OX4 3JR. 0865 775476.

Bowdown Woods
`1`

Map 174 SU50-65- 55 acres (22 ha)
2 miles south-east of Newbury. Turn east off A34 south of Newbury to Greenham
village. Drive along Bury's Bank Road with Greenham Common on your right.
After Newbury and Crookham Golf Club turn left down steep gravel track with
old mill-stone at top. SSSI. Wet and dry deciduous woodland, heathland, ponds.

Access   AYR on foot from CP at SU501656 on good, way-marked, paths.

Information   Good boards in CP with map. There is a small shelter in the
wood.

History   The reserve drops down a wooded north-facing slope to the valley
of the River Kennet. The gravel on the plateau on the south side supports dry
heathland and oak woodland with wild cherry, rowan and occasional hazel and
birch. Lower down, the London clay below the gravel is exposed and here the
woodland changes to ash and field maple with hazel, crab apple and blackthorn.
Spring-fed streams have cut small valleys into the slope where much of the
ground is waterlogged and carries fine stands of alder most of which have been
coppiced in the past.

What to See   Spring flowers include Solomon's-seal and early-purple orchid
whilst heather and bell heather colour the heathland in autumn. White admiral
and purple hairstreak are amongst the many species of butterfly regularly seen.
Dragonflies are conspicuous in summer along with day-flying moths such as
brown silver-lines and the distinctive speckled yellow. The quiet visitor is very
likely to see roe deer, and possibly muntjac—but the mud around the ponds will
certainly carry their signs. Dormice also occur amongst the hazels.

Dinton Pastures Country Park
`2`

Map 175 SU78-71-274 acres (111 ha)
4 miles south-east of Reading, west of B3030 between Winnersh and Twyford
Country Park.

Access   AYR on foot from CP at SU785718 along well defined and maintained
paths.

Information   Leaflet for nature trail from small Information Centre by CP.
Open 9.30 a.m.–5 p.m. daily.

History   The Park, which lies in the valley of the River Loddon, has been
developed in worked-out gravel pits excavated in the 1970s to build the adjacent
motorways. Much creative planting of native trees, shrubs and wild flowers has
taken place to produce woods, hedges and grassland. An additional 40 acres to
the north, Lavell's Lake, has been set aside as a conservation area with restricted
access to hides overlooking a wader scrape and tern island.

What to See   Summer snowflake, known locally as Loddon lily, grows at the water's edge whilst the Loddon pondweed lies submerged in the River Loddon which flows along the western boundary. About 50 species of bird regularly breed here including redshank, little ringed plover, common tern and kingfisher. Winter wildfowl include occasional goldeneye, goosander and scaup as well as large numbers of grebes, swans and the common ducks. Insect populations are growing steadily with over 30 species of butterfly and 16 species of dragonfly so far recorded.

T[D]. Refreshments.

Wheelchairs have access along good paths and to a hide.

Inkpen Common   ▣3

Map 174 SU38-64- 26 acres (11 ha)

1½ miles south of Kintbury, 1¼ miles east of Inkpen village. Take road to East and West Woodhay from Kintbury: after 1¼ miles bear right at Rooksnest Farm. The common is on the left just after the Inkpen village sign. SSSI. Heather and gorse covered heath with encroaching birch and oak.

Access   AYR on foot from CP on road verge at SU382643.

Information   Notice board with map and description at post box adjacent to entrance. Information sheet from BBONT.

History   The current common is a remnant of Inkpen Great Common, formerly kept open by local people who had the right to graze stock, collect firewood, heather and bracken (for bedding) and gorse (for heating their bread ovens). Now much overgrown, particularly on the perimeter, though gorse and birch are being cut back to allow the heather, bell-heather and cross-leaved heath to grow better.

What to See   In addition to common gorse there is dwarf gorse, which flowers in late summer, along with lousewort, purple moorgrass and pale dog-violet in its only Berkshire locality. A small valley bog holds bog asphodel where meadow thistle, ragged-Robin, marsh-marigold, lesser spearwort and petty whin are also abundant. The scrub is an excellent nesting site for yellow bunting, linnet, garden, grasshopper and willow warblers, tree pipit, woodcock. Sparrowhawk and kestrel are regularly seen.

Moor Copse   ▣4

Map 175 SU63-74- 67 acres (27 ha)

East of A340 ½ mile south of Tidmarsh between Theale and Pangbourne. At the rise to cross the M4 turn into the lay-by on the left opposite Tidmarsh village sign. SSSI. Ancient woodland, meadow and river.

Access   AYR on foot through the stile from CP area at SU634739 along the well-marked paths which run beside River Pang for ¼ mile.

Information   Notice board at entrance with map.

History   The wood near the entrance, Hogmoor Copse, is a wet alder/ash/willow woodland on peat and gravel, formerly coppiced but now much overgrown. Park Wood, entered by a bridge over the Pang, is a fine example of coppice-with-standards—standard oaks over coppiced ash, alder and hazel. Moor Copse itself in the south-east corner is an alder/ash/hazel coppice with standards of oak and ash and is separated from Park Wood by a 5-acre field.

What to See   The primroses and bluebells make a dramatic display in Park Wood in spring when early-purple orchids are abundant in Moor Copse. In summer the River Pang is lined with drifts of the carmine-coloured common comfrey and hemp agrimony. Mayfly are abundant on this stretch in May and June when brown trout may rise to them. In this very varied reserve insects in general are abundant with over 250 species of moth recorded: the white admiral butterfly may be seen in July and early August.

Seven Barrows   5

Map 175 SU32-82- 13 acres (5 ha)
2½ miles north of Lambourn. Follow B4001 from Lambourn for 1¼ miles to Mile End then fork left on to the minor road to Kingston Lisle to the reserve on the right at the left-hand bend after 1 mile. SSSI. Ancient Monument. Unimproved chalk grassland.

Access   AYR on foot from cars parked on roadside at the entrance to the bridleway at the south corner at SU329828. Please do not drive across the grass.

Information   Notice board with map at entrance.

History   Whereas most of the Berkshire Downs are now under the plough this site has survived because it contains about 40 burial mounds of various kinds, including disc and bell barrows, mostly dating from the Bronze Age, and has never been ploughed. The flat turf is mown twice a year and the reserve is grazed by sheep over the winter.

What to See   The herb-rich grassland includes such increasingly rare plants as horseshoe vetch, common rock-rose, saw-wort and clustered bellflower with a total of over 150 species recorded from the site. These provide food for a large butterfly population amongst which are chalkhill blue, small blue, brown argus, dark-green fritillary and marsh fritillary.

Buckinghamshire

Buckinghamshire falls into three very distinct areas which are themselves more often associated with neighbouring shires. The north of the county, which is within 6 miles of Northampton, is mainly on oolitic limestone although, sadly, intensive agriculture has left no large areas of limestone grassland and the landscape is not drawn in stone walls. However, there are still large tracts of oak woodland, notably *Salcey Forest* which straddles the border with Northamptonshire and where there is a reserve run jointly by BBONT and the Northamptonshire Wildlife Trust. Other woods act as reservoirs for wildlife which were left during the development of Milton Keynes.

The building of that city has itself produced habitats which are now managed, in part, as nature reserves. Gravel in the valley of the River Great Ouse has been excavated to provide materials for roads and houses and, in two cases, reinstatement has created areas attractive to wildfowl. One is the ARC Wildfowl Centre at Great Linford near the northern edge of the city which is run by the Game Conservancy as a research and education reserve with limited access. The second is at *Stony Stratford* to the west where BBONT has a reserve which is leased from Milton Keynes Development Corporation, and part of which is open throughout the year.

Milton Keynes is built on the Oxford clay and this and other clays underlie the Vale of Aylesbury. This is also a highly agricultural region where formerly there were many permanent herb-rich grasslands but the majority of these have been ploughed or improved. However, a fine example can still be seen in *Bernwood Meadows* near the county boundary only six miles north-east of Oxford. These hay meadows, which are a wonderful sight in June, are adjacent to *Bernwood Forest*, a Forest Nature Reserve with remnants of former oakwood, which is rapidly becoming one of the best sites for butterflies in the county. Other woodlands can be seen at Finemere Rushbeds and *Boarstall* though, at the latter the fascination is the opportunity to see one of only four working duck decoys in Britain in action.

The southern third of Buckinghamshire contains the chalklands of the Chilterns. The chalk itself is only exposed to produce typical grassland on that narrow escarpment which dominates the horizon from the plain below. The best is to be found between *Ivinghoe Beacon* and the Chequers estate to the south-west and includes one of the three remaining areas of England where box may be native. Unless the chalk is grazed it rapidly reverts to scrub—a fate which was, until recently, overtaking *Dancersend*, near Tring, even though it has been a nature reserve for over 60 years. The trend has been reversed by the introduction of sheep, so that the future of the Chiltern gentian and other rare plants which grow there, is assured.

The chalk immediately south-east of the scarp is covered in a thick layer of clay-with-flints on which develop the cathedral-like beech woods which are a lasting memorial of this county. Some of these can still be seen at *Dancersend* though much timber was felled here during the Second World War. Going still further south towards the River Thames the chalk is covered by Tertiary sands and gravels which are most famously represented by the acid woods of Burnham Beeches, north of Slough. Despite their closeness to London, the Chilterns are still a tangle of small villages and narrow roads which form an invaluable screen of unspoilt countryside into which it is possible to disappear.

● Berkshire, Buckinghamshire and Oxfordshire Naturalists' Trust (BBONT), 3 Church Cowley Road, Rose Hill, Oxford OX4 3JR. 0865 775476.

● The Game Conservancy, Fordingbridge, Hampshire SP6 1EF. 0425 52381.

Bernwood Forest ⑥

Map 164 SP61-11- 1000 acres (400 ha)
6 miles north-east of Oxford on minor road between Horton-cum-Studley and Oakley. Follow signs for Horton from roundabout on Oxford's eastern ring road at Headington. Turn right in Horton and, after 1 mile, turn left at T-junction to entrance in 200 yds. SSSI. Forest Nature Reserve. Mixed woodland with wide rides, butterflies.

Access   AYR on foot from CP at SP611117 on excellent way-marked paths.

Information   Butterfly trail leaflet from dispenser in CP gives details of a 1—1½ hour walk through the forest.

History   Ancient woodland mentioned in the Domesday Book and part of the Royal Forest of Bernwood during the middle ages when some areas were managed as wood pasture. Coppice-with-standards became more prevalent from the sixteenth century onwards but ceased at the end of the nineteenth century. Much of the best timber was felled soon after the Second World War. Taken over by the Forestry Commission in 1952 it was replanted with a mixture of oak and, mainly, Norway spruce.

What to See   The wide rides are especially important for the large butterfly population: 40 species have been recorded including marsh and pearl-bordered fritillary, dingy skipper, black, purple and brown hairstreaks, wood white, purple emperor, white admiral and Duke of Burgundy.
  Picnic site.
  Wheelchairs have access to much of the trail from CP.

Boarstall Duck Decoy ⑦

Map 164 SP62-15- 17 acres (7 ha)
Off B4011 Bicester to Thame road 6 miles south-east of Bicester. A man-made decoy pond and mixed woodland.

Access   Via track from Manor Farm, Boarstall to CP at SP624150. Open Easter–end August W/Es and BHs 10 a.m.–5 p.m.; Weds 2–5 p.m. Free for BBONT and NT members, otherwise there is a small charge.

Information   Guide book and check-list of birds from Information Centre in CP from which a nature trail leads. Demonstrations of duck decoying are given at 11 a.m. and 3 p.m. at W/Es and BHs when decoyman and dog are available.

History   One of four working decoys left in Britain. This method of catching wild ducks for the table was introduced from Holland in the seventeenth century. The shallow, 2½ acre pond has curving, narrowing channels or 'pipes' radiating from it. One pipe is maintained here. It is covered with netting stretched over hoops and has, on one side, a row of overlapping reed screens tall enough to hide the decoyman but with gaps large enough for a dog or piper to squeeze through. This activity attracts the ducks which swim into a trap net at the narrow end. They now have their legs, rather than their necks, ringed.

What to See   Ducks which visit the decoy include teal, wigeon, pintail, garganey, shoveler, pochard and tufted. In spring bluebells and primroses carpet the ground beneath the old oak, cherry and birch whilst blackcap and nightingale sing in the blackthorn thicket. Tracks of badger and muntjac deer are frequent. A wild pear provides food for blackbirds and migrating fieldfare in winter.

Wheelchairs have access to the trail.

Dancersend

8

Map 165 SP90-09- 79 acres (32 ha)

2 miles south-west of Tring. Turn south off A4251 from Tring town to Aylesbury at SP915110 via Duckmore Lane under A41. Keep right at first junction, continue until road joins from right from Aston Clinton. Keep left and, after 300 yds, stop when road swings left round pond in front of Pond Cottage. Park at entrance to field on right. SSSI. Deciduous woodland, chalk grassland and scrub.

Access   AYR on foot up the track to the right of Pond Cottage to the entrance after 400 yds.

Information   Details in BBONT Handbook and a good information board at the entrance.

History   The native woodlands of beech with some oak were clear-felled during the Second World War and the area was then colonized by scrub. This part was leased to the Forestry Commission for 150 years in 1957. They have either planted beech with a nurse crop of larch or spruce or allowed self-sown ash to grow. Much of the grassland is threatened by invasion of dogwood and hawthorn but sheep are now being used to graze small meadows to re-establish good chalk grassland.

What to See   The wide rides and woodland margins attract many species of butterfly including dark-green fritillary and green hairstreak and have a large population of common spotted-orchid in June. Wood vetch and yellow bird's-nest occur in the woodland whilst the very rare Chiltern gentian is a feature of the chalk grassland in August and September. The grassland also contains a large number of ant-hills made by the yellow ant.

Ivinghoe Beacon

9

Map 165 SP96-16- 1000 acres (400 ha)

South of B488 Tring to Dunstable road midway between the two towns on minor road to Ashridge. SSSI. Chalk grassland and scrub.

Access   AYR on foot from CP at top of the hill on the east of the road after climbing through a beech copse at SP961162. Paths lead to the summit of the Beacon in around half an hour's walk.

Information   None available.

History   Though formerly heavily grazed by sheep which produced a short turf rich in wild flowers, much has been undergrazed in recent times and tall grasses and scrub, including hawthorn, wayfaring-tree and whitebeam, have become widespread. By scrub control and the introduction of cattle grazing, it is hoped this trend will be reversed but erosion from public pressure is an increasing problem.

What to See   Most of the Beacon is chalk grassland with good areas of kidney and horseshoe vetch, food plants for small and chalkhill blue butterfly larvae respectively, accompanied by species such as salad burnet, rock-rose, cowslip, milkwort, yellow rattle and, occasionally, adder's-tongue. At the top of the hill, from which there are superb views over the Vale of Aylesbury, there is a capping of clay-with-flints with gorse amongst the scrub.

Picnic site.

Wheelchairs have limited access from CP.

Salcey Forest

See under Northamptonshire

Stony Stratford   10

Map 152 SP78-41-57 acres (23 ha)
2 miles north-west of Milton Keynes. From roundabout on A5 turn south towards Stony Stratford, after ½ mile fork left down Queen Eleanor Way then turn left after another ½ mile into lane which ends in CP. Bird reserve developed from old gravel workings.

Access   AYR on foot on good paths from CP at SP792410 to the north part of reserve and to public hide on the north side.

Information   Notice boards near entrance.

History   Alluvial flood meadows of the River Ouse, rich in gravel, were excavated in the 1970s during the construction of the A5 through Milton Keynes. However, excavations and reinstatement were conducted to a prearranged design to form a wetland for birds with shallow and deep lagoons, and islands suitable for nesting wildfowl.

What to See   Waders such as ringed plover, curlew and redshank are regular visitors whilst waterfowl include mute swan, great crested grebe, Canada goose, coot and moorhen. Banks have also been constructed to attract sand martin and kingfisher.

Picnic site.

Wheelchair access along good paths.

Hampshire and the Isle of Wight

It is not possible to cross Hampshire with your feet or your wheels on the ground without passing over the chalk. From the outskirts of Farnham in the east to the Wiltshire border at Tidworth—over 35 miles in a straight line—it is solid chalk all the way: and, if you start down the A34 from Newbury and continue to the sea at Southampton, two thirds of your route will be over the chalk. It also forms the backbone of the Isle of Wight, uninterrupted from The Needles to Culver Cliff.

At the time when Gilbert White was writing his letters from Selborne or W.H.Hudson was enthusing about a 'green country', much of the chalk was still covered in herb-rich grassland or ancient beech and ash woods, but planting, ploughing and improving have now changed the character of the landscape: the flat tops and gentler slopes are generally cultivated and the best which remains is often on the steeper hillsides. Nowhere is more typical, or more aptly named, than *Selborne Hanger*, the deciduous wood which hangs above and behind the house where White lived and wrote, where birds still sing in the light shade of stately beech and ash. There could be no greater woodland contrast than to go straight from the airy hanger to the intense shade of the yew wood on *Old Winchester Hill* where nothing grows beneath the canopy. Outside, the south-west slopes have some of the finest chalk grassland left in England. This and Martin Down, on the Wiltshire border south of Salisbury, are the gems of the Hampshire chalk, but they are not alone: Stockbridge Common Down, St Catherine's Hill and Butser Hill to name but a few.

Despite the bareness of much of the chalk and the relative infrequency of large areas of woodland on it, Hampshire still manages to hold 10 per cent of England's ancient woodland—and the reason for this must be, in the main, the New Forest. Here nearly 10,000 acres of ancient woodland still exist within its 50,000 acres of unenclosed vegetation which contribute to making the whole one of the outstanding areas for wildlife in the lowlands of northern Europe. Nowhere else can such an intimate mixture of deciduous woodland, pine woods, acid grassland, heath and bog be found. This is a vast area to discover and there is no better place to start than the Museum and Visitor Centre in the centre of Lyndhurst in the centre of the Forest. Whilst open access for the visitor to all these unenclosed acres is such a joy the equally open access for ponies and other grazing animals means that many of the woodland plants do not survive.

An ungrazed wood complete with flowers can best be seen where it has been fenced to exclude stock for a long time: the Hampshire Trust provides such an opportunity in *Roydon Woods*, an unbelievably beautiful reserve just outside the New Forest perambulation, as its boundary is called.

Whilst the unique importance of the New Forest cannot be denied it is not the only part of Hampshire to have an international status—the other is the many shallow-water bays that punctuate the coastline on both sides of the Solent between Hampshire and the Isle of Wight, from Keyhaven in the west for 35 miles to the Sussex border in Langstone Harbour, which have a combined total of nearly 22,000 acres of intertidal mud flats, sand and saltmarsh attracting up to 40,000 wildfowl at their peak. Many of these bays are now protected as nature reserves on both sides of the Solent and some of the best are on the north shore of West Solent, at *Keyhaven Marshes*, in the shelter of that astonishing shingle spit of Hurst Castle.

In complete contrast to the soft coast of the Solent side of the Isle of Wight, its south side is an almost continuous stretch of formidable and variable cliffs. The most significant are at the west end beneath *Compton Down*, the finest example of maritime influence on the chalk flora in England.

If botanists are attracted to the chalk, and ornithologists to the coast, then to entomologists, and those other countrymen who understand flies, fishermen, Hampshire's greatest attraction must be its world-famous, clear-running, trout streams—the Test and the Itchen. The fish are at the top of a food-chain which teems with all forms of wildlife. This wildlife can best be observed at the two Hampshire Trust reserves *Winnall Moors* on the Itchen, almost in the centre of Winchester, and the *Lower Test* on the western outskirts of Southampton. Elsewhere access to the trout streams may be limited and a long walk beside either stream difficult. For the unimpeded pleasure of a waterside walk the north of the county offers the Basingstoke canal: for stretching your legs the section west of Fleet is better but for spotting dragonflies the *Basingstoke Canal Flashes* to the east is one of the best places in the county.

● Hampshire and Isle of Wight Naturalists' Trust (HIOWNT), 71 The Hundred, Romsey, SO5 8BZ. 0794 513786/830070.

Basingstoke Canal Flashes   11

Map 186 SU84-52- 3½ acres (1½ ha)
3 miles east of Fleet north of A323 to Aldershot. Part SSSI. Open water, aquatic plants, dragonflies.

Access   AYR on foot to viewing points over:

1. Eelmoor Flash from the parking space by Eelmoor Bridge at SU842528 across the bridge and left along the towpath.
2. Claycart Flash from the parking space in the large sandy area on the north side of A323 opposite Claycart Road at SU852524 and taking the path to the left on the south side of the canal.

Information   Nothing at site: leaflet from HIOWNT.

History   These Flashes were constructed when the canal was built to act as reservoirs to augment the water supply: they were originally much larger and deeper. When the canal ceased to be used the Flashes became havens for wildlife harbouring many rare species. However they gradually silted up and by 1970 Claycart had reverted to dry woodland. Now the canal is being restored for navigation the Flashes are being used as reservoirs for wildlife. Claycart has been dredged and stocked with rare plants from the main canal.

What to See   Because Eelmoor Flash has never dried out it has retained a remarkably rich population of dragonflies, with 24 species recorded including the rare brilliant emerald, ruddy darter and the hairy dragonfly. Rare aquatic plants include water-soldier, frogbit, flowering-rush, narrow-leaved water-plantain and water-violet. Palmate newts breed in the water whilst nightingales sing in the dense woodland nearby.

Compton Down

12

Map 196 SZ36-85- 133 acres (54 ha)
Due east of Freshwater, Isle of Wight, north of A3055. SSSI. Chalk grassland.

Access   AYR on foot from the parking space at the east side of Freshwater Bay at SZ349858 onto the track which runs along the crest of the Down to Shalcombe 3 miles to the east.

Information   Nothing on site.

History   Because it is part of the most southerly chalk outcrop in England and has steep south-facing slopes to the sea this is our best example of chalk grassland affected by the sea: the sward is very open with considerable areas of chalk rubble which restricts the growth of course grasses and allows many small flowers, including annuals, to flourish. Elsewhere, on deeper soils, there are patches of gorse and occasional hawthorn. The flowers attract butterflies including migrants which make their first landfall here.

What to See   Amongst the wild flowers are horseshoe and kidney vetches, squinancywort, clustered bellflower, early gentian, early-purple, green-winged and pyramidal orchids. The butterflies include Adonis, small and chalkhill blues, dark-green fritillary and an occasional Glanville fritillary whose caterpillars feed on plantains on the undercliff and which occurs only in the Isle of Wight in Britain, where it flies in June. Migrating clouded yellows are most likely to be seen between mid-July and October. The cliffs have nesting sea-birds including fulmar and kittiwake, with a few pairs of guillemot, razorbill and puffin.

Keyhaven Marshes

13

Map 196 SZ31-91- 686 acres (278 ha)
1 mile south-east of Milford-on-Sea on the east side of Hurst Spit. SSSI. Mud flats, shingle bank and beach.

Access   AYR on foot from car parking space in Keyhaven village at SZ306915 onto public footpath along the sea-wall and out to Hurst Castle.

Information   Nothing on site.

History   Hurst Spit is a 1½ mile shingle ridge and forms the western boundary of the reserve. In its shelter a large area of mud flats and shingle banks have developed with the area immediately inside the ridge forming a narrow zone of salt marsh. There are also a few pools behind the sea-wall with areas of reed-bed.

What to See   Salt marsh plants include annual sea-blite, marsh mallow, golden samphire, Danish scurvygrass, sea-lavender and sea-pink whilst the shingle on the sheltered side and around the castle has little-Robin, yellow horned-poppy and sea kale. In autumn large numbers of Brent geese, shelduck and teal are present with smaller flocks of ducks such as long-tailed, goldeneye, pochard and wigeon and there is a gathering of red-breasted merganser in November. The spring migration may bring red-throated diver, arctic and great skuas and black tern, with waders such as black and bar-tailed godwits, common and curlew sandpipers, ruff, little stint and whimbrel in the autumn. Little, common and Sandwich terns all breed here in moderate numbers.

Lower Test   `14`

Map 196 SU36-14- 270 acres (110 ha)
On the west side of M271 between Southampton and Totton. Leave M271 at Exit 1 and turn south onto the minor road: after 200 yds, park, cross over railway onto the reserve. SSSI. Reed-beds, water meadows, river banks, brackish grassland, salt marsh.

Access   AYR on foot from CP at SU367150 onto the public footpaths and hide on the west side. The reserve can also be viewed from CP on the south side at Redbridge on A35 at SU369137.

Information   Interpretation boards near the entrance.

History   The marshland near the mouth of the River Test is subject to periodic flooding and inundation by the sea. The latter is becoming more frequent as the south coast of Britain slowly sinks into the sea at over 7 inches per century, so there is now less grazing than there was previously. Some areas have become overgrown and reed-beds have expanded to become some of the largest on the south coast. For over 25 years the reeds have been harvested for thatching.

What to See   Sedge and reed warblers breed every year in the reed-beds whilst lapwing, curlew, redshank and snipe nest in the old hay meadows. In autumn bearded tit and bittern arrive and, later still, marsh harrier may be seen. Winter brings masses of dunlin, wigeon and teal, and a flock of the unusual water pipit. The long list of plants (over 450) has several of great interest particularly those of brackish areas such as wild celery, bulbous foxtail and brookweed: there is a small clump of green hellebore. Marsh-orchids are a feature of the marsh with meadowsweet, marsh valerian, purple-loosestrife, marsh-marigold and green-winged orchid.

Picnic site in summer.

Old Winchester Hill `15`

Map 185 SU64-20- 151 acres (61 ha)
2 miles west of West Meon off the A32 Alton to Fareham road. Leave West Meon on minor road on the south side of the river bridge named Station Road: reserve is on the left after 2 miles. NNR. Chalk grassland, scrub, woodland.

Access AYR on foot from an almost continuous series of lay-bys, starting at SU645215, which run along the ridge parallel to the reserve. The part nearest the road is a picnic site with superb views over the New Forest to the Isle of Wight.

Information A nature trail guide is available from a dispenser at south end of lay-bys at SU647210. The 1-mile trail leads to an Information Centre and wild flower garden with labelled plants. To find the Centre turn right down the hill just before the yew wood at the south end.

History An area of outstanding chalk grassland, yew woodland and scrub managed to maintain a balance which not only produces a wide range of plants, including 14 species of orchid, but provides habitats for over 30 species of butterfly. The scrub, which includes a large area of juniper, is cut over a 30-year rotation but the dense yew wood is unmanaged and many of the trees are 200–300 years old.

What to See South-west-facing grassy slopes are extraordinarily colourful from May onwards with violets, horseshoe and kidney vetches, yellow rattle and autumn gentian: there is also a very large population of round-headed rampion, at its best in July. Butterflies include chalkhill blue, ringlet, dark green fritillary, marbled white and Duke of Burgundy. The scrub attracts many warblers and the yew berries redwing and fieldfare in winter. The yews also shelter over a dozen badger setts.

Wheelchairs have access to grassy tracks along the hill-top from a special parking area at the south end of the lay-bys.

Roydon Woods `16`

Map 196 SU31-00- 850 acres (344 ha)
1 mile south of Brockenhurst east of A337 towards Lymington. SSSI. Ancient woodland, heath, grassland, river.

Access AYR on foot via the bridle path to the south of Filly Inn on A337 at SU302003 or from the parking space in the lane at SZ314995 through the gate and across the field to the entrance to the reserve after 200 yds onto a network of well-walked paths. Please keep to the paths and away from the river banks.

Information Leaflet from HIOWNT.

History Although adjacent to the New Forest with vegetation typical of that area, these fine woods have never been part of it and domesticated grazing animals have long been excluded. As a result the ground flora is much richer than that in the Forest proper.

What to See   Woods ranging from oak/ash coppice-with-standards to beech/hornbeam with occasional wild-service tree and, in damper areas by the streams, alder and willow carr. Shrubs include field maple, spindle, alder buckthorn, dogwood and guelder-rose. Amongst the rarer plants are royal fern and narrow-leaved lungwort. Buzzard, hobby and sparrowhawk may be seen and a small herd of red deer visits the reserve.

Selborne Hanger   `17`

Map 186 SU73-33- 240 acres (97 ha)
¼ mile west of Selborne on B3006 from Alton to Liss. SSSI. Ancient woodland.

Access   AYR on foot by a path from CP behind the Selborne Arms in the middle of the village at SU742336 which leads to the foot of the famous 'zig-zag', constructed in 1753. After a short, sharp climb this leads though the Hanger to the Common above. Alternatively cars may be parked in Newton Valence, 1¼ miles west of Selborne at SU742327 from which a bridleway goes on to the Common avoiding any climbing.

Information   Leaflet showing paths through the reserve, and others in the village, on sale in Wakes Museum 100 yds north of CP: open daily (except Tues) 12 noon–5.30 p.m. or from the Selborne Cottage Shop next door. Museum also has displays on the surrounding area.

History   The surroundings inspired Reverend Gilbert White to write letters to two naturalist friends which later became his *Natural History and Antiquities of Selborne* when published in 1788. White, whose grandfather was Vicar of Selborne, first knew the area as a boy and returned in 1751.

What to See   The Hanger is a beech wood on the steep chalk slope south-west of the village. In its majestic shade are ash, young beech, dogwood, hawthorn, hazel, holly, spindle, wayfaring-tree and yew. Sadly many of the finest trees were felled by the hurricane of October 1987 but the ground flora still contains wood melick, spurge laurel, nettle-leaved bellflower and Solomon's-seal: ferns are numerous on this shady slope. The Common on the plateau above varies from open scrub round grassy clearings to high forest: the acid-loving flora has gorse, broom and bracken.

T[D] in CP. Refreshments in village.

Wheelchairs have access to the bottom of the zig-zag path.

Winnall Moors   `18`

Map 186 SU48-30- 40 acres (16 ha)
¼ mile north-east of the centre of Winchester east of North Wall Recreation Ground which is at the end of Park Avenue. SSSI. Water meadows, reed-beds, fen carr, river banks.

Access   AYR on foot through the Recreation Ground to the far end where there is a bridge over River Itchen leading on to about 1 mile of surfaced paths and a hide overlooking a small pond.

Information   Leaflet, including map, from TI Office in Broadway, Winchester or from HIOWNT. Notice board at entrance draws attention to wildlife in season.

History   The area was farmed as water meadows along the Itchen until abandoned in the 1930s and most of the rich, tall, fen vegetation with extensive beds of reeds and sedges has developed since then. It was established as a nature reserve in 1981. A further area of over 60 acres lies to the north but is not open to the public.

What to See   The River Itchen is famous for its salmon and trout which thrive in its clear, lime-rich water, but it also supports large numbers of duck including breeding tufted duck and mallard which are joined in winter by pochard and gadwall. Coot, moorhen, little grebe and mute swan nest amongst the sedges and reeds in which sedge, reed and grasshopper warblers sing in summer. Waterside plants include hemp-agrimony and great willowherb: an unusual plant of late summer is green-flowered helleborine.

Wheelchairs have no access via the footbridge but there is another (locked) entrance in Durngate, east of the Police Station which can be opened by arrangement with HIOWNT.

Oxfordshire

Two physical features give a special character to Oxfordshire and dominate its landscape—the River Thames or Isis into which almost all its streams and small rivers flow—and the geology which, from the lower Jurassic in the north-west to the upper Cretaceous in the south-east, has provided an almost continuous series of lime-rich rocks, banishing heather and heathland to a few isolated patches on the plateau of the Chilterns.

These features can perhaps be best appreciated from the city of Oxford which stands on the Thames almost midway between the north-west and south-east borders of the county. Most of the colleges which have made Oxford world-famous have been built of the honey-coloured, oolitic limestone quarried in the Cotswolds which rise to over 800 ft near Chipping Norton north-west of the city. Here are many pretty stone villages though the landscape never quite achieves the grandeur of the Gloucestershire Cotswolds further west and most of it is under intensive agriculture. Remnants of the once widespread limestone grassland are now confined to old quarries and railway lines, some of which were built to carry the stone away, either for building or to extract the iron, far beyond the county boundary. Such a complex can be seen at *Horley* whilst one of the best exposures through the Jurassic is in the abandoned Hook Norton railway cutting four miles north-east of Chipping Norton.

Oxford is set in a plain of Jurassic clays—Oxford and Kimmeridge—through which the Thames and its tributaries meander. Meads, meadows and fens line their banks or are covered by their waters in winter. Many are public open spaces within the city limits—Iffley Meadows, Magdalen Meadow, Port Meadow—and, only a mile or so to the north, lie Pixey and Yarnton Meads. Smaller examples set aside as nature reserves include *Tuckmill Meadow* near the Wiltshire border.

Separating the two Jurassic clays is a narrow band of harder rock, full of fossils, the eponymous Corallian. The lower strata are somewhat sandy and these are exposed a few miles south-west of Oxford near Sandleigh and *Dry Sandford*—names reflecting the rarity of the habitat.

To the south and east of Oxford the great band of the chalk commands the horizon except where the Thames breaks through the Goring Gap north-west of Reading at a point where the well-wooded escarpment of the Chilterns gives way to the more rounded, down-like, barer hills which run west into Berkshire. The chalk of the Chilterns generally only comes to the surface along the escarpment: behind, it is overlain by a thick layer of clay-with-flints to which are added Tertiary deposits such as the mixed clay and sand of the Reading beds. These increase in depth as the altitude falls towards the River Thames in the south-east corner of the county.

The complex of chalk and clay, chalk grassland and woodland may be appreciated to the full on *Chinnor Hill*. Similar complexes can occur on the dip slope where valleys are deep enough to cut through the clay capping to expose the chalk on their flanks as occurs at Bix Bottom north-west of Henley which cradles the *Warburg Reserve*, perhaps the most rewarding and unexpected of all the wildlife areas still to be found in this part of middle England.

- Berkshire, Buckinghamshire and Oxfordshire Naturalists' Trust (BBONT), 3 Church Cowley Road, Rose Hill, Oxford OX4 3JR. 0865 775476.

Chinnor Hill   19

Map 165 SP76-00- 70 acres (28 ha)
1000 yds south-east of Chinnor Church. Follow minor road to Bledlow Ridge, take first turn left and then left fork into Hill Top Lane to CP in 500 yds. SSSI. Chalk grassland, scrub and mixed deciduous woodland. Fine view.

Access   AYR on foot from CP at SP766003 along well-marked paths.

Information   None on site.

History   This reserve on the Chilterns escarpment demonstrates the two kinds of soil for which it is renowned: clay-with-flints on the top, with the chalk exposed on the north-west facing slopes below. The clay-with-flints is dominated by oak/ash woodland, with small areas of beech wood on the crest and, here and there, groups of whitebeam or wild cherry. The chalk, once grazed by livestock and rabbits, began reverting to scrub in the 1950s overwhelming the native juniper. Now scrub is being cleared and sheep grazing has been introduced.

What to See   Chalk grassland with common rock-rose, wild thyme, wild candytuft, autumn gentian, bee, frog and pyramidal orchids, and scrub with several different wild roses, as well as wild privet, spindle, buckthorn, wayfaring-tree and the now rejuvenating juniper. This scrub attracts many nesting birds including seven species of warbler as well as food for winter visitors such as redwing and fieldfare.

Wheelchairs have access through the woods.

Dry Sandford Pit   20

Map 164 SU46-99- 20 acres (8 ha)

2 miles north-west of Abingdon at the east end of Cothill village. On the south side of the road opposite a curio shop enter a lay-by which leads up slope to CP. SSSI. Geological site with dry grassland, scrub, fen and pond.

Access   AYR on foot from CP at SU466997. Please do not collect fossils from friable cliffs or walk in the fragile fen area.

Information   Board with illustrations near entrance.

History   An old sand and stone quarry in the Corallian limestone excavated in the 1930s which is rich in fossils of ammonites and belemnites as well as coral. It had become overgrown with scrub and coarse grasses which are now being kept in check by periodic visits by BBONT sheep.

What to See   The fen area has early marsh-orchid, common spotted-orchid and marsh helleborines and is one of only two sites in South England for the rare variegated horsetail. This wet area also attracts frogs, toads and newts whilst kingfisher are seen quite frequently. Glow-worms may be seen and the great green bush-cricket heard on warm summer nights when, by day, the marbled white butterfly may be on the wing.

Horley   21

Map 151 SP41-43- 30 acres (12 ha)

3 miles north-west of Banbury via A41 and then A422 to Wroxton: take third turn right onto minor road at the west end of village. Reserve is on right at cross-roads after ½ mile. Abandoned railway line and ironstone quarry with grassland, scrub and woodland.

Access   AYR on foot:

1. from parking space by cross-roads at SP407428 along an uneven path.
2. from parking space at junction of Wroxton—Horley road and turn to Hanwell at SP417430 through entrance 100 yds up road to Horley on left.

Information   Notice board at entrances at both access points.

History   This area on the oolite was mined for ironstone until about 60 years ago. This was carried away south eastwards on a mineral railway to connect with the main line at Banbury. When mining was abandoned the natural succession of scrub invasion began which has now developed into some tall woodland. In addition two areas were planted with larch which now have an understorey of hazel, elder, holly and some introduced grey elder. Rough grassland remains in a few areas where it is kept open by public pressure.

What to See   Characteristic plants of limestone grassland including large patches of greater knapweed and lady's bedstraw. In all a total of 170 different plant species have been recorded along with 43 species of breeding bird and numerous butterflies including the marbled white.

Wheelchair access from the east end. Disabled may be taken by car to park at scout camp site which is signposted off the Horley road.

Tuckmill Meadow   22

Map 174 SU23-89- 13 acres (5 ha)
½ mile north of Shrivenham off minor road to Watchfield. Take track to Bremhill Golf Club: 100 yds beyond entrance to Golf Club there is a gate on right into CP at SU238897. SSSI. Limestone grassland, fenland, hedgerows and coppice.

Access   AYR on foot from CP.

Information   Nothing at site.

History   The name Tuckmill refers to a fulling mill which once stood on the north bank of the brook at the far end of the reserve from the CP. Tucking is the old local word for fulling which is the processs whereby cloth is beaten with a mixture of Fuller's earth and water to increase its density. Fuller's earth is still dug locally from the Middle Jurassic beds at Baulking 3½ miles east. This site was overgrown but is now being restored by cattle and sheep grazing.

What to See   Species-rich limestone grassland at the south end gives way to a rushy fenland beside the stream with meadowsweet, southern marsh-orchid, marsh valerian and great willowherb. The thick hedges have nesting chiffchaff and spotted flycatcher whilst sedge and reed warbler and reed bunting nest elsewhere. Kingfisher are regularly seen and there are good populations of dragonflies and damselflies.

Warburg Reserve   23

Map 175 SO71-87- 257 acres (103 ha)
4 miles north-west of Henley-on-Thames. Follow A423 and after 1½ miles fork right onto B480. After ¾ mile turn left at the north end of Middle Assendon and follow twisting lane for 2 miles to reserve entrance shortly after the lane becomes a track. SSSI. Ancient deciduous woodland, glades and grassland.

Access   AYR on foot from CP through gate on right at SO720879 on good way-marked paths.

Information   Booklet and nature trail guide from shelter in CP. Interpretative display and other information from Visitor Centre across lane from CP open daily 10 a.m.–5 p.m. except Thurs and Fri.

History   The Warburg Reserve lies in Bix Bottom, a dry winding valley through the chalk with mixed woods of oak, ash, beech, birch, field maple and yew with an understorey of hazel, dogwood, wild privet, spindle, wayfaring-tree and hawthorn. Formerly much overgrown and planted with conifers and other aliens such as Turkey oak and sycamore, these are now being removed and openings created which will be maintained as grassland by grazing sheep. An old rifle range is managed particularly to encourage butterflies and nearly 40 species have been recorded.

What to See   One of the richest woods in southern England. The 450 higher plants include 15 different orchids and 50 indicators of ancient woodland such as yellow archangel, columbine, wood barley, green hellebore, herb-Paris and Solomon's-seal. Breeding birds include redstart, kestrel, sparrowhawk, willow and marsh tit, wood warbler and woodcock.

T in Visitor Centre.

Wheelchairs have limited access.

Wiltshire

For the visitor there can be little doubt that for scenery and history, both archaeological and natural, it is the chalk which is the major attraction of Wiltshire. Geologically two-thirds of the county consists of chalk and, even though some is buried beneath superficial deposits of varying thickness, there are two distinct and extensive areas where the chalk is at the surface—Salisbury Plain in the south and the Marlborough Downs to the north, each embracing ancient monuments and ancient chalk grassland which are some of the most important in the country.

The *Pewsey Downs*, south-west of Marlborough, look south into the Vale of Pewsey and the headwaters of the Bristol Avon, and north-west to Avebury with its stone circle, perhaps the centre of Neolithic Britain. Eighteen miles south stands the even more impressive monument of Stonehenge in the centre of Salisbury Plain, where military training has helped to protect the landscape but made it more difficult to enjoy. Down in the Vale the Bristol Avon flows through clay-lined water meadows where the grass grows lusher and provides food for cows whose surplus milk is converted into cheese. This contrast between the grasslands of the Downs and the clay vales led to Wiltshire being dubbed the 'land of chalk and cheese'.

Without proper management these water meadows rapidly become overgrown and revert to valley fens fed by the lime-rich water coming off the chalk. This is the history of *Jones's Mill*, a mile upstream from Pewsey, which has become the best wetland site of its kind in the county in the 100 years since the water meadows were abandoned.

In the chalk uplands too, the lime-rich waters were exploited in the valley bottoms—the streams were dammed and widened to create water-cress beds. Many of these have also been abandoned and provide a vivid contrast with the grassland and woods which hang on the steep slopes above. Such a kaleidoscope in a small space is beautifully demonstrated, on the edge of the Marlborough

Downs above Swindon, at the Wiltshire Trust's *Clouts Wood* reserve.

Near Swindon the typical Wiltshire landscape changes to one more akin to the Vale of Aylesbury—a wide level plain drained by the Upper Thames or Isis. This river is now so feeble that it often runs dry in summer but, in winter, it revives and is still capable of overflowing its banks and flooding the hay meadows alongside, some of which remain as the finest examples in Britain. *North Meadow, Cricklade*, in addition to its dazzling display of fritillaries in spring, has so many wild flowers in its hay that the seed is harvested and sold as 'Cricklade Mixture'.

Going south-westwards the plain narrows until, at Chippenham, it is only a short hop to the, perhaps unexpected, Wiltshire Cotswolds—honey-coloured stone villages nestling in wooded valleys. Can there be a more beautiful walk anywhere in England than the one which starts beside the By Brook as it runs through the middle of enchanting Castle Combe? The path climbs the gentle wooded slopes of *Rack Hill* and then drops into the hollow which shelters the picturesque hamlet of Long Dean—and such woods these are on the oolite, with the excitement of knowing that lily-of-the-valley, Solomon's-seal and herb-Paris might all be seen.

If Cotswold limestone is a surprise in the extreme north-west then there is, perhaps, an even greater one for those who visit the extreme south-east, for suddenly you are on the edge of the Hampshire Basin and the soils are a mixture of acid sands over the Reading Beds and impermeable London clay: birch and bracken alternate with sallow and alder. Such mixtures make for species richness and none more so than in *Blackmoor Copse*, where the rides are alive with butterflies and birds on the wing in the spring.

Whilst in Wiltshire the chalk hills hold centre stage, some of its most seductive pleasures are found in the wings.

● Wiltshire Trust for Nature Conservation (WTNC), 19 High Street, Devizes, SN10 1AT. 0380 725670.

Blackmoor Copse   24

Map 184 SU23-29- 77 acres (31 ha)
5 miles east of Salisbury via A30 towards Winchester. After 2 miles take the turning on the right to Pitton: passing through Pitton and Farley to East Grimstead, turn left at north end of that village to reserve at next T-junction after ½ mile. SSSI. Ancient woodland, pond, butterflies.

Access   AYR on foot from the parking space on the roadside at the T-junction at SU234288 onto good, but sometimes muddy, paths for about 1½ miles.

Information   Nothing on site: nature trail leaflet and reserve guide from WTNC and Salisbury TI Office.

History   The northern part of the reserve is ancient woodland whereas the southern part was once common land, which may have been managed as wood pasture where commoners grazed their stock and areas were fenced to protect the trees and coppice. It is probable that this southern part had been clear-felled by the nineteenth century. During and immediately after the Second World War, many old oaks were felled and the wood neglected. It was bought by RSNC in 1956 who leased it to WTNC in 1963. The whole wood is largely situated on London clay and slopes towards the south-east which makes that corner particularly wet, with many sedges and rushes. There is also a pond which is important as a drinking area for birds and mammals.

What to See   An oak/ash wood with birch and some field maple, and an understorey of coppiced hazel, with alder and willow in wetter areas. Woodland flowers include sheets of bluebells and wood anemone with meadowsweet, bugle, dog-violet, yellow pimpernel, ragged-Robin, wood and water avens and black bryony. The birds include several warblers, great spotted woodpecker, treecreeper, nuthatch, and woodcock in winter. Amongst 32 species of butterflies recently recorded purple emperor and pearl-bordered fritillary are of particular interest. Other notable species are silver-washed fritillary, white admiral and purple hairstreak. Mammals include dormouse and roe deer.

Clouts Wood   `25`

Map 173 SU13-79- 33 acres (13 ha)
3 miles south of Swindon on A4361 to Avebury 1 mile south-west of Wroughton. SSSI. Ancient woodland, hazel coppice.

Access   AYR on foot from layby on the north side of A4361 at SU136800 to entrance 50 yds towards Wroughton on opposite side of road signposted to Clouts Wood. Then follow good path for 600 yds to horse chestnut, bridge across stream and lime tree at entrance. Way-marked paths are steep and often muddy.

Information   Notice board near entrance: nature trail leaflet and reserve guide from WTNC and from PO in Wroughton.

History   An ancient oak/ash woodland managed as coppice-with-standards it lies on the edge of the chalk. Below the chalk a band of Upper greensand overlies impermeable Gault clay and there is a line of springs in the valley opposite leading into the stream which flows through the bottom of the wood. Early in the twentieth century this was widened into a series of ponds to create water-cress beds. Since the Wiltshire Trust took over the wood in 1983 earlier plantings of conifers and beech are gradually being converted back to native woodland and a coppice cycle is being restored. Wych elm on the steep slopes was ravaged by Dutch elm disease: some dead trees have been left standing as roosting sites for owls and bats.

What to See   Other trees and shrubs include field maple, wild cherry and traveller's-joy whilst the ground flora has spiked star-of-Bethlehem, wood vetch, nettle-leaved bellflower and herb-Paris with hemp-agrimony along the stream. Characteristic woodland birds occur: woodpeckers, tits, treecreeper and nuthatch with redwing and fieldfare in winter. Marbled white and ringlet butterflies may be seen in the valley below and roe deer visit the wood.

T [D]. Refreshments, picnic site at Barbury Castle via B4005 east of Wroughton.

Jones's Mill   26

Map 173 SU16-61- 29 acres (12 ha)
¾ mile north-east of Pewsey via B3087 towards Burbage turning left after ½ mile at the crossroads down Dursden Lane signposted to Milkhouse Water. Pass over railway bridge and park immediately on left. SSSI. Valley fen, willow carr, pond.

Access   AYR on foot from the parking space at SU170611 to a sunken lane after 100 yds on the left which leads to the reserve where the paths are usually wet.

Information   Nothing on site: reserve guide from WTNC.

History   Jones's Mill on the Hampshire Avon and a windmill built north of the reserve were used to control water flowing along the Kennet and Avon Canal. Meadows beside the River Avon which flows through the reserve were managed until about 1850 as water meadows: these were flooded from nearby springs by a system of sluices and drains and the water, rich in nutrients and warmer than the land, promoted the growth of an early bite for grazing animals. Later some springs were used as water-cress beds but production ceased soon after the Second World War. Now fenland plants have colonized the old meadows with rushes and sedges and alder and willow carr.

What to See   Fenland flowers include common-spotted and southern marsh-orchid, marsh valerian, bogbean, greater tussock-sedge and bottle sedge. The river and nearby canal attract kingfisher, heron, moorhen and tufted duck whilst reed and sedge warbler chatter in the fen and snipe may zig-zag away. Water vole and water shrew inhabit the banks whilst butterflies on the wing may include ringlet, speckled wood and purple hairstreak.

North Meadow, Cricklade   27

Map 163 SU09-94- 109 acres (44 ha)
½ mile north-west of Cricklade on the road leading north from town centre to A419 to Cirencester, between River Churn and River Thames. NNR. Ancient hay meadow.

Access   AYR on foot from parking space by entrance at SU 100943 to public footpaths which cross the site. In summer please keep to the paths or walk round the edge: from hay-making to April there is open access.

Information   Leaflet from the Warden, Greywethers, West Overton, Marlborough SN8 1QE.

History   A meadow which has been managed for hay for at least 800 years as a result of an unusual form of land tenure. Citizens of Cricklade are entitled to graze 10 horses or cattle and 20 sheep during autumn and winter up to 12 February. Then it reverts to the owners who 'own' the hay: this is now sold as a standing crop to local farmers by NCC. Lying between two rivers the meadow is sometimes flooded in winter which deposits fertile silt and inhibits frost. The floor of the valley consists of gravels and clays derived from the oolite and they are therefore lime-rich.

What to See   Pride of place goes to the fritillary—several million plants of this handsome flower make a brave display in late April and early May: most are mauve but 1 or 2 per cent are white. In addition cowslip, adder's-tongue, great burnet, ragged-Robin, betony and meadow-rue occur. The river banks harbour kingfisher and reed bunting and, in winter, grey wagtail and green sandpiper. When the meadow floods snipe, teal, redshank and golden plover move in whilst, in summer, hedges are alive with blackcap and treecreeper with orange-tip, small copper, small skipper and ringlet amongst the butterflies.

Pewsey Downs

28

Map 173 SU11-63- 422 acres (170 ha)
5 miles south-west of Marlborough via A4 to Fyfield taking left turn at the west end of village for Lockeridge and Alton Barnes: reserve is on both sides of road at hill crest. NNR. Chalk grassland.

Access   AYR on foot from limited car parking space on the roadside to a network of footpaths and bridleways with freedom to visit any part of the reserve, but please keep dogs on a lead.

Information   Leaflet from the Warden, Greywethers, West Overton, Marlborough SN8 1QE.

History   One of the finest areas of chalk grassland left in England with a long history of continuous grazing by sheep and, more recently, cattle. It lies on the south edge of the Marlborough Downs looking into the Vale of Pewsey to the south and is within a few miles of Avebury, at the centre of Neolithic Britain.

What to See   The special interest is the large concentration of species confined to ancient grassland such as bastard-toadflax, chalk milkwort, burnt orchid, field fleawort, horseshoe vetch, round-headed rampion, squinancywort, knapweed broomrape, early gentian and tuberous thistle. These support a brilliant display of butterflies, notably brown argus, chalkhill and small blue, dingy skipper, green hairstreak and marsh fritillary: there are a large number of hills made by the yellow meadow ant. Birds of open grassland—skylark and meadow pipit—are abundant as are badger with over 150 holes in the hillside round six large setts.

Rack Hill

29

Map 173 ST84-76- 20 acres (8 ha)
5 miles north-west of Chippenham leaving A420 to Bristol at Ford, turning north between the bridge over By Brook and the church to the parking space on the

road at the south end of Castle Combe village. SSSI. Ancient limestone grassland, scrub.

Access   AYR on foot from parking space at ST842768 or in village at top of hill over old stone bridge across the By Brook onto well-marked path.

Information   Nature trail leaflet from PO in Castle Combe, TI Office in Chippenham or WTNC.

History   The reserve takes its name from the medieval practice of cleaning woollen cloth with a solution of Fuller's earth clay. When the fulling was complete the cloth was stretched out on racks to dry in the sun: the south-westerly slopes of this hill were suitable—hence Rack Hill. The antiquity of the turf is indicated by the large ant hills—some over 50 years old. Until recently, when sheep grazing was restored, there was only light cattle grazing which allowed scrub to spread providing shelter for small song birds.

What to See   Downland flowers include clustered bellflower, fairy flax, common rock-rose, wild thyme, fragrant and pyramidal orchids. Many species of butterfly occur such as chalkhill blue and marbled white. Heron, kingfisher and dipper feed in the brook and green woodpecker on the ant hills, whilst chiffchaff and long-tailed tit sing in the scrub.

SOUTH-EAST

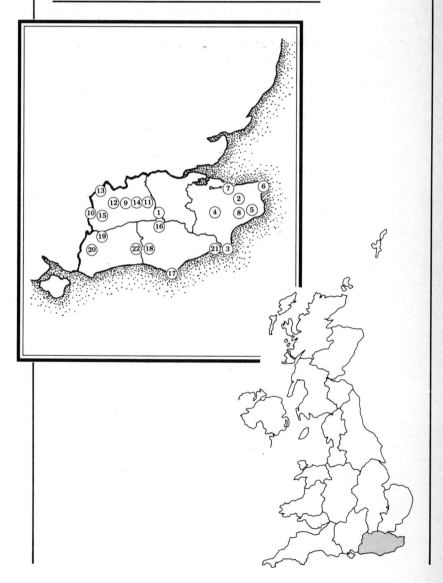

Kent

Despite the growing pressures on the Kent countryside from the development of the Channel Tunnel and its rail link with London, which adds to the ravages of over 100 miles of motorway already built, it still retains a wealth and variety of sites for wildlife.

Variety is well demonstrated on the coasts of Kent. Along the north coast the rise and fall of the tides in the Thames estuary has produced a landscape of mud flats and creeks backed by salt marshes and grazing meadows which have remained unchanged for centuries. Though much has been drained and reclaimed the Swale between the Isle of Sheppey and the mainland to the south is of such importance for birds that it has been recognized as a wetland of international importance under the 1973 Ramsar Convention. This wilderness can be entered only 3 miles from the end of the M2 in the *South Swale* reserve of the Kent Trust for Nature Conservation.

On the east coast the mud gives way to sand—not unexpectedly—in *Sandwich Bay*. Whilst golf courses like Royal St George's occupy most of the dunes they also protect a wonderful display of wild flowers and provide a protected landfall for birds from the Continent during migration.

The most prominent feature of the south coast, and the most important site for sea-birds in South-East England, is *Dungeness* where flints from the eroding chalk cliffs, where the South Downs meet the sea further west, have been rounded and thrown up by wave action over thousands of years.

The best-known feature in Kent must nevertheless be where the North Downs meet the sea in the white cliffs of Dover. These downs dominate the northern half of the county and fragments of the once almost continuous chalk grassland still remain to provide a haven for wild flowers and butterflies which is hardly equalled anywhere else in Britain. One of the nearest to the white cliffs is at *Lydden* only 4 miles north-west of Dover. However not all the chalk was cleared of the original forest cover and there are still many areas of ancient woodland, especially on steeper slopes and summits—a fine example can be seen at *Yockletts Bank* south of Canterbury. To the north and west of Canterbury, on the London clay, is one of the most extensive areas of almost continuous woodland in the south-east—Blean Woods with access at *Church Wood* and *East Blean* reserves.

The well-wooded Weald which lies between the North and South Downs is an area of contrasts between heavy clay soils and narrow bands of acid greensand. The oak/ash woods of the clays give way to birch, pine and bracken on the sands and occasionally, as at *Hothfield Common*, valley bogs are preserved to provide a New Forest landscape in miniature.

Though development has defaced the Kentish countryside there can be compensations—disused gravel workings at *Dungeness* are an asset to that reserve, and residents in the west of the county can enjoy watching wildfowl and waders in quantity at *Bough Beech Reservoir* where there are now about twice as many species of breeding birds as there were before the reservoir was built.

● Kent Trust for Nature Conservation (KTNC), 1a Bower Mount Road, Maidstone, ME16 8AX. 0622 753017.

Bough Beech Reservoir

Map 188 TQ49-48- 82 acres (32 ha)
2 miles south of Ide Hill, bisected by a minor road to Winkhurst Green which goes from B2042 at TQ489501 to the B2027 east of Bough Beech. Open water and muddy shores for birds.

Access   The reserve can be viewed from the road where there is room for parking. To enter the reserve a permit is necessary from the Warden via the Trust office.

Information   Leaflets, nature trail guides and a booklet 'Birds of Bough Beech' from a Visitor Centre in the old oast house at the north end of the reservoir: open April–October 11 a.m.–4 p.m. Weds, Sat and Sun. The Centre also houses displays on the history and early land use of the Eden valley in which the reservoir lies, and on the functions of the oast house.

History   The reservoir was built in the mid-1960s. Water is pumped into it from the River Eden, a tributary of the River Medway, during the winter only. By the autumn large areas of silt and mud are exposed which attract large flocks of migrating birds. Before the reservoir was built about 35 species of birds bred in the area but this has now increased to over 60 species. Though much of the 300 acres of water are used for sailing and angling these activities are not allowed in the reserve.

What to See   In summer lapwing and little ringed plover are nesting on the banks whilst grey wagtail and kingfisher may be seen by a diverted stream between the lake on the east side of the road and the main reservoir. In winter Canada goose and many species of duck including shoveler, gadwall, pochard and goldeneye are regularly seen. In autumn there are numerous greenshank and green sandpiper and, in most years, a passing osprey.
   T at Visitor Centre.
   Wheelchairs have good access and viewing.

Church Wood, Blean

Map 179 TR11-59- 440 acres (176 ha)
At Rough Common 1 mile north-west of Canterbury on a minor road linking the A2 London road with the A290 Whitstable road. There is a 'Nature Reserve' signpost in Rough Common 100 yds north of the Post Office. SSSI. Sessile oak and chestnut woods, coppice and heath, rides and ponds.

Access   AYR via a good gravel road from Rough Common to CP at TR120595. From here three way-marked walks lead off into the wood on good paths.

Information   Direction board with map inside entrance with dispenser for a good guide to the reserve, also leaflets on birds and general information.

History   Church Wood is part of a 7000 acre area known as Blean Woods which lie in an arc from the north-east to south-west of Canterbury. Much is still ancient sessile oak woodland but the rise of the hop industry in Kent in the seventeenth century led to a demand for long poles to support these climbing plants. Native trees were cleared and sweet chestnut, an alien from the uplands of South Europe, was planted in their place and coppiced on a 15-year cycle. Now the hop trade has dwindled and chestnuts are being replaced by conifers. Church Wood reflects all three types of woodland.

What to See   To date 49 species of bird have been recorded breeding on the reserve including the scarce hawfinch, redstart and wood warblers as well as considerable numbers of nightingale, blackcap and garden warbler. The ground flora in summer has large patches of common cow-wheat, the food-plant of the caterpillars of the rare heath fritillary. Management of suitable open areas saw the population rise from 200 in 1983 to 1800 in 1987, but there was a crash to below 200 again in 1988. The nests of black wood ants are also a feature of the woodland floor.

Wheelchairs have some access.

Dungeness   3

Map 189 TR06-18- 2029 acres (821 ha)
2 miles south-east of Lydd, south of the road to Dungeness village. SSSI. The most important sea-bird reserve in South-East England.

Access   Via signposted track to CP at TR068185. Open from 9 a.m.–9 p.m. (or sunset when earlier) daily except Tues. Charge of £2 for non-members of RSPB includes free reserve guide.

Information   Leaflet from Information Centre at CP. A new centre, opening shortly, will have a shop and light refreshments. A way-marked trail leads to four hides overlooking a large area of man-made pits.

History   Dungeness is the largst shingle ridge in Europe. It has developed over 3000 years and is a pebble desert which contains a large sea-bird colony and many fascinating plants adapted to its windswept and often inhospitable climate. This is RSPB's oldest reserve—the first land purchase by the Society was made here in 1931. There has been a full-time warden since 1952.

What to See   In summer there are up to 350 pairs of common tern and Sandwich tern breeding on islands in disused gravel pits overlooked by the hides. There are also a few breeding pairs of common gull and Mediterranean gull. Oystercatcher, ringed plovers, lapwing and redshank breed on the islands and along the shore-line whilst wheatear, skylark and meadow pipit nest on the gravel ridges. In natural hollows reed-beds and marshes attract reed and sedge warbler and the elusive water rail. In winter the pits shelter large numbers of diving and dabbling duck including goldeneye and smew, whilst black-necked, red-necked and Slavonian grebes also occur. In spring and autumn the major attraction is migrating waders and small birds.

T[D].

Wheelchair access to hides.

Hothfield Common ▪4

Map 189 TQ96-45- 139 acres (56 ha)
3 miles north-west of Ashford on the west side of A20 to Charing. SSSI, LNR. Acid bog, heath and birch woodland.

Access AYR on foot from main CP south of junction of minor road to Hothfield village and A20 at TQ971459.

Information There are notice boards with maps and leaflet dispensers at several points on the west side of the minor road. Dispensers have a general leaflet and a nature trail guide to a way-marked route of about 1 mile. The paths can be muddy after rain.

History The Common lies on the edge of a gently sloping plateau. Beneath the sand are impermeable clays. Water passes through the sand but cannot penetrate the clay and so emerges as acid springs. This has led to the creation of valley bogs, four of which occur on the reserve. Too infertile to cultivate the villagers of Hothfield had rights to graze stock and take firewood or peat from the Common. The use of these rights lapsed after the Second World War and much of the area, formerly open heath, has been invaded by bracken and birch.

What to See The bogs are of outstanding interest. The main one can be viewed from a wooden causeway built across it. Bog asphodel, marsh St John's-wort, heath spotted-orchid, common sundew and cross-leaved heath are abundant and, in summer, the wetter areas are white with cottongrass. In addition 12 species of *Sphagnum* moss are found at Hothfield. Visitors are asked to keep to the causeway—the bog is deep and damaged by trampling. Grass snake and common lizard live on the Common whilst fox, badger, weasel and stoat are regularly seen. Amongst the dragonflies is the very local keeled skimmer.

T at CP. Picnic site.

Wheelchairs have access to shortened nature trail.

Lydden ▪5

Map 179 TR27-45- 53 acres (21 ha)
3½ miles north-west of Dover north of the B2060 (old A2) between Lydden and Temple Ewell. On the north side of railway bridge over road take narrow pot-holed lane going north-west parallel with railway for 400 yds. There is adequate car parking space on the left. SSSI, LNR. Chalk grassland.

Access AYR on foot a few yards down lane from CP on the right to the entrance to the reserve, marked by a notice board at TR275451.

Information   Leaflet in dispenser on notice board with a map of the site and up-to-date wildlife facts for the month.

History   Like many other areas of chalk grassland normally maintained by sheep and cattle grazing, the problem is to keep coarse grasses, like torgrass, under control whilst not destroying the wild flowers. This reserve has been divided into three paddocks which are grazed on a rotational system—one in spring and early summer, another from July to February and the third from October to February. This last controls the grasses and produces the ideal conditions.

What to See   One of the few sites in Kent for the burnt-tip orchid and one of the best for early spider-orchid with well over 1000 in good years. Other noteworthy plants are squinancywort, chalk milkwort, dyer's greenweed and autumn lady's-tresses. Butterflies are an important feature: this is now the only Kentish site for the silver-spotted skipper, whilst Adonis blue, chalkhill blue and marbled white also occur. The other outstanding insect is the great green bush-cricket whose song is to be heard in scrub or long grass in late summer.

Sandwich Bay   6

Map 179 TR34-62- 1000 acres (400 ha)
On the coast between the Hoverport in Pegwell Bay and the south end of Sandwich Flats. SSSI. Sand dunes, dune grassland, salt marsh and mud flats.

Access   The reserve is divided into two by the mouth of the River Stour:

1. access to the northern part in Pegwell Bay from Pegwell Bay Picnic Site CP at TR344636 just after derestriction sign on A256 to Sandwich. CP open 9 a.m.–dusk (except 25 December). Parking fee. Good paths along shore to the south.
2. access to the southern part is via a minor road from Sandwich through the Sandwich Bay estate and then north along the coast to CP at TR356592. There is a toll charge of £2.50 entering the estate.

Information   Notice board and KTNC leaflet at Pegwell Bay Picnic Site CP. Hide overlooking reserve 600 yds south of CP is good for evening viewing. KTNC notice board and map at south section of CP.

History   The last remaining area in Kent of a complex of sand dunes, salt marsh, mud flats and dune grassland. The dunes have grown enormously in the last 400 years leaving Sandwich town nearly 2 miles from the sea—and growth continues.

What to See   The sands are full of shells making them lime-rich and attractive to many wild flowers: pyramidal orchid, lizard orchid, yellow-rattle, and adder's-tongue. The salt marsh species include sea blite, sea-lavender, and much sea-purslane bordering the creeks. The shore line has a number of local species notably sea kale and sharp rush. This range of habitats provides suitable conditions for thriving populations of invertebrates and nesting sites for birds such as little tern, ringed plover, shelduck and redshank. The winter brings sanderling and grey plover, snow bunting and hen harrier whilst whimbrel and short-eared owl are amongst those which pass through in autumn. Also passing through are migrant butterflies e.g. clouded yellow and painted lady.

T[D] at Pegwell Bay. Picnic Site.

South Swale   7

Map 179 TR05-64- 1032 acres (413 ha)
South bank of River Swale north of Graveney via the road signposted from the roundabout at the end of M2 to Homestall and Graveney. SSSI, LNR and Ramsar Site. International importance for birds.

Access   AYR on foot along the Saxon Shore path which runs along the south side of the reserve which can be reached from Ye Olde Sportsman Inn at TR060647 or from Nagden at TR030631 via two paths: there is room for parking at both these points (Inn charges £1). Visitors are asked to avoid bird-breeding sites from April–August, particularly around Castle Coote 1½ miles west of the Inn and not to disturb birds on the foreshore at any time.

Information   Notice boards at all entrances have maps and leaflets are available from a dispenser.

History   The reserve is part of the large Swale SSSI and was declared an LNR by Kent County Council in 1969. Management is undertaken by KTNC which owns part of the site. The dykes along the boundary are drainage channels for adjacent farmland but liaison with the Internal Drainage Board has ensured they are managed in a way beneficial to wildlife.

What to See   The reserve includes some 900 acres of mud flats, 40 acres of shingle, 22 acres of salt marsh, 50 acres of grassland and 20 acres of reed-beds and dykes. Its major importance is as an overwintering site for wildfowl and waders—up to 1000 Brent geese gather at times feeding on the eelgrass beds at low water. Waders include redshank, dunlin, knot, curlew and both bar-tailed and black godwit. The shore-line attracts snow bunting in winter and large flocks of linnet, goldfinch, greenfinch and twite, often feeding on the mixture of salt marsh and shingle flowers which occur: sea-lavender, sea aster, thrift, golden-samphire, viper's-bugloss and yellow horned-poppy. Little tern and bearded tit breed on the reserve.

T and Refreshments from Inn.

Yockletts Bank   8

Map 179 TR12-47- 62 acres (25 ha)
5 miles south of Canterbury ½ mile west of B2068 Canterbury to Hythe road turning down the lane at TR137490. SSSI. Mixed deciduous woodland on the chalk with orchids.

Access   On foot from the parking space at the bottom of the lane by turning to Yockletts Farm. There is a small CP in the south part of wood near the entrance at TR124478 but it is only open when the Warden is present. Good way-marked paths lead off from the entrance to the north and south parts of the wood.

Information   Notice board with map at entrance. Some 50 yds into the wood at the exit from CP there is a shelter with a dispenser for leaflets about the reserve and a board with up-to-date news about the wildlife.

History   Situated on the chalk of the North Downs with a capping of clay-with-flints, the natural woodland is ash, hornbeam, field maple, beech and hazel with lime-loving shrubs such as dogwood and spindle. Most parts have been coppiced, especially hazel and hornbeam, but some areas were open grassland until recently and these are managed to safeguard species like common rock-rose and yellow oat-grass. Other openings were created by the great storm of October 1987.

What to See   The reserve is famous for its orchids—lady orchid in late spring is followed by white helleborine, fly orchid, common spotted-orchid, pyramidal orchid, greater butterfly-orchid and broad-leaved helleborine. Woodland birds are plentiful—nightingale, blackcap and chiffchaff are heard singing whilst woodpeckers, nuthatch and treecreeper are often seen.

Surrey

Surrey is a county with a varied geology in a small space which produces a landscape of great contrasts. The chalk hills of the North Downs form a continuous wedge running right across from the 'thin-end-of-the-wedge' of the Hog's Back west of Guildford to the broad end, about 7 miles across, at the Kent border south of Croydon. To the north-west are the sands and gravels of the Bagshot Beds which now support large areas of heathland and ever-expanding housing estates: to the north-east is the London clay surrounding Cobbet's great 'Wen'. South of the chalk the Weald begins with the narrow contrasting bands of Gault clay and greensand, and then the wider expanse of the well-wooded Wealden clays which extend well across the border into Sussex.

Proximity to London has led to the destruction of wildlife habitats in three ways: through the building of houses, roads and factories; through increased public pressure on fragile sites; and more subtly, deterioration because traditional agriculture, which used to help manage the sites, has ceased on the urban fringe and open sites are overwhelmed by the invasion of scrub . For this last reason very few areas of chalk grassland, formerly grazed by sheep or cattle, remain and even the best and most dramatic, on *Box Hill*, suffers from recreational use especially near the car parks. Similarly thousands of acres of heathland are rapidly changing to birch and pine woods. These dry areas are also endangered by frequent fires which kill many of the heathland animals which were once widespread but are now restricted to a few scattered localities: the future for sand lizards, smooth snakes and natterjack toads in Surrey is precarious despite efforts made by conservation organizations in and around protected areas like *Frensham Country Park*. The problems of lizards and heathland wildlife generally are beautifully demonstrated in the new Heathland Visitor Centre at *Lightwater Country Park*.

Not all Surrey is threatened: some of the Commons like Bookham are so extensive that there are remote corners rarely visited. One, *Thursley Common*, is so important that it is a National Nature Reserve with more species of dragonfly than any other site in Britain, yet it is only 35 miles from the centre of London.

There is also extensive, though often fragmented, woodland, especially in a broad band from Epsom to Haslemere and, with 18 per cent still covered in woods, Surrey remains one of the most forest-covered counties in England. One of the most accessible woods is the Surrey Wildlife Trust reserve at *Nower Wood* near Leatherhead, which sits on the heavy clay-with-flints overlying the chalk.

In contrast the Trust's other wood, the *Graeme Hendrey Reserve* south of Godstone, is on the greensand and supports acid loving species. Both here and at *Home Farm Wood*, *Effingham*, visitors may still experience a woodland walk in peace and solitude. Surrey is indeed a county of contrasts.

● Surrey Wildlife Trust (SWT), Powell Corderoy Annexe, Longfield Road, Dorking RH4 3DF. 0306 743404.

Box Hill Country Park   9

Map 187 TQ17-51- 800 acres (324 ha)
1 mile north-east of Dorking. The summit can be reached by road via the zigzag which is first turn right going north to Mickleham from the Burford Bridge roundabout. SSSI. Chalk grassland, scrub, and deciduous woodland with box and yew.

Access   AYR on foot on numerous way-marked trails from CP at the summit at TQ178512. For alternative, quieter, access take the second turn on the right going north to Mickleham past Juniper Hall and enter NT CP on the right at TQ176529.

Information   Display room, maps, teachers' guide and nature walks from Visitor Centre at CP, open Easter to early November, Weds–Sun and BHs 1.30–5.30 p.m.; early November–mid December, Weds, Thurs, Sat and Sun 2–4 p.m.

History   The south-facing chalk escarpment is cut through by the River Mole. On the warm, dry slopes above woodland of yew and giant box trees has developed with patches of chalk grassland and lime-loving shrubs. On the top are plateau deposits of clay-with-flints on which heathland, dominated by heather, bracken and birch wood, is widespread.

What to See   Wild flowers of the steep slopes include marjoram, horseshoe vetch, man, musk and bee orchids as well as the rare cut-leaved germander and ground-pine. The beech and oak woods of the summit include, besides yew and box, large quantities of holly and a few trees of large-leaved lime, which may be native here. Woodland herbs include white helleborine and stinking hellebore. The hill is particularly rich in invertebrates, notably a large colony of Roman snails, and numerous butterflies including silver-spotted skipper and chalkhill blue.

T[D] and refreshments at Visitor Centre.

Wheelchairs have access to special ½-mile path.

Frensham Country Park   10

Map 186 SU84-40-782 acres (325 ha)
Astride the A287 4 miles south of Farnham. SSSI. Heath, birch wood, large ponds.

Access   AYR on foot from CP in Bacon Lane, Frensham on the west side of Common at SU844407 for Frensham Great Pond, or from CP in Priory Lane on the east side at SU856419 for Frensham Little Pond.

Information   Leaflets, including map of whole area showing footpaths and a nature trail around Little Pond, from the Information Centre beside the Great Pond CP or direct from Waverley District Council, The Burys, Godalming GU7 1HR. 0483 861111.

History   This typical area of Surrey heathland has developed on the Folkstone Beds of the lower greensand and embraces two ponds, Great and Little, with sandy, beach-like shores. It lies within the Surrey Hills Area of Outstanding Natural Beauty and is itself a justification for that designation.

What to See   Pine/birch woodland with areas of open heath with gorse and bell heather. Notable as one of the few inland sites in Britain where our three rarest amphibians and reptiles, smooth snake, sand lizard and natterjack toad may still be found. Breeding birds include hobby, woodlark, tree pipit, stonechat and Dartford warbler.

T at Great Pond CP.

Wheelchairs have access to track round Little Pond.

Graeme Hendrey Reserve   11

Map 187 TQ34-50- 25 acres (10 ha)
On Tilburstow Hill 1 mile south of Godstone via A22 forking right immediately to Blindley Heath. Turn right at first crossroads to public CP on left after 400 yds at TQ349501. Mixed deciduous woodland.

Access   AYR on foot from CP, another 220 yds to the gate on the right into the reserve at the south-west corner.

Information   Way-marked trail through wood. Leaflet from Trust.

History   This woodland is situated in an old sand quarry on the lower greensand ridge which was producing sand for the upkeep of local roads until earlier this century. The resulting humps and hollows now have to be negotiated by steps built by local volunteers.

What to See   This mixed deciduous wood has a fine array of shade-loving species including bitter-vetch, broad-leaved helleborine, early-purple orchid, moschatel and common wintergreen: in damp hollows lady fern and hard and soft shield-ferns may be seen with large numbers of bird's-nest orchid. The view to the south from the CP is particularly fine.

Home Farm Wood, Effingham   12

Map 187 TQ10-53- 10 acres (4 ha)
¾ mile west of Effingham Church at the end of Orestan Lane. Mixed deciduous woodland with some introduced trees

Access   AYR on foot from the parking space at junction of Orestan Lane and Calvert Road at TQ108536, westwards along bridle path towards the wood which is entered through a gap in wooden railings after 200 yds.

Information   Nature trail guide from shops in Effingham village, from SWT or from Guildford Borough Council, Millmead House, Guildford GU2 5BB.

History   Home Farm Wood, some of which is of ancient origin, sits on the edge of a clay and gravel deposit overlying the chalk. The original woodland is characterized by large trees of oak, beech, ash and maple. Elsewhere hazel has been planted and managed as coppice. Other introduced trees include Turkey oak, sweet chestnut, Scots pine and rhododendron. About 5 per cent of the trees were damaged by the great storm of October 1987—most have been left to rot where they fell and natural regeneration is now beginning.

What to See   In spring there is a fine display of bluebell, lords-and-ladies, wood anemone and dog's mercury. Chiffchaffs sing in the trees whilst treecreeper and nuthatch work old bark hunting for insects. Roe deer visit the wood and grey squirrels are all too frequent.

Wheelchairs have access to most of village trail.

Lightwater Country Park   13

Map 175 SU92-62- 143 acres (57 ha)
1 mile south of Bagshot at the end of The Avenue off the A322 to Guildford from Exit 3 on M3. Heathland, pine wood, meadow, bog and ponds.

Access   AYR on foot from CP near the entrance at SU913616 to a complex network of bridleways and footpaths.

Information   From the Warden (tel: 0276 79582) or from SWT's new and exciting Visitor Centre by CP which has exhibits including a talking lizard, A/V display and leaflets and nature trail guides. Open April–October: Tues–Fri 12 noon–6 p.m., W/Es and BHs 10 a.m.–6 p.m. November–March: W/Es and BHs only (tel: 0276 51605).

History   Part of Bagshot Heath, an area dominated by birch, two species of gorse and three species of heather. Formerly a Royal hunting ground and reputed, without much foundation, to have been one of the two main haunts of Dick Turpin. The park is now managed to retain a variety of habitats which include ponds, a meadow, an acid bog and a pine wood.

What to See   In early summer the meadow is full of the mixed colours of ragged-Robin, heath spotted-orchid, oxeye daisy and St John's-wort. The largest pond, Hammond's Pond, named after a local eighteenth century curate, has breeding mute swan and visiting heron fishing for roach and carp which swim between the white and yellow water-lilies. The banks are fringed with the highly aromatic bog-myrtle. In the bog itself there are several species of *Sphagnum* moss and the round-leaved sundew. On the drier heath large piles thatched with pine needles are the homes of wood ants, the largest British species.

T[D] at CP. Picnic site.

Wheelchairs have some access on good paths.

Nower Wood   14

Map 187 TQ19-54- 83 acres (33 ha)
2 miles south-east of Leatherhead north of Mill Way on B2033 Headley road. Educational Reserve, ancient woodland with ponds.

Access   On foot from CP at TQ192545 which is open most school days March–November or AYR via the gate off the bridleway, Langley Lane, on the south-east side.

Information   This is primarily an educational reserve: leaflets and nature trail guides from the Field Centre 300 yds from CP up steps.

History   An ancient woodland mentioned, though not by name, in the Domesday Book. It lies on a chalk outcrop capped by clay-with-flints which means most of the soils are acid. Over the centuries it has been managed for timber and game and, more recently, to create a variety of wildlife habitats. Three ponds and a swamp have been made as particular attractions and a deer-watching hide erected.

What to See   In spring a colourful display of bluebells, primroses and anemones beneath a canopy of oak/birch full of the sounds and sights of nightingale, wood warbler, woodpeckers, woodcock, sparrowhawk, blue tit and nuthatch. The ponds are always alive—full of newts, frogs and toads and are visited by grass snake, mallard and heron whilst damselflies and dragonflies skim the surface. Badgers live in the wood and roe deer may be seen by the quiet and patient.

T near the Field Centre.

School parties are welcome but must be booked in advance via SWT Education Officer on 0372 379509.

Thursley Common   15

Map 186 SU90-40- 900 acres (360 ha)
4 miles south-west of Godalming off A3 through Thursley village. NNR. Dry and
wet heathland, woodland, bogs and pools.

Access   AYR on foot from CP at The Moat, a small pond on the Thursley–
Elstead road at SU899415. A track from the south-east corner of the pond leads
through a narrow belt of pines to an area of wet peat bog. Part of the site is used
for military training: beware of any metal objects found.

Information   Nothing on site. Reserve leaflet from the Warden, 8 Homefield
Cottages, Highfield Lane, Thursley.

History   A superb area managed by controlled burning and raising of water
levels to retain an intimate mixture of woodland, heath, bog and open water
which is a home for 65 species of breeding birds, 26 species of dragonfly (more
than any other single site in Britain) and perhaps 10,000 different insects.

What to See   Dry heath with heather, bell heather, common and dwarf gorse:
wet heath and bog with cottongrass, bog asphodel, brown and white beak-sedge
and oblong-leaved and round-leaved sundews: pools with lesser bladderwort and
bogbean and a fringe of marsh St John's-wort. Curlew nest on the bog, Dartford
warbler on the heath whilst hobby breed in the trees and feed on dragonflies
and small birds over the pools. Interest continues into winter with snipe,
woodcock, and occasional hen harrier, merlin, short-eared owl or great grey
shrike.
    Wheelchairs have easy access to Moat Pond from CP.

Sussex

Sussex is the southern part of the Weald of South-East England. The varied
geology is reflected in the strongly contrasting landscapes of the chalk hills of
the South Downs, the heaths and birchwoods of the acid sands around Ashdown
Forest and the oak woods on the heavy Wealden clays north-west of Brighton.
The whole long county is underlined, as it were, by a coastline of equal
contrasts—mainly chalk in the west, mainly sands in the east. The latter makes
resorts like Hastings attractive but also produces the shingle beaches of *Rye
Harbour* which continue east to Dungeness in Kent.
    The chalk rises from the sea west of Eastbourne to form the impressive cliffs
of *Beachy Head and the Seven Sisters* giving over seven miles of unspoilt
coastline. It then rises to over 800 ft north of Brighton where, from *Ditchling
Beacon*, which is on the South Downs long distance footpath, there are
wonderful views across the Weald to the North Downs. Further west still, as they
approach the Hampshire border, the Downs swing inland and rise to the giddy
height of 836 ft north-east of Chichester. On their southern slopes north-west
of Chichester is found one of the most remarkable features on the chalk anywhere

in England—*Kingley Vale*, a yew wood in a great horseshoe curve from which Sir Arthur Tansley, father of British ecology and conservation, considered the view to be the finest in the land.

North of the otherwise mainly treeless chalk, the Weald forms the most wooded area in Britain and, especially in West Sussex, there are still thousands of acres of mature oak forest including the nature reserves of *Ebernoe Common* and The Mens, north-west of Pulborough. The importance of oak as a source of timber and as a habitat for other species of wildlife is beautifully exhibited in the appropriately named *Woods Mill*, the headquarters of the Sussex Wildlife Trust. Alongside, in a small woodland reserve, the art of coppicing is demonstrated. This has been practised in some areas since Roman times to provide a continuous supply of small wood for heating and charcoal production: the latter was of great importance for the smelting of iron which went on for over 1000 years in South-East England.

Another area which, as its name suggests, was once equally well-wooded is *Ashdown Forest* west of Crowborough. This former Royal Hunting Forest has been cleared and grazed to the point where 60 per cent is open heathland and represents the largest single area of undeveloped countryside with open access in South-East England, covering over 10 square miles. This is now threatened by nature itself—the spread of bracken and rhododendron smothers smaller plants growing beneath so that control by cutting or herbicides is a major task for the conservation organizations.

But this landscape, where A.A. Milne brought up Winnie the Pooh, lies astride the Brighton road and is now threatened by easy access from South London: the author who wrote *Now We Are Six* could well be horrified 'now we are 600,000'.

● Sussex Wildlife Trust (SWT), Woods Mill, Shoreham Road, Henfield, West Sussex BN5 9SD. 0273 492630.

Ashdown Forest   16

Map 187 TQ4-3- 6250 acres (2500 ha)
On either side of the A22 between East Greenfield and Maresfield. Common Land, most SSSI. Oak woodland, heath, valley bogs.

Access   AYR on foot from numerous CPs on roads radiating from Wych Cross on the A22, as at Hindleap TQ405322 or Churlwood TQ417311. There is also access to the Old Lodge Nature Reserve of SWT from CP at TQ470306 on B2026 Hartfield to Maresfield road: it has a way-marked trail but dogs are not permitted.

Information   From Ashdown Forest Centre, in charming vernacular buildings with heather garden, ¾ mile east of Wych Cross at TQ 4340323 which sells guides and maps of the Forest, has A/V display and is the starting point for a way-marked trail. Open 2-5 p.m. weekdays, 11 a.m.–5 p.m. W/Es and BHs.

History   The Forest is the largest area of South-East England never to have been ploughed. It was once covered in oak wood but much was cleared to make charcoal for the Wealden iron industry and for timber for buildings like the Forest Centre. Subsequent grazing by commoners' cattle, sheep and pigs as well as Royal deer created the heathland which covers 60 per cent of the forest today.

What to See   In drier parts broom, heather, bell heather, dwarf gorse and bracken are abundant but give way to cross-leaved heath, bog-asphodel, cottongrass and round-leaved sundew in boggy hollows. In spring the wooded areas are alight with wood anemones and primroses whilst blackcap and nightingale sing in the scrub, which also attracts woodcock and nightjar.

Areas of pine and birch are hunting grounds for sparrowhawk and provide shelter for a herd of fallow deer. Adder and common lizard inhabit the drier heaths whilst many species of dragonfly breed in the wetter areas including the rare small red damselfly.

T[D] at Forest Centre and at Forest Row 2 miles north of Wych Cross.

Wheelchairs have access to view points from many CPs.

Beachy Head and Seven Sisters   17

Map 199 TV55-96- 4000 acres (1600 ha)
South of A259 between Seaford and Eastbourne. Mostly SSSI. Cliffs, chalk grassland, shingle beach.

Access   AYR on foot to most of the area, which includes a coastal footpath, from CPs of Seven Sisters Country Park Centre at Exceat at east end of bridge across Cuckmere Haven at TV519995, or from Beachy Head Countryside Centre in former Signalman's Cottage on the south side of road from Beachy Head Hotel at TV590956 being developed by SWT.

Information   Leaflets and guides from Country Park Centre: open daily Easter to end October 11 a.m.–5.30 p.m., November to Easter W/Es only 11 a.m.– 4 p.m. and from Countryside Centre: open daily mid-April–end September 11 a.m.–5 p.m..

History   This landscape of chalk cliffs and downland cut through in the west by the flat-bottomed valley of the Cuckmere River and towards the east by the Birling Gap is one of the best-loved in Britain as well as being a large and very diverse nature reserve.

What to See   Superb chalk grassland with rare species such as field fleawort, burnt orchid, round-headed rampion, moon carrot, least lettuce, red star-thistle and small hare's-ear. At Cuckmere Haven a shingle beach is covered in sea beet and sea-kale as well as being the nesting site for common tern and ringed plover. Fulmar nest on the cliffs which are occasionally visited by peregrine. Beachy Head is a vantage point for watching migrating birds such as nightingale, redstart, ring ouzle- and pied flycatcher with an occasional hoopoe or serin in spring and firecrest in autumn.

T[D] at Country Park and Beachy Head.

Wheelchairs have access to 1 mile of good roads.

Ditchling Beacon 18

Map 198 TQ33-13- 50 acres (20 ha)
6 miles north of Brighton and 1 mile south of Ditchling on the minor road to
Brighton. SSSI. Chalk grassland and scrub.

Access   AYR on foot from NT CP on the west side of the road at TQ333130.
A path leads downhill off the South Downs Way from the site of the Beacon which
is in the reserve a short distance north-west of CP.

Information   Nothing on site: way-marked trails through the reserve. Leaflet
from SWT.

History   The Beacon is Common Land which was once grazed by sheep
tended by shepherds. But since these days were over 50 years ago and the area
could not be fenced the only grazing has been by rabbits which have not
prevented the extension of scrub of hawthorn, dogwood, wayfaring-tree and
whitebeam over the grassland which has become dominated by coarse grasses
in some areas. The remains of former chalk quarries can be seen above the road
on the north side.

What to See   Over 200 species of wild flowers have been recorded including
early-purple, pyramidal and bee orchids. They are host to at least 26 species of
butterfly amongst which green hairstreak, brown argus, painted lady and chalkhill blue are the most noteworthy. The scrub provides shelter for small birds such
as blackcap, whitethroat and corn bunting whilst kestrel hover overhead.

Ebernoe Common 19

Map 197 SU97-27- 180 acres (72 ha)
4 miles north of Petworth 1 mile east of A283 on minor road signposted to Balls
Cross and Ebernoe. SSSI. Oak/beechwood, scrub, open grassland, ponds.

Access   AYR on foot from CP outside Trinity Church at SU975278 on well-
maintained paths which lead to all parts of the reserve.

Information   Nothing on site: trail leaflet from SWT.

History   An area of Common Land which was heavily grazed by cattle until
early this century and was probably a fine example of wood pasture. Since
grazing ceased oak/beech woodland has extended over most of the reserve. A
brickworks was functioning from the early eighteenth century until the 1930s
making use of local clay and firewood for fuel: two buildings, a kiln and a
moulding shed, have recently been restored.

What to See   One of the few areas of ancient Wealden woodland left in Sussex
over a wide range of soils with areas of open grassland scrub and two ponds which
attract heron and kingfisher. Wild daffodils and violets carpet the woodland floor
in early spring to be followed by bluebell and primrose: 400 species of fungi have
been recorded. The butterflies include brown hairstreak and purple emperor, the
emblem of the Sussex Wildlife Trust. Sunny glades with blackthorn and sallow
are maintained to encourage these insects.

Kingley Vale 20

Map 197 SU82-10- 363 acres (146 ha)
4 miles north-west of Chichester off B2178 to Funtington at East Ashling to CP at West Stoke. NNR. Yew forest, scrub, chalk grassland, chalk heath.

Access AYR on foot on a footpath from CP at SU824088 to the entrance in ¾ mile.

Information Nothing on site: trail guide from R.C.C. Williamson, Keeper's Cottage, West Dean Woods, Chichester PO18 ORO. 0243 59286.

History This area contains the finest yew forest in Europe, some of the trees are over 500 years old and grow so close together that no other plants grow in the darkness beneath their canopy. The yews grow in a chalky valley carved out during the last Ice Age 10,000 years ago.

What to See A superb view across farmland and woodland of Chichester Cathedral, with the sea and the Isle of Wight beyond. At one's feet a wide range of chalk habitats from grassland with 11 species of orchid, yellow horseshoe and kidney vetch contrasting with blue round-headed rampion and clustered bellflower, to scrub including buckthorn, dogwood, juniper, spindle, wayfaring-tree and whitebeam: chalk heath with heather grows on the summit ridge. Butterflies are abundant—amongst 38 species recorded are many blues, fritillaries and skippers whilst 56 species of birds breed on the reserve.

Rye Harbour 21

Map 189 TQ94-18- 880 acres (356 ha)
Between A259 south of Rye and the sea to the east. SSSI and LNR. Saltmarsh, foreshore, shingle and gravel pits.

Access AYR on foot from CP by Martello Tower at TQ943189 along a good road beside the River Rother from which much of the reserve can be viewed and from which there is access to two hides.

Information Information Centre in CP has display and maps: open daily April–September 10.30 a.m.–5.30 p.m., W/Es October–March Noon–4 p.m. (not Christmas). Guided walk and other leaflets from TI Office in Rye or from Warden, 2 Watch Cottages, Nook Beach, Winchelsea TN36 4LU. 0797 223862.

History Over 3000 years ago the coastline was some 3 miles inland from Rye Harbour. Since then the sea has created a large area of gravel between Winchelsea and the mouth of the River Rother. Much has been exploited leaving a series of pits which, with the shingle ridges, foreshore and saltmarsh beside the river, combine to produce a wide range of habitats for plants and birds.

What to See The saltmarsh contains sea aster, sea purslane and sea-heath whilst the shingle carries yellow horned-poppy, sea pea, sea-kale and sea wormwood. In summer little and common tern both breed along with ringed plover, oystercatcher, redshank and little grebe. In winter a large number of waders may be seen: dunlin, golden plover, curlew, sanderling and snipe amongst them, accompanied by ducks in large numbers such as pochard, shoveller, wigeon, eider, goldeneye and gadwall. The noisy marsh frog, introduced to Romney Marsh in 1935, has spread and is now established on the reserve.

T[D] on corner where the road from Rye meets the harbour.

Wheelchairs have excellent access to roads with views and hides.

Woods Mill   22

Map 198 TQ21-13- 35 acres (14 ha)

1 mile south of Henfield on A2037 road to Brighton at junction with Horn Lane to Woodmancote. Woodland, meadow and pond.

Access   From CP in Horn Lane at TQ219139 to the reserve and Countryside Centre.

Information   Guide to nature trail round reserve, exhibition on Sussex wildlife, A/V display from Countryside Centre: open mid-April–end of September Tues, Weds, Thurs and Sat 2–6 p.m., Suns and BHs 11 a.m.–6 p.m.

History   Woods Mill, an eighteenth century watermill, is the headquarters of SWT as well as a Visitor Centre with educational facilities and a series of events throughout the year.

What to See   The exhibition includes a replica of a 25 ft oak tree, a vivarium for harvest mice and an observation beehive whilst the water wheel and machinery are in working order. The trail goes round a lake and dipping pond, with nets provided, and continues through a small wood typical of those on the damp Wealden clays, of which part is managed as hazel coppice. There is also a hay meadow which is being traditionally managed to increase the variety of wild flowers. Great spotted woodpecker, nuthatch and treecreeper breed in the wood where white admiral butterflies also occur. Kingfisher and, occasionally, water rail also breed on the reserve.

T[D]. Shop.

Wheelchairs have access to part of the trail.

EAST ANGLIA

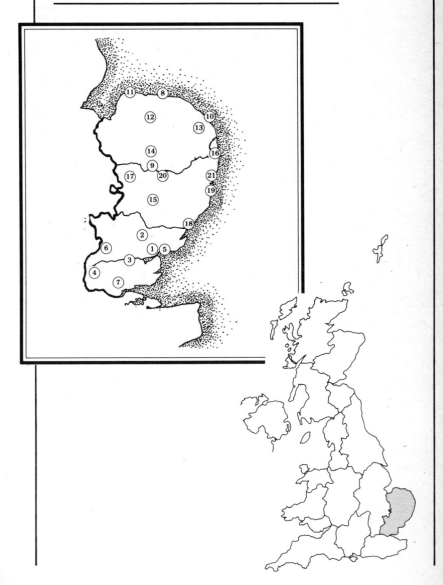

Essex

Essex, away from the capital and the Thames estuary, is a remarkably rural county with country lanes and cows within a dozen miles of Tower Bridge. It may lack the varied topography of all the other Home Counties—no sweeping North Downs or Chiltern escarpment on the skyline, no vast expanses of uncultivated Surrey commons—but this very unspectacular nature may have given it a measure of protection and restrained the urban sprawl.

As any gardener brought up in the county knows, with few exceptions, the soils are either derived from the London clay or from Boulder clay over it—the exceptions are where the chalk reaches the surface in both north and south, but in the north, round Saffron Walden it is mostly under Boulder clay and in the south around Thurrock it has nearly all been turned into cement.

The great contrast then is between the heavy clays inland and the muddy east coast estuaries—and on those clays it is the woods which are the features of greatest national importance. *Epping Forest* can be claimed as one of the first wild areas in Britain which was conserved for the benefit of the public when attempts to enclose it were overthrown on 24 November 1874. Ever since then it has been managed by a group named the Conservators 'who shall at all times as far as possible preserve the natural aspect of the forest'. Although at its southern end it is only six miles from the City it still gives sanctuary to such a declining treasure as round-leaved sundew.

If the importance of Epping Forest was appreciated as early as 1874 it is perhaps odd that an even more important Essex forest should have been largely unappreciated for a further century. Not until November 1971 when Oliver Rackham was taken to *Hatfield Forest* for the first time did its true significance begin to appear and it must now be regarded as the finest example in Britain of a medieval forest for deer.

The combination of wood and pasture at Hatfield which was so important for the rural economy is also important for wildlife producing a range of niches which attract many species. This same mixture, though of a different origin, is found around *Danbury* where there are numerous woods, heaths, marshes and pools which make it one of the richest areas for wildlife in the county—conveniently placed near the centre.

Epping, Hatfield and Danbury all demonstrate this mixture of habitats—and it happens yet again in the south near Brentwood where the *Thorndon Country Park*, adjacent to the fine Georgian house of Thorndon Hall, retains ancient oak and hornbeam woods alongside heathy grassland and natural and man-made lakes. All four of these areas are spacious, pieces of landscape perhaps rather than nature reserves. In contrast *Chalkney Wood* is discrete—an ancient wood with well-defined boundaries—near the Suffolk border. It is a characteristic coppice-with-standards Boulder clay woodland with close affinities to nearby woods in Cambridgeshire and Suffolk—though it lacks the oxlips which are their particular joy.

The coast creeps up creeks a long way into Essex—not just up the Thames past the Isle of Dogs, but up the Crouch to Battlesbridge, the Blackwater to Maldon and the Colne to Colchester carrying the call of ducks and geese miles inland. And when there is calm water, with shelter and food, birds escaping the rigours of a northern European winter come and stay. So it is that *Abberton Reservoir* south of Colchester, only three miles from the Blackwater and the Colne has become, in 50 years, the most important wintering place for ducks in Britain—and the new Visitor Centre now makes visiting even more enjoyable.

On the shores of the Colne estuary the Essex Wildlife Trust has long welcomed visitors to the area and provided an introduction to the wildlife of the whole county at *Fingringhoe Wick*, their flagship and their headquarters. This has given thousands an insight into the further riches which await the naturalist who is prepared to look more closely at a county which may look superficially similar but has a wealth of variety beneath the surface.

- Essex Wildlife Trust (EWT), Fingringhoe Wick, South Green Road, Fingringhoe, Colchester CO5 7DN. 020628 678.

Abberton Reservoir ■ 1

Map 168 TL96-18- 1210 acres (470 ha)
5 miles south-west of Colchester on both sides of B1026 through Layer de la Haye. SSSI. Ramsar Site. Reservoir for wintering duck.

Access   AYR from viewing points on B1026 at CP at TL962185 where there is a hide and from minor road to Layer Breton, 1 mile west.

Information   Leaflets and information from Wildfowl and Visitor Centre by CP: open daily (except Mon) 9 a.m.–5 p.m.

History   The reservoir, first flooded in 1940, has become the most important reserve in Britain for wintering duck; it regularly attracts 10–15,000 principally because it is only 3 miles from the coast and access is limited to its mainly shallow water which is ideal for diving ducks, and there is also a wide grassy shoreline for dabbling species. Abberton is a ringing station run by the Wildfowl and Wetlands Trust where over 75,000 ducks have been ringed in the last 35 years with recoveries from as far away as Iceland, Azores, Senegal and Siberia.

What to See   Winter duck include over 1000 each of mallard, teal, wigeon and tufted duck, and hundreds of gadwall, shoveler, pochard and goldeneye. Abberton is the most important site for goldeneye in Britain. There are also smaller numbers of pintail, goosander, shelduck and smew. Large numbers of greylag and Canada geese are regularly seen with Bewick's swan, white-fronted and Brent geese. Migrant waders such as turnstone and little stint appear in autumn and spring. A curiosity is the cormorants which nest in trees between the two roads across the reservoir. 100–200 mute swan come here to moult in late summer.

T[D] at Visitor Centre.

Wheelchairs have excellent viewing from roads.

Chalkney Wood   2

Map 168 TL87-27- 63 acres (25 ha)
1½ miles south-east of Earls Colne on south side of River Colne: take Tey Road from A604 at the east end of Earls Colne towards Great Tey to entrance on left in 1 mile. SSSI. Small-leaved lime wood, ancient coppice-with-standards.

Access   AYR on foot from the parking space on the roadside at TL872272.

Information   Nothing on site.

History   An ancient woodland on the Boulder clay, with boundary banks and an irregular outline, which appears on a map of 1598: it was recorded as being used as a swine-park in 1500. The wood is bisected by a massive hollow way which is part of the course of an Iron Age road from Cambridge to Colchester. The north-east two-thirds has been planted with conifers but the south-west third is a coppice of small-leaved lime with ash and oak standards where coppice-with-standards management is being reintroduced.

What to See   Other trees and shrubs include field maple, hazel, birch, sweet chestnut, hornbeam, aspen and, rarely, wild service. The ground flora in spring is dominated by dog's mercury, bluebell, primrose, dog-violet and red campion. Later the rare violet helleborine may be found. The mixed coppice is an ideal habitat for nesting birds which include warblers, tits and a good nightingale population.

Danbury   3

Map 167 TL78-04- 436 acres (178 ha)
5 miles south-east of Chelmsford around the village of Danbury north and south of A414: a complex of 12 reserves. SSSI. Deciduous woodland, scrub, heath, valley bog, pools.

Access   AYR on foot on a complex of paths, often way-marked, from numerous CPs e.g. to:

1. The Backwarden at TL780043 on minor road from Danbury to Bicknacre or
2. Scrubs Wood at TL788057 in Runsell Lane ½ mile along the Danbury to Little Baddow road on the right.

Information   Leaflets from EWT.

History   This varied group of reserves stands on a ridge above the River Chelmer to the north and which slopes towards the River Crouch. The lower parts are on the London clay but the top is capped by glacial gravels and Boulder clay. Springs at the junction of the glacial deposits create wet, boggy areas. There are extensive oak woods with coppiced hazel, hornbeam and sweet chestnut whilst on open Commons there is heathland with heather and scrub with gorse and broom. There are also small valley bogs with active growth of *Sphagnum* moss and some ponds created by former marl or gravel workings.

What to See   The more local plants include greater butterfly-orchid, broad-leaved helleborine, lily-of-the-valley, marsh fern, greater and lesser spearwort, striated clover, pignut, wood melick, marsh pennywort, skullcap and lesser skullcap, lousewort, trailing St John's-wort and climbing corydalis whilst the shrubs include wild-service, alder buckthorn and creeping willow. Amongst nesting birds are marsh and willow tits, treecreeper, great spotted woodpecker, chiffchaff, blackcap, willow and garden warblers, hawfinch and nightingale. Brambly clearings attract many butterflies such as gatekeeper, comma, small copper, Essex skipper, speckled wood, ringlet, and green and purple hairstreak. Mammals include dormouse, yellow-necked mouse and water shrew whilst adder and common lizard also occur.

T[D] at Danbury Country Park on minor road to Sandon at TL775048.

Epping Forest

Map 177 TQ4-9- 6000 acres (2430 ha)
10 miles north-east of London on both sides of the A104 between Chingford and Epping. SSSI. Ancient pollard, scrub, heath, acid grassland, marsh.

Access   AYR on foot from a complex of roads and paths.

Information   Leaflets and guided walks from the Epping Forest Conservation Centre at High Beech at TL412980 behind the King's Oak Hotel. Well signposted from roundabouts on A104 at Robin Hood at TL411971 going north, or at Wake Arms at TL426994 going south. Centre open: Easter–October Weds–Sats 10 a.m.–5 p.m., Suns 11 a.m.–5 p.m., November–Easter W/Es 11 a.m.–5 p.m. (closed for lunch).

History   An ancient wood pasture on the London clay where cattle were free to graze anywhere and the trees were cut, pollarded, so high that the young shoots were out of reach of browsing animals. Many of the pollards are of beech and hornbeam. The Forest was saved for the nation in 1878 and given to the City of London to protect. Since pollarding ceased much of the wood has become very dense and the ground flora is poor. When old pollards die natural regeneration occurs and birch replaces it: there is a danger that the birch is also over-running the heathy areas. Some experimental pollarding is taking place near the Conservation Centre.

What to See   Proximity to London means that wild flowers are in danger of over-collection but primrose, wood anemone, dog-violet, greater stitchwort, bog St John's-wort, round-leaved sundew, wood sorrel, petty whin, moschatel, bell heather and cross-leaved heath still occur. The usual woodland birds are found including nuthatch, treecreeper and all three types of woodpecker whilst redpoll, hawfinch and redstart are also frequent. Butterflies include a number of skippers—small, large and Essex, as well as common and holly blues and purple hairstreak. Slow worm, common lizard, toad, frog and all three types of newt survive but, apart from muntjac, larger mammals have largely disappeared.

T[D] at King's Oak by Conservation Centre.

Wheelchairs have access to special path through the Forest from the Conservation Centre.

Fingringhoe Wick

Map 168 TM04-19- 125 acres (50 ha)

5 miles south-east of Colchester on the west shore of the Colne estuary via minor road from Colchester through Old Heath to Fingringhoe village then follow signs for the Wick and entrance at TM041195. Mud flats, salt marsh, heath, pools.

Access AYR on foot from CP at Visitor Centre at TM049192 onto a complex of trails with seven hides and several seats.

Information Trail guides, plant and animal lists and booklet on reserve from Visitor Centre: open daily (except Mon, other than BHs, and 25 and 26 December) 9 a.m.–5 p.m. Centre has displays on wildlife of area: there is also a special caravan for WATCH members, the junior arm of the RSNC.

History The reserve was created in an area worked for gravel from 1921-59 and was acquired by the Trust in 1961 for £4000. The lake was used as part of the process of washing the gravel in freshwater. The Visitor Centre was opened in 1975 and amenities for the public have been steadily improved since then.

What to See 13 ferns and their allies occur including stag's-horn clubmoss, royal fern and adder's-tongue with other unusual plants such as mousetail, soft hornwort, bird's-foot and bee orchid. Birds are abundant: in the wooded part there are seven species of warblers and up to 30 pairs of nightingale whilst the lake has kingfisher, little grebe, great crested grebe, tufted duck and pochard. In winter over 1000 Brent geese are present on the nearest part of the Colne estuary when wigeon, teal, gadwall, pintail, shoveler and goldeneye are amongst many other visitors to the reserve. Migrants which may be seen, especially in autumn, are knot, ruff, snipe, whimbrel, greenshank, green and common sandpiper. The butterfly list of over 20 species has purple hairstreak, Essex skipper and speckled wood.

T. Shop in Visitor Centre.

Wheelchairs have access to good paths and a hide: there is a special trail with guide for the disabled.

Hatfield Forest

Map 177 TL54-19- 1046 acres (420 ha)

3 miles south-east of Bishop's Stortford via A120 towards Dunmow turning south at Takely Street to entrance leading to CP. SSSI. Ancient woodland, grassland, lakes.

Access Forest open AYR on foot from CP at TL540199 (charge to non-members of NT) to nature trail with hide.

Information   Trail guide from shop in eighteenth century Shell House by the lake.

History   A remarkable forest, recently studied in depth by Oliver Rackham, with documentary evidence dating back nine centuries and with boundaries hardly altered in that period. All the elements of a medieval forest survive here: deer, cattle, coppiced woods, pollards, scrub, timber trees, open grassland and fen as well as a seventeenth century lodge and a rabbit warren. The forest originated as an area for keeping deer in about 1100, a mixture of woods and plains, a pattern which still remains with only a few areas of more recent plantations.

What to See   Native trees include pedunculate oak, ash, field maple, hazel, hornbeam, alder, goat willow, spindle, crab apple, elder, beech, two species of birch and two hawthorns. Notable woodland flowers are broad-leaved and violet helleborines, herb-Paris, goldilocks buttercup and greater bird's-foot trefoil. The plains are rather plain but have some lady's bedstraw, meadow barley and cuckoo-flower with upright chickweed, wild thyme, heath dog-violet and small-flowered buttercup in an old gravel pit. The lake and marsh have gipsywort, fleabane, cyperus sedge, marsh arrowgrass and lesser water-parsnip whilst the birds include reed bunting and snipe with nightingale in the woods. Butterflies include Essex skipper, orange tip and common blue.

   T[D]. Refreshments, Shop.

   Wheelchairs have access to good paths.

Thorndon Country Park   7

Map 177 TQ60-91- and TQ62-89- 357 acres (144 ha)
2 miles to the south-east of Brentwood off A128 road to Tilbury: for Thorndon North Country Park take first right ½ mile beyond railway bridge to entrance in 1 mile: for Thorndon South CP continue on A128 for 2 miles through Ingrave and Herongate to entrance on right. Part SSSI. Woods, acid grassland, ponds.

Access   AYR from 8 a.m.–dusk on foot from CP in Thorndon North through Lion Lodge Gate House at TQ607915 and from CP in Thorndon South at TQ632899. (There is a small charge on Sundays.)

Information   Leaflet and booklet at new Countryside Centre in Thorndon North CP.

History   An ancient deer park created with permission from Edward III in 1363 which still has areas of ancient woodland, acid grassland and a number of ponds and old gravel workings. The woods are dominated by pollarded oak and hornbeam whilst the heath has small areas of heather and gorse. Recent gales have felled many trees which have been salvaged for use in building the Countryside Centre.

What to See   Other trees include beech, birch and sweet chestnut whilst amongst the other wild plants are moschatel, wood-sorrel, pendulous sedge, hard fern and matgrass. There are many woodland birds such as long-tailed tit and goldcrest whilst heron and kingfisher visit the ponds. Badger and fox also visit the park.

T[D] at Countryside Centre. Picnic site.

Wheelchairs have good access on smooth, wide tracks.

Norfolk

Often seen by outsiders as an area of intense arable farming, Norfolk remains a county of immense interest for wildlife, scarcely surpassed anywhere else in lowland England. It contains three outstanding and contrasting areas each with large numbers of almost continuous nature reserves: the Broads, the Breck and the Coast—BBC—and like that other BBC, of both national and international importance.

The Broads east of Norwich form a series of shallow lakes and pools, often interconnected, which lie in the flood plain of three rivers, the Bure, Yare and Waveney, and their tributaries which converge on Great Yarmouth. They have resulted from medieval peat-diggings abandoned as the sea-level rose and they became flooded. They are surrounded by reed-swamp, fen, wet alder woodland (carr) and grazing marshes and together produce a kaleidoscope of wetland habitats rich in plants, insects and birds alike.

Unfortunately increased recreational use and run-off of agricultural chemicals have combined to pollute many of the lakes and interconnecting waterways so that there has been a dramatic decline in submerged aquatic plants within the last 25 years. Nevertheless the guided trail by boat at *Hickling Broad* is a thrilling experience whilst landlubbers can still go afloat by visiting the Broadland Conservation Centre on *Ranworth Broad*.

Across the county near its south-west corner, within about a nine mile radius of Thetford, lie the dry, sandy heaths of Breckland where lines of pines prick out the landscape. Until early this century this was a wide open expanse of sheep-walks and rabbit warrens, but intensification of agriculture during two World Wars and the arrival of the Forestry Commission have broken it into smaller, isolated areas. Ironically military requirements have also served to save some corners of the Breck—notably the Stanford Training Area from which 1000 people were temporarily removed in 1942—never to be allowed to return. Though the Training Area is not generally open to the public some of the best reserves lie immediately to the east. *Thompson Common* has an excellent nature trail through a maze of pools called pingos, relicts of the last Ice Age, whilst larger pools, or meres, are a feature of *East Wretham Heath* at the south-east corner.

Despite the splendours of the Broads and the Breck it is doubtful whether even they can compete with the wonders of the wildlife wilderness which is the North Norfolk Coast extending almost uninterrupted through a series of nature reserves managed by RSPB, NCC, NT and the Norfolk Naturalists Trust for nearly 25 miles from *Holme Dunes* in the west to *Cley and Salthouse Marshes* in the east. The range of habitats is immense embracing the shingle spits of Blakeney Point and Scolt Head, the salt marshes which run from Blakeney to Wells and from Burnham to Holme. Behind the shore-line interrupted or sluggish streams produce a network of brackish and freshwater marshes, as at Titchwell and Cley, which attract immense numbers of birds at all seasons of the year many of which can be seen at even closer quarters at *Pensthorpe Waterfowl Park* only 10 miles inland.

• Norfolk Naturalists Trust (NNT), 72 Cathedral Close, Norwich NR1 4DF. 0603 625540.

Cley and Salthouse Marshes   8

Map 133 TG05-44- 776 acres (312 ha)
North of A149 between Cley next the Sea and Salthouse. SSSI. Ramsar Site. A wetland of international importance for birds.

Access   From Visitor Centre at TG054441 on landward side of road 200 yds east of turning to Holt, or from North CP at end of Beach Road at TG060449. Permits are necessary to visit any of the 11 hides: £2 for full day from Visitor Centre or North CP. The cafe is open 10 a.m.–5 p.m. April–Oct, closed Mondays (except BHs). At other times contact the Warden at house dated '1936 NNT', west of Holt turn by Visitor Centre.

Information   Leaflet from Visitor Centre and North CP.

History   In the sixteenth century the marshes were saltings covered by the sea at spring tides and beyond them lay a navigation channel connecting the port of Salthouse with the sea at Blakeney. Since then the shingle shore has been moving landwards about 3 ft a year and much of the original marshland is under the sea. Today there are brackish pools on the seaward side of the main drain, but the marshes on the landward side are maintained by freshwater springs which feed drains running into the Cley channel. The area was bought by Dr Sidney Herbert Long and friends in 1926: the NNT was formed to administer it and it was therefore the first Wildlife Trust reserve to be established.

What to See   Amongst a long plant list are two species on the shingle ridge at their northern limit in Britain, shrubby seablite and grey hairgrass. The birds are outstanding: Brent geese and whooper swan in winter; Sandwich tern, Kentish plover and black tern on spring migration; bearded tit, bittern, avocet and black-tailed godwit breeding and a continuous stream of waders migrating southwards in autumn. There is always the chance of seeing something unusual and exciting such as wryneck, bluethroat or barred warbler. For all these reasons Cley has become an all-year-round mecca for bird-watchers in Britain.

  T at north CP with refreshments (excellent chocolate cake).
  Wheelchair access to hide: Key from Visitor Centre.

East Wretham Heath

Map 144 TL91-88- 363 acres (147 ha)
3 miles north-east of Thetford on A1075. SSSI. Heath, woodland and meres.

Access   On foot from CP at Warden's house on the west side of road at TL913887 where permits are issued. Charge for non-NNT members. Open 10 a.m.–5 p.m. daily except Tues. The reserve can also be viewed from Drove Road (rough track) which leaves A1075 300 yds south of CP.

Information   Leaflet from Warden's house for way-marked nature trail which includes hide overlooking Langmere and details of trail for the visually handicapped which starts from stone cairn on Drove Road ⅓ mile west of the main road.

History   This is the heart of Breckland. 'Breck' is a Saxon word for strips of land cleared in the forest for growing crops or grazing cattle. When crops failed on this poor, sandy soil ancient farmers moved on to clear more forest and the whole area changed to heathland. Here the heath surrounds two attractive meres beside which scots pines were planted during the Napoleonic Wars and hence called Waterloo Plantation. The diverse habitats of heath, pine woods and the crumbling runways of a Second World War aerodrome combine to harbour over 250 species of wild flowers whilst approximately 130 species of bird are recorded annually. The reserve was acquired by the Trust in 1939.

What to See   Chalk-loving flowers such as dyer's greenweed, musk mallow and wild mignonette thrive where the sand is shallow, whilst golden dock and knotted pearlwort grow round the fringe of the meres. Crossbill feed in the pines, hawfinch in an area of hornbeam where ringlet and speckled wood butterflies fly in summer. Adder, grass snake and common lizard may be seen and there is a resident population of roe deer.

Hickling Broad

Map 134 TG41-21- 1356 acres (549 ha)
1 mile east of A149 between Potter Heigham and Stalham. Follow signs for Hickling Green: there turn east at Greyhound Inn, then left at signpost 'No access to Broad NNT'. After 1 mile turn right at sign 'NNT' for CP at lane end at TG428221. NNR and part of Ramsar Site. International importance for birds.

Access   AYR (except Tues) on walking trails which begin at Warden's office in CP. A water trail of 2¼ hours operates from May–October and starts from the Pleasure Boat Inn, Hickling Heath, at the north end of Broad at TG409225: book at hut near Inn or telephone Hickling 503 9 a.m.–6 p.m.

Information   Leaflet and trail guide from Warden's office. Educational visits arranged for school parties.

History   2000 or so years ago there was a broad river estuary with its mouth extending from Waxham to Winterton which reached inland to Heigham Sound at the south end of the reserve. When coastal changes blocked the mouth mud flats were turned into marshland and peat deposits built up to the west. In medieval times the peat and clay was dug to a depth of 3–4 ft, and it is these flooded workings which form most of Hickling Broad today.

What to See   Holly-leaved naiad was once abundant but is now confined to a few small areas. Fortunately milk parsley has not declined and still provides plentiful food for the caterpillars of the swallow-tail butterfly which is on the wing in June to be followed by purple hairstreak in August. The resident birds include bittern, bearded tit, and marsh harrier. They are joined by common and little tern, ringed plover and avocet in summer. Many waders are regular visitors, especially in autumn when pectoral, broad-billed and buff-breasted sandpiper are joined by osprey, spoonbill and black tern.

Holme Dunes
11

Map 132 TF70-44- 550 acres (223 ha)
3 miles north-east of Hunstanton off the A149. Follow the sign to the NNT Reserve at the west end of Holme next the Sea village. After ½ mile turn right at sign 'Police Notice—No Parking—Car Park Ahead' and follow gravel track through gate to NNT CPs after ⅓ mile or 1 mile beside Warden's house at TF714449. SSSI. Sand dunes, salt marsh and grazing meadows.

Access   Open daily 10 a.m.–5 p.m. Permits for visiting seven hides from Warden's house, 'The Firs', tel: 0485 25240.

Information   Leaflet from shop in Warden's house which also has small exhibition and notice board carrying topical information.

History   The coastline at Holme was formerly further north: the woodland which grew there has been buried by the rise of the sea since 2000 BC but remains of forest peat can be seen at low water. During the Second World War the area was used for gunnery practice—the blockhouses remain. It became a nature reserve in 1965.

What to See   2 miles of superb coastal sand dunes are backed at either end by large areas of salt marsh and, in the middle, by grazing marshes. Open water occurs in dune slacks and in a string of brackish and freshwater pools. Notable plants include, in the dunes, sea holly and sea bindweed, and, in the slacks, marsh and bee orchids and marsh helleborine. 280 species of birds have been recorded with incredible numbers of migrants specially in spring and autumn when harriers, osprey, and rough-legged buzzard are regularly seen. In winter snow bunting, twite, Brent goose and short-eared owl are frequent with huge flocks of waders.

Pensthorpe Waterfowl Park and Nature Reserve
12

Map 132 TF94-29- 200 acres (80 ha)
1 mile south-east of Fakenham south of A1067 Norwich road. Clearly signposted

from A148 Fakenham bypass. Part SSSI. Lakes, river, marsh and wet woodland.

Access   Open daily 11 a.m.–5 p.m. Easter–New Year's Day: W/Es only Jan 1–Easter. Walks lead off from Visitor Centre around Waterfowl Park and to a nature trail (1 hour) through the reserve. Groups of schoolchildren by appointment.

Information   Guide to the Waterfowl Park and nature trail guides from the shop. The Visitor Centre includes extensive displays on archaeology and natural history.

History   The Park has been developed from worked out gravel pits which were landscaped to produce a series of lakes and ponds which now house one of the largest collections of waterfowl in the world with over 120 species of ducks, geese and swans.

What to See   In addition to foreign waterfowl, such as whistling duck, red breasted goose and king eider, British species including avocet, ruff, turnstone and redshank can be watched in natural surroundings at close quarters. The nature trail meanders along the River Wensum, one of the purest freshwater rivers in East Anglia.

T[D]. Refreshments. Children's play area.

Wheelchairs have access to 1 mile of tarmac and gravel paths.

Ranworth and Cockshoot Broads   13

Map 134 TG35-15- 306 acres (124 ha)

1½ miles north-west of South Walsham on the B1140 Norwich to Acle road. Part of Bure Marshes. NNR and a Ramsar Site. Open water, fen, scrub, wet woodland.

Access   On foot along road for ¼ mile from CP at TG361146 near The Maltsters Inn in Ranworth village, then along nature trail to floating Broadland Conservation Centre moored at the east end of Ranworth Broad. Centre open 10.30 a.m.–5.30 p.m. daily except Fri (Sat 2–5.30 p.m.). Nature trail open AYR. Boating visitors can moor at the staithe in Ranworth close to CP and then walk.

Information   Leaflets and trail guides at Conservation Centre which also houses an exhibition on problems of wildlife conservation in Broadland.

History   Like most broads these are flooded peat cuttings which were excavated between the ninth and fourteenth centuries when the sea-level was lower. The sea rose at the end of the fourteenth century and the flooded excavations were abandoned. These two broads then became famous for wildfowl: a duck decoy was built and earlier this century it was a favourite Royal shooting area. However all that ceased when the reserve was given to the NNT in 1949.

What to See   The nature trail illustrates natural succession in Broadland from open water through swamp, open fen, scrub and wet woodland to dry oak wood. Rare plants include marsh pea, milk parsley (the food of the swallow-tail caterpillar), cowbane, bog myrtle and marsh sow-thistle. Swallow-tails fly in June but other butterflies include holly blue and painted lady. In winter ducks dominate: wigeon, tufted, pochard, shoveler, gadwall, mallard, teal and goldeneye are abundant. Ranworth has the largest inland roost of cormorant in the British Isles and up to 20,000 gulls. Common tern, pochard, shoveler and shelduck all breed here whilst bittern, marsh harrier and osprey occasionally call in.

Thompson Common

14

Map 144 TL93-96- 309 acres (126 ha)
West of A1075 3 miles south-east of Watton. SSSI. Wet woodland, heath, marsh and ponds (pingos).

Access   AYR on foot from CP off A1075 in the old station yard at Stow Bedon TL940967 where the Great Eastern Pingo Trail of up to 8 miles begins.

Information   Explanation board in CP. Leaflet to way-marked trail from the farm shop by the start, or at the Post Office and shops in Stow Bedon village.

History   Pingos are shallow, crater-like depressions formed on the edge of the ice-sheet at the end of the last glaciation. They vary in size from about an acre to only a few feet across and the largest are filled with water. There are about 300 in this area and, together with Thompson Water, an artificial lake created in 1845, and areas of open heath and grassland grazed by Shetland ponies and roe deer, they form a fascinating mixture of scenery and habitat.

What to See   Pingos with a wide range of water plants look especially attractive in spring with large stands of water-violet, bogbean and marsh-marigold. Water meadows are later bright with ragged-Robin and marsh-orchids. Thompson Water has breeding populations of great crested grebe, mallard, teal, pochard, shoveler, and tufted duck whilst the surrounding reeds and willows attract sedge and reed warblers and reed bunting.

Suffolk

Suffolk is a county of contrasts. In the north-west where it borders Cambridgeshire and Norfolk the climate is severe—the nearest approach to a continental type in the country with low rainfall combined with low winter temperatures, but on the coast, 50 miles to the east, average winter temperatures may be a few degrees centigrade higher and oceanic plants prosper.

Although the majority of the county is intensively farmed and most of the once dominant woodland has been removed a number of areas remain, where cultivation has been impossible or proved to be impracticable, which are extraordinarily rich, often exhibiting a wide range of habitats in a small space.

Outstanding amongst these is the Breckland. This amazing area has a kaleidoscope of soil types where the underlying chalk is covered by sand of varying thickness, left by the retreating ice after the last Ice Age, which has since been blown by the wind. Where the chalk is at or near the surface lime-loving plants characteristic of chalk grassland abound—but a few yards away, where acid sand has accumulated in a hollow, heather and bracken are dominant. Whilst much has been lost to agriculture and forestry, areas remain between Bury St Edmunds and Brandon where this unique landscape can still be enjoyed. It is at its very best at the *Cavenham Heath NNR* astride the River Lark at Icklingham.

Heathland is also a feature of a narrow strip inland from the coast—the Sandlings, which runs for over 30 miles from Kessingland south to Felixstowe lying on considerable depths of glacial sands and gravels. This can be explored most easily in the Westleton area where Westleton Heath NNR, the NT property at Dunwich Common and the RSPB reserve at *Minsmere* are all adjoining.

Minsmere, like the Breck, is a superb example of many habitats in a small space—wetland, woodland and heath—and it also demonstrates how the exits of many Suffolk rivers have been blocked or diverted by the southward shift of coastal gravels resulting in a wetland delta. These make wonderful havens for birds and can also be seen at Thorpeness to the south and at Walberswick, Benacre and Kessingland to the north.

Shifting sands and gravels have been responsible for the build up of coastal spits like the 8 miles of Orford Beach at the mouth of the Ore and of *Landguard Point* at the mouth of the Orwell. The latter is much the more accessible and a fine place to watch shore-nesting and migratory birds—as well as ships coming and going from Harwich and Felixstowe Docks.

Wetlands are, of course, particularly associated in East Anglia with the Norfolk Broads—but Suffolk also has its Broads at its north-east boundary around Lowestoft. *Carlton Marshes* lie along the south side of Oulton Broad inland from Lowestoft and are connected to the River Waveney. The plants and animals here are similar to those found in the Fens which just touch the western border of the county near Lakenheath. The majority of fens have been drained so that the best areas of this type of vegetation which remain are now to be found in the Waveney Valley. Outstanding are *Redgrave and Lopham Fens* near the source of the river west of Diss, though there is a danger that extraction of water from a nearby borehole has lowered the water-table and is causing them to dry out. Today, however, there is an intimate mixture of pools, sedge fen and fen woodland or carr.

Elsewhere in Suffolk large areas of ancient woodland, which must once have dominated the heavy Boulder clay which covers most of the county, are rare. Near the east coast, only 3 miles from Southwold is a small fragment, *Reydon Wood*, from some of which all the mature trees were felled and the rest planted with conifers. This is now being restored by the SWT.

The largest remaining woodland nature reserve in the county, *Bradfield Woods* is, however, so splendid as to be some compensation for the losses elsewhere. But even this 161 acres is only part of a once much larger area, and was saved when it was purchased by RSNC in 1970 following the clearance of a large section of Monk's Park Wood for agriculture.

Much earlier, in 1938, RSNC (then the Society for the Promotion of Nature Reserves) purchased a 4½ acre meadow at Mickfield in the Deben Valley to protect its magnificent colony of fritillaries. This was the first Suffolk nature reserve and is a wonderful sight for a few days each spring when the flowers are at their best.

● Suffolk Wildlife Trust (SWT), Park Cottage, Saxmundham, Suffolk, IP17 1DQ. 0728 603765.

Bradfield Woods 15

Map 155 TL93-57- 161 acres (65 ha)
6 miles south-east of Bury St Edmunds on a minor road which leaves A134 at the north end of Great Welnetham for Bradfield St George, Felsham and Gedding. SSSI. Ancient coppice-with-standards—one of the richest woods in Britain.

Access   AYR on foot from CP off the road at TL934581.

Information   Leaflet with map from dispenser at CP. Information Centre open at the W/E.

History   The reserve consists of 103 acres of Felsham Hall Woods and 58 acres of Monk's Park Wood. They were bought by RSNC in 1970 following the destruction of around 130 acres of Monk's Park Wood for agriculture. Both woods were owned by the Abbey of Bury St Edmunds in the Middle Ages and are among the very few in Britain where the ancient practice of coppicing has continued from medieval times—the first record dates from 1252.

What to See   The soils are very variable with acid sands close to alkaline clays. There is thus a great variety of trees including ash, elm, maple, dogwood, spindle and guelder-rose in alkaline areas and hazel, birch, alder, holly and small-leaved lime in acid ones. Amongst the flowers are herb-Paris, oxlip, wood spurge and water avens. Breeding birds include tawny owl, woodcock and nightingale whilst redpoll, brambling and siskin come in winter. Fallow, roe, red and muntjac deer have all been reported.

Carlton Marshes 16

Map 134 TM50-92- 112 acres (45 ha)
On the south side of Oulton Broad on the west outskirts of Lowestoft at the north end of Burnt Hill Lane off A146 ¾ mile west of Oulton Broad station. SSSI. Broadland with grazing marsh, dykes, pools, fens and reed beds.

Access   AYR on foot from CP at White House Farm TM509920.

Information   Leaflet with map from Visitor Centre in CP which has an exhibit on the Waveney Valley. Open 9 a.m.–5 p.m. daily.

History   In Roman times the area where the reserve lies was part of a huge estuary. On a clear day an ancient sea-cliff can be seen at Burgh St Peter across the valley to the north-west whilst the shells of cockles and mussels are found when dykes are dredged. Peat was dug for fuel in medieval times: the abandoned diggings have filled with water to form two areas of open water—mini-broads—called Sprats Water and Round Water.

What to See   A rich fen supports marsh sow-thistle, flowering-rush, milk-parsley and greater spearwort with greater bladderwort in the pools and dykes full of water-soldier and water-violet. Marsh harrier breed here most years whilst Cetti's warbler bred for the first time in 1974. In winter waders probe the wet grassland whilst short-eared owl and hen harrier hunt above. Grass snakes, harvest mice and water voles all live on the reserve where 13 species of dragonfly have been recorded.

T[D]. Shop in Visitor Centre.

Wheelchairs have some access.

Cavenham Heath   17

Map 144 TL75-72- 336 acres (140 ha)
1 mile west of Icklingham at end of by-road which leaves A1101 Mildenhall to Bury St Edmunds road 100 yds west of the church at the Mildenhall end of the village. NNR. Breckland heath, acid woodland and fen.

Access   AYR on foot from CP on the far side of Temple Bridge over River Lark at TL757727: only the area south-west of the bridge is open.

Information   Notice boards with maps at access points. Leaflets from NCC, 60 Bracondale, Norwich NR1 2BE. 0603 620558.

History   One of the finest remaining examples of the once extensive Breckland heaths with a sequence of soils from dry acid sands and shallow lime-rich soils to reed, sedge and damp willow carr beside the River Lark which flows through the reserve.

What to See   Heather dominated heathland includes occasional dodder, petty whin and the tiny mossy stonecrop, plentiful on well-trodden paths. More calcareous areas have dwarf thistle and maiden pink whilst marsh fern is frequent in the willow carr. Nightjar nest here with tree pipit, linnet and reed bunting, whilst a small herd of roe deer grazes the area. Grass snakes and adders may be seen and grayling butterflies are on the wing from mid-July to the end of August.

Wheelchairs have limited access.

Landguard   18

Map 169 TM28-31- 40 acres (16 ha)
Off the road to the docks 1 mile south-west of Felixstowe at the end of Manor Terrace. SSSI and LNR. Coastal plants and sea birds.

Access   AYR on foot from CP at TM289329 across public open space to reserve entrance 600 yds to the south-west.

Information   Leaflet with map from Bird Observatory on the west side of reserve or from warden on site during the summer.

History   For over 400 years Landguard was used by the Military. Fortifications were first built in 1540 and replaced by more solid defences in the eighteenth century. Bunkers, gun batteries and blockhouses were added during the two World Wars. The fort is now an ancient monument part leased to the Landguard Bird Observatory which looks down on a windswept shingle spit built up by wind and waves beating down the North Sea from the north-east.

What to See   The beach is dominated by sea-kale, sea sandwort and yellow horned-poppy: other local plants include sea pea and many grasses such as great brome, bearded fescue, hard fescue, dune fescue, bulbous meadow-grass and curved hard-grass. Little tern and ringed plover nest on the shingle whilst the dense tamarisk scrub inland attracts rare migrants and vagrants: bluethroat, wryneck, ortolon bunting, icterine warbler and firecrest occur most years and black redstart regularly breed here. Butterflies abound and migratory painted ladies and clouded yellows pass through.

Minsmere

19

Map 156 TM47-66- 1470 acres (630 ha)
East of B1122 from Leiston to Westleton, from south via East Bridge at TM452660, from north via B1125 Westleton to Dunwich road—then follow RSPB signs to Reserve Centre. SSSI. Ramsar Site. Birds of coast and marshland with many spring and autumn migrants.

Access   AYR except Tuesdays. By permit issued on arrival from Reserve Centre at CP at TM472671 on a first come first served basis from 9 a.m.–9 p.m. or sunset if earlier. Only RSPB and YOC members on Sundays and BH W/Es. Charge for non-members. There is a public hide at TM477662, open AYR, which can be reached from NT CP at the south end of Minsmere Cliffs by walking for ½ mile along the beach.

Information   Leaflet from Reserve Centre with guidance to way-marked trails to eight hides. Up-to-date information boards. Warden: 0728 73281.

History   One of Britain's most important bird reserves where over 280 species have been recorded of which about 200 are seen each year and up to 100 in a day. Between the Centre and the sea a scrape has been created—an area of shallow water and mud with many small islands designed to attract breeding birds. There are also large stretches of mixed woodland and over 400 acres of heath.

What to See   The second largest British colony of breeding avocets occupies the scrape from April–September, where little tern also breed. Bitterns may be heard, but not seen, at this season. Marsh harriers are, however, regularly visible. Bearded tits are common with over 1000 in the reed-beds in autumn, whilst Savi's, Cetti's and grasshopper warblers all regularly occur. Out on the heath woodcock and nightjar come in small numbers whilst grey herons and the occasional purple heron fly overhead. In spring and summer spoonbills normally appear, often staying for many weeks.

T[D].
Wheelchair access to three hides.

Redgrave and Lopham Fens   20

Map 144 TM04-79- 304 acres (123 ha)
4 miles west of Diss south of the A1066 Diss—Thetford road. Take turning to Low
Common ½ mile east of South Lopham, straight over crossroads after ½ mile,
follow road for another ½ mile to signpost to CP. SSSI. Reed-beds, pools, heath,
fen woodland and alder carr.

Access   AYR on foot on a wide selection of way-marked trails.

Information   Notice boards in CP with map and details of walks. Leaflet from
Warden at Reserve Office at TM053803 just after sharp bend south of crossroads
en route. Tel: 037 988 618 (daytime).

History   A valley fen which contains the source of the River Waveney.
Maintained for centuries by the cropping of reed and sedge for thatching and
animal bedding and by the digging of peat for fuel. These activities declined and
the fen was in danger of encroachment by scrub until acquired by the Suffolk
Trust in the mid 1960s.

What to See   Outstanding is the presence of Britain's largest spider, the great
raft spider, found here in 1956 and, until 1989, not known anywhere else in the
country. It occurs in pools on either side of the path leading from the east end
of the CP. Greater bladderwort flowers here in summer whilst on the fen margin
another insectivorous plant, butterwort, still occurs with grass-of-Parnassus. In
heathy areas common cottongrass, lousewort and cross-leaved heath grow
together. Kingfisher may sometimes be seen flashing along the river.

Reydon Wood   21

Map 156 TM47-78- 40 acres (16 ha)
½ mile east of Wangford off the B1126 taking minor road to Frostenden opposite
Reydon Hall. Park on corner when wood is in front and road turns sharp right.
Ancient wood of ash, hazel and hornbeam.

Access   AYR on foot along a lane to entrance at TM476787 100 yds after
reaching the corner of the wood.

Information   Leaflet with map to way-marked trail from wooden hut inside
entrance. Also up-to-date notice board.

History   The remains of a once much larger ancient wood. The original south
and west boundaries are marked by earthworks and a sinuous margin, but with
straight edges without banks on the north and east sides where the wood was
grubbed up and converted to agriculture in the nineteenth century. In the 1960s
all the remaining mature trees were felled and replaced by conifers: it was then
left untouched until bought by SWT in 1984. They are gradually removing the

conifers and restoring the former coppice regime. It is now run as a community woodland with much help in management from local volunteers.

What to See   Coppice of various ages produces a variety of light conditions in which five species of orchid occur including bird's-nest orchid and greater butterfly-orchid. In spring the west side of the wood is a carpet of bluebells, greater stitchwort and yellow archangel. Ponds, with boggy margins, support fine-leaved water-dropwort, water-violet and water-crowfoot as well as frogs, toads and newts. Woodcock nest on the ground in the darker, older, coppiced areas.

EAST MIDLANDS

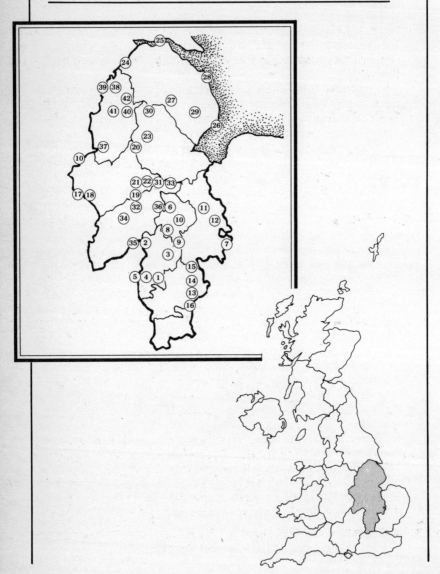

Bedfordshire

Geologically Bedfordshire can be divided into three parts which run from north-east to south-west. Right across the middle from Potton in the east to Leighton Buzzard in the west lies a thin slice of Lower Greensand about 3 miles wide. On either side are clays—the Oxford clay to the north which covers nearly half the county and, to the south, the almost indistinguishable Ampthill clay. The third part is in the extreme south where, for about 8 miles, the chalk escarpment of the Chiltern Hills crosses the county between Hertfordshire and Buckinghamshire reaching its highest point just below 800 ft on the Dunstable Downs.

Superimposed on this simple outline and cutting a tortuous path through the northern clays is the River Great Ouse on its way from its source near Brackley in Northamptonshire to the Wash. The gravel terraces of the valley have long been exploited as a source of building material.

Happily, in Bedfordshire, there are nature reserves with open access where the different habitats, which the three geological features and the Ouse valley support, can be seen and enjoyed.

Ancient woodland was typical of the heavy clay lands before they were cleared but, compared with other counties, few of these woods have survived. However a good example can still be visited at *Bramingham Wood* on the north edge of Luton.

In complete contrast are the dry, acid birch and oak woods on the Greensands. The most accessible are those in and around *Stockgrove Country Park* and those which surround the headquarters of the Royal Society for the Protection of Birds at *The Lodge, Sandy*: both these areas also have heath dominated by bracken and heather—the latter a very rare plant in the county confined to the Greensand band.

Few areas of natural wetland now remain in the valley of the Bedfordshire Ouse—instead wildlife habitats are being created and managed within areas such as worked-out gravel pits. A good example is found at *Felmersham* which was abandoned nearly 40 years ago and is now a valuable educational reserve. Another area, 1¼ miles east of Bedford town centre, has become Priory Country Park where the local office of the Bedfordshire and Cambridgeshire Wildlife Trust is situated.

However there is little doubt that for scenery and wildlife the best in the county is still to be found in that small area of chalk in the south either on the heights of Dunstable Downs on the way to Whipsnade or on the lower outlier of *Totternhoe Knolls* which sits on the edge of the Aylesbury Plain on the Buckinghamshire border and where you can still look out from the mound of a Norman castle like our forebears 900 years ago.

- Bedfordshire and Cambridgeshire Wildlife Trust (BCWT), Priory Country Park, Barkers Lane, Bedford MX41 9SH. 0234 64213.

Bramingham Wood ▮1

Map 166 TL06-25- 45 acres (18 ha)
North-west outskirts of Luton ½ mile west of A6. Turn into Icknield Way then
fork right after ½ mile, then take the next right into Northwell Drive and then
right at the roundabout into Lygetun Drive; the wood is at the far end.
Community Woodland. Deciduous woodland, ponds.

Access   AYR on foot from parking space at TL071255 onto well-maintained
paths for a circular walk taking about 1 hour. The south end is used by Girl Guides
and there is no public access.

Information   Leaflet from Woodland Trust.

History   Ancient woodland with records going back to 1227 when the tenant
planted a hedge round the wood. More recently it has become surrounded by
housing and was subject to vandalism. In 1985 it was transferred to the Woodland
Trust and is now managed as a Community Woodland with the involvement of
local volunteers. This has led to a reduction in damage to trees and less rubbish
dumping. A coppice-with-standards management system is being restored on a
15-year cycle and the ponds have been improved.

What to See   Woodland flowers begin with snowdrop, followed by colt's-foot,
primrose, wood anemone, bluebell and red campion, with twayblade appearing
in cleared areas. There are resident tawny owls, great spotted woodpecker,
nuthatch, treecreeper, sparrowhawk and woodcock whilst blackcap, willow
warbler and spotted flycatcher join them in summer. The ponds attract heron
and teal and support smooth newts and frogs. Less common butterflies to be seen
are speckled wood and comma with gatekeeper and ringlet in sunnier spots. Shy
muntjac deer inhabit the wood throughout the year.

Felmersham ▮2

Map 153 SP99-58- 52 acres (21 ha)
In the valley of River Ouse ¼ mile north of Felmersham village. SSSI. Gravel pits
and old grassland.

Access   AYR from CP on the north side of the reserve on the west side of the
road from Felmersham to Sharnbrook at SP987583.

Information   Leaflets available from BCWT.

History   The gravel pits forming the reserve were dug in the late 1930s and
40s for building roads and airfields: they subsequently filled with water. The
overburden was left in lines which now form linear islands attractive to wading
birds. The gravel beds date from the Pleistocene period. An Iron Age settlement
was found during the gravel digging.

What to See   The pits were dug in flood meadows and some of the species
of old grassland remain including yellow-rattle and red bartsia whilst orchids
such as bee orchid and broad-leaved helleborine may be found. Some boundary

hedges of old fields remain and are rich in shrubs including spindle, grey willow, field maple and hazel. There is a well-developed aquatic and marsh flora amongst which greater bladderwort, bogbean, marsh stitchwort and arrowhead are noteworthy. The variety of habitats attracts many breeding birds—little grebe, great crested grebe and kingfisher amongst them. Overwintering wildfowl include tufted duck and pochard whilst sandpiper and little ringed plover are occasional visitors.

The Lodge, Sandy   3

Map 153 TL18-48- 104 acres (42 ha)
1 mile east of Sandy south of B1042. Part SSSI. Birds for all seasons, heath and woodland.

Access   On foot from CP at entrance by gatehouse at TL192486. Open daily throughout year 9 a.m.–9 p.m. (or sunset if earlier). Charge for non-members.

Information   Guides to four trails and leaflets from Visitor Centre and shop at entrance open 9 a.m.–5 p.m. weekdays; 10 a.m.–5 p.m. W/Es; 12 noon–4.30 p.m. Christmas–Easter. Hides with views over lake and small pond.

History   The Lodge is a Victorian house built in 1870 for the son of Sir Robert Peel. It was bought by the RSPB, with the surrounding estate, in 1961. Though the house itself is encircled by formal gardens this soon gives way to extensive woods and heathland on the light acid soils of the Lower Greensand which gave the town of Sandy its name. The Greensand is exposed in the remains of a quarry which forms a sheer cliff on the west edge of the reserve.

What to See   By planting trees, creating ponds, erecting nest boxes and feeding in winter The Lodge is of major interest for birds at all seasons. Nuthatch, treecreeper, woodcock, spotted flycatcher and great spotted woodpecker occur. Kingfisher and green sandpiper visit the lake whilst tree pipits nest on the heath. Aquatic life is abundant in the lake where dragonflies, including the handsome Emperor, hawk over the water in summer and toads and newts come to breed. Natterjack toads have recently been established in a shallow pool dug on the heath. Muntjac deer are often to be seen.

T at CP [D at The Lodge]. Shop.

Wheelchair access to hide and special CP for disabled.

Stockgrove Country Park   4

Map 165 SP91-29- 74 acres (30 ha)
West of A418 2½ miles north of Leighton Buzzard just north of the village of Heath and Reach: signposted from the A5. Part SSSI. Ancient woodland, heath, stream and lake.

Access   AYR on foot from CP at SP919294.

Information   Leaflets and guides at small Visitor Centre by CP.

History   The Park lies on both sides of a small valley running north-south which has cut through Boulder clay into the underlying Lower Greensand. Baker's Wood which clothes the slope to the east is an ancient oak woodland formerly coppiced to produce fencing and firewood. To the west open heath and grassland rise to a gorse and bracken-covered plateau. The stream in the valley bottom rises in springs near the CP and flows through marshland to an artificial lake in the grounds of Stockgrove House to which the Park was formerly attached. The house still stands beyond the western boundary and is used as a residential school.

What to See   There is a fine display of bluebells in Baker's Wood in spring accompanied by some wood anemone and followed by yellow archangel and nettle-leaved bellflower. Tormentil and lesser stitchwort grow on the heath whilst marsh bird's-foot trefoil, wild angelica and yellow loosestrife occur beside the stream. This area also has the last surviving colony of wood vetch in the county. Nesting birds include blackcap, kestrel, nuthatch, redstart and willow warbler whilst crossbill, goldcrest and siskin are amongst others which may be seen. Water shrew and water vole both occur and badger and muntjac deer are regularly reported. The wide range of habitats supports 23 species of butterfly including brown argus, speckled wood and green hairstreak.

T[D]. Refreshments in summer.

Wheeelchair access to some good paths.

Totternhoe Knolls   5

Map 165 SP98-22-34 acres (14 ha)
2 miles west of Dunstable on a minor road off B489 to the north, well signposted to 'Nature Reserve'. Turn in immediately after the bus stop on the right. LNR and SSSI. Ancient Monument. Chalk grassland and scrub.

Access   AYR:

1. from CP at the west end of Totternhoe village at SP986215. Clearly marked paths through the reserve are shown on board in CP.
2. by footpath opposite the Cross Keys Pub at SP980218.

Information   Board at entrance to Wildlife Trust part of the reserve.

History   The Knolls were formed from the Lower Chalk and have been quarried and affected by earth moving since Saxon times. The reserve rises to 525 ft with extensive views over the Aylesbury Plain. A castle was constructed on the top by the Normans with a wooden keep on a mound (a motte) surrounded by two yards or baileys. The inner bailey can be seen in the scrub-covered earthworks whilst the outer is the large rectangular field on the south-east side.

What to See   The flowers of this chalk grassland include sainfoin, clustered bellflower, wild thyme, as well as kidney vetch and horseshoe vetch, food plants of the caterpillars of the small blue and chalkhill blue butterflies respectively. A number of species of orchid occur.

Picnic site.
Access for disabled to edge of reserve by car.

Cambridgeshire

Present-day Cambridgeshire includes the once separate local authority areas of Huntingdonshire and the Soke of Peterborough. The latter, which lies north of the River Nene on the Jurassic limestone, is included in the chapter on Northamptonshire to which it is historically and geologically much more closely related.

The remainder of Cambridgeshire falls easily into three very distinct landscapes; the chalk, the clays and the fens.

The chalk, which is a north-easterly extension of the Chilterns, forms a belt about 6 miles wide which runs through the whole of the south of the county from Steeple Morden near Royston in the south-west to the outskirts of Newmarket on the Suffolk border. It is perhaps most obvious to the visitor in the Gog Magog Hills which reach the comparatively high altitude of 234 ft 4 miles south of Cambridge.

The chalk forms a very thick filling to a sandwich of clay. To the south-west, from Linton to Cheveley, the chalk is overlain by a thick deposit of Boulder clay: to the north-west, from Cambridge through Huntingdon almost to Peterborough, the Boulder clay overlies the Gault, Oxford or Kimmeridge clays—clay on clay.

Finally, in this flat, low-lying, northern part of the county where the clays have been periodically flooded by the overflowing River Ouse and its tributaries or by inundations of the sea from the Wash, there is the Fenland basin, with its black, peaty soils at the southern end and its silts in the north around Wisbech.

One of the best ways of appreciating these three landscapes would be to walk along that magnificent pre-Saxon monument, the *Devil's Dyke*, the very existence of which was determined by their characteristics. The dyke runs from Wood Ditton ('wood ditch end') to Reach in the fens.

The Devil's Dyke begins on Boulder clay soils which are extremely wet and difficult to work and were, before Saxon times, almost completely covered in deciduous woodland which formed an impenetrable barrier at this south-east end. Though most of the woodland was subsequently cleared individual blocks remained, often to meet the needs for timber of particular parishes after which they were named such as Ditton Park, Balsham and Hildersham Woods on the east side; Waresley, Eversden and Kingston on the west. Of all these the most celebrated is *Hayley Wood* in the parish of Little Gransden, a fine example of an ancient wood famous for its spring display of oxlips, which are only found in this part of England. Twenty miles to the north-west, on the other side of Huntingdon and outside the oxlip zone, but with an equally ancient origin, stands *Aversley Wood*.

Within a mile of its beginning the Dyke starts to cross the open chalk country where, if there are woods, they are recent plantations, usually of beech which is not native to Cambridgeshire. Standing on top of the Dyke where it crosses Newmarket Heath, and closing one's eyes to the grandstand in the distance across the race courses, it is still possible to envisage the bare open countryside across which the Dyke was built to control movement of men and beasts.

The open countryside continues downhill into the fens at Reach—not, apparently, impenetrable today as tractors race along the straight laid roads. Only 2 miles away, at the end of Reach Lode, *Wicken Fen* begins, a relict of the wet, boggy vegetation which made Ely an island and a refuge for Hereward until it was drained. This and Wood Walton Fen NNR near Ramsey are all that is left to remind us why the Devil's Dyke ends where it does.

But the major period of fen drainage, from the seventeenth century onwards, brought one enormous, though accidental bonus—it created the *Ouse Washes*. The Washes are 11,600 acres of shallow lake in winter and rough grazing in summer, which has become a site of international importance for birds and is amongst the top ten of such sites in the British Isles.

More recently the need to drain has been replaced by a need to store water. The construction of *Grafham Water* in the 1960s when conservation issues were beginning to attract attention meant that, by design rather than accident, that reservoir rapidly became attractive to birds and is now an SSSI.

Agriculture in Cambridgeshire has always depended on raising crops rather than livestock so that grassland is rare and unimproved grassland extremely so. Only fragments have survived but some, recently discovered near St Ives, *Houghton Meadows*, are now safely secured as a nature reserve.

The traveller rushing through Cambridgeshire may indeed get the impression that it is a dull area with wall-to-wall wheat and barley but, in a county which can still point to sites of international and national importance like *Ouse Washes*, *Wicken Fen*, *Hayley Wood* and the *Devil's Dyke*, it is surely worth pulling into the slow lane and then stopping for a few days.

- Bedford and Cambridgeshire Wildlife Trust (BCWT), 5 Fulbourn Manor, Fulbourn, Cambridge CB1 5BN. 0223 880788.

Aversley Wood ▮6

Map 142 TL16-81- 152 acres (62 ha)
1 mile south of Sawtry west of the A1. SSSI. Ancient woodland, pond, marsh.

Access AYR on foot ½ mile along the path going south-west from CP in St Judith's Lane, Sawtry at TL170829 to an entrance which leads to a number of rides on the east and south sides.

Information Nothing on site: leaflet on history with recommended walks from Woodland Trust.

History   The north part of the wood is the oldest, having probably existed since the end of the last Ice Age. The southern third across a well-marked boundary bank was under the plough at Domesday (1086) and distinct ridges and furrows can be seen within the wood. It probably reverted to woodland after the Black Death, since so many people were killed, the land was no longer required for food production. In the south-easterly corner is an armed pond which was needed to water the 200,000 cattle which passed along the adjacent Bullock Road each year on their way to London markets.

What to See   In this wood of many habitats—dense shade, lighter coppice, wide rides, ponds and marshes—the most interesting tree is the wild service which is confined to ancient woodland. Some areas of dense shrubs such as spindle, elder, honeysuckle, and wayfaring-tree harbour nightingale in summer and large numbers of tits and warblers. The sheltered rides can be a blaze of colour, especially in spring and early summer, with bugle, cowslip and cuckoo-flower.

Devil's Dyke   7

Map 154 TL56-56- to TL65-58- 85 acres (34 ha)
2 miles south-east of Newmarket and running for 7½ miles from Wood Ditton to Reach. SSSI. Chalk grassland, scrub, woodland.

Access   AYR on foot from the parking space on the roadsides at Wood Ditton and Reach or from roads which cut through it onto a public footpath. The best for access and parking are B1102 between Swaffham Prior and Burwell at TL580649, a minor road from Dullingham to Chevely at TL641596 and from the roundabout at junction of A1303 and A1304 near the Race Course at TL617612.

Information   Notice board at Race Course entrance: leaflet from BCWT.

History   A great linear earthwork dating from the fourth to the seventh centuries and one of the most spectacular monuments of its kind in Britain. It runs across the open chalk country from the Fenland at Reach to the once wooded, and equally impenetrable, Boulder clay on the plateau near Wood Ditton. It was probably built to hinder communications. It was colonized by lime-loving plants which then grew on the chalk plain which it crossed. Most of that was ploughed after nineteenth century enclosures, though the adjacent Newmarket Heath race courses still give a wonderful impression of the former landscape.

What to See   Among the more interesting flowers on a long list are pasqueflower, spotted cat's-ear, bloody crane's-bill, bastard toadflax, rare spring-sedge, purple milk-vetch and horseshoe vetch. The moss flora is also rich with a number of species found nowhere else in the county.

The butterflies include common and small blues, brown argus and dingy skipper. It was once an area for red-backed shrike but the numbers have declined here, as elsewhere in Britain, and breeding is now extremely rare.

Grafham Water   8

Map 153 TL14-68- 370 acres (148 ha)
3 miles south-west of St Neots and north of B661 between Buckden on A1 and
Staughton on A45. SSSI. Open water, marsh, rough grassland, woodland, birds.

Access   AYR on foot:

1. from main CP (Mander) on the south side of reservoir west of Perry at
   TL143672 onto trails which lead to two hides on good paths and woodland
   walks in the BCWT reserve.
2. from Plummer CP east of Perry at TL163665 with adjacent hide.
3. from Hill Farm CP on north side of reservoir west of Grafham village at
   TL148683 where another trail starts.

Information   Leaflet and bird lists from Fishing Lodge shop at east end of
Mander CP: open daily.

History   Built between 1962 and 1966 Grafham Water covers about 1600 acres
and has a shore line of 9 miles. The reserve at the west end was set aside during
construction and opened in 1968. It includes not only the man-made shore line,
some grassland and new plantations but also two areas of ancient woodland. Two
creeks on the reserve are closed to anglers and sailors and these regularly attract
over 60 per cent of the waterfowl in autumn.

What to See   Large numbers of duck in winter—1500 mallard, 1000 wigeon,
2000 tufted duck and 500 teal with smaller numbers of pochard, goldeneye and
goosander occasionally accompanied by Bewick's swan, red-necked and
Slavonian grebes, scaup and eider. In summer tufted duck, shoveler, gadwall and
shelduck breed with a few pairs of redshank, lapwing, and ringed and little
ringed plovers. In late summer up to 250 mute swan gather to moult. The best
ancient woodland is in Littless Wood where the canopy of oak, ash and field
maple covers a woodland floor including wood spurge, nettle-leaved bellflower
and spurge-laurel.
     T[D] in Mander and Plummer CPs. Refreshments at Fishing Lodge.
     Wheelchairs have access to hide in Plummer CP.

Hayley Wood   9

Map 153 TL29-52- 122 acres (49 ha)
12 miles west of Cambridge on B1046 1½ miles after it crosses A14 at Longstowe.
The path to the entrance begins opposite a black water-tower. SSSI. Ancient
woodland, coppice-with-standards, glades, pond.

Access   AYR on foot from parking space by road at TL295537 between hedges
down Hayley Lane to entrance in 200 yds onto network of well-managed paths
which can be muddy. Dogs are not welcome.

Information   Notice board at entrance: leaflet from dispenser or from
Interpretative Centre which has a display on woodland history and
management. A tree-top walk and hide will be available from 1992.

History   One of the finest coppice-with-standards oak/ash woods in the country. It was acquired by the Wildlife Trust in 1962 when a 14-year coppicing cycle was restored in one-acre plots on the two sides of the main ride. The first part of the wood from the entrance, the Triangle, was farmland until 1920 but has reverted to woodland since.

What to See   Famous for its spectacular display of oxlip in the spring when the woodland floor is also carpeted in wood anemone, bluebell and early-purple orchid with some herb-Paris: later in the summer the wood margin holds crested cow-wheat and, on the old railway line alongside, clustered bellflower and greater burnet-saxifrage. The central glade has centaury, betony, wild basil and several orchids. There is a large population of woodland birds: great and lesser spotted woodpeckers, marsh and willow tits, blackcap, chiffchaff, willow and garden warblers and nightingale. A herd of about 40 fallow deer is frequently seen in the wood and leaves tracks in and around the pond: there are also up to a dozen muntjac.

Refreshment (pubs) in Longstowe, Gransden and Waresley.

Houghton Meadows   10

Map 142 TL29-71- 19 acres (8 ha)
North of River Ouse ½ mile east of Houghton Church. SSSI. Ancient ridge and furrow herb-rich meadows.

Access   AYR on foot from the parking space in Houghton village, along Thicket Road for 400 yds to entrance on south side.

Information   Notice board at entrance: leaflet from BCWT.

History   Ridge and furrow meadows on the first terrace of the river gravel on the north side above the flood plain of the River Ouse. The ridges are almost exactly 1 furlong in length and of great width—up to 14 yds across. They were created by a plough team of eight oxen yoked in pairs. Corn was grown on the ridges which here are not quite straight, having the shape of a reversed 'S'. This form of cultivation probably ceased with enclosure in the middle of the seventeenth century when mixed hedges, mainly of hazel, were planted across the ridges.

What to See   Pride of place must go to green-winged orchid, a species declining everywhere, and to large bitter-cress but, amongst the other 90 species of flowers recorded are crosswort, yellow-rattle, cowslip, meadowsweet, cuckooflower, salad burnet and meadow crane's-bill. Kingfisher, woodpecker, tawny owl, kestrel, sparrowhawk and cuckoo all occur whilst the damp grass attracts frog, toad, great crested newt and grass snake.

Ouse Washes   11

Map 142 TL4-8- 2200 acres (887 ha)
15 miles strip across the Fens from Mepal in Cambridgeshire to Denver, near Downham Market in Norfolk. SSSI. Ramsar Site of international importance for wildfowl, aquatic and marsh plants.

Access   AYR on foot from CP at Welches Dam, 4½ miles east of Chatteris via Manea, at TL470860 to paths to 11 hides over a 3 mile section of the Barrier Bank.

Information   Leaflets and guides from Visitor Centre 100 yds beyond far end of CP: open W/Es and BHs throughout the year 10 a.m.–5 p.m. or from RSPB Warden's house by entrance to CP. Visitor Centre has exhibition on the origin of the Washes and on their wildlife. Notice board in CP shows location of hides and gives up-to-date information. Also from Wildfowl and Wetlands Trust Centre at Welney, TL540934.

History   The construction of the Washes as part of a system devised by the Dutch engineer, Cornelius Vermuyden, was begun early in the seventeenth century. It now consists of two parallel, artificial rivers ½ mile apart which by-pass the meandering River Ouse and carry water in a straight cut, 20 metres wide, enclosed between high banks. Sluices at the south end make it possible to flood the grassland between the banks when the amount of water is too great for the 'rivers'. It is this area of shallow, flooded meadows which is so important for wildfowl in winter. In summer the washes are grazed by sheep and cattle and become attractive for ground nesting birds.

What to See   The birds are phenomenal. In January 1990 there were over 6000 Bewick's swan, about 20 per cent of the world population, and a staggering 50,000 wigeon, over 20 per cent of the British population: in addition 3000 pintail, 1000 shoveler, 5500 pochard, 7000 mallard and 7500 teal are regularly counted. In summer breeding birds include black-tailed godwit, ruff, redshank, shoveler and up to 800 pairs of snipe: spotted crake also nest occasionally. The submerged aquatic plants in the ditches and drains are noteworthy and include nine pondweeds, fringed water-lily and flowering-rush whilst meadows have marsh yellow-cress and meadow-rue.

T in CP at Welches Dam and Welney.

Wheelchairs have access to viewing from top of Barrier Bank at Welches Dam and to the hide at Welney.

Wicken Fen   12

Map 143 TL55-70- 730 acres (295 ha)
11 miles north-east of Cambridge on B1085 near the west end of Wicken village down lane signposted to Wicken Fen. CP is 200 yds on left. SSSI. Fen woodland, carr, reed-beds, marsh, lake, pools, waterways.

Access   AYR (except 25 December) on foot from CP at TL564706 to well-marked (but often wet) paths leading to tower hide overlooking a mere. There is also a ¾ mile boardwalk suitable for all seasons.

Information   Leaflets and trail guide from Visitor Centre beyond CP at entrance to Fen (charge to non-NT members). There is a display on the history of the Fen in the Visitor Centre: open April–November.

History   One of the best remaining examples of the original uncultivated peat fens which once covered most of this part of the county and probably Britain's oldest nature reserve, the first plot being acquired in 1896. It is now surrounded by arable land which has been drained and is some 5 ft below the level of the Fen. Wicken owes its preservation to its use as a catchwater into which flood water from the uplands could be discharged to prevent flooding of the arable land round about.

What to See A windmill, an example of the hundreds once used to drain the farmland, is here used to pump water into the Fen to maintain the water level. This helps in the management of the vegetation, particularly of the sedge, dominated by the great fen-sedge, which was cut as a crop for thatching every 4 years. Amongst a very long list of rare or local plants are frogbit, greater bladderwort, greater spearwort, milk parsley, marsh fern and bog-myrtle. Bird life is rich throughout the year: many species breed in the sedge including Cetti's and Savi's warblers and bearded tit. In winter bittern, short-leaved owl, great grey shrike and hen harrier are a feature.

T[D] at Visitor Centre.

Wheelchairs have access to ¾ mile boardwalk trail.

Hertfordshire

'London 10 miles' reads the sign on the A1 at Borehamwood on Hertfordshire's southern boundary—and this closeness to the capital has had a profound effect upon the county's character. It lies across all the most important road and rail links in the country. Not only the A1(M) but also the M1, M10 and M25 criss-cross like a cat's cradle between Hemel Hempstead and Hatfield and, whether you leave Euston for Birmingham, St Pancras for Sheffield, King's Cross for Edinburgh or Liverpool Street for Cambridge, some 20 miles of your journey will be through this one small county—less than half the size of Essex to the east.

Not surprisingly good communications attracted industry and housing. The New Town concept first took root here at Letchworth and Welwyn Garden City; Stevenage followed. Now, throughout its southern half, most of the countryside is in islands surrounded by suburbia. But, in spite of these pressures, Hertfordshire still retains many unspoilt rural areas and places for wildlife of the highest national importance across a wide range of soils; wet and dry, acid and basic.

In the north-east is an area 15 miles square where there are no towns and scarcely a village with over 1000 people—this is where the chalky Boulder clay overlies the chalk and produces deep soils and gentle hills suited to modern agriculture: hedges have been removed and fields enlarged so that wildlife is mainly confined to the woods.

In the north and west, from Tring to Royston, the chalk is freed of its clay mantle and carries the Chiltern landscape into East Anglia, along a prehistoric, literal highway, with Neolithic long barrows and Bronze Age round barrows on its route at *Therfield Heath* which, despite its name, is one of the finest pieces of ancient downland left in England with an assemblage of lime-loving wild flowers.

Elsewhere in the county the clays predominate again—clay-with-flints over the Chiltern plateau, the London clay across the south. These heavier soils were too intractable for medieval ploughs to tackle and carried coppice-with-standards woodlands as a source of fuel and timber. Many survived and the county is still well-wooded, especially in the area between Hatfield and the Essex border where Northaw, Hoddesdon Park Wood and *Wormley Wood*, oak woods with coppiced hornbeam, are of national significance.

In some places Tertiary gravels of the Reading Beds overlie the clays and there are small pockets of wet and dry heathland such as Bricketwood Common, near St Albans, and the Hertfordshire and Middlesex Wildlife Trust Reserve on *Hertford Heath*. Other, less acid, wetland habitats are found in the valleys. Nearly all the county's streams and rivers flow south and east to the Colne and the Lea, tributaries of the Thames. The valley of the Lea has retained some of the finest wet meadows in South-East England several of which are nature reserves now traditionally managed—Sawbridgeworth Marsh, Hunsdon Mead, *Rye House Marsh* and the adjacent Rye Mead. Because the Lea valley runs north-south it is also an important flyway of special interest to migrating birds.

- Hertfordshire and Middlesex Wildlife Trust (HMWT), Grebe House, St Michael's Street, St Albans AL3 4SN. 0727 58901.

Hertford Heath   `13`

Map 176 TL35-10- 62 acres (25 ha)
1½ miles south-east of Hertford on both sides of the A602 to Hoddesdon. SSSI. Deciduous woodland, scrub, wet and dry heath, ponds.

Access   AYR on foot from the parking space near East India College Arms at TL349111 to two separate parts on either side of A602. Please do not park on the private road at the Roundings.

Information   Notice boards with map at entrances.

History   The heath lies on pebble gravel over the London clay and consists of wet, acid, heathy grassland, one of the best examples still remaining in the county, and an area of woodland with oak, beech and hornbeam with an understorey of holly, hazel, blackthorn, hawthorn, birch and rowan with bracken beneath.

What to See   Plants of particular interest are petty whin, heather, common cow-wheat, sneezewort, lousewort, compact rush, oval, pill and common sedges, velvet bent, matgrass, heath grass and purple moorgrass with pools containing water-violet, water spiders, large red damselfly and great crested newt.

Rye House Marsh   `14`

Map 177 TL38-10- 17 acres (7 ha)

1 mile north-east of Hoddesdon opposite Rye House station on Toll Road to Stanstead Abbots. SSSI. Marsh, reed-beds, lagoons, willow carr.

Access   W/Es only 9 a.m.–9 p.m. (or sunset when earlier) on foot from CP at TL387099 to south hide (and others occasionally). At other times on written application to the warden at 4 Cecil Road, Rye Park, Hoddesdon EN11 0JA.

Information   Leaflet from Information Centre on site or from RSPB.

History   Rye House Marsh, in the Lea valley, was the site of a large sewage works which has attracted birds and birdwatchers for many years and is the headquarters of a ringing group. The reserve lies on a migration route and many passing birds drop into the pools and lagoons.

What to See   Interesting plants in the marsh include common meadow-rue, meadowsweet, wild angelica, common valerian, comfrey, adder's-tongue and lesser pond-sedge. Migratory birds include little ringed plover, redshank, common and green sandpipers and yellow wagtail. In winter come snipe, jack snipe, water rail, teal, shoveler and pochard with occasional bittern and bearded tit. Reed bunting, reed and sedge warblers breed here and there are common terns on rafts in the lagoons.

T[D] near Rye House station.

Wheelchairs have access along an 80-yd paved track from CP to hide overlooking marsh.

Therfield Heath   `15`

Map 154 TL33-39- 417 acres (169 ha)
1 mile west of Royston at the roundabout on A505 either taking turning to Therfield to the parking space on the roadsides or the road back to Royston to CP near a pavilion. SSSI, LNR. Chalk grassland.

Access   AYR on foot from parking space at TL 336400 or from CP at TL348405 onto the open heath, but beware of low-flying golf balls.

Information   Notice boards near entrance.

History   One of the richest areas of ancient chalk grassland in the country forming a link between the Chilterns and Cambridgeshire: the area round Church Hill on the west side of the Therfield road is particularly important. Much of the heath is managed as a golf course and the variety of cutting regimes help maintain the rich flora: where no cutting occurs upright brome is dominant and flowers few.

What to See   Rare and local wild flowers to be found include pasqueflower, purple milk-vetch, horseshoe vetch, bastard toadflax, spotted cat's-ear, squinancywort, clustered bellflower, lesser meadow-rue, dropwort and field fleawort: six species of orchid have been recorded. The butterflies attracted to this rich array include brown argus, common, chalkhill and holly blues, Essex, small, large and dingy skippers. Birds of the open downland are frequent: meadow pipit, skylark, yellowhammer and corn bunting.

T at pavilion CP.

Wormley Wood ■ 16

Map 176 TL31-06- 336 acres (136 ha)

2½ miles north-east of Cheshunt, west of A10 and A1170 reached by taking Little Berkhampstead turn off A1170 between Wormley and Broxbourne along White Stubbs Lane to CP on left after 2 miles. SSSI. Oak/hornbeam coppice-with-standards, high forest.

Access AYR on foot from CP at TL317063 on the path to the kissing gate which is the entrance to the wood.

Information Leaflet from Woodland Trust.

History A large ancient wood which is part of a more extensive area of adjoining woods covering over 1400 acres. The wood is on London clay which here has superficial gravel deposits producing a mosaic of woodland types. The dominant tree is sessile oak which in most parts stands over a coppice of almost pure hornbeam but there are also some areas of high forest with mixed oak and hornbeam standards. In the late 1970s one third of the wood was felled and replanted with conifers but these are being removed and broad-leaved woodland restored.

What to See Amongst other trees are ash, pedunculate oak, holly, aspen and birch whilst the ground flora consists largely of bramble, wood anemone, bluebell, great woodrush and honeysuckle with some lemon-scented fern in its only locality in the county. There are also some lime-rich areas with woodruff, yellow archangel and pendulous sedge. Birds are numerous with hawfinch, spotted flycatcher and all three woodpeckers amongst more notable species.

Leicestershire and Rutland

Leicestershire and the old county of Rutland have suffered more than most parts of England from the hand of man. The generally gently rolling surface has been easy to farm and has developed a landscape of well-kept hedges surrounding arable or ley grassland famous both for its fox-hunting and its fat cattle. But in the north-west this landscape has been disfigured by seven centuries of coal-mining which has left a complex of old spoil heaps and, in the east on the Jurassic limestone, by quarries which have gouged great holes in the hills to create cement for building and ballast for roads. Roads have added to the destruction of the countryside such as the M1 and M69 to the west of Leicester and the A1 along the eastern flanks.

However, there are still havens of wildlife where these pressures of industrial Britain can quickly be forgotten—though paradoxically some of the best are by-products of the expansion of industry and the growth of towns in neighbouring counties. This applies particularly to the two reservoirs in the south-east of the county.

Eye Brook Reservoir was built in 1942 to supply water for the growing steel-works of Corby just across the River Welland in Northamptonshire and rapidly became the foremost ornithological site in the county: it was only demoted to second place when *Rutland Water*, 6 miles to the north-east, was created in 1975 to supply water for the new or expanding towns of Corby, Daventry, Milton Keynes, Peterborough and Wellingborough.

These expanses of open water with their marshy margins are some compensation for the loss of wetland habitats in the county generally early in the twentieth century—losses which were also partly offset by the building of canals and railways in the nineteenth century. Four major canals cross the county: the two westerly ones, the Ashby Canal and the Grand Union Canal, are still in daily use but a 9-mile stretch of the latter, from a few miles south-east of Leicester to Foxton Locks near Market Harborough, is an SSSI for most of its length. Not now open to navigation and much less disturbed is the *Grantham Canal*, particularly the 11-mile section in the north-west from Harby to Grantham just across the county boundary in Lincolnshire where kingfishers flash by and the air is full of dragonflies in summer.

Railway lines, especially those long disused, form a network of linear links for wildlife with their intimate mixture of dry grassland, damp woodland and even marsh in borrow-pits beyond the fence. One of the most readily accessible is *Shenton Cutting* near Market Bosworth which is an integral part of the Bosworth Battlefield Trail.

Also adjacent to the Bosworth Trail and commanding the view south from the Visitor Centre is *Ambion Wood*—an old woodland which has certainly been in existence on the site for over 600 years. Even older and with a large area which has never been clear-felled is *Prior's Coppice* where traditional coppice-with-standards management is being restored after a lapse of nearly 50 years. This wood is typical of a number still found on the heavy Lias clays which stretch southwards across the River Welland into Northamptonshire where they underlie Rockingham Forest.

One part of Leicestershire stands out from the rest—Charnwood Forest. This unique area is spread over 30 square miles just north-west of Leicester. It is a buried mountain of hard pre-Cambrian rocks which produce highly acid, unproductive soils. There are still considerable areas of unenclosed moorland dominated by heather and bilberry with cottongrass and cross-leaved heath in boggy hollows. However this very proximity to Leicester means that much of it is in danger of destruction by the feet of an excessive number of visitors.

A similar flora and a great range of habitats can be found only 10 miles away just west of Junction 2 on the M69: here is more unenclosed land on Burbage Common where those willing to walk a little way can roam through ancient woods rich in wild flowers and butterflies with much less human pressure.

There are no shortages of wildlife treasures in Leicestershire so long as you are prepared to search them out.

- Leicestershire and Rutland Trust for Nature Conservation (LRNTC), 1 West Street, Leicester LE1 6UU. 0533 553904.

Ambion Wood and Shenton Cutting

17

Map 140 SP40-99- 50 acres (20 ha)
Between Shenton and Sutton Cheney 2 miles south of Market Bosworth, adjacent to Bosworth Battlefield Country Park. Coppice-with-standards wood, scrub, pond, herb-rich grassland.

Access AYR to Shenton Cutting from CP in old station yard at SK397003. From Battlefield Centre CP (small charge) open 22 March–31 October, weekdays 2–5.30 p.m., Suns and BHs 1–6 p.m., follow Battlefield Trail south-west along the north side of the wood into Shenton Cutting. There is no access to Ambion Wood except on the Battlefield Trail.

Information Leaflets and guides to waymarked trails from Battlefield Centre in CP: also numerous notice boards with maps.

History Ridge-and-furrow in the wood suggests it was once under the plough, but perhaps not since the fourteenth century and the Black Death. Now privately owned part will be leased to LRTNC who will keep the ride open by controlling vigorous blackthorn scrub. The railway cutting was constructed in 1831 and closed in the 1960s: it is now being managed to maintain open areas of herb-rich grassland.

What to See Native trees in the wood include ash, field maple and oak with much hazel beneath where meadowsweet and early-purple orchid colour the ground. Two other orchids, twayblade and common spotted, grow in the cutting with cowslip and hairy violet. Amongst larger birds jay and green woodpecker may be seen and heard. The rides and the cutting can both be alive with butterflies including brimstone, common blue and purple hairstreak.

T[D]. Refreshments, picnic site.
Wheelchair tracks round the Battlefield Trail.

Burbage Common and Woods

18

Map 140 SP44-95- 180 acres (75 ha)
South of A47 1 mile north-east of Hinckley. Part SSSI. Woods, heath, rough grassland, ponds.

Access AYR on foot from CP by Charlston Inn on the main road at SP446955 or 500 yds up Burbage Common Road to SP449952.

Information Maps in CPs and at other access points. Leaflet from Visitor Centre at main road CP. Open: Easter–end September 9 a.m.–6 p.m., October–April Mon–Weds 9 a.m.–1 p.m., Sats 2—5 p.m., Suns/BHs 2–6 p.m.

History The two woods on either side of the Leicester–Birmingham railway line, Burbage and Sheepy, are both ancient with ash, oak and field maple with an understorey of hazel. Burbage Common stands on glacial sand and gravel supporting a complex of dry heath, scrub and some marshland.

What to See In spring the woods are carpeted with wild flowers including woodruff, yellow archangel and moschatel with five species of orchid including greater butterfly. The common has numerous acid-loving species such as mat-grass, heather and oval sedge but elsewhere more lime-demanding species, great burnet, bulbous buttercup and cowslip, occur. Adder's-tongue, spiny restharrow, and saw-wort are amongst the rarer species to be found. This varied flora supports 19 species of butterflies including purple hairstreak.

T in CP. Light refreshments at Woodhouse Farm across the railway line or from the Inn near CP.

Eye Brook Reservoir   `19`

Map 141 SP85-95- 385 acres (160 ha)
4 miles north-east of Corby off the A603 Corby to Uppingham road. Aquatic and shore birds and marshland.

Access   AYR. Though permits are needed to enter the reservoir area itself there are splendid view points from the minor roads on the west and north sides, e.g. at SP847950, 845965 and 850966 as well as from the bridge over the Eye Brook at the north end which overlooks a marsh where waders gather in winter.

Information   Nothing on site: details from Leicester and Rutland Ornithological Society, 31 Tysoe Hill, Glenfield, Leicester LE3 8AR. 0533 873896.

History   The reservoir was opened in 1942 to serve the growing needs of the Corby steel-works but it is now a major centre for trout fishing where the absence of sailing maintains undisturbed conditions over much of the area.

What to See   Until the flooding of Rutland Water in 1975 Eye Brook was the most important site for bird-watchers in Leicestershire and Rutland. Even now it is visited by large numbers of waterfowl and waders with most continuing to increase—notably in winter with hundreds of mallard, wigeon, teal, pochard and tufted duck and regularly smaller numbers of pintail, shoveler, gadwall, goldeneye, goosander and ruddy duck. Small flocks of Bewick's swan may occur in winter along with golden plover, green sandpiper and jack snipe. Hobbies are regularly seen in spring and early summer and osprey on autumn passage when little stint and curlew sandpiper are amongst the waders on the muddy shore.

Excellent viewing for disabled.

Grantham Canal   `20`

Maps 129 and 130 SK74-31 to SK90-35- 11 miles in length
From Harby 7 miles north of Melton Mowbray to Grantham in Lincolnshire. Part SSSI from the west end of Harby to Redmile. Water plants, reed-swamp, grassland, hedges.

Access   AYR at many points on foot from road crossings.

Information   LRTNC Reserves Handbook.

History The canal was built between 1793 and 1797 and operated commercially until the 1960s. Since then it has remained closed though there are plans to reopen it for recreational purposes.

What to See A very diverse flora includes lesser water-parsnip, flowering-rush, arrowhead, branched and unbranched bur-reed. These species provide food and shelter for many birds and insects, with a large number of dragonflies. The very slow-moving water supports significant populations of frogs, toads and water voles.

Prior's Coppice
21

Map 141 SK83-05- 69 acres (28 ha)
  3 miles south-west of Oakham. Leave Braunston village on minor road to Brooke and Leighfield. After 1 mile take right turn to 'Leigh Lodge no through road' for 500 yds to reserve entrance on the right at SK832049. SSSI. Ancient coppice-with-standards wood.

Access AYR on foot (muddy) from parking space in lane along well-maintained network of way-marked rides.

Information Leaflet from LRTNC.

History A relic of the primeval woodland of the area on heavy clay soil. Formerly managed as coppice-with-standards, the west part was clear-felled during the Second World War but has regenerated into an even-aged ash woodland: here a small demonstration coppice plot will be restored. The east end is still a complex of trees of various ages which will be managed in future to maintain its interest as high forest.

What to See The ground flora below the ash, sallow, oak and field maple includes herb-Paris, violet helleborine, hard shield-fern, water avens, common spotted-orchid and ragged-Robin. About 35 species of bird breed in the wood including nuthatch and the three species of woodpecker whilst badger, fox and stoat are regular visitors.

Rutland Water
22

Map 141 SK89-05- 500 acres (200 ha)
1 mile south-east of Oakham. SSSI. Aquatic and shore birds, marshland, grassland, woodland.

Access

1. via Egleton village from which a track runs east to CP and Information Centre at SK878075. Open 9 a.m.–5 p.m. Weds, W/Es and BHs.
2. via road from Manton to Edith Weston on track leading north for 1 mile east of Manton signposted to 'Nature Reserve' to CP and Visitor Centre at SK894058. Open 9 a.m.–5 p.m. W/Es and BHs and also, Easter–October, Tues–Thurs.

Information   Leaflets with maps and guides to footpaths, trails and hides from Information and Visitor Centres.

History   The reserve is unique in that it was declared before the reservoir was built in 1975 and is now managed for Anglian Water by LRTNC. It has become internationally important for winter wildfowl with a December count of approximately 21,500 and has the largest number of gadwall, 1550 in 1985, in Britain.

What to See   Rarer wintering birds include Bewick's swan, smew, scoter and long-tailed duck whilst rare grebes, black-necked, red-necked and Slavonian, regularly occur. Birds-of-prey hunt over the marshland with frequent sighting of short-eared owl and hen harrier. In summer hobbies chase martins and swallows across the water. Shoveler, shelduck, teal, garganey, pochard, and ruddy duck are amongst the ducks which now breed here. The meadows round the lake are full of flowers including ragged-Robin, meadow saxifrage and marsh-orchids providing food for an increasing number of butterflies—large, small and Essex skippers are amongst the 24 species recorded.

T[D]. Shop, picnic site.

Wheelchair access to Information and Visitor Centres and to hides.

Lincolnshire

Lincolnshire has suffered more than most counties from the agricultural revolution with vast fields of wheat stretching from foot to horizon. However, it still retains a long and largely unspoilt coastline running for over 100 miles from the tidal flats of the River Humber in the north to the seal-strewn sands and muds of the Wash near the outfall of the River Nene. In between are some of the finest sand dune and salt marsh nature reserves in Britain such as *Gibraltar Point* and *Saltfleetby-Theddlethorpe*.

The chalk hills of the Wolds lie inland from the coast. Little remains of the sheep-grazed grassland which covered them before 1750 and not all of the soils are lime-rich. The tops are overlain with glacial Boulder clay and drift whilst the slopes are of the lower Cretaceous strata which are often impervious or acidic. This can be seen at *Snipe Dales*, a valley complex on the southern edge of the Wolds east of Horncastle, whilst west of Barton upon Humber, at the northern edge, the clay at the base of the chalk has been exploited for brick-making leaving a series of water-filled pits which form the heart of the *Far Ings* reserve.

The south-east quarter of Lincolnshire, around the Wash, was once undrained fenland: of that vegetation almost nothing now remains. There are still a few fragments left in the other fen area, the Isle of Axholme in the north-west, between the River Trent and the Yorkshire border. These, including Epworth Turbary, can be seen from the disused *Axholme Line* reserve running north from Haxey.

The loss of these wetlands has been partially compensated for by the creation of gravel pits in the river valleys. There is a large complex in the Witham valley south-west of Lincoln where a small group have been made into *Whisby Nature Park* with easy access from the A46.

On the other side of Lincoln, about 10 miles to the east on the heavy clays, lie remains of one of the most important and celebrated of all the county's wildlife habitats—the Lincolnshire Lime Woods—a group of these in Bardney Forest is managed by the Forestry Commission. *Little Scrubbs Wood*, south of Wragby, is an easily accessible example and has alongside it a small but very fine example of old, species-rich meadows, most of which have been ploughed up since the 1950s.

The limestone grassland of the county, which was once widespread on the Jurassic ridge from Stamford to the Humber near the Trent mouth, is also now reduced to a handful of sites but happily an example full of flowers still remains in the *Ancaster Valley* reserve between Grantham and Sleaford.

● Lincolnshire and South Humberside Trust for Nature Conservation (LSHTNC), The Manor House, Alford, Lincoln LN13 9DL. 0507 463468.

Ancaster Valley · 23

Map 130 SK98-43- 24 acres (10 ha)
South side of A153 Grantham to Sleaford road 100 yds east of its junction with B6403 at Ancaster. SSSI. Limestone grassland, woodland.

Access   AYR via a signposted bridleway to the reserve entrance 200 yds up the track at SK985432. Cars are best parked in the village.

Information   Nothing at site.

History   When the reserve was acquired in 1982 large areas of steep banks were overgrown with scrub of hawthorn and gorse. Much of this has now been cleared and restoration of limestone grassland has been achieved by a combination of late cutting of hay in July followed by sheep-grazing. Woodland on the east side of the valley is being managed and planted with oak, ash and field maple to fill in gaps.

What to See   This narrow, steep-sided valley is over ½ mile long. It is one of the finest sites for limestone grassland in Lincolnshire and contains such rare and beautiful species as pasqueflower, dyer's greenweed, dropwort and spring cinquefoil. The woodland harbours yew, wayfaring-tree and traveller's-joy on its edge with violets and early-purple orchids covering the ground in the spring.

Axholme Line · 24

Map 112 SE77-01- 34 acres (14 ha)
North of Haxey for 1½ miles along the disused Axholme Light Railway track, parallel to and west of the A161. CP in Haxey village close to the junction of Blackmoor Road and Marlborough Road at SE773000. Scrub and grassland with many butterflies.

Access   AYR on foot from the entrance 150 yds west of Kings Arms at SK773997 or along the footpath from Low Burnham at SE780021 to the north end of the reserve.

Information   Nothing at site.

History   When the Trust acquired the reserve in 1978 much of the track had become overgrown with hawthorn: this has now been cleared and grassland re-established on the banks.

What to See   The first mile from Haxey is a cutting through the base-rich Keuper marl which supports many species of shrubs including aspen, oak, and field maple. The speciality of the reserve is the green-winged orchid which grows in large numbers on the banks and in the ballast. The dingy skipper is amongst the 18 species of butterfly recorded.

Wheelchairs have access to a good level track once padlocked gates or stiles have been negotiated.

Far Ings

25

Map 112 TA01-23- 115 acres (46 ha)
On the south shore of the River Humber west of Barton upon Humber. Turn left off A15 1 mile south of Humber Bridge onto A1077 to Scunthorpe. Almost immediately turn north following signs for Clay Pits View Point. At bottom of hill turn left for CP at TA011229. SSSI. Salt marsh, reed-beds, open water.

Access   AYR on foot from CP on well maintained way-marked paths which lead to five hides overlooking the main areas of interest.

Information   Leaflet and guides from Visitor Centre in CP open daily.

History   A brick and tile industry flourished for 4 miles of the Humber bank from west of Barton upon Humber to New Holland from the Middle Ages to early in the twentieth century. Since then cement-making has added to the number of flooded clay-pits which have been left. These pits have developed extensive beds of reeds and bulrushes and a wide range of aquatic habitats. These supplement the salt marshes which continue to line the Humber shore.

What to See   Birds are the outstanding feature and it is one of the few breeding sites in Lincolnshire and South Humberside for bearded tits, whilst other notable nesting species include pochard, shoveler and water rail. Reed and sedge warblers are abundant in the reed-beds in summer whilst lapwing and redshank have already raised young around new scrapes made in 1986. Winter brings diving ducks, goosander, merganser and occasional smew and bittern.

T[D] at Visitor Centre. Shop.

Wheelchairs have access to hides on good tracks.

Gibraltar Point

26

Map 112 TF55-58- 1057 acres (428 ha)

3 miles south of Skegness, east of Gibraltar Road and north of the mouth of the River Steeping at Wainfleet Haven. NNR. Sand dunes, salt marsh, shingle, scrub and sea birds.

Access   AYR:

1. from main CP by Visitor Centre at the south end of Gibraltar Road at TF556581.
2. from CP at Seacroft Esplanade, east of Seacroft Golf Course at TF565610.
3. From CPs on the east side of Gibraltar Road ½ mile north of Visitor Centre close to a hide overlooking a mere.

Information   Map and nature trail guide from Visitor Centre: open daily 1 May–31 October, W/Es 1 November–30 April 10 a.m.–dusk. Centre includes fine display on wildlife of reserve . Many plants on trail are labelled in spring and summer.

History   This vast area of sand dunes and salt marsh is growing rapidly: the present coastline is over 500 yds further seawards than it was in 1825 and a new spit over 600 yds long has developed at the southern end enclosing more salt marsh. Wainfleet, 5 miles to the west, was a flourishing port in medieval times.

What to See   One of the best places on the east coast to see a wide range of sea-shore life in mud, sand dunes, salt marsh and scrub at various stages of development. Unusual plants include sea-heath, and shrubby sea-blite at its northern limit in Europe. The birds are outstanding: it has breeding little tern, ringed plover, redshank and shelduck. In winter regular visitors include Brent goose, snow bunting, fieldfare and twite.

T[D] Shop.

Wheelchairs have access on good tracks.

Little Scrubbs Wood and Meadow   `27`

Map 121 TF14-74- 45 acres (18 ha)
2 miles south-south-east of Wragby on road to Langton from the B1202 Wragby to Bardney road. AA signs to 'Forest Walks' may be in place. Forest Nature Reserve. Ancient lime wood, old herb-rich meadow.

Access   AYR on foot from CP beyond the FC Bardney Forest HQ at Chambers Farm at TF149738. Walk up woodland ride opposite CP and pick up the blue trail which leads first through coniferous woodland to the meadow and then into Little Scrubbs Wood: 1¼ miles long.

Information   Open days are frequently held on which a comprehensive leaflet is available on site.

History   The woodland is part of the 4000 acre Bardney Forest which includes several areas of what are known as the Lincolnshire Lime Woods, broad-leaved woods in which the small-leaved lime is abundant, which represent examples of ancient woodland which developed on the site after the last Ice Age: they are being managed as coppice-with-standards to protect their structure of high canopy, understorey and ground layer.

What to See   The meadow is species-rich: full of green-winged orchid in May and June, it becomes a sea of purplish-blue saw-wort and devil's-bit scabious in August and September. Amongst the butterflies to be seen are large and small skipper and white admiral, whilst five species of tit may be seen and heard. In spring the wood is filled with the songs of blackcap, chiffchaff, robin, wren and willow warbler.

Wheelchairs have limited access.

Saltfleetby—Theddlethorpe Dunes   `28`

Map 113 TF47-90- 1185 acres (480 ha)
Coast running south for 4 miles from Saltfleet Haven to about 1 mile north of Mablethorpe east of A1031. NNR. Sand dunes, salt marsh, scrub.

Access   On foot from CPs in four places at the end of lanes off A1031. From north to south:

1. Sea View to TF465924 (lane is opposite turning to Louth on B1200).
2. Churchill Lane to TF478901.
3. Brickyard Lane to TF483893.
4. Sea Lane to TF489882 following signs 'To Sea and Car Park'. The CPs are joined by a footpath and there is open access elsewhere except to a 'Danger Zone'—visitors must comply with safety regulations.

Information   Notice boards near CPs give map and details of the reserve.

History   The oldest landward dunes may have been created before the fourteenth century when the Great Eau, a stream which separates Saltfleetby All Saints and Theddlethorpe All Saints, was channelled northwards to Saltfleet to keep the haven free of silt. A second ridge of dunes nearer the sea encloses a freshwater marsh which is widest at the northern end.

What to See   The old dunes, where grazed, are rich in wild flowers including common centaury, field mouse-ear, viper's-bugloss and pyramidal and bee orchids. In the absence of grazing sea buckthorn, hawthorn and elder are dominant. The younger dunes are colonized by sea couch and stabilized by marram and sand fescue. The marsh in between is a little brackish and sea club-rush is often abundant but, in shorter vegetation, there are spectacular displays of marsh-orchids in June and early July as well as lesser spearwort, lesser water-plantain, bog pimpernel and the very rare marsh pea. Salt marsh on the foreshore has sea arrowgrass, thrift and some sea-lavender. Green hairstreak butterflies are a feature of early summer when natterjack toads may be breeding in shallow pools. Breeding birds include shelduck, redshank and short-eared owl whilst in winter waders in large numbers feed on the shore and birds of prey, including harriers, appear.

Snipe Dales   `29`

Map 122 TF32-68- 121 acres (48 ha)

5 miles east of Horncastle, north of A1115 at Winceby between Horncastle and Spilsby Statutory Nature Reserve. Scrub, dry grassland and marsh.

Access   AYR on foot from CP at TF319683 along well-marked trail.

Information   Notice board with map in CP and nature trail with many explanatory boards.

History   The Dale is a steep-sided valley traversed by streams which cut through the soft Spilsby sandstone into the Kimmeridge clay below. At the junction of the sandstone and clay a spring line produces small streams and flushes.

What to See   Dry slopes covered in bracken and rosebay willowherb lead down to valley bottoms full of meadowsweet, great willowherb and great horsetail and areas of alder and willow. Stream-side flowers include ragged-Robin, water avens and water figwort. Snipe and meadow pipit breed in the shorter grassland of a paddock grazed by cattle and sheep. Barn owl, short-eared owl and kestrel regularly hunt over the valley and green woodpecker may be heard. At one point in the valley not far along the trail an old hydraulic ram thuds regularly pumping water up to a farm on the hill by the CP.

T[D]. Picnic site at Country Park ½ mile to the east at TF330682.

Whisby Nature Park   30

Map 121 SK91-66- 145 acres (59 ha)

5 miles south-west of Lincoln to the west of A46 down Moor Lane signposted to 'Nature Park' and Thorpe-on-the-Hill. Worked-out gravel pits with lakes, grassland, scrub and marsh.

Access   On foot from CP at SK914660 a number of attractive way-marked walks of varying length lead off along good paths. A railway line crosses the park so children must not be allowed to stray. Open daily 9 a.m.–dusk.

Information   There is an explanatory board in CP and a leaflet is available on site or from the TI Office in Lincoln. There are two hides on the largest of the southern lakes.

History   The Nature Park consists of a series of pits left from excavations over the last 40 years of sand and gravel deposited in the valley of the River Witham by the ice retreating after the last glaciation.

What to See   In summer great crested grebe, mallard, and moorhen nest round the pits whilst willow tit, nightingale, reed and sedge warblers, whitethroat and lesser whitethroat are amongst the birds nesting in the scrub and copses nearby. Common tern may be seen hovering over the water or sparrowhawk hunting for prey. Amongst the 300 wild flowers so far recorded are water-plantain, gipsywort and marsh-orchids. Dragonflies and damselflies are abundant and 16 species are known to occur. Small copper and common blue butterflies may also be seen.

T[D] in CP.

Wheelchairs have access to excellent paths.

Northamptonshire and the Soke of Peterborough

To many outsiders Northamptonshire may suggest tail-backs on the M1 or the industrial East Midlands towns of Kettering, Northampton and Wellingborough and, until recently, the belching chimneys of the steel-works at Corby. But, away from these few centres, the rest of the county retains a quiet rural charm and can justifiably boast of a higher percentage of unspoilt villages than most other parts of Britain.

Much of the landscape too, has been protected, as it falls within some of the great estates like Althorpe, Boughton, Drayton and Rockingham where tree planting and hedgerow management are sympathetically promoted.

The character of the county changes markedly from east to west. Along the eastern boundary are the Oxford clays—heavy land now mostly under the plough. This drops down into the valley of the Nene, the main river, which flows from the highest part of the county near Daventry north-east towards Peterborough. Much of the valley floor is alluvial gravel which has been extensively exploited for building expanding towns like Northampton. The gravel pits which have been left are becoming of increasing importance to wildlife and the *Titchmarsh* reserve between Thrapston and Oundle is a fine example of how planning and forethought can create new habitats even though the last dragline did not leave until 1985.

Higher up the valley, north of Peterborough, gravel workings at *Peakirk*, which were abandoned in the nineteenth century and were later planted as osier beds, have been developed into attractive waterfowl gardens.

Immediately across the Nene lies the oolitic limestone and the character of the landscape changes abruptly. Grey stone villages flank its western bank and the value of this most durable of building materials is proclaimed by the soaring spires of churches like St Peter's, Oundle which rises to 215 ft. Quarrying began as early as the Roman period and the National Nature Reserve of *Barnack Hills and Holes*, developed on the site of quarries abandoned about 1450, is now one of the few places on the limestone where species-rich old grassland still survives. Much younger examples now occur all round Corby where quarrying of ironstone took place from the 1930s to the 1980s and several are already managed as Country Parks and small reserves.

Corby itself was built in the heart of Rockingham Forest which, with *Salcey* and Whittlebury Forests to the south, was created as a Royal Forest at the time of William the Conqueror. Much of Rockingham has now been cleared or changed to conifers but a number of ancient woods remain including *King's Wood* only a mile from Corby town centre.

Where the ironstone came near the surface it was quarried in the past and provides the warm brown stone which is such a feature of the villages on the west side of the county.

The population of Northamptonshire has been one of the fastest growing in Europe. People need water and several new reservoirs have been built to meet the demand. The largest of these is at *Pitsford* which, since it was opened in 1955, has become a major bird reserve.

Thus, though man has been disturbing the natural features of Northamptonshire for nearly 2000 years, this has often led to the creation of habitats which have been taken over by the wildlife and now provide many opportunities for its enjoyment.

● Northamptonshire Wildlife Trust (NWT), Lings House, Billing Lings, Northampton NN3 4BE. 0604 405285. This is also a nature reserve and Information Centre: it is in Lings Way due east of the Weston Favell Centre at SP803638.

Barnack Hills and Holes   31

Map 142 TF07-04- 55 acres (22 ha)
South-west edge of Barnack village, 2 miles east of A1. NNR. Limestone grassland.

Access   AYR on foot from CP at the north-west corner at TF073047. Dogs must be kept under strict control especially when sheep are present.

Information   Leaflets from dispensers at entrance or NCC.

History   A stone quarry from Roman to medieval times: the source of materials for cathedrals and abbeys at Ely, Bury St Edmunds, Peterborough and several Cambridge colleges. The hummocks left were sheep-grazed and have prevented ploughing. Now one of the richest areas of limestone grassland in England.

What to See   In spring pasqueflower, cowslip and early-purple orchid are abundant, to be followed in summer by horseshoe vetch, purple milk-vetch and squinancywort, with four orchids—man, bee, pyramidal and fragrant. Large numbers of knapweed broomrape arise, parasitizing the greater knapweed. The chalkhill blue butterfly, which feeds in the caterpillar stage on the horseshoe vetch and the Duke of Burgundy fritillary whose caterpillars feed on cowslip, both occur. 50 species of birds include nesting skylark and yellow-hammer.

King's Wood   32

Map 141 SP86-87- 65 acres (31 ha)
1 mile south-west of Civic Centre of Corby north of A6014 to Great Oakley. LNR. Ancient ash-hazel-maple woodland.

Access   AYR on foot from the limited parking on the south and east sides in Colyers Avenue and Alberta Close.

Information   Four-page leaflet from NWT or District Council Office, Civic Centre, Corby NN17 1QB. 0536 402551.

History   Fine remaining example of the once extensive Royal Rockingham Forest which provided shelter for the King's deer and grazing for livestock from neighbouring townships. Following deforestation in the nineteenth century it survived because of its value as a game preserve. It was the first LNR to be declared in the county.

What to See   Over 250 species of wild flowers are found including wood anemone, primrose, bluebell, yellow archangel and wood-sorrel, with ragged-Robin in the wet areas. Guelder-rose, dogwood and common and Midland hawthorn occur in the understorey. The wood supports a good variety of birds including tree creeper, nuthatch, tawny owl and all three woodpeckers. Migrant warblers inhabit young coppice in summer whilst siskin and redpoll feed in a group of alders in winter. Considerable areas of open grassland in and around the wood are managed in a mosaic of tall and short swards attractive to insect life.

Wheelchairs have easy access from adjacent roads.

Peakirk   33

Map 142 TF16-06- 17 acres (7 ha)
5 miles north of Peterborough and north of B1443 Glinton—Thorney road. Wildfowl reserve, wildfowl collection, ancient duck decoy, wetland.

Access   From CP on road north from Peakirk village. Open daily 9.30 a.m.–6.30 p.m. or dusk if earlier. Closed 24 and 25 December.

Information   Leaflets and guide to trail from Reception Centre in CP.

History   One of seven Wildfowl Centres set up by the Wildfowl and Wetlands Trust this one dates from 1956. Peakirk is situated in an old osier bed on an island in the Fens where local inhabitants formerly lived on ducks and eels.

What to See   The collection contains over 700 wildfowl of some 112 species from all over the world. The grounds are a beautiful combination of water and woodland whilst a wader scrape attracts a wide variety of migrant birds. One may also see kestrel, barn owl, tawny owl, kingfisher and many other land birds throughout the year. The reserve is being extended to include a wetland area designed to attract wild birds.

T[D]. Refreshments and shop.

Wheelchairs have easy access on good paths.

Pitsford Reservoir   34

Map 141 SP78-70- 480 acres (194 ha)
6 miles north of Northampton east of A508 at Brixworth and crossed by minor road from Brixworth—Holcot at SP780702 (Holcot Causeway). SSSI. Aquatic birds.

Access

1. picnic site (SP760686) with views over southern half and gull roost.

2. Holcot Causeway with views over the nature reserve and central area.
3. limited number of permits to visit the nature reserve from NWT.

Information   Four-page leaflet from NWT.

History   Built in 1950 to supply drinking water to Northampton.

What to See   Winter visitors include over 1000 wigeon, large numbers of teal, tufted duck, gadwall, pochard and shoveler with a few pintail, goosander and goldeneye. Bewick's and whooper swans may also occur. In spring sandmartins, swallows, yellow wagtails and wheatears arrive. Several species of tern, including occasional black tern, pass through whilst willow warbler, chiffchaff, blackcap, sedge warbler and occasional grasshopper warbler move in to breed in the woodland around the water's edge. Coot, great-crested grebe, mallard and tufted duck also breed here. In autumn, if the water level is low, shallow bays attract passing waders including greenshank, spotted redshank, ringed plover, dunlin, little stint and ruff. Plants which colonize bare mud in dry years include golden dock and water-crowfoot.

Wheelchair passengers have excellent viewing from Holcot Causeway.

Salcey Forest   35

Map 152 SP81-51- 34 acres (14 ha)
6 miles south of Northampton west of B526 Northampton to Newport Pagnell road taking turning to Hartwell to CP on left after ½ mile. SSSI. Ancient oakwood with butterflies, deer and wild flowers.

Access   AYR on foot from CP at SP811509 along the ride on the opposite side of the road to the reserve entrance.

Information   From FC picnic site on road south of Quinton near north-west corner at SP 793518.

History   Remarkably unchanged since its creation as a Royal Forest by William the Conquerer: Salcey Lawn was always an integral part. The name means willow wood and many areas are still very wet.

What to See   Home of such rare butterflies as black hairstreak, purple emperor, white admiral and wood white. Mammals include fallow and muntjac deer and innumerable grey squirrels, whilst amongst the 52 species of birds which breed here are nightingales, blackcap, chiffchaff, redstart and spotted flycather. The wild flowers include several orchids such as early-purple, common spotted and greater butterfly.

Wheelchairs can gain access at various points from roads through the wood.

Titchmarsh   36

Map 141 TL00-80- 180 acres (73 ha)
1 mile north of Thrapston west of A605. Part SSSI, and LNR. Aquatic birds and heronry.

Access   AYR on foot to west side of main lake via bridle path from Islip at SP990799 or from Aldwincle at TL007813: to the east side via track from A605 at TL014802 where there is some space for cars and a path leads to a hide at the north end of the lake. Visitors are asked to keep well away from the wooded area, the heronry, from February to July.

Information   Information boards at access points and leaflets from dispensers or from NWT.

History   The open water is derived from gravel pits worked out in the 1980s. They have been landscaped and planted to make them attractive to wildfowl. The heronry has been established in a plantation which surrounds an old duck decoy created by Lord Lilford in 1885.

What to See   In winter flocks of mallard, shoveler, wigeon and teal feed in shallow areas, whilst little grebe, great-crested grebe, goldeneye, pochard, goosander and tufted duck occupy the deeper water. In spring up to 40 pairs of heron are at their nests and many migrants pass through including black tern, wheatear, bar-tailed godwit and numerous other waders. There are resident breeding populations of Canada geese, mute swan, common tern, ringed plover, little ringed plover and oystercatcher. Autumn migrants include many species of wader with occasional avocet, Kentish plover, ruff and whimbrel. Otters have been seen recently in the small lake and along the River Nene.

Nottinghamshire

Nottinghamshire is a generally low-lying, egg-shaped, Midland county with a pronounced north–south axis. The highest land in the west does not exceed 660 ft and the altitude falls gently eastwards: over a third of the county is below 100 ft. The yolk of the 'egg' is the Bunter sandstone, an area of dry, acid, pebbly soils, on which lay the Royal hunting forest of Sherwood, perhaps the county's most famous landmark.

The Bunter sandstone extends north from the outskirts of Nottingham to the county boundary at Bawtry and beyond. Once covered by open forest much has altered since it began to be enclosed in the middle of the seventeenth century. It was then that the great estates like Clumber, Thoresby and Welbeck were created and the area was given the name The Dukeries, which it retains to this day. Elsewhere coniferous plantations have changed the character of the landscape so that it is only in a few areas that the structure of the medieval Royal Forest remains. This can best be seen at *Sherwood Forest Country Park* north of Edwinstowe where, legend has it, Robin Hood and Maid Marian were married and where the Major Oak still persists. Acid soils do not support a wide variety of wild flowers so the woodland floor has little excitement. It is the old decaying oaks which are so important with over 250 species of insect depending upon them for food.

However immediately to the west the woods are brighter: here there is a long narrow outcrop of Magnesian limestone which often lies astride the county boundary with Derbyshire and Yorkshire and on which the woodland flowers are found in much greater profusion. A typical example persists in the north-west, to the west of Blythe, where the ash and wych elm dominated *Dyscarr Wood* is a feast of spring colour with large patches of woodruff, ramsons and yellow archangel followed in summer by stinking iris and giant bellflower.

But the finest and largest blocks of woods left in the county are those on the other side of the Bunter 'yolk'—on the Keuper marl or Mercia mudstone ridge which runs north–south between the River Idle and the River Trent to the east. This weathers to a heavy, reddish, poorly-draining clay difficult to work and on which most parishes retained some woodland as part of their rural economy. Some, like Eaton and Gamston, have been heavily planted with conifers, but others like *Kirton* and *Treswell Wood* are examples of coppice-with-standard in the process of being restored by the Nottinghamshire Wildlife Trust.

The River Trent is the major aquatic artery of the county—and its valley cuts through the middle of these Triassic marls whilst at the same time creating its own deep alluvial soils over the glacial gravels which it brought down during the last Ice Age. Because the valley runs south-west to north-east and then north it acts as an important flyway for migrating birds going south in autumn or coming north in spring.

There has been a continuous demand for the gravel for buildings and roads, especially in the Nottingham area but, with careful forethought and design, these workings have become of benefit to wildlife. Thus it is that the *Attenborough Reserve*, 5 miles south-west of the centre of Nottingham, has become one of the best bird-watching sites in the county. Two much smaller areas, the lakes at *Daneshill*, which were also excavated from glacial gravel, are of growing importance for birds and can just be glimpsed to the right of the line as your Inter City 125 rushes between East Retford and Bawtry. It's worth stopping off to enjoy this and the many other sites tucked away just over the rolling Nottinghamshire horizon.

- Nottinghamshire Wildlife Trust (NWT), 310 Sneinton Dale, Nottingham, NG3 7DN. 0602 588242.

Attenborough 37

Map 129 SK52-34- 360 acres (146 ha)
5 miles south-west of the centre of Nottingham south of A6005 road to Long Eaton at the end of Attenborough Lane. SSSI. Flooded gravel pits, aquatic and marshland birds and plants.

Access AYR on foot from CP at SK521343, or from Beeston Rylands or Long Eaton along the River Trent tow-path.

Information Leaflets and guide to a way-marked nature trail from Information Caravan in CP, open W/Es, or from Works Office.

History Until 1929 Attenborough was surrounded by wet grassland grazed by cattle in summer, and willow holts harvested for the basket-making trade.

A series of gravel pits was dug betweenn 1929 and 1951. Recolonization over 30–60 years has created a wide range of aquatic and wetland habitats as well as areas of scrub and grassland. The reserve was established in 1966 and is being continuously improved with the creation of reed-beds, further ponds and lagoons, and by willow coppicing and ride clearance.

What to See In winter the reserve holds a large proportion of the county's shoveler and diving ducks with large numbers of teal and occasional wigeon. Sawbills and sea-ducks occur regularly and all the British grebes have been recorded. In summer shelduck, little ringed plover and common tern are breeding around the open water whilst reed, sedge and grasshopper warblers and chiffchaff will also be present. The numerous dragonflies include four-spotted chaser, southern and brown hawkers. The rich aquatic flora includes flowering-rush, unbranched bur-reed, lesser bulrush and several pondweeds whilst the marshland has round-fruited rush and brown sedge. There is old grassland with meadow saxifrage, meadow crane's-bill and great burnet.

Refreshment caravan may be present.

Daneshill Lakes 38

Map 120 SK66-86- 120 acres (48 ha)
1 mile east of A638 East Retford to Bawtry road at Torworth, immediately beyond the level-crossing. LNR. Flooded gravel pits, aquatic and marshland birds.

Access AYR from CP at SK669865 on the south side of the road 300 yds east of level-crossing to:

1. Daneshill South 80 acres—unrestricted with recreational facilities.
2. Daneshill North—40 acres with access on paths only.

Information Leaflets from Information Centre by lake at Daneshill South open most days. Educational facilities for schools including well-marked trail.

History Former gravel workings in glacial deposits which have been abandoned for over 20 years. Recent reshaping and tree planting have enhanced the quality of the area which now has open water, wet grassland, scrub and some rapidly growing carr woodland.

What to See In summer the woods are alive with whitethroats, willow warbler and blackcap, replaced by siskin, goldcrest and water rail in winter. All three woodpeckers may be seen as well as the occasional kingfisher. Other water birds include snipe, redshank, greenshank, ringed plover and little ringed plover. Wildflowers include southern marsh-orchid, weld and goat's-rue which attract a good number of butterflies—gatekeeper and ringlet amongst them.

T. Picnic site.

Wheelchairs have easy access to Daneshill South.

Dyscarr Wood

39

Map 120 SK58-86- 42 acres (17 ha)

½ mile west of Langold 5 miles north of Worksop on A60. Turn down Church Street at the south end of village by Victorian church, now a conveyor-belt factory, following signs for Langold Lake to CP in this Country Park at SK580866. Most SSSI, part LNR. Ash, wych elm wood, scrub and marsh.

Access

1. to CP in Country Park—open daily 9 a.m.–dusk.
2. to Dyscarr Wood AYR on good well-marked paths.

Information   Leaflets from Information Office by CP describes vegetation of Dyscarr Wood and gives three routes round Country Park. Fact Sheet on wood from NWT.

History   An ancient ash, wych elm wood on soils developed from the upper Magnesian limestone, though many of the trees have been killed by Dutch elm disease. An old ditch and bank on the west edge of the wood marks the county boundary with South Yorkshire.

What to See   Trees include oak, birch, cherry and yew with alder and crack willow in damper areas, and an understory of hazel, hawthorn, blackthorn, field maple, privet and dogwood. The rich woodland flora boasts woodruff, ramsons, yellow archangel, broad-leaved helleborine and twayblade with meadowsweet and lesser spearwort in marshy places. Over 50 species of birds have been recorded with sparrowhawk, little and tawny owls, woodcock and hawfinch amongst them. There is open scrub to the north-west which is excellent for butterflies where small copper, orange-tip and migrant painted lady may be seen.

T in Country Park. Picnic site, refreshments.

Wheelchair access along good paths in wide rides in wood and round Country Park.

Kirton Wood

40

Map 120 SK70-68- 46 acres (29 ha)

On minor road 1 mile east of Kirton which is 3 miles west of Tuxford on A6075 to Ollerton. SSSI. Ash, wych elm wood with rich shrub layer.

Access   AYR on foot from CP inside the entrance at SK708687: if the gate is locked, park on verge opposite the entrance.

Information   Booklet and Fact Sheet from hut 100 yds inside reserve on open days, or from NWT. Way-marked trails on good paths (muddy).

History   Lying on the clay soils of the Triassic Keuper marl it is in part an ancient wood going back over 2000 years but much of it was clear-felled in the 1930s. It was subsequently managed for shooting until bought by NWT from the Coal Board in 1983. It has been damaged by Dutch elm disease so that considerable replanting has now been undertaken by the Trust and Tooley tubes are frequent.

What to See The right-hand boundary near the entrance has numerous wild service-trees whilst guelder-rose is a feature of the ride margins and spurge-laurel of the deeper shaded areas: spindle, dogwood, field maple and privet also occur. Some of the stools of coppiced ash are enormous. Wild flowers include woodruff, yellow archangel, ramsons and primroses with occasional greater butterfly-orchid. Woodpeckers, sparrowhawk and woodcock are regularly seen and there is a large population of breeding tits, finches and warblers including garden warbler.

T at Visitor Centre, 1 mile SE in yard of Dovecote Inn, Laxton.

Wheelchair access is good along main ride of wood.

Sherwood Forest Country Park   41

Map 120 SK62-67- 450 acres (202 ha)
2 miles west of Ollerton on B6034 Edwinstowe to Budby road. LNR. Open oak woodland, park and heath.

Access AYR on foot from CP at SK627677.

Information Leaflets and guides to several way-marked trails, which also have panels along the route, from Visitor Centre, open daily 9 a.m.–1 p.m.,2–5 p.m. There is an exhibition, an A/V display and an educational pack for schools.

History Sherwood was a Norman Hunting Forest which, at the beginning of the thirteenth century extended from Nottingham in the south to the Meden valley north of Mansfield covering some 100,000 acres. Following the death of Richard II in 1399 the popularity of Sherwood for hunting declined and from the seventeenth century onwards much of this former Crown Land was sold. However the importance of the fragments which now remain was appreciated and were scheduled as an SSSI in 1954.

What to See Half a mile from CP is the Major Oak, a massive old tree with a hollow trunk 12 yds round, which is one of many such ancient, stag-headed trees, perhaps suffering from a reduction in their water supply. Elsewhere sessile and pedunculate oak and birch predominate with much bracken beneath their light canopy. Over 60 species of bird are known to breed in the Park and the insect population associated with the old trees is specially important. Herds of red and fallow deer may still be seen through the trees.

T[D]. Picnic site, shop, refreshments.

Wheelchair access on good paths, blind trail.

Treswell Wood   42

Map 120 SK76-79- 118 acres (48 ha)
3 miles east of East Retford following signs to Grove 50 yds north of Fina petrol

station on A638 on the south side of town. After 1½ miles follow sign to Grove and Treswell. The wood is 1½ miles beyond Grove. SSSI. Coppice-with-standards, oak, ash, field maple wood with rides and pond.

Access AYR on foot from CP inside entrance or from verge outside if gate locked. Visitors must keep to paths. There are special Open Days on second Sun each month April–Sept.

Information Booklet and Fact Sheet from NWT or from wood on Open Days.

History One of the best examples of primeval woodland on the Triassic Keuper marl in the county which formed part of the nearby Grove Estate until it was broken up in 1946. The ash dominated canopy also includes oak, field maple, aspen, wych elm, birch, crab apple and wild cherry: the presence of wild service-tree confirms its ancient origin. Much was clear-felled at the time of the First World War and most of the rest of the large timber was taken out before 1960. It was bought by NWT in 1973 which has since set about restoring the traditional coppice-with-standards management regime.

What to See The rich ground flora includes some ancient woodland indicators e.g. woodruff, wood-sorrel, wood anemone, herb-Paris and early-purple orchid whilst the pond harbours marsh-marigold, yellow iris and water-crowfoot as well as all three species of newt. Woodland birds are numerous and include woodcock, nuthatch, and, in summer, spotted fly-catcher, garden warbler and blackcap. A speciality is the speckled bush cricket here at the northern limit of its range in Britain and another old woodland indicator: being flightless it cannot recolonize areas totally cleared of forest.

WEST MIDLANDS

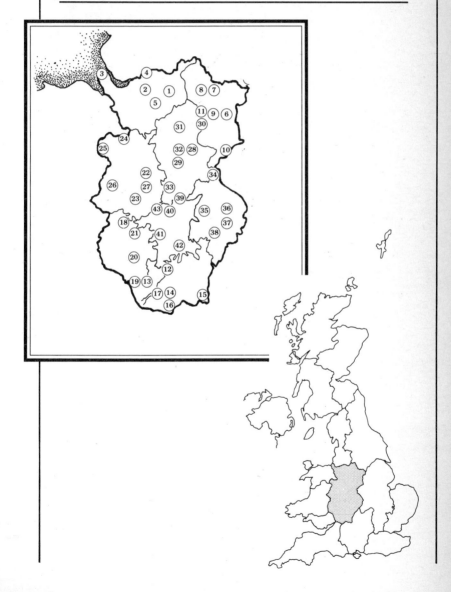

Cheshire

The greater part of Cheshire consists of a plain of post-glacial clays and sands overlying Triassic rocks of varying depths. The county divides naturally into three landscapes. In the west are the red sandstones which outcrop in the Wirral Peninsula and form the mid-Cheshire ridge. This rises to over 500 ft near Duckington and in Delamere Forest. In the east, towards the Peak, are the Millstone grits on the flanks of the Pennines between Macclesfield and Buxton, rising to 1834 ft on Shining Tor. In between these two, on the salt-bearing marls, are the meres and the remains of many peat mosses.

This once glaciated landscape left a series of hollows some of which are filled by natural meres today. A fine example can be seen in *Marbury Country Park* which contains Budworth Mere, over 100 acres in extent. This includes what is perhaps one of the two oldest nature reserves in the county in the 14 acres of woodland and reed-bed at the western end which was bought in 1934, together with Cotterill Clough, as a memorial to Cheshire naturalist T.A.Coward.

Other hollows have gradually filled with vegetation to form the peat mosses which were once a widespread feature but which have now been largely drained or cut over. The best of those which remain, Wybunbury Moss south of Crewe, is too fragile and dangerous for visitors, having at its centre only a thin crust of peat floating over water. However it is possible to visit, under guidance and on safe paths, *Risley Moss* near Warrington where management to restore it as a living example is being undertaken.

To natural hollows have been added artificial ones, particularly where subsidence has occurred following the exploitation of salt deposits in the Keuper Marls which have beds over 2000 ft thick. These hollows are specially frequent round Northwich, Middlewich and Sandbach: four in the latter area have been recognized as the *Sandbach Flashes* SSSI, where salt marsh plants thrive inland and many aquatic birds come to breed, visit or pass the winter.

Set in the plain as a vantage point from which to witness the changes below, the mass of *Alderley Edge* stands over 300 ft above the surrounding countryside and has been occupied by man since at least the Bronze Age in 1500 BC.

Twenty miles to the west what there is of the Cheshire coastline can be seen on a clear day where the bird-rich estuaries of the Dee and Mersey are shared, from the Wirral Peninsula, with Lancashire and Clwyd. The Lancashire side facing Liverpool is almost completely covered by industry or houses, but the west and north still have space for golf and gulls, and for natterjack toads which have an isolated population in the pools behind the dunes of *Red Rocks Marsh* near Hoylake from where, if you want to walk away from it all, you can leave Cheshire behind by taking a 3-mile walk across the sands to Hilbre Island.

- Cheshire Conservation Trust (CCT), Marbury Country Park, Northwich CW9 6AT. 0606 781868.

Alderley Edge

Map 118 SJ86-77- 218 acres (88 ha)
4 miles north-west of Macclesfield on B5087 to Wilmslow. SSSI. Deciduous woodland, conifers, heathland.

Access   AYR on foot from CP at SJ860771 onto a network of well-maintained paths.

Information   Leaflet from Information Centre in CP.

History   Alderley Edge is a 300 ft high ridge, with extensive views over the Cheshire plain to the Pennines, capped by a resistant bed of coarse, pebbly, Triassic sandstone which protects the softer marls and sandstones beneath. Copper mining here goes back at least to Roman times and there are still traces of old mine shafts scattered over the hill. The Edge was a sandy heath in the Middle Ages but was enclosed in 1779. Scots pine and beech were planted and today form a mixture with the native oak and birch. It was given to the NT in 1947.

What to See   The acid woodland has a restricted ground flora of bluebell, pignut, bilberry, wavy hairgrass, heath bedstraw and common cow-wheat. The woodland birds include warblers, tits, nuthatch, treecreeper and great spotted woodpecker.
  T[D] in CP. Refreshments.
  Wheelchairs have good access on special paths to view points and there is a special CP for the disabled.

Marbury Country Park and Reed Bed

Map 117 SJ65-76- 188 acres (76 ha)
1½ miles north of Northwich between A559 and A533. The entrance is well signposted and is in Marbury Road, south of Comberbach. SSSI. Lake, reed-bed, deciduous plantation, canal bank.

Access   AYR on foot from CP in Country Park at SJ651763 to a network of paths with the hide overlooking Budworth Mere and the reed-bed.

Information   Leaflets and lists of plants and animals from Information Centre north of CP. Other enquiries from CCT HQ nearby: open Mon–Fri 9 a.m.–5 p.m.

History   The Park once surrounded the early Victorian 'chateau' of Marbury Hall which was pulled down in 1968. The landscaped grounds include Budworth Mere which has, at its west end, a 15 acre woodland and reed-bed owned by RSNC and managed by CCT. The woodland, planted in the 1850s, now has a selection of woodland flowers, especially in the spring, and attracts a long list of birds and insects. The Trent and Mersey canal, which runs along the southern boundary of the Park, adds further to the variety.

What to See   About 80 native and introduced trees and shrubs grow in the Park and have attracted native wild flowers such as wood-sorrel, wood anemone, yellow archangel, opposite-leaved golden-saxifrage, giant bellflower, bluebell and red campion whilst the Mere has flowering-rush and marsh cinquefoil along its margins or in the reed-bed. The reed-bed is the most important bird habitat with nesting reed and sedge warblers, and great crested and little grebes. In winter the Mere attracts tufted duck, wigeon, pintail, pochard, shoveler and goldeneye with sanderling, redshank and curlew amongst the waders. The woods hold large numbers of tits, warblers, treecreeper, nuthatch, tawny owl and great spotted woodpecker with smaller numbers of lesser spotted woodpecker, siskin and whitethroat.

T in Information Centre.

Red Rocks Marsh 3

Map 108 SJ20-88- 10 acres (4 ha)
½ mile to the north of West Kirby at the north-west corner of Wirral, west of A540 Meols Drive. SSSI. Foreshore, dune slacks, reed-bed, lime-rich grassland.

Access   AYR on foot from:

1. CP in Dee Lane near West Kirby station at SJ211868 then north along foreshore.
2. car parking space in Stanley Road, Hoylake reached by turning off A540 at roundabout near Hoylake station and turning left in 200 yards then south along the foreshore. There is no access to the reed-bed.

Information   Notice board on site: leaflet from CCT.

History   The reserve consists of a low fore-dune and two parallel dune ridges with a reed-bed, dune slacks and pools in between. The main importance is having the only breeding colony of natterjack toads in the Wirral Peninsula. The water levels of the pools are maintained to provide good conditions for breeding: conditions exploited by common toads and frogs as well. At the north end is an outcrop of Triassic sandstone which continues northwards to Red Rocks.

What to See   The fore-dunes are colonized by limegrass and marram with sand sedge, sea sandwort, sea-holly, sea rocket, and sea milkwort. The slacks have a range of marsh-orchids, meadow crane's-bill and Danish scurvygrass with pools fringed by gipsywort, yellow iris, alder and willow. Drier areas have kidney vetch, restharrow and quaking-grass. Migrant birds shelter in the reeds.

T in Albert Road, Hoylake which is first right from roundabout off A553 to Wallasey, and at the north end of Marine Lake west of CP in West Kirby.

Risley Moss 4

Map 109 SJ66-92- 220 acres (82 ha)
4 miles north-east of Warrington via A574, Ordnance Avenue towards Exit 11 of M6 – the entrance is at Moss Gate off last roundabout before M6. SSSI. Nature Park. Woodland, remnant of raised peat bog, pools.

Access   AYR on foot from CP at SJ660922 onto a complex of paths leading to two hides and a 20 ft high observation tower: there are guided walks to the Moss, which is a conservation area with restricted access.

Information   Leaflets from Visitor Centre near CP where arrangements for guided walks can be made. The Centre has A/V displays and an exhibition on the history of the Moss: open Mon–Thurs 9 a.m.–4.30 p.m., W/Es 9 a.m.–5 p.m. (not 25 December).

History   The Moss is one of the few remnants of the many raised bogs which once covered much of the Mersey Valley from Warrington to Manchester. It has been heavily cut over and drained. The drier parts are now dense birch and willow woodland with some oak, ash, alder and elm, with clearings and pools. On the east side the Moss is being encouraged to return to open peat bog by maintaining a high water table and by removing birch and bracken.

What to See   Cottongrass, purple moorgrass, heather and bog mosses are frequent on the Moss with, rarely, royal fern. Elsewhere are red campion, ragged-Robin, bluebell and tufted vetch. Open pools attract grebes, teal, mallard, curlew, snipe and woodcock which breed here whilst golden plover, green sandpiper, redshank and whimbrel visit during the winter with pink-footed geese, shoveler, pintail and tufted duck. In the woodland six species of warblers, spotted flycatcher, treecreeper, great spotted woodpecker, tawny owl, redpoll, willow and long-tailed tits breed whilst little owl, barn owl, short-eared owl, kestrel and sparrowhawk are regular visitors. As many as 12 species of dragonfly have been recorded which have attracted predatory hobby.

T [D] Refreshments, shop at Visitor Centre, Picnic site.

Wheelchairs have access to Centre and onto good paths.

Sandbach Flashes   5

Map 118 SJ72-60- 126 acres (51 ha)
3 areas about 2 miles west of Sandbach on the west side of the Crewe to Manchester main line. SSSI. Wet woodland, marshland, open water.

Access   AYR on rights of way overlooking:

1. Fodens Flash: leave A533 at Elworth north of Sandbach station down Moss Lane over the canal and forking right into Oakwood Lane which leads to CP at SJ729613.
2. Watch Lane Flash: down Watch Lane over the canal keeping straight on and turning left into Watch Lane after ¼ mile and then right at T-junction to CP in ¼ mile on the left at SJ726606.
3. Elton Hall and Railway Flash: return to Watch Lane turning but continue straight on into Red Lane which follows east side of Watch Lane Flash round to T-junction, turn right into Hall Lane and, after 600 yds, turn left at the crossroads into Clay Lane which crosses Elton Hall Flash for parking at SJ725595.

Information   Nothing on site.

History   These flashes are part of a chain of pools and marshes created by subsidence following solution of salt beds beneath during brine pumping operations. The shallow water is somewhat saline and the wet meadows contain a number of salt marsh plants which are unusual inland.

What to See   Watch Lane has the highest salinity in the area and it supports sea aster and lesser sea-spurrey: elsewhere alder and willow line pools with bulrushes. Nesting birds include little grebe, tufted duck, little ringed plover, redshank, common sandpiper, reed and sedge warblers and reed bunting with willow warbler, blackcap, chiffchaff, whitethroat and willow tit in the woodland. Winter visitors include curlew, dunlin, ruff, green sandpiper, greenshank and shy water rail with shelduck, pochard, tufted duck, shoveler and pintail amongst the wildfowl.

Wheelchair visitors have good views from CPs and in Clay Lane.

Derbyshire

Derbyshire is a Midland county which, within its modest bounds, contains highly contrasting landscapes. These are as different as uplands of over 2000 ft with the feel of the north of England, and plains with sluggish, meandering rivers with the feel of the southern lowlands.

South of Derby lies the Trent valley where most of the land is used for agriculture. The sand and gravel deposits of the valley floor have long been exploited, and those not filled with fly-ash from nearby coal-fired power stations, have become refuges for nesting and breeding birds. Reservoirs to provide water for the industrial Midlands have also contributed to the creation of bird habitats, as for example at Staunton Harold on the Leicestershire border and where nearby, on a small outcrop of Millstone Grit, *Spring Wood* is a fine example of a lowland, acid birch wood—and both are within a mile of historical Calke Abbey.

Carboniferous rocks dominate Derbyshire geology—particularly in the uplands of the north and west much of which falls within the Peak National Park. Here the Millstone Grit is the major geological formation: these acid rocks predominantly underlie the high, peaty moorlands which have given the area its name—the Dark Peak. These grits form an almost complete circle, broken only in the south-west corner, round the central core of the White Peak, a plateau of Carboniferous limestone, cut through by valleys which have become the Derbyshire Dales.

The moors start above 1000 ft and stretch for nearly 20 miles across the Pennines from Sheffield to Manchester reaching their highest and wildest round Kinder Scout and Bleaklow at over 2000 ft. The characteristic sheep-grazed heather with bilberry and crowberry, and shining white patches of cottongrass, are a feature of the National Trust's *Longshaw Estate* only three miles from the western edge of Sheffield. Most of the Peak District was once covered in dense, sessile oak woodland: little now remains but, at Langshaw, there are relics— particularly in the Padley Gorge.

Dramatic as these uplands are, the woods and moors are poor in species. In contrast, the White Peak is the richest area for wildlife in the county. Much of the plateau, which lies at about 1000 ft, is permanent hay or grazing meadows set in square, stone-walled fields which give a special character to the area. The majority of fields have been improved—cultivated and/or fertilized and reseeded—but, here and there, fragments full of flowers have survived as at *Rose End Meadows*, near Matlock.

The Dales have not been so heavily exploited for agriculture due to their often steep, craggy sides, though some sheep and cattle grazing does occur. The result is often an intimate mixture of grassland, scrub and woodland which is characteristic of the dales, many of which have become linear nature reserves— Monsal Dale, Lathkill Dale and *Miller's Dale*, where the Derbyshire Trust reserve, within a relatively small area, demonstrates this range of habitats and, in addition, has the River Wye running along its northern boundary where kingfishers flash and dippers bob, whereas most of these valleys are dry.

Linear reserves seem to be a speciality of Derbyshire, both natural and man-made. The abandoned *Cromford Canal*, in the Derwent Valley south of Matlock, provides one of the most charming and peaceful wildlife walks in the county— and the nearby, active railway is a bonus—travellers from Derby and the lowlands beyond can enjoy a towpath walk between stations as well as visiting the Derbyshire Trust's Whistlestop Visitor Centre in Matlock Bath station buildings.

Abandoned railways also make fine linear trails—and there can be few finer in Britain than the *Tissington Trail* where the railway cuts through the Carboniferous limestone creating an artificial dry valley. If Tissington is visited at Ascensiontide there is the additional attraction of seeing the art of 'well-dressing', unique to Derbyshire, which started in this sheltered, grey-stone, dale village.

- Derbyshire Wildlife Trust (DWT), Elvaston Castle Country Park, Derby DE7 3EP. 0332 756610.

Cromford Canal　　　　　　　　　　6

Map 119 SK 332543 to 348519 12 acres (5 ha)
4 miles south-east of Matlock and east of the A6 between Whatstandwell and Ambergate. SSSI. LNR. Open water, grassland, woodland.

Access　　AYR on foot:

1. from parking space at Whatstandwell on the north side of B5035 between railway and canal at SK332543.
2. from CP at Crich Chase on the east side of canal via minor road 1 mile south of Whatstandwell at SK340530.
3. from parking space at Ambergate on the east side of railway bridge up the lane north of the junction with A610 to Ripley at SK348519.

Information   Nothing on site: leaflet from DWT Visitor Centre at Matlock Bath station.

History   The canal, which was last used in 1944, is an isolated section which formerly linked with the Nottingham Canal near Ilkeston, via a tunnel north of Ripley.

What to See   The towpath runs between the clear water of the canal, herb-rich grassland and light woodland. Rare aquatic plants for this area include flowering-rush, sweet-flag and arrowhead whilst stone walls carry English stonecrop and lamb's-lettuce. Six species of dragonfly breed in the canal, and grass snakes are frequent on the banks. Kingfishers occur and, in winter, there are redpoll and siskin in the alders. The best section begins from Crich Chase: there are also extensive walks in the birch/oak woods of the Chase, with magnificent bluebells in May.

Wheelchairs have limited access at Whatstandwell.

Longshaw Estate   7

Map 119 SK26-79- 1600 acres (630 ha)
7½ miles west of Sheffield south of A625 Sheffield to Hathersage road: CP is 200 yds south of Fox House Inn on west side of B6055. Part SSSI. Oak woodland, moorland.

Access   AYR on foot from CP at SK266801 down slope to the west over footbridge to the Information Centre at the north-west corner of Longshaw Lodge.

Information   Leaflet on many walks of varying lengths from Information Centre: open daily 3rd Mon in July–2nd Sun in September from 11 a.m., otherwise W/Es and BHs.

History   Longshaw Lodge was built about 1827 as a shooting lodge for the Duke of Rutland. Longshaw Sheep Dog Trials, held here early in September, began in 1893 and are the oldest in the land.

What to See   The higher ground up to 1250 ft is sheep-grazed heather moorland with cowberry and bilberry but lower down, in Padley Gorge in the valley of the River Derwent, are areas of ancient woodland dominated by sessile oak which harbour wood warbler, redstart, pied flycatcher and all three species of woodpecker.

T[D]. Refreshments, shop at Information Centre.

Wheelchairs have access to some paths.

Miller's Dale   8

Map 119 SK14-73- 60 acres (24 ha)
5 miles to the east of Buxton following A6 and B6049 through Blackwell into Miller's Dale. After passing the church take the minor road to Litton Mill at the

fork; the reserve entrance is immediately on the right via the public footpath across the river. SSSI. Ash woodland, limestone grassland, spoil heaps.

Access   AYR on foot from CP at SK143733 over footbridge across River Wye and a disused railway to entrance and a public footpath which leads through to the eastern part of reserve. Entrance to the western part is 500yds west on B6049 on south side of road bridge across the River Wye and leads to a ½ mile circular walk through woodland. Please keep to the paths some of which are very steep.

Information   Nothing on site: leaflet from DWT.

History   The old quarries in the Carboniferous limestone have a fine example of vegetation and wildflowers of the Dales. The western end is ashwood with an understorey of hazel and guelder-rose which existed before the quarrying began and has some areas of limestone grassland. The eastern end, the quarry floor, contains many large spoil heaps.

What to See   The woodland has bird cherry, wych elm and aspen with occasional mountain currant and shelters globeflower and columbine. The quarry floor supports cowslip, early-purple, fragrant, common spotted and bee orchids as well as grass-of-Parnassus and lesser meadow-rue. The waste heaps have wild thyme, marjoram, goldenrod and limestone bedstraw. The River Wye on the northern boundary has dipper, grey wagtail and kingfisher whilst redstart, treecreeper, spotted flycatcher and great spotted woodpecker inhabit the woodland. Jackdaws nest and bats roost in the quarry face.

Refreshments from Angler's Rest Inn at road fork by CP.

Rose End Meadows   9

Map 119 SK29-56- 19 acres (8 ha)
2 miles south of Matlock, turning off A6 on to B5036 through Cromford village: reserve is on the west side of road on Cromford Hill. Limestone grassland, spoil heaps, hedgerows, scrub, woodland.

Access   AYR on foot from parking space on right immediately after leaving A6 at SK295570 and taking second turning right, Alabaster Lane, to entrance to reserve in 300 yds on left which leads onto public footpath across reserve. Beware of old mine shafts.

Information   None on site: leaflet from DWT Visitor Centre at Matlock Bath Station.

History   A series of small enclosures on the Carboniferous limestone which has been mined for lead in the past leaving spoil heaps and mine shafts but the majority of the reserve is unimproved, species-rich grassland. There are also small areas of oak/ash wood, scrub and some large, mature hedges.

What to See   The grassland contains cowslip, meadow saxifrage and betony with bee, frog, common spotted and pyramidal orchids whilst the spoil heaps harbour spring sandwort and alpine penny-cress. The woodland has an understorey of hazel with bluebell, wood-sorrel, giant bellflower, moschatel and toothwort beneath. Butterflies include common blue, meadow brown and small skipper. Amongst woodland birds are tawny owl, great spotted woodpecker and nuthatch with tree pipit, linnet and goldfinch prominent in the scrub and meadows. Hawfinch are regular visitors.

Spring Wood   `10`

Map 128 SK37-22- 50 acres (20 ha)
On the Leicestershire border 2 miles south of Melbourne and west of B587: turn right at signpost to Calke to reserve entrance on right after 500 yds. SSSI. Birch/oak woodland, streams, open water.

Access   AYR, with a permit in advance from DWT, on foot from the parking space by the road at SK379220 onto the path which leads through the wood to the hide overlooking Staunton Harold Reservoir. Please keep away from the water's edge. The reservoir is also visible from CP at SK375226, reached by continuing on the road over the bridge over the reservoir arm to T-junction and turning right.

Information   Nothing on site: leaflet from DWT.

History   The reserve, which lies on the Millstone Grit, is part of a much larger wood. It is a damp, acid birch wood with oak, ash and some alder and an understorey of hazel with some guelder-rose, holly and rusty willow. There are several streams through the reserve and some large clearings dominated by bracken.

What to See   In spring opposite-leaved golden-saxifrage, dog's mercury, bluebell and yellow pimpernel occur, followed by foxglove, greater bird's-foot-trefoil, wood sage and adder's-tongue. In late summer broad-leaved helleborine may be seen. Woodland birds include lesser spotted woodpecker, treecreeper and nuthatch which are joined in summer by grasshopper, garden and sedge warblers, blackcap and whitethroat. In autumn and winter goldfinch and siskin arrive. At that time interest builds up on the reservoir which has teal, wigeon, shoveler, pochard, goldeneye and goosander in addition to resident great crested grebe, tufted duck and mute swan. Hornets nest on the reserve and brown hawker dragonflies may be seen.

T[D]. Information room, refreshments, shop at Calke Abbey.

Wheelchairs have access to view point over reservoir from CP on west side.

Tissington Trail   `11`

Map 119 SK18-52- 17 acres (7 ha)
To the north and south of Tissington village on the old railway line from south-east corner of the village clearly signposted. Limestone woodland, scrub.

Access   AYR on foot from CPs at:

1. SK178520 in the village onto path under the bridge to the north into Tissington Station Cutting which runs for ½ mile to end of cutting: then after further ½ mile into another cutting east of Crakelow Farm.

2. SK166502 at the former Thorpe Cloud station off a minor road from Tissington to Thorpe 200 yds north into Fenny Bentley Cutting.

Information   Leaflet from National Park Information Centres.

History   Old railway line which cuts through the Carboniferous limestone. A woodland flora rich in ferns has developed under a canopy of ash with occasional wych-elm. Invasive sycamore and hawthorn are being controlled by the Derbyshire Wildlife Trust.

What to See   Sheets of cowslip, early-purple orchid and wood forget-me-not in spring are followed by meadow crane's-bill, giant bellflower and orpine. Wetter areas have ragged-Robin, water avens and meadowsweet with polypody, hart's-tongue and lady-fern amongst the ferns. Butterflies include common blue and orange tip whilst woodland birds such as willow warbler, tree pipit, linnet and whitethroat are in constant motion across the trail.

T[D] in CP at entrance to Tissington Station Cutting.

Gloucestershire

Gloucestershire is a remarkable county which falls naturally into three regions, each extremely different in character and each having affinities with other adjacent parts of Britain.

In the west, between the Wye and the Severn, lies the Forest of Dean, an area which, climatically and physically, is an extension of the Welsh Hills into England with its tradition of mining and tight local communities. Narrow valleys with steep sides have left little space for cultivation and it remains one of the most heavily wooded parts of the country. Here, on mainly acid soils derived from the Devonian Old Red sandstone and grit stones of the coal measures of the Carboniferous period, large tracts were originally covered in sessile oak wood with abundant bracken and foxglove beneath. The pedunculate oak which now occurs has been introduced with increasingly large areas of conifer plantations. The full range of the many kinds of woodland can be seen on the various walks which radiate from the *Dean Heritage Centre* whilst some of the finest and least spoilt line the limestone cliffs which hang above the *Wye Valley* on the border.

In the east, across the Severn, the Cotswolds stretch from the Oxfordshire border down to Somerset: steep and fortress-like on the west side but sloping gently on the east towards the juvenile streams of the Upper Thames where the landscape belongs firmly to southern England. Where slopes are naturally steep or have been created by quarrying, herb-rich limestone grassland persists with species like pasqueflower which are now almost confined to places where the sward has never been ploughed. Some areas have escaped cultivation in part because they are commons: one of the largest concentrations is that on the south side of the valley from Stroud including *Rodborough*, Minchinhampton and Selsley.

The characteristic woods of the escarpment are either pure beech, where the soils are thin, or on deeper soils or where there are deposits of clay or sand, mixtures of ash, oak and beech. The finest beech woods, here almost at their western limit in Britain, lie between Cranham and Dursley. In the *Frith Wood* reserve of the Gloucestershire Trust both kinds of woodland can be seen alongside each other. Some of these mixed woods are extraordinarily rich in wild flowers: orchids are in abundance including green-flowered, narrow-lipped, broad-leaved, red and white helleborines.

Below the Cotswolds, between Cirencester and Lechlade, alluvial deposits in the Upper Thames valley have been excavated for gravel for over 70 years leaving behind a landscape of nearly 100 artificial lakes. Many are already used, or are scheduled to be used, for recreation whilst others have become nature reserves, especially for waterfowl, as at *Keynes Country Park* near Ashton Keynes.

But one of the finest places for wildfowl in the world is at *Slimbridge* in the Severn valley. This tidal funnel at the head of the Bristol Channel pushes salt water upstream as far as Framilode, 5 miles south-west of Gloucester, and the famous 'bore' sends a wall of water right through the county into Worcestershire by which it is connected to the Midland Plain to the north. However it is the inter-tidal muds and the salt marshes covered at least by spring tides, which have attracted thousands of waterfowl and, in consequence, millions of visitors from all over the world. Freshwater plants are more abundant near the Severn north of Gloucester and here, as so often is the case elsewhere in the Midlands, it is a disused canal which provides the county's best example of freshwater plants: *Coombe Hill Canal* near Cheltenham.

It has been said, with evident truth, that if a person were to travel in a straight line the 45 miles between Burford on the Oxford border and the Wye at Monmouth, he would pass through countryside more diverse than on any other journey of similar length in England.

● Gloucestershire Trust for Nature Conservation (GTNC), Church House, Standish, Stonehouse, Gloucester GL10 3EU. 0453 822761.

Coombe Hill Canal   `12`

Map 163 SO88-27- 33 acres (13 ha)
5 miles to the north-west of Cheltenham down a track from the point where the A4019 from Cheltenham meets the A38 at Coombe Hill. SSSI. Aquatic and bankside plants, beetles, water birds.

Access   AYR on foot down lane from car parking space at top at SO887273, then good towpath for a 6-mile walk to the River Severn and back along the north side of the canal.

Information   Leaflet from GTNC.

History   The canal was built between 1792 and 1796 to carry coal coming from the Forest of Dean up the Severn to Wainlode and then the 3 miles to Coombe Hill. A proposed extension to Cheltenham was thwarted. Trade declined with the advent of railways in the 1840s and the canal eventually closed in 1876.

What to See   Prominent aquatic plants are purple — loosestrife, yellow loosestrife, water-plantain, grey club-rush, fine-leaved water-dropwort, great yellow-cress, flowering-rush, cyperus and bladder sedges, and the very rare greater dodder which parasitizes nettles at the water's edge.

Birds are abundant in the tall vegetation by the canal and in summer include grasshopper, sedge and willow warblers whilst, in winter, if the meadows on either side are flooded, there are good opportunities to enjoy fine views of waterfowl from the slightly elevated level of the towpath above the valley : white-fronted goose, pintail, wigeon, teal, shoveler, pochard, gadwall, garganey, shelduck and a few Bewick's swan may be seen. The canal is also one of the most important beetle sites in the county with 27 rare or local species recorded.

T. Refreshments at Red Lion Inn, Coombe Hill.

Wheelchair access along towpath with difficulty.

Dean Heritage Centre   13

Map 162 SO66-10-

2 miles south of Cinderford on the west side of B4227 to A48 at Blakeney. Part SSSI. Ancient woodland, heath, bogs, ponds.

Access   AYR on foot from CP at Heritage Centre at SO663107 to four way-marked trails of varying length.

Information   Leaflets, trail guides and specialist wildlife pamphlets from Centre, open daily (except 25 and 26 December) April–October 10 a.m.–6 p.m., November–March 10 a.m.–5 p.m., and from TI Office in Tintern. Exhibition in old buildings of Camp Mill on the history and relationship of harvesting timber and mining coal and iron in the Forest of Dean.

History   The Soudley valley cuts through the Old Red sandstone, known locally as Brownstones, laid down 380 million years ago. The forest round about is mainly pedunculate oak and beech with rowan, holly, sweet chestnut, ash, wild cherry, field maple, whitebeam and yew with alder and willow in damper places. For hundreds of years, until the mid 1800s, the forest was exploited as a source of charcoal for iron-making. Since then conifers have been widely introduced though the first, some Weymouth pines, were planted in Foundry Wood in 1781. Many of these plantations help to hide the scars of quarries and mines from which stone and coal and iron have been extracted, the latter since Roman times. In the nineteenth century a series of fish ponds was created: now known as Soudley or Sutton Ponds their clear, unpolluted water supports a large variety of insect life.

What to See   Uncommon plants include autumn crocus, herb-Paris and bird's-nest orchid. There are a large number of different woodland birds: chiffchaff, willow warbler, goldcrest, redstart, all three types of woodpecker, pied flycatcher and many different tits. Heron and little grebe may be seen on the ponds with raven in the sky overhead. At least 30 species of butterfly occur with five species of fritillary amongst them: dark green, high brown, pearl-bordered, small pearl-bordered and silver-washed. Herds of fallow deer roam the forest whilst small numbers of polecat and otter still occur.

T[D]. Refreshments, picnic site.

Wheelchairs have access to level paths on a nature trail.

Frith Wood—Morley Penistan Reserve ▪14▪

Map 163 SO87-08- 58 acres (24 ha)

3 miles north-east of Stroud on B4070 at Bull's Cross. SSSI. Beech, oak and ash woodland.

Access   AYR on foot from the car parking space at the entrance to the wood at SO876087 on good paths.

Information   Nothing on site: included in *Wildlife Walkabouts: South Cotswolds and North Avon* by Rosemary Teverson under 'Slad Valley', from local bookshops. Leaflet from GTNC.

History   A Cotswold beech wood which lies on either side of a limestone ridge between the Slad and Painswick valleys. The trees are even-aged and were probably planted into an open 'wood pasture' (frith) early in the nineteenth century. Near the plateau top is an area of oak and ash which may represent the native ancient woodland. The understorey has numerous lime-loving smaller trees and shrubs: whitebeam, field maple and traveller's-joy which are now being encouraged by the progressive felling of mature trees. The wood is also known as the Morley Penistan Reserve in memory of a much-loved former Chairman of GTNC.

What to See   Amongst the wild flowers agrimony, wood spurge, spurge-laurel and broad-leaved helleborine are noteworthy with pendulous sedge and great willowherb in wetter places. The thick understorey is attractive to woodland birds: tree creeper, nuthatch, great spotted and green woodpeckers, whitethroat, blackcap, chiffchaff, willow warbler and several species of tits regularly occur. Amongst invertebrates a survey of snails has identified several species which are indicators of ancient woodland whilst speckled wood, gatekeeper and silver-washed fritillary are some of the butterflies which may be seen.

Keynes Country Park ▪15▪

Map 163 SU02-95- 143 acres (57 ha)

4 miles south of Cirencester off Spine Road from A419 Swindon road signposted to South Cerney and Ashton Keynes. Continue over crossroads at Ashton Keynes. Keynes Country Park is first turning right after 1 mile. Entrance on right after 800 yds. SSSI. Part of proposed NNR. Waterfowl.

Access   AYR on foot from CP at SU026958 with circular walks round two lakes.

Information   Leaflet about Water Park and walks in the area from Ranger's Office. Explanatory boards at entrance to Coke's Pit on the west side of road at SU027953 which is managed as a nature reserve by GTNC.

History   The Country Park is at the centre of the west section of the Cotswold Water Park which has been formed as the result of gravel extraction over the last 70 years around Ashton Keynes and South Cerney in the west and Fairford and Lechlade in the east. Nearly 100 lakes have been created and, whilst many are used for water sports some, like these, have been set aside for wildlife conservation and quiet enjoyment of the countryside. Many of the abandoned pits are rich in calcium and have developed into marl lakes.

What to See   The lakes attract waterfowl at all seasons: great-crested grebe, coot, mute swan, and tufted duck are frequent breeding species and are joined in winter by wigeon, teal, goldeneye, gadwall, shoveler and large numbers of pochard, some feral greylags and more than enough Canada geese. In summer hobbies hawk for dragonflies over the lakes.

T[D]. Picnic site, refreshments.

Wheelchairs have good access to lake sides.

Rodborough Common

16

Map 162 SO85-03- 241 acres (97 ha)

1 mile south of Stroud on either side of minor road which crosses Common between Rodborough and Rooksmoor. SSSI. Limestone grassland, scrub.

Access   AYR on foot from numerous parking places along a network of roads over the Common: a convenient starting place is at the north end, just inside the cattle grid, at SO847042 below Rodborough Fort. No parking is allowed more than 15 yds from the road.

Information   Nothing on site: included in *Wildlife Walkabouts: South Cotswolds and North Avon* by Rosemary Teverson, from local bookshops.

History   Rodborough, together with Minchinhampton to the south and Selsley to the west, form a group of three commons in the Cotswolds south of Stroud which are relics of the time when the use of these rough hilltops was enjoyed for grazing animals and gathering firewood by the villagers from the valleys below. Rodborough bears the scars of hundreds of years of quarrying which has added to the variety of soils and exposures on this oolitic limestone.

What to See   Limestone grassland with horseshoe and kidney vetch, small scabious, common rock-rose, clustered bellflower, wild thyme, wild basil and marjoram: here and there some scrub which includes small amounts of juniper and yew. Birds of the open grassland predominate—skylark and meadow pipit with green woodpecker attracted by hills of the yellow meadow ant on south-facing slopes. The herb-rich sward provides food for butterflies and their progeny: meadow brown, chalkhill blue, marbled white and dark green fritillary all thrive here.

T. Refreshments at the Bear Inn at the south end of the common at SO853027.

Wheelchairs have many good paths and tracks.

Slimbridge 17

Map 162 SO72-04- 1200 acres (800 ha)

By the River Severn 10 miles south-west of Gloucester, west of A38 from which it is signposted: leave M5 by Exit 13 going south and by Exit 14 going north. SSSI. Part of Severn Estuary Ramsar Site. Mudflats, saltmarsh, meadows and lagoons of international importance for wildfowl: collection of wildfowl.

Access   From CP 1½ miles beyond Slimbridge village at SO722049. Open daily (except 24 and 25 December) 9.30 a.m.–6 p.m. (or dusk if earlier). There are numerous hides and two towers in the grounds which can be reached on good paths with views over lagoons, marshes and the River Severn.

Information   There is a Visitor Centre with an exhibition, A/V display and a large selection of leaflets and books about the collection of wildfowl and the nature reserve.

History   Sir Peter Scott began buying property at Slimbridge in 1946 and here founded the Wildfowl (and Wetland) Trust. Now the pools and pens created round the site of the old farm buildings house the greatest collection of wildfowl in the world—some 2500 birds of nearly 200 species. In addition the Trust controls a large area of marshland where enormous flocks of wild birds gather in winter, including Bewick's swan and white-fronted geese from Siberia.

What to See   Winter brings, in addition to swans and geese, wigeon, teal, pintail, gadwall, shelduck and shoveler among the duck, and waders such as bartailed godwit, curlew and dunlin. Other waders come as autumn migrants: black-tailed godwit, greenshank, ruff and spotted redshank are then regular visitors joining resident short-eared and barn owls which hunt over nearby hedgerows—hedgerows which fieldfare and redwing flock to for their crop of berries later in the year. Such a congregation of small birds naturally attracts predators and peregrine may be seen on the attack. In summer water rail, sedge and reed warblers and spotted flycatcher may be watched from a hide near an old duck decoy.

T [D]. Refreshments, Shop.

Wheelchairs have first-class facilities including access to hides.

Herefordshire

Old Herefordshire, like Worcestershire to which it was artificially joined in 1974, is a basin-shaped county with the cathedral city sitting in the centre. The city of Hereford is completely surrounded by hills and in the south-west, by mountains, which all reach 800 ft or more with the highest point, 2306 ft, in the Black Mountains overlooking Hay-on-Wye. It is the River Wye and its tributaries, the Lugg and the Arrow, which occupy the lower ground.

The Wye and its banks together form one of the most important river habitats in Britain; few others have been declared as SSSIs. The flood meadows alongside are almost equally important, representing a habitat which has declined dramatically in area since the Second World War as river drainage, ploughing and reseeding, and the increased application of artificial fertilizers has changed herb-rich grassland into uniform stands of perennial rye-grass and white clover. Fortunately not all have met this fate and, on the eastern outskirts of Hereford, the Lugg meadows, a vast area of Common Land, have survived as one of the few areas in Britain where fritillaries flower in the spring.

The timber for the local black-and-white houses came from woods on the higher ground around and, whilst much has been cleared, there are still significant tracts where forestry is the major form of land management.

In the north-west, on the Welsh and Shropshire border, lies an upland area underlain by Silurian limestones. Here the steep north-facing scarp of Leinthall Common is crowned by the Iron Age fort of *Croft Ambrey*: on the dip slope *Bircher Common* overlooks the Leominster lowlands. These hills fall within a belt of woodland which runs 15 miles south-westwards between Ludlow and Presteigne.

Midway between Leominster and Hereford, mainly on Old Red sandstone rocks, runs another belt of hills with steep, wooded slopes, from Hope under Dinmore on the River Lugg to Byford on the River Wye. Though some has been cleared to create a fascinating Arboretum fine examples of the ancient oak wood of Dinmore Hill can now be enjoyed in *Queenswood Country Park*.

Silurian limestone appears again in the Woolhope Hills south-east of Hereford. Two parallel ridges of limestone practically encircle the central hill on which stands the 800-acre block of Haugh Wood owned and managed by the Forestry Commission. The Hereford Nature Trust owns several smaller reserves in this area a feature of which is the dense yew woods on the steep slopes as at *Nupend Wood*. Yew is also a feature of the somewhat similar woods which lie on the Carboniferous limestone of the Little and *Great Doward* at the southern tip of the county perched above the Wye only 3 miles from Monmouth.

Finally, in this circuit of woods round Hereford, come those on the Old Red sandstone on either side of the Golden Valley eight miles south-west of the city. Nearby on the Wye valley side of the ridge separating the Golden Valley from the Wye Valley persists one of the most remarkable and important wildlife sites in the county—Moccas Park, an ancient Deer Park, one of the finest remaining in Britain with its gnarled, mis-shapen oaks set in grassland grazed by fallow deer. This combination of trees and grass in the unpolluted air of west Herefordshire has allowed large numbers of species of lichen and insects to thrive, for which it is now famous. Although not generally open to the public, the extraordinary trees and the antique deer-fence of cleft-oak stakes can be seen from the B4352 road at SO34-42-.

● Hereford Nature Trust (HNT), Community House, 25 Castle Street, Hereford HR1 2NW. 0432 356872.

Bircher Common and Croft Ambrey

18

Map 137 SO46-65- 1400 acres (565 ha)
5 miles north-west of Leominster, north of B4362: signposted to Croft Castle from A49 and A4110. Upland grassland, mixed woodland.

Access   AYR on foot from CP at Croft Castle SO451656 to Croft Ambrey: also from three access roads off B4362 to Bircher Common.

Information   Map and guided walk leaflet from Croft Castle: open April–October 2–5 p.m., W/Es and BHs, also Weds–Fri May–September. Information boards in CP and at Croft Ambrey.

History   Croft Ambrey is an Iron Age hill-fort crowning a 1000 ft Aymestry (Silurian) limestone ridge with views over 14 counties, weather permitting. Bircher Common is an area of upland grassland still grazed, in common, by sheep and cattle belonging to local people.

What to See   Buzzards circle over the woods which are rich in birds including goldcrest and pied flycatcher, whilst hawfinches may be seen feeding on the hornbeams on Croft Ambrey. Amongst the butterflies the presence of high brown fritillary at Croft Ambrey is of particular interest. The estate has fallow deer, stoat, weasel and even polecat.

T. Picnic site, refreshments at the Castle.

Wheelchairs have access to good paths in Castle grounds.

Great Doward Reserves

19

Map 142 SO54-15- 49 acres (20 ha)
1 mile south of Whitchurch, East of the A40. Take the turning to Doward and Crockers Ash passing Doward Hotel on left, follow signs to Heritage Museum, at left hand U-turn after 1 mile park at head of track to The Biblins. SSSI. Mixed deciduous woodland, scrub, limestone grassland.

Access   AYR on good way-marked paths to two reserves:

1. White Rocks: entrance is by small yew tree on the right on leaving CP at SO548157.
2. Leeping Stocks: entrance is on the left 200 yds further on up road.

Information   Booklet and trail leaflet from HNT.

History   The Great Doward is the larger of the two hills of Carboniferous limestone which rise above the winding Wye valley at the southern tip of the county—it reaches an altitude of 661 ft: the lesser hill, unreasonably named Little Doward, is higher by 65 ft though smaller in area. Once covered by mixed woodland with yew amongst the oak, beech, wild service, field maple, whitebeam and elm, much has been cleared and quarried and some has since been used for tipping. The result is an attractive, intimate mixture of woodland, scrub and limestone grassland.

What to See   Many lime-loving shrubs occur: wild privet, wayfaring-tree, traveller's-joy, spindle and dogwood. In grassland and shady clearings a wide array of flowers such as deadly nightshade, yellow-wort, columbine, white helleborine, blue fleabane, bee orchid and meadow saffron occur.

Woodland birds are numerous including, pied flycatcher and, occasionally, nightingale whilst holly blue, silver-washed and pearl-bordered fritillary, marbled white and white admiral head the butterfly list.

Nupend Wood

`20`

Map 149 SO58-35- 12 acres (5 ha)
6 miles south-east of Hereford off B42244 at Fownhope. Take turning to Woolhope at crossroads at the west end of village, after ¾ mile reserve is on the left through large wooden gate; park just inside but do not obstruct the track. SSSI. Yew and mixed deciduous oak wood.

Access   AYR on foot from CP at SO581351 along the track on the left side of wood for 100 yds to stone steps past memorial stone onto blue way-marked trail.

Information   Booklet from HNT.

History   A ridge of Wenlock (Silurian) limestone, covered on the dip slope with a dense stand of yew and, on the scarp, by coppiced oak with some mixed deciduous woodland of ash, beech, hazel and field maple. The property was bought in 1969 from a fund subscribed to by patients and friends in memory of a local GP, Dr Beach of Leintwardine.

What to See   The dense yew wood and drier parts of the oakwood have few wild flowers but elsewhere stinking iris is abundant and, in open areas, stinking hellebore is a spring delight and there are numerous trees of wild service. Resident birds include sparrowhawk, tawny owl, nuthatch and all three types of woodpecker. Grasshopper warbler may be heard in summer whilst flocks of mistle thrush feed on yew berries in autumn. Butterflies are numerous with pearl-bordered and silver-washed fritillaries and four species of skipper on a long list. Earth-stars and morels are amongst the fungi which occur.

Queenswood Country Park

`21`

Map 149 SO50-51- 170 acres (69 ha)
6 miles south of Leominster on A49 at top of Dinmore Hill ½m south of Hope under Dinmore. Country Park, part SSSI which is an LNR oak woodland.

Access   AYR on foot from CP at SO506515 on good paths.

Information   Leaflet with map to two way-marked trails and *Guide to the Trees* from new Visitor Centre in CP which contains an exhibition on the Park and sales area, open daily 10 a.m.–5 p.m. Braille and large-print guide leaflets available on loan.

History   Dinmore Hill is made of Old Red sandstone and was formerly covered in natural oak woodland. This still remains at either end, north and south, and is scheduled as an SSSI. However the middle area has been developed as an

Arboretum since 1953 and now contains examples of over 400 species and varieties of trees from all over the world.

What to See   A rich woodland flora includes wood vetch and stinking iris: bluebells and primroses make a fine display in spring, giving way to common spotted-orchid, greater butterfly-orchid and devil's-bit scabious in summer. Sparrowhawk and woodcock may be seen and heard and signs and smells of fallow deer, fox and badger are clear.

T[D]. Picnic site, refreshments.

Wheelchairs have access to good paths.

Shropshire

Shropshire is a county of contrasts divided into two by the River Severn. To the north and east a low-lying, predominantly arable landscape is broken by isolated small hills and hollows left by retreating ice after the last glaciation. The latter filled with water and either remain today as the meres around *Ellesmere* or have become overgrown with vegetation to form peat bogs such as Wem and Whixall Mosses near the Clwyd border. To the south and west is the hill country: a series of ridges of hard rocks running from the north-east to the south-west including, in the Wrekin and the Long Mynd, pre-Cambrian formations laid down over 600 million years ago, which are some of the oldest in Britain.

Because of its literary associations with the poet A.E.Housman *Wenlock Edge* is perhaps the best known of all these ridges: made of a hard limestone it dominates the eastern skyline as it runs straight and level from Much Wenlock down to Craven Arms. South of Much Wenlock and east of the Edge rise the prominent round-topped peaks of Brown Clee and Titterstone Clee, both emphasized by radio masts. *Brown Clee*, at 1772 ft, is the highest point in the county—a windswept bilberry and bracken covered hill typical of the acid rocks of south Shropshire, but broad enough on top for boggy pools to develop.

From the summit of Brown Clee there is a view to the west over Wenlock Edge to the Long Mynd, an extensive upland heather moor with grouse seeking cover on the ground and merlin ready to strike from the air.

Beyond the Long Mynd, and only a few feet lower than Brown Clee, is the rugged, rocky outline of the *Stiperstones*, with tors reminiscent of Dartmoor fashioned into outlines which have attracted such evocative names as Cranberry Rocks, the Man Stone and the Devil's Chair. This wild country was an inspiration to the novelist Mary Webb who lived for a year in an isolated hill cottage on the northern slopes of the Stiperstones.

Into these ridges of pre-Cambrian, Ordovician and Silurian age volcanoes have erupted and given rise to a number of rounded hills with familiar outlines: Breidden, which looks over the Severn valley west of Shrewsbury, is just in Wales: it is on the edge of the plain and is yet part of the hill country: a beacon beckoning to the delights of both.

The north-west of the county is resplendent with Welsh names like

Llanymynech and Llynclys. The former is a wonderful area of Carboniferous limestone, one of the richest for plants in Britain, with a steep, wooded escarpment to the west and dramatic cliffs facing east and looking like a bastion built by the Welsh to keep the English out. These cliffs are partly man-made as the limestone was quarried and carried away along the Montgomery arm of the Shropshire Union Canal at the foot (see Powys p. 235).

Quarrying and mining, from Roman times onwards, have scarred the Shropshire landscape, especially the lead mines around the Stiperstones where few plants can grow on the bare white tailings. The impact of man is evident in the extreme in the Ironbridge Gorge, heart of the Industrial Revolution. *Benthall Edge* on the south side of the Gorge is now clothed in trees but beneath their shade lie the mine shafts, railway tracks and quarries of the eighteenth and nineteenth centuries when many of the woods in this area were exploited to make charcoal for the iron furnaces.

Thankfully many of the scars have been healed and have become official and unofficial nature reserves adding to the immense range given to the county naturally by its varied geology and topography.

● Shropshire Wildlife Trust (SWT), St George's Primary School, Frankwell, Shrewsbury SY3 8LG. 0743 241691.

Benthall Edge   22

Map 127 SJ66-03- 100 acres (40 ha)
On the south side of the River Severn at Ironbridge. SSSI. Deciduous woodland with some coppice, old quarry.

Access   AYR on foot from the south side of the Iron Bridge where a nature trail leads off from a picnic site at SJ672032.

Information   Nature trail guide from a kiosk on the south side of bridge.

History   These Severn valley woods have been exploited for timber since Saxon times and were later a source of building materials for Buildwas Abbey 1 mile upstream. With the advent of the Industrial Revolution the demand for fuel grew and many of the trees were felled for charcoal. Nowadays Benthall Edge wood is being coppiced on a 10–15 year cycle to produce wood for the manufacture of chairs and bowls in Telford.

What to See   The woodland occurs on both limestone and sandstone rocks and contains a wide range of trees and shrubs. Noteworthy are some magnificent beeches, frequent native yews, a small group of wild service and several spurge-laurels. The woodland floor is carpeted with wood anemones, bluebells, wood-sorrel, dog-violets, and lesser celandine in spring, but over the more acid sandstone bilberry occurs. In wide rides and open glades such as a limestone quarry near the west end butterflies including comma, large and small skippers, speckled wood and wall brown, as well as at least seven species of dragonfly which breed in the Severn below, may be seen.

T 30 yds east of the north end of the Iron Bridge.
Wheelchairs have access along old railway line for ½ mile from CP.

Brown Clee

23

Map 138 SO59-86- 100 acres (40 ha)
8 miles south-west of Bridgnorth, west of B4364 at Cleobury North. From Ditton
Priors via Hillside or from Cleobury North to Forest Trail CP under the trees at
SO607871. Deciduous and coniferous woodland, heather moor, upland pool.

Access   AYR on foot from CP and the picnic area via a gate and stile. The path
swings left to a stone cairn which marks the first stop on a nature trail.

Information   Trail guides from the stone cairn, from Estate Office at
Burwarton, 1 mile south of Cleobury North, or from Bear Steps, Fish Street,
Shrewsbury.

History   The highest hill in Shropshire rising to 1772 ft is made from Old Red
sandstone less than 400 million years old with a capping of dolerite. The lower
slopes were planted with Sitka spruce in 1947. Above lies a treeless hillside with,
at the summit, the remains of the Iron Age hill-fort of Abdon Burf, one of three
on the hill, and many relicts of former coal mining.

What to See   On the trail, which does not include the summit and is an easy
walk along woodland rides and roads, many birds may be seen or heard including
jay, buzzard, raven, goldcrest, firecrest and tree pipit. The summit, which is
reached through areas of marsh with alder and willow thickets, is dominated
by heather and bilberry and there is a large pool.

Ellesmere and the Meres

24

Map 126 SJ40-34- about 250 acres (100 ha)
16 miles north-west of Shrewsbury on A528 and 9 miles north-east of Oswestry
by A495. Part SSSI. Canal banks, lakes, marsh and wet woodland.

Access   AYR:

1. to the shores of The Mere, Ellesmere from CP at SJ406345.
2. to Blake Mere, SJ41-33- from bridge at SJ413330.
3. to Colemere, SJ43-33- from CP at SJ435328.

Information   The Meres Visitor Centre by the CP has an exhibition on the
natural history of the area and there is a small viewing place. Leaflet including
map of the canal-side walk from the Centre: open Easter—end October Mon–Fri
12 noon–4 p.m., Sat 12 noon–5 p.m., Sun and BHs 11 a.m.–5 p.m. Times are
flexible according to demand. Leaflet also from TI Office or from Bear Steps, Fish
Street, Shrewsbury.

History   Meres are lakes formed at the end of the last Ice Age around 12,000
years ago following the melting of the glaciers into clay-lined depressions in an

undulating landscape. They filled with nutrient-rich water which attracted colonizing plants and animals.

What to See   Canal banks have frequent water dock, hemlock water-dropwort, yellow iris and yellow water-lily. In summer tufted duck, great crested grebe and heron are frequent with visitors such as reed, sedge, willow and garden warblers: during migration occasional white-fronted and pink-footed geese may be seen whilst, in winter, Ellesmere has a large gull roost.

T near Visitor Centre. Picnic site at Colemere.

Wheelchairs have access for short distance along canal towpath from the Wharf, Ellesmere.

Llanymynech Rocks   `25`

Map 126 SJ26-21- 62 acres (25 ha)
West of A483 between Oswestry and Welshpool ½ mile north of Llanymynech village. Take lane opposite the Pant Cafe at SJ272219 which leads to CP. SSSI. Limestone grassland, cliffs and scrub.

Access   AYR on foot from CP over a stile along good but undulating paths.

Information   Nothing at site.

History   This abandoned quarry in the Carboniferous limestone straddles the England/Wales border. Thousands of tons of stone were excavated leaving soaring limestone cliffs and spoil heaps which have created a fascinating range of habitats. The stone was burnt to make agricultural lime in summer or cut for building materials in winter.

What to See   Amongst the 120 species of wild flowers recorded are yellow-wort, autumn gentian and blue fleabane whilst six orchids including autumn lady's-tresses may be found. On sunny days the air is full of bees and butterflies: amongst the latter brown argus, dingy and grizzled skipper. Kestrel, jackdaw and rock dove nest on the cliffs which are also used by lesser horseshoe bats.

Other interest   On the left of the track, near the end of the quarry face, are the remains of an old 'gin' from which wagons full of stone were attached by a rope to a beam between the massive walls, and lowered down an inclined plane into barges on a section of the Shropshire Union Canal below.

Stiperstones   `26`

Maps 126 and 127 SO36-98- 1080 acres (437 ha)
10 miles south-west of Shrewsbury east of minor road from Snailbeach to The Bog. NNR. Heather moorland, wooded valleys, holly wood.

Access   AYR on foot from CP, which is at an altitude of over 1400 ft, at the south-east corner of reserve at SO369976. There are many paths within the reserve and one can walk through it and on along the ridge to Snailbeach about 5 miles away. The paths are often very rocky so strong boots are advisable but there are no steep climbs.

Information   Notice board with map in CP. Leaflet from NCC, Attingham Park, Shrewsbury SY4 4TW.

History   The ridge is formed of quartzite of the Ordovician age and is around 480 million years old. It was subjected to alternate freezing and thawing during the last Ice Age which split the rocks that now form stripes of stone and scree on the hillside. More durable rocks were left as a series of tors which dominate the skyline and have been given names referring to their shapes such as the Devil's Chair and the Man Stone.

What to See   The main ridge, which rises to 1762 ft, is covered in heather moorland with large amounts of crowberry and cowberry or cranberry which gives the name to another feature, Cranberry Rock, at the southern end. On the western slopes are steep wooded valleys or 'dingles' whilst at the Hollies at the northern end lies an open area of large holly trees of ancient origin. The descent to Snailbeach passes through oakwoods formerly coppiced as a source of wood for charcoal for smelting. Birds of the open moorland include grouse, meadow pipit and raven.

T at Snailbeach Village Hall.

Wenlock Edge Woodlands   27

Map 138 SO60-99- 296 acres (120 ha)
½ mile south-west of Much Wenlock on B4371 to Church Stretton. Part SSSI. Oak/ash woods and limestone banks.

Access   AYR on foot from CP on the north side of B4371 at SO610996 or from another at SO582975 2 miles to the south-west.

Information   National Trust leaflet, from Much Wenlock Museum and TI Office in Shrewsbury, gives details of way-marked trails. The Museum has displays and sells a guide, *Geology of the Wenlock Edge District*.

History   Much of the area has been quarried for Wenlock limestone of Silurian age which contains brachiopods and polyzoans as well as 'ball-stones', remains of coral reefs, prominent at Ippikin's Rock (SO569965) and Major's Leap (SO600991). This last marks the spot where the Royalist Major Smallman is said to have jumped down the escarpment with his horse to escape his parliamentarian pursuers.

What to See   Lanes with limestone grassland banks harbour salad burnet, lady's-mantle, yellow-rattle, goldilocks buttercup, columbine and cowslip. They lead to oak/ash woods with herb-Paris, yellow archangel, ramsons, sanicle, yellow pimpernel and woodruff. Overhead buzzard, kestrel and sparrowhawk take to the sky whilst the sound of woodpeckers fills the air. Mammals include badger and yellow-necked mouse.

T in Much Wenlock.

Wheelchairs have limited access from CPs and viewpoints on B4371.

Staffordshire

Staffordshire has many faces. In the north, on the Millstone Grit, are the wild, bleak moorlands rising to nearly 1700 ft north of Leek, at the southern end of the Pennines. Only 10 miles away to the east are the Staffordshire Dales with clear streams and rivers flowing peacefully towards the Trent along steep-sided, well-wooded valleys. In the lowland particularly on the east side are stretches of countryside as lovely and unspoilt as any in England with many large, beautifully landscaped estates.

This is in stark contrast to the great conurbations centred on the two coalfields—the Potteries and the Black Country—which must represent some of the most spoilt, satanic landscapes in the land, albeit now improved by such initiatives as the Stoke Garden Festival of 1986 and many other land reclamation schemes.

For the millions cramped into narrow streets and high-rise blocks Staffordshire provides wonderful, relaxing, open spaces: and none more important to them than *Cannock Chase*, on the northern edge of the Black Country, less than 10 miles up the A34 from Birmingham. Here are 26 square miles of woods and heath rightly recognized as an Area of Outstanding Natural Beauty. Much of Cannock was Common Land and the county is fortunate that over 5000 acres of Commons remain. Many of these areas with open public access are in the south-west, on the edge of the Black Country. One of the best, only 10 miles from the centre of Wolverhampton, has been bought by the County Council to become *Highgate Common Country Park*—another area of heath and birch woodland which, like Cannock, has developed over the poor soils of the Bunter sandstone.

Doxey Marshes are almost in the centre of Stafford—a green wedge of space along the River Sow which attracts exciting birds despite being bounded on two sides by the M6 and a main line railway. For quieter birdwatching in a gentler landscape the *Blithfield Reservoir*, 10 miles east across the Trent valley from Stafford, has considerable charms. Because Birmingham and the Black Country take most of their water from Wales there are not many man-made lakes in the area: Blithfield Reservoir and Belvide on the A5 south of Stafford are the richest of them.

For an ornithological feast and a wildlife treat, the best of the county must be in those north-eastern valleys. Here again the variety and contrast of Staffordshire are displayed. *Castern Wood* in the Manifold Valley is a fine example of the riches of the limestone whilst the *Churnet Valley Woods*, which embrace an RSPB reserve as well as Consall Nature Park, are on the more acid Coal Measures.

Any unfavourable impression of Staffordshire gained during a journey up the M6, past the Black Country and Stoke-on-Trent, would be totally overturned if the journey were made up the east side rather than the west. From the spires of Dr Johnson's Lichfield to the valleys round Leek by way of Abbots Bromley is a progress of delight enhanced by some fine reserves.

● Staffordshire Wildlife Trust (SWT), Coutts House, Sandon, Stafford ST18 0DN. 08897 534.

Blithfield Reservoir   28

Map 128 SK05-23- 790 acres (324 ha)
3½ miles north of Rugeley on B5031 to Abbots Bromley and Uttoxeter. SSSI.
Open water, marsh, willow carr, deciduous woodland.

Access   AYR public viewing from B5013 which crosses the reservoir dividing it into northern and southern halves. Access by permit only to 9 mile shoreline walk with seven hides, mainly in the northern half. It is possible to obtain a permit from West Midland Bird Club, 6 Lloyd Square, 12 Niall Close, Edgbaston, Birmingham B15 3LX.

Information   Nothing on site.

History   This reservoir was formed in 1952 by damming the River Blith, a tributary of the Trent which it meets at Kings Bromley 4 miles to the south-east. Sailing is confined to the southern end but there is fishing from boat and bank in the northern half. Despite this disturbance it provides a winter roost for large numbers of gulls and attracts many wildfowl in winter.

What to See   One of the largest concentrations of ruddy duck in the Midlands sharing with Belvide Reservoir, south of Stafford, over 40 per cent of the British population. Also notable in winter are the large number of mallard, teal, wigeon, pochard and tufted duck with smaller concentrations of shoveler, goldeneye and goosander with occasional gadwall, pintail, common scoter, scaup, red-necked grebe and great northern diver: the gulls include Iceland and glaucous. Autumn brings osprey and peregrine on passage with ringed plover, dunlin, little stint, curlew sandpiper, jack snipe and spotted redshank. Redpoll and siskin feed in the surrounding trees in winter where sparrowhawk and lesser spotted woodpecker breed in summer. Canada geese are all too common at all seasons.

Cannock Chase   29

Map 139 SJ91 and SK01 1200 acres (3000 ha)
On both sides of the A460 between Cannock and Rugeley Country Park. An Area of Outstanding Natural Beauty. Deciduous woods, conifer plantations, heath, damp grassland, valley bogs.

Access   AYR on foot from numerous CPs scattered throughout the park to hundreds of miles of paths.

Information   From two Visitor Centres:

1. The Country Park Centre at Marquis Drive on Brindley Heath 1½m north of Hednesford at SK005152: open daily 10 a.m.–6 p.m., June–September and W/Es 2–5 p.m. October–May. Has a display on the Chase and leaflets on geology, history and natural history.

2. The Forest Centre off Penkridge Bank 1 mile south-west of Rugeley at SK019170: open 7.30 a.m.–4 p.m. weekdays, 2–5 p.m. W/Es. It has a wildlife display and information leaflets. Permits to visit wildlife conservation area with hide for deer-watching from FC Office in CP, weekdays only.

History   A Royal Forest at the time of William the Conqueror, much of the natural oak woodland was cleared to make charcoal for iron smelting in the sixteenth century. Sheep were then introduced creating the heathland which still covers much of the area. This was used for military training during both World Wars but this has been gradually reduced by afforestation with conifers since planting began in the 1920s.

What to See   Vast areas of broad-leaved woods, conifer plantations, heaths, damp grassland and valley bogs make the Chase a rich reservoir of plant and animal life. Amongst the heather, a blaze of autumn purple, a rare hybrid between bilberry and cowberry may be found, whilst wetter areas hold southern marsh-orchid near its northern limit and marsh hawk's-beard near its southern limit. The herd of fallow deer is a major attraction, but a few red deer may also be seen and muntjac are increasing. A small number of red squirrel survive in the conifers. Notable birds include occasional hen harrier in autumn and winter and, in summer, despite recent rapid decline, nightjar may still be heard on calm evenings.

T [D] at Marquis Drive and at Milford Common on A513 at SJ972211. Wheelchairs have access to many good paths.

Castern Wood

30

Map 119 SK11-53- 51 acres (20 ha)
6 miles north-west of Ashbourne in the Manifold Valley off a minor road running south-east from Wetton village for 1½ miles. SSSI. Deciduous woodland, scrub, limestone grassland.

Access   AYR on foot from CP at SK119537, which is at end of track through gate on right at end of the minor road, onto a well-marked path.

Information   Nature trail leaflet from TI Office in Leek or from SWT.

History   This area of mixed deciduous woodland, scrub and grassland on the Carboniferous limestone was long used for lead mining—the spoil heaps remain: beware of mine shafts. Halfway down the hillside are moss-covered stones, the remains of a small-holding: the reserve was once called John O'Clamps Wood after a former resident. Many prehistoric, Roman and Anglo-Saxon finds have been made in the caves of the valley below the wood.

What to See   Cowslip is widespread in spring whilst in summer spoil heaps are covered in rock-rose, wild thyme and biting stonecrop whilst eyebright, harebell and carline thistle colour the grassland. The woodland of ash, elm and sycamore grows sparsely on the scree above a shrub layer including hazel and dogwood. Butterflies are numerous: of special interest in June is the northern brown argus of which the caterpillar feeds on rock-rose. Birds include all three types of woodpeckers, redstart, pied flycatcher, blackcap and several warblers. Sparrowhawk, tawny owl and woodcock also occur.

Churnet Valley Woods · 31

Map 119 SJ99-48- 430 acres (175 ha)
6 miles east of Stoke-on-Trent via A52 towards Ashbourne and, 1 mile after the crossroads at Cellarhead, turning left onto A522 signposted to Consall and Nature Park. Go through Consall village down the private road to CP. SSSI. Deciduous woodland, ancient grassland, heath, ponds, river.

Access   AYR on foot from CP at SJ990489 on the way-marked paths through Consall Nature Park to RSPB Churnet Valley Woods reserve which begins across the Caldon Canal at SK000490.

Information   Leaflets and trail guides from Visitor Centre in CP which also has a display on the history of the valley and its wildlife: open April–September Mon–Sat 10 a.m.–6 p.m., Sun 9 a.m.–8 p.m.

History   Iron-working in the valley goes back to 1290 or earlier and much timber was felled to produce charcoal for smelting. Water power from the River Churnet was harnessed to a hammer mill and a forge. In the eighteenth century smelting was replaced by mining ironstone which was carried by barge 2 miles down the Caldon Canal to Froghall. Since the industry ended nearly 100 years ago mixed ash, oak and birch woodland has recolonized the spoil heaps.

What to See   In spring the woods are bright with bluebell, wood anemone, moschatel and ramsons with marsh-marigold in wet areas: giant bellflower and broad-leaved helleborine follow in summer. There are a large number of migratory birds including wood, garden and willow warblers, whitethroat and lesser whitethroat, chiffchaff and blackcap. All three types of woodpeckers, treecreeper and nuthatch, redstart and five different tits, tree pipit, pied flycatcher, woodcock, dipper and kingfisher also occur with raiding sparrowhawk. The butterflies have green hairstreak, small pearl-bordered fritillary and white-letter hairstreak on the list whilst palmate newts appear in the pools.

T[D] at Visitor Centre.
Wheelchairs have some access from special CP.

Doxey Marshes · 32

Map 127 SJ90-24- 180 acres (70 ha)
Immediately north-west of the centre of Stafford off A5013 Eccleshall Road turning left 400 yds before M6 Motorway down Creswell Farm Drive to CP at end. SSSI. Dry meadows, damp meadows, ditches, marshes, reed-beds, open water.

Access   AYR on foot from CP at SJ904249 or up the old railway line where it is cut by Doxey Road at SJ915234.

Information   Leaflet from TI Office in Stafford or SWT.

History   The construction of a town mill in Stafford and its associated drain dug in the eleventh or twelfth centuries was a major factor in the formation of the marshes. Brine pumping below in the 1950s and 60s caused subsidence and flooding: pumping ceased in 1970 leaving a number of pools or flashes. There is a complete progression of habitats from dry meadows through marshes and reed-beds to open water overlooked by a hide 800 yds south-east of the CP.

What to See   In summer redshank, snipe, yellow wagtail, sedge warbler, pochard, ruddy duck and water rail may be seen or heard. Garganey and shelduck visit the flashes in spring, Bewick's and whooper swan in winter. Amongst interesting plants are lesser spearwort, flowering-rush, tubular water-dropwort and meadow-rue.

Highgate Common

`33`

Map 139 SO83-90-278 acres (111 ha)

6 miles west of Dudley between A458 and B4176. Turn south off B4176 at Halfpenny Green to Common. Country Park. Heath, birch wood, pools.

Access   AYR on foot from numerous CPs on roads crossing the Common. Way-marked trails begin at Birch Coppice CP on the east side at SO843900.

Information   Leaflets from site or local TI Offices.

History   An area of acid heathland on the Bunter sandstone once kept open by rabbits which occupied an enormous warren. Since myxomatosis birch and oak have repopulated the area. There has been some planting with lodgepole pine by the Forestry Commission and, in another area, hazel is being regularly coppiced. Several ponds were dug in 1981 and 1982 and had trees planted round them by local Scouts.

What to See   Heathland plants include heather, bell heather, cross-leaved heath, bilberry, tormentil, heath groundsel and wavy hairgrass. Meadow pipit and skylark, yellowhammer, chiffchaff and even woodcock breed on the heath: wheatear and whinchat rest here in spring and redwing and fieldfare feed here in autumn. Siskin and redpoll are attracted to a line of alders in winter. Grass snake, lizard and slow worm may be seen on the ground whilst skippers and speckled wood butterflies and the broad-bodied chaser and Emperor dragonflies, both near their northern limit in Britain, may be seen in the air. Frog, toad and great crested newt inhabit the pools.

  T at south-west corner in Triangle CP at SO835893. Refreshments.

Warwickshire

Warwickshire lies in the heart of England, the county of Shakespeare and radio's 'the Archers'. A lowland shire with very few steep hills or hard rocks to make cultivation difficult, it has been developed by agriculture into a gently rolling patchwork of arable crops and pastures with many fields still surrounded by hedges. Little remains of the Forest of Arden which inspired the Duke in *As You Like It* and once spread from Stratford to Nuneaton. Warwickshire, with 3.5 per cent covered by woods, is now one of the least well-wooded counties in the country. The swans survive on the southward flowing Avon as threats from fishermen's lead weights recede, but the River Tame, which rises in the Black Country and passes through the north of the county on its way to the River Trent, is often polluted by overloaded sewage farms and industrial waste.

History has not left many large areas of wilderness and, where wildlife persists, it is often in small pockets left accidentally as a by-product of other human activity. A notable exception is the group of woods south-east of Coventry, on the Keuper Marl, where the Warwickshire Trust and the Forestry Commission control over 460 acres including Wappenbury Wood and the Trust's *Ryton Wood* reserve where they are actively restoring traditional coppice-with-standards management. The privately owned Ufton wood, five miles to the south, is also managed on a long coppice rotation. On the other side of the county, on the Worcestershire border, the Trust owns *Clowes Wood*, much more acid in character with occasional glades—one carrying a fragment of heathland which is an extremely rare habitat in the county. The only significant area of heath, and bog, remains in Sutton Park just six miles to the north-east of Birmingham and one of the City's playgrounds, not recommended at weekends or on bank holidays!

Public pressure like this has persuaded local authorities to establish a number of Country Parks and Nature Trails. One of these has long been a lung for the natives of Stratford—somewhere to retreat to when the coach crowd crush is at its most ferocious. *Welcombe Hills* rise 200 ft only a mile north of the town centre and a crowning obelisk helps to point the way.

A Country Park at Alvecote Priory is a convenient starting place for visiting the county's largest man-made reserve, *Alvecote Pools,* at the north end of the Warwickshire coalfield—and a relict of mining—a combination of wetland caused by subsidence and mounds formed from spoil. The pools have become one of the most important sites in the Midlands for wintering wildfowl and migrating waders, but the adjacent canal and old tips attract a wide range of plants and animals tolerant of neutral or somewhat acid conditions.

'Mining' in limestone rocks has been the origin of another area which has now become an attractive reserve—*Ufton Fields* near Leamington. This too is an intimate mixture of habitats—a situation which creates the maximum opportunity for large numbers of different species to occur side by side.

Although such sites do not have the historical dimension which gives our dwindling numbers of ancient woodlands and old meadows such an appeal *Alvecote* and *Ufton* represent an opportunity and a challenge and are the kind of reserves which can only increase in number in the future so long as organizations like WARNACT will take the areas on.

● Warwickshire Nature Conservation Trust (WARNACT), Montague Road,

Warwick CV34 5LW. 0926 496848. Trail guides and other information also available from the two WARNACT shops:
- Wildlife Gifts, 7 Old Square, Warwick CV34 4RA. 0926 410312.
- The Wildlife Gift Shop, 11 Shrieves Walk, Stratford-on-Avon CV37 6GJ. 0789 414667.

Alvecote Pools   34

Map 140 SK25-03- 664 acres (264 ha)
3 miles east of Tamworth via B500 to Polesworth and Atherstone: after 2 miles turn north onto minor road, Robey's Lane, to Alvecote. Reserve is on right between Coventry Canal and railway line. SSSI. Open water, marsh, river and canal banks, old coal tip.

Access   AYR on foot from CP in Alvecote Priory Country Park, on right on the south side of canal bridge at SK250042, across bridge to entrance to Pooley Fields on right and then along way-marked paths. There is only limited access on public footpaths to the rest of the reserve which lies to the north of the railway line.

Information   Nothing on site: nature trail booklet from Country Park and from WARNACT.

History   The reserve lies over the Coal Measures and the pools are the result of mining subsidence, being formed mainly from 1940–45. Their origin is remembered by naming the outward section of the nature trail 'The Miners' Path' along which coal miners used to travel to and from work. The River Anker flows through the three largest pools . It has been a nature reserve since 1958 and has been an SSSI since 1955. Over the last 30 years a rich wetland and marsh flora has developed.

What to See   The wetland flora includes bladderwort and a large colony of southern marsh-orchid: arrowhead grows in the canal. Breeding birds in and around the pools include reed-warbler, great crested grebe, little ringed plover, snipe, redshank, pochard and tufted duck, with less frequent success by common tern, oystercatcher and ringed plover. Kingfisher and garganey may also be seen. In winter the pools provide food for many teal and wigeon with smaller numbers of shoveler, goldeneye and ruddy duck. Autumn brings large flocks of migrating waders. 14 species of dragonfly and 20 species of butterfly have been recorded whilst a black (melanic) form of wolf spider lives on the coal tip.

Clowes Wood   35

Map 139 SP10-74- 73 acres (30 ha)
4 miles south-west of Solihull west of B4102 Shirley to Earlswood road. Turn right at crossroads passing Earlswood Reservoirs on the left, then left at next crossroads into Wood Lane where there is parking space at SP101743. SSSI. Oak/birch wood, alder wood, heath, meadow and pond.

Access   AYR on foot by path from Wood Lane via the bridge over a ditch into the north part of the reserve called Little Clowes. The larger southern part, Big Clowes, is over railway line via a footbridge on the west boundary, *not* by the level-crossing.

Information   None on site.

History   Big Clowes is an even-aged oak wood with a thin understorey of birch, holly and alder buckthorn and a ground cover of bilberry and bramble. Little Clowes is more varied with beech amongst the oak, some wild service and small-leaved lime and areas where coppicing of hawthorn and hazel occurs, and a number of clearings and pools surrounded by alder, rushes and sedges. There is also a small area of heathland. The meadow on the east side has marshy hollows and has been mown and grazed continuously for 200 years.

What to See   One of the few sites in Warwickshire for lily-of-the-valley: other local plants include cyperus sedge, common cow-wheat, elongated sedge and wood melick. Clearings provide habitats for chiffchaff, willow and wood warblers and four species of tits whilst nuthatch, woodcock, sparrowhawk and all three types of woodpecker are regularly reported. The ponds harbour newts and frogs, and wood mouse and bank vole are frequent on the woodland floor.

Ryton Wood   `36`

Map 140 SP38-72- 210 acres (85 ha)
1½ miles north-west of Princethorpe up track to the west of A423, 200 yds north of Old Bull and Butcher Inn. SSSI. Coppice-with-standards oak/hazel/lime woods, glades.

Access   AYR on foot from CP at end of track at SP382730 on way-marked trails.

Information   Nothing on site: nature trail guide from WARNACT.

History   One of the finest examples of a coppice-with-standards oak/hazel woods in the county now being managed to restore its original character. Grassy glades are being created to attract butterflies and provide food for muntjac deer though young coppice has to be protected from them.

What to See   In May it is a staggering sight with carpets of bluebells studded with the white stars of batchelor's buttons (greater stitchwort). All three species of woodpecker and woodcock occur whilst nightingale have bred along the northern edge. Over 30 species of butterfly have been recorded notably purple emperor, brown hairstreak and white admiral. The pool is alive with dragonflies and grass snakes are often seen here.

T. Refreshments at Old Bull and Butcher.

Wheelchairs have access to good paths from CP.

Upton Fields   `37`

Map 151 SP37-61- 77 acres (30 ha)
Between Leamington and Southam ½ mile south-east of Ufton village off A425.

Take minor road to Harbury: the road turns sharp left and then sharp right to CP on left. LNR and SSSI: limestone grassland, pools, marshland, scrub.

Access   AYR on foot from CP at SP378315 on way-marked nature trail of around 1 mile (please keep to paths).

Information   Notice board near entrance: nature reserve guide from WARNACT.

History   A quarry in the limestone of the Lower Lias was worked here between 1952 and 1954. The excavation left spoil heaps forming 23 parallel ridges covering half the site with six large pools and numerous smaller ones in between over the rest. Some areas are maintained as dry limestone grassland but scrub of hawthorn, ash, guelder-rose and privet has encroached and many of the pools are now fringed by alder and willow. Sheep have been introduced to help retain a balance.

What to See   Six species of orchid have been recorded including bee and man, whilst yellow-wort, wild basil, eyebright, small scabious and common centaury are frequent. Grasshopper, reed and sedge warblers are amongst the breeding birds with chiffchaff, reed bunting and tree pipit. Winter brings lesser redpoll and occasionally siskin and long-eared owl. Amongst the large number of butterflies are green hairstreak, small blue and marbled white whilst some 250 species of moth have been recorded here. Other notable insects are ruddy darter dragonfly and the variable damselfly.

T[D] at CP. Picnic site.

Wheelchairs have some access on good paths.

Welcombe Hills   38

Map 151 SP20-56- 333 acres (135 ha)

1 mile north of Stratford-on-Avon off A46 to Warwick turning left after Welcombe Hotel towards Snitterfield to CP on the left opposite Ingon Bank Cottages. Pasture, scrub, parkland and woodland.

Access   AYR on foot up the lane from the CP at SP215573 to the entrance gate after 600 yds.

Information   Notice board at entrance: nature trail leaflet from District Council, 5 Tyler Street, Stratford-on-Avon 0789 67575.

History   An area on the edge of Stratford used in the past for woodcutting, hunting and farming. Relicts of medieval cultivation can be found in the many ridges and furrows created by ox-drawn ploughs. However, as no ploughing has taken place since, this old grassland is rich in wild flowers, with cowslip and field woodrush in spring.

What to See   Areas of planted woodland are mainly of beech and oak with some ash, lime, hornbeam, horse-chestnut, larch and sycamore with an understorey of privet, traveller's joy and elder where violets, lesser celandine and lords-and-ladies flourish in spring. Nuthatch, treecreeper, great spotted and green woodpecker may be seen or heard and several warblers breed here. Meadow brown and small heath butterflies are amongst the many which occur.

Picnic site, good views as far as Edgehill to the south-east.

Worcestershire

The old county of Worcestershire is topographically like a basin with the low-lying ground in the centre and the hills around the circumference. Through the centre, from Bewdley in the north to Tewkesbury in the south, the River Severn meanders collecting, through tributaries like the Teme, the Stour and the Avon, almost all the rain which falls on the county. The peripheral hills often have outlines which make them familiar landmarks and there are few parts of Worcestershire when one or the other is not in view.

The south-western boundary with old Herefordshire is marked by the 10-mile long north-south ridge of the Malvern Hills made of hard pre-Cambrian rocks and rising to 1394 ft near the town of Malvern. The south-eastern boundary towards Gloucestershire is dominated by the great, round, comfortable mass of Bredon Hill, an outlier of the Cotswolds which overlooks the Vale of Evesham and its apple orchards. In the north-east the Lickey and *Clent Hills*, which reach over 1000 ft, provide an effective screen between the West Midlands and Kidderminster and lungs for the millions who live within easy reach.

A lower screen of a different kind separates Kidderminster and Stourport from Shropshire to the west: for here is that green expanse of the ten square miles of the *Wyre Forest,* one of the largest but least well known of Britain's forests, much of it still retaining many indicator species of ancient woodland. The countryside west of Worcester, which lies between the Wyre and the Malverns, has a character which has echoes of the landscapes of South Shropshire, North Herefordshire and even of the Welsh borderland beyond. It is a tight little world of small hills and narrow, wooded valleys which can be enjoyed to the full round Alfrick, where *The Knapp and Papermill* reserve protects landscape as well as wildlife.

These upland areas, except for Bredon, are almost all made of old rocks of Carboniferous or earlier periods—some pre-Cambrian—which frequently produce acid soils: the woods of oak and birch include much rowan and holly with bilberry, bracken, bluebells and heather beneath. In the Severn plain such acid soils are rare but, just south of Stourport, and within half a mile of the river's eastern bank, lies *Hartlebury Common*, heathland which has developed on sand blown over the top of the Bunter sandstone which forms a wedge in the north between the Lickeys and the Wyre Forest.

The only large area of lime-rich soils occurs in the south-east and though most of these are on the heavy Lower Lias clays around Bredon, they do give rise to species-rich woods and meadows, a few of which still survive as at *Tiddesley Wood* beside the River Avon west of Pershore and in Tunnel Hill Meadow west of Evesham. These sites are overlooked by the great, round mound of Bredon standing on the Gloucestershire border and where, in Housman's words:

In summertime on Bredon
The bells they sound so clear;
Round both the shires they ring them
In steeples far and near,
A happy noise to hear.

- Worcestershire Nature Conservation Trust (WNCT) Lower Smite Farm, Smite Hill, Hindlip, Worcester WR3 8SZ. 0905 754919.

Clent Hills `39`

Map 139 SO93-80- 425 acres (171 ha)
South of A456 Birmingham to Kidderminster road 2 miles east of Hagley. Country Park. Acid grassland, coniferous and deciduous plantations.

Access   AYR on foot from CP at Nimmings Visitor Centre in Hagley Wood Lane at SO938807. Also from Walton Hill in the east at SO943803 and Adam's Hill in the west at SO923797.

Information   Leaflet with map from refreshment counter at Nimmings Centre open daily Easter—end October 9.15 a.m.–6 p.m., otherwise at W/Es, depending on weather at site.

History   The Clent Hills date from the late Carboniferous period but are made up of fragments of much older, pre-Cambrian, rocks called 'breccias' which were deposited by torrential streams. With an altitude of 1035 ft they are the second highest hills in the county. The rocks produce red, acid soils which support slopes covered in bracken and gorse with large areas of matgrass into which plantations of pine, larch and broad-leaved trees have been introduced.

What to See   In spring bluebells colour the ground beneath the trees: later, in summer, the blue bells of the harebell colour the grassy slopes along with foxglove and heath bedstraw. Nesting birds in summer include tree pipit, yellowhammer, redstart and sparrowhawk, whilst winter brings siskin and redpoll which feed on the pine cones. Badgers have several setts on the hill and a herd of fallow deer come in from the Park at Hagley Hall: their hoof-marks may be seen along damp tracks.

T[D] at Nimmings Centre, Walton Hill and Adam's Hill CPs.

Wheelchairs have access to gentle slopes specially designed for them.

Hartlebury Common `40`

Map 139 SO82-71- 216 acres (91 ha)
½ mile south of Stourport-on-Severn on both sides of A4025. LNR and SSSI. Heath, scrub, woodland, bogs and pools.

Access   AYR on foot from numerous CPs off A4025 and B4193 to the north and off interconnecting roads.

Information   Notice boards in CPs show maps and a leaflet can be obtained from Hereford and Worcester CC, Spetchley Road, Worcester WR5 2NP. 0905 763763 extn 3553.

History   This Common lies on the east side of the Severn valley and is made of wind-blown sand overlying gravel. In the eighteenth century it was used as a 'Warren for Conies' (rabbits) but has now become dominated by broom, gorse and heather and is one of the most important areas of heathland left in the West Midlands.

What to See   On the heath small amounts of bell heather occur and some of the gorse is western gorse which is in full flower in the autumn when it contrasts brilliantly with the purple heather. In spring sand bared by rabbits carries tiny annuals like changing forget-me-not, shepherd's cress, bird's-foot and silver hair-grass. Birds include kestrel and sparrowhawk and, in winter, flocks of redpoll and occasional siskin. Amongst common visitors are wood, willow and garden warblers, blackcap, whitethroat and chiffchaff. Hillditch Pool on the east side is particularly attractive: terrapins have been introduced and appear to be thriving.

Picnic sites.

Wheelchairs have difficult access in sand.

The Knapp and Papermill   41

Map 150 SO74-51-62 acres (24 ha)
7 miles west of Worcester at Alfrick Pound on minor road which leaves A4103 Worcester-Hereford road at Bransford. SSSI. Species-rich, deciduous woodland, meadow, marsh and brook.

Access   AYR on foot from car-parking space east of the bridge across Leigh Brook at SO751521 to entrance to the west of the bridge, through wild flower garden which leads to the house called The Knapp which has an information room. Small CP for disabled at entrance.

Information   Guide to way-marked nature trail from Information Room open AYR. There is a small display area where guides to other WTNC reserves are sold. Visitors are asked to sign the book.

History   The reserve is in a wooded valley through which the Leigh Brook flows. It lies mainly on rocks of Silurian limestone but there are small areas of Keuper marl and sandstone. The valley sides have areas of ancient woodland with large and small-leaved lime and wild service trees. The floor has herb-rich meadows which lead down to streamside marshes beside the brook across which a weir was built over 200 years ago to provide power for a mill which was in use until 1973. In a wet depression above the weir is a large pool: a breeding site for frogs.

What to See   Interesting woodland plants include alternate-leaved golden-saxifrage, spurge-laurel, toothwort, greater broomrape., small teasel, monk's-hood, wild daffodil and both violet and broad-leaved helleborine. The Papermill meadow at the south end has around 120 species including greater butterfly-orchid, lady's-mantle and adder's-tongue. Dipper and kingfisher feed in the brook whilst spotted flycatcher and green woodpecker also occur. Yellow-necked mice and dormice sometimes use nest-boxes in winter.

T at The Knapp and at Ravenshill Wood, a mixed woodland reserve 1 mile NW at SO739537.

Wheelchairs have limited access at both.

Tiddesley Wood · 42

Map 150 SO92-45- 185 acres (75 ha)
1 mile west of Pershore. Take A44 to Worcester, just before the town boundary fork left onto minor road to Besford and Croome. In ½ mile park near entrance to lane on left at SO929462 which leads to wood. SSSI. Ancient woodland.

Access   AYR (except 25 December) on foot down gated track to wood. There are two further entrances off the A4104 Pershore—Defford road: ¼ mile after the cemetery on the right at SO933450 or at the southern tip of the wood at SO929444. There is no access to a fenced-in Rifle Range at the south-westerly corner.

Information   Leaflet with map from TI Office in Pershore.

History   There has been woodland on this site for 7–8000 years and it contains several indicator species characteristic of ancient woodland such as small-leaved lime, wild service-tree, wild pear, herb-Paris and violet helleborine. Clearance in the area began about 5000 BC and a polished Neolithic axe was found in the 1970s in the valley of the Bow Brook which forms the western boundary of the wood. The wood was mentioned in the Domesday Book when it belonged to Westminster Abbey. The freehold belonged to the Church for 1000 years until bought by WTNC in 1985.

What to See   Other interesting wild flowers include bird's-nest orchid, goldilocks buttercup, yellow-wort, narrow-leaved everlasting pea, meadow saffron and adder's-tongue. In spring and summer bird song fills the wood notably nightingale, garden and willow warblers and blackcap: sparrowhawk regularly nest. Nearly half of Britain's butterfly species occur, amongst them comma, white admiral and, in July and August, white letter hairstreak.

Wyre Forest · 43

Map 139 SO7-7- 6000 acres (2650 ha)
North and west of Bewdley off A456. FNR and NNR. Ancient woodland, plantations, meadows, streams.

Access   Most of forest open AYR with numerous access points and picnic sites.

Information   Leaflet to way-marked trails from FC Visitor Centre at SO759743 1 mile west of the roundabout at the west end of Bewdley by-pass.

The Centre also contains exhibition on forestry including a live wood-ants nest, A/V display and computer game. Open daily Mon–Fri 11 a.m.–4 p.m., W/Es 11 a.m.–5 p.m. The Teachers' Centre may be booked. Leaflet on Fred Dale Nature Reserve of WTNC from Trust HQ or Knapp and Papermill Reserve. A nature trail starts on Dowles Road 1½ miles north-west of Bewdley at SO776763, 100 yds west of bridge over Dowles Brook where there is a CP and informative map.

History   One of the best remaining large areas of woodland in Britain, the forest lies on the Coal Measures which here exhibit a wide range including sandstones, conglomerates, marls and some bands of limestone. This variety is reflected in the forest cover which has tracts of both sessile and pedunculate oak and numerous small-leaved lime and wild service-tree whilst the valley of the Dowles Brook through the centre, flowing east to the River Severn, is lined with alder and willow. Much of the ground flora is of acid-loving species—bilberry, bracken, heather, common cow-wheat and wood sage but, where limestone predominates, there are often small meadows with betony, common bird's-foot-trefoil and wild thyme. Much of the forest was formerly coppiced and the 'crop', taken every 20 years on a rotational basis, was used for fuel, charcoal, and oak bark for tanning.

What to See   Unusual plants include lily-of-the-valley, green-winged orchid and meadow saffron as well as mountain melick and wood crane's-bill which are here at their southern limit in Britain. Amongst the notable birds are dipper, kingfisher and grey wagtail along the brook, with pied flycatcher, wood and grasshopper warblers, woodcock, sparrowhawk and long-eared owl elsewhere. The insect list is enormous with over 25 species of butterfly regularly seen including high brown and silver-washed fritillary and green and purple hairstreak. Adder and grass snake both occur: the deer of Wyre are fallow.

T[D]. Picnic sites, refreshments at FC Visitor Centre.

Wheelchairs have access on good paths from Visitor Centre.

NORTH-WEST

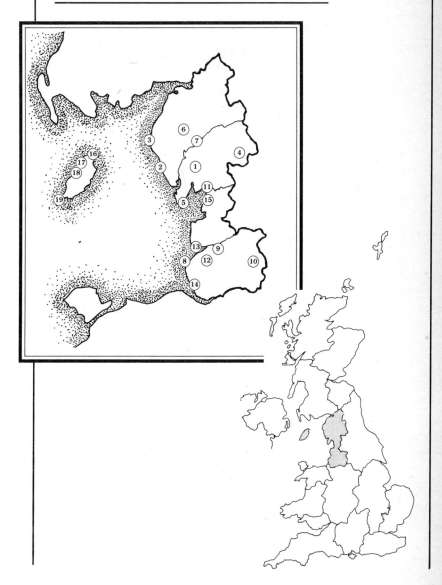

Cumbria

The millions of visitors who pour into Cumbria from the south and east each year still find a county of unmatched beauty. The ravages of industry have left a few scars but these are confined to the west and north, round Barrow-in-Furness, the coastal coalfield north of St Bees, and Carlisle—parts the average tourist does not reach. The main attraction for tourists, as it was for the writers who popularized the area over two centuries ago, remains the Lake District though this occupies less than one third of the county.

To the north lie the flat and fertile farmlands of the Solway plain whilst, to the east, beyond a band of upland limestone, the broad valley containing the River Eden stretches from Kirkby Stephen to Carlisle and then the Pennines, where the peat hags of Crossfell almost reach 3000 ft.

The south of the county is a mixture of limestone hills and woods overlooking the alternating sea and sand banks of the great estuary of Morecambe Bay, whilst the west coast beyond the Lakes is of astounding variety: sand, shingle, and marsh culminating in the mighty cliffs of *St Bees Head*.

For wildlife it is the west coast of Cumbria which is of widest renown—the two extensive estuaries of the Solway, shared with Scotland to the north, and Morecambe Bay, shared with Lancashire to the south, are both of great significance. Morecambe is the most important intertidal area in Britain, attracting up to 200,000 waders in winter, and some of the best viewing is from the CWT reserve on the west side at *South Walney*. This has the advantage of having, on its other side, the Irish Sea. Here, and at *St Bees Head*, there is the opportunity of watching sea-birds of the north and west which are rarely seen further south, such as black guillemot and arctic skua.

This west coast is also famous for its many miles of unspoilt sand dunes, safe from the masses of bucket-and-spade holidaymakers and day-trippers who besiege the Lancashire coast: there are still fine reserves here where the natural succession from shifting sand to mature dune grassland is protected—notably round the mouth of the River Esk at Ravenglass where CWT has its *Eskmeals Dunes* reserve.

Though the lakes and mountains which have shielded this west coast have not been spoilt by industry in the normal sense, they have been attacked by the afforestation of conifers: millions of these 'strange foreigners' have been planted on the lakeland fells, and none more densely than in the *Thornthwaite Forest* in the Whinlatter Pass west of Keswick. However, now that they have become a major tourist attraction, these artificial and renewable woods can help to take the pressure off more sensitive and precious native woods elsewhere.

Such serene woods may be viewed, or passed through, along the shores of that most beautiful of all the Lakes, *Ullswater*. To walk along the eastern side with Hellvelyn mirrored in its depths and return by motor yacht must be one of the world's most outstanding delights.

A shorter passage over water can be enjoyed on Windermere. Those who cross from Bowness in search of the homeland of the writer Beatrix Potter can visit a charming wildlife garden, *Ash Landing*, run by CWT to demonstrate, in a small space, the wide range of wildlife habitats to be found in the Lake District as a whole. There can be no better place in which to begin an understanding of the riches of a county the casual visitor never sees.

One such to be treasured, for its mixture of railway and natural history, is the *Smardale Line* where nineteenth century engineering and ancient limestone woods contribute to an absorbing walk away-from-it-all in a lakeless district of unknown Cumbria.

- Cumbria Wildlife Trust (CWT), Church Street, Ambleside, LA22 0BU. 05394 32476.

Ash Landing

Map 97 SD38-95- 6 acres (2.5 ha)
On the west side of Lake Windermere across the ferry from Bowness on B5285 to Far Sawrey 600 yds from the landing stage. Woodland, hedgerows, meadow, bog, pond.

Access   AYR on foot from CP on the east side at SD386951 on well-marked paths.

Information   Reserve guide from Information Centre on site: open Thurs 11 a.m.–4 p.m., or from CWT.

History   Until recently a garden nursery overrun by rhododendron, the area is now being run by CWT to create as diverse a range of wildlife habitats as possible including deciduous woodland, coppice, marshes, meadows, hedges and ponds. There is also a nursery where native plants are raised for use here and in other reserves in the county.

What to See   Native trees include oak, ash and birch with honeysuckle and coppiced hazel under which bluebell and foxglove thrive. Greater spearwort is a feature of the ponds which have a flourishing population of dragonflies and damselflies, frogs and toads. Woodland birds include blackcap, chiffchaff and several different tits which are expected to increase as the site matures.

Eskmeals Dunes

Map 96 SD08-94- 167 acres (68 ha)
½ mile south of Ravenglass on the south side of estuary of River Esk via turning off A595 at Lane End, Waberthwaite to the west side of Esk railway viaduct. SSSI. Sand dunes, salt marshes, meadow, pools.

Access   AYR on foot from parking space on road near viaduct to entrance along bank of River Esk. The reserve may be inaccessible for a short time at very high tide: it is often closed on weekdays when firing is taking place at a nearby gunnery, indicated by yellow flags flying at the entrance (ring 06577 629 on weekdays to check the position).

Information   Reserve guide from CWT.

History   One of the least spoilt sand dune systems in Britain forming part of a complex which includes the Ravenglass dunes on the north side of the Esk. This south peninsula consists of a series of parallel shingle ridges which have been deflected into the estuary forcing the River Esk to turn north before reaching the sea. Lime-rich sand has been blown onto these ridges which has been stabilized by marram grass.

What to See   Dune flowers include sea holly, sea spurge, sea bindweed, wild pansy, restharrow, carline thistle and the rare fern, moonwort. A marshy meadow has a fine population of marsh-orchids, adder's-tongue and royal fern. These flowers attract many butterflies, notably small pearl-bordered and dark green fritillary, both on the wing in June. Skylark and meadow pipit are common with frequent partridge, stonechat and linnet whilst the salt marsh areas attract waders such as curlew, dunlin, turnstone, oystercatcher and ringed plover. In summer whimbrel arrive and in autumn, common sandpiper, bar-tailed godwit and greenshank. Wigeon and a few goldeneye appear in winter. However the most important animal on the reserve is the endangered natterjack toad which breeds in carefully managed ponds.

St Bees Head   3

Map 89 NX94-13- 55 acres (22 ha)
3 miles south-west of Whitehaven via B5345 to St Bees: cross staggered crossroads in village, after 400 yds turn right at T-junction to CP on beach after ½ mile. SSSI. Cliffs with nesting sea birds.

Access   AYR on foot from CP at NX961119 from which cliff path leads 2½ miles to North Head lighthouse with good viewing points *en route*. Please keep to the path.

Information   Leaflets on site: RSPB summer warden April–August.

History   A stretch of sheer New Red sandstone cliffs up to 300 ft high, which are topped with areas of gorse and grassland. It holds over 5000 breeding sea-birds as well as other cliff and rock breeding species. The Head is also a good place for sea watching, especially in late summer and autumn.

What to See   Breeding auks include large numbers of guillemot, some razorbill and small numbers of puffin and the only English colony of black guillemot. There are also fulmar, shag, kittiwake, jackdaw, raven, kestrel, rock pipit and stonechat whilst peregrine, merlin and sparrowhawk may hunt over the reserve. Offshore gannet, terns, Manx and sooty shearwaters, common scoter, red-throated diver and occasional skuas may be seen. The list of colourful plants includes bloody crane's-bill, kidney vetch, orpine, meadow saxifrage and rock samphire.

T in St Bees beach CP.

Wheelchairs have access by car along private road to North Head lighthouse from Sandwith at NX965147.

Smardale Line 　　　　　　　　　　　　　　　　　4

Map 91 NY72-06- 90 acres (36 ha)
3 miles to the west of Kirkby Stephen north of A685 to Newbiggin-on-Lune. SSSI.
Limestone woodland, open scrub, grassland.

Access　　AYR on foot from parking space in Newbiggin via lane on the north
side of village opposite a telephone box which reaches a disused railway line in
½ mile. There is then good path to Smardale in 3½ miles passing through woods.
Please keep to the path. The Smardale Gill Viaduct on the line reopens after
repairs in 1991. During repairs the viaduct is impassable.

Information　　Nothing on site: leaflet from CWT.

History　　The old railway was the Kirkby Stephen to Tebay branch of a line
to join the ports of the North Sea and the Irish Sea. It was opened in 1845 and
closed in 1960. The ash/birch woods lie on the Carboniferous limestone on the
steep east slopes of the valley of the Scandal Beck, a tributary of the River Eden
to the north. There is a limestone quarry to the west of the line from which stone
to build the viaducts was hewn: it contains a huge double limestone kiln.

What to See　　Interesting trees and shrubs are spindle, aspen and hazel with
bluebell, bugle, herb-Paris and primrose beneath their shade. On the old line
and its embankments are bird's-eye primrose, common rock-rose, melancholy
thistle, bloody crane's-bill, twayblade, common wintergreen, fragrant orchid
and broad-leaved helleborine. Heron and dipper frequent the Beck, whilst great
spotted and green woodpeckers, tawny and short-eared owls, treecreeper,
redstart, garden and willow warblers and goldcrest are amongst breeding
species.

South Walney 　　　　　　　　　　　　　　　　　5

Map 96 SD21-62- 230 acres (92 ha)
5 miles south of Barrow-in-Furness at the southern tip of Walney Island reached
by crossing the bridge from Barrow, turning left at the traffic lights, following
along Promenade and Ocean Road which swings right at King Alfred Hotel, and
then taking the fifth on the left, Carr Lane, through farmland to the road's end
after 5 miles. SSSI. Mud flats, sand dunes, salt marsh, meadows, pools.

Access　　AYR except Mons (but open BHs) 10 a.m.–5 p.m. (–4 p.m. September-
April): there is a small charge. Two way-marked nature trails include four hides
with views over the Irish Sea and one looking over Morecambe Bay.

Information　　Leaflets and guides from Information Centre by CP: open daily
(except Mons other than BHs) summer 10 a.m.–5 p.m., winter 10 a.m.–4 p.m.,
or from CWT.

History　　Walney Island is built of red Boulder clay deposited by retreating
glaciers, over which sands have been blown to create a dune system. The Boulder
clay is exposed along the highly eroded western shore. The shape of the Island
is constantly changing and it is frequently breached during storms. The southern

end, which has been a reserve since 1963, was exploited for salt about 100 years ago and, more recently, for gravel extraction. This has left many ponds, pits and trenches which are attractive to birds.

What to See Marram dominated dunes have wild pansy, biting stonecrop, sea bindweed, hound's-tongue and sea spurge with, rarely on the shore, oysterplant. Elsewhere yellow horned-poppy, henbane and great mullein may be found. The major ornithological importance is the largest mixed breeding colony of herring gull and lesser black-backed gull in Europe with 27,000 pairs in total, with a few great black-backed, shelduck, oystercatcher, ringed plover, little and common terns and the most southerly breeding eider on the west coast. Winter brings large numbers of teal and wigeon whilst merlin and peregrine are daily visitors: there are also red-throated diver and occasional common scoter, red-breasted merganser and goldeneye. Spring and autumn bring many migrants especially willow warbler, goldcrest, redstart and flycatchers.

T in CP.

Thornthwaite Forest 6

Map 89 NY20-24- approximately 6500 acres (3000 ha)
4 miles west of Keswick on both sides of B5292 through Winlatter Pass to Lorton and Cockermouth. Coniferous woodlands.

Access AYR on foot from CP at the Visitor Centre on the north side of B5292 at NY207245 onto six way-marked walks of 2¾–7½ miles, including Grizedale Pike at almost 2600 ft.

Information Leaflets and trail guides from Visitor Centre which also has A/V displays and computer games: open daily (except 25 and 26 December and all of January) 10 a.m.–5.30 p.m. Information boards on the trails.

History Thornthwaite is part of Britain's oldest man-made National Forest. The Forestry Commission was set up in 1919 and some of the first trees were planted across the road from the Visitor Centre.

What to See Most of the trees are planted conifers which include Norway Spruce, Corsican pine, Scots pine, western red-cedar, western hemlock, Douglas fir and sitka spruce. There is an oak plantation at Noble Knott which overlooks Bassenthwaite with Skiddaw beyond.

T[D]. Refreshments, shop at Visitor Centre. Picnic site at Noble Knott 1 mile towards Keswick at NY221245.

Wheelchairs have good access on paths from Visitor Centre.

Ullswater Trail 7

Map 90 NY394161–443199 7 miles (12 kilometres)
To the east side of Ullswater from Patterdale to Howtown. Lakeside, meadows, wet flushes, scree, deciduous woodland.

Access   AYR on foot from the parking space in Patterdale across Goldrill Beck following a good path via Side Farm and Silver Point above the lake shore: then climbing above Sandwick through Hallinhag Wood to the pier at Howtown where a steamer can be taken back to Glenridding, 1 mile from the starting point.

Information   Trail guides from TI Offices in Glenridding, Ambleside etc. and from CWT.

History   Ullswater is one of the most beautiful of the English lakes. Patterdale at the head is close to Glenridding from which motor yachts ply to Pooley Bridge at the north end, calling at Howtown *en route*. The footpath crosses a wide range of lakeland habitats including bracken-covered slopes, open birch wood with juniper, and sessile oak wood.

What to See   Interesting plants on the way include heath milkwort, lady's-mantle, betony, wood crane's-bill and, in wet flushes, lesser spearwort, round-leaved sundew and common butterwort. Frequent woodland birds are spotted and pied flycatchers, treecreeper, redstart, coal tit, willow warbler and jay: numerous becks and the water's edge attract pied and yellow wagtail, whilst cormorant, heron and red-breasted merganser may be seen on the lake. Holly blue butterflies are on the wing in May.

Lancashire

The major attraction of Lancashire must be its coast—the golden sands of Southport, Blackpool and Morecambe: the challenging links of Royal Birkdale and Lytham St Anne's. However the annual invasion of holidaymakers has not deterred the millions of other visitors to these shores who were coming regularly, long before the invention of the charabanc or the game of golf—the gulls, waders and waterfowl which feed and breed around the bays and estuaries of Liverpool, the Ribble and Morecambe, each with their own reserves.

The most surprising, because it is on the edge of Liverpool, is *Seaforth Docks*, one of the best places to watch gulls in Britain. The Ribble estuary is one of the most important places in Britain for waders, supporting internationally recognized populations of nine species in winter, including bar-tailed godwit, knot and sanderling. The *Ribble Marshes* NNR on the south side now protects much of the area though it was nearly lost in 1978 when it was bought by a Dutch farmer who intended to embank and drain over 5000 acres for agriculture. After a year-long national furore it was bought by the government to become a National Nature Reserve.

Morecambe Bay vies with the Wash for the distinction of being the largest intertidal area in Britain and, for birds, is the most important with over 200,000 waders in winter. The shoreline from Fleetwood to Silverdale provides numerous vantage points including the RSPB Morecambe Bay reserve which is continuous with their *Leighton Moss* reserve near the Cumbria border. This wonderful reserve produces birdwatching thrills at all seasons, none greater than the biggest booming collection of bittern anywhere in Britain.

Botanists can be equally excited by the riches of the sand dunes further south. Between Formby and Southport lies an almost continuous series of reserves over a seven mile stretch of shore where the lime-rich sands provide habitats for such national and local treasures as dune helleborine, baltic rush, lesser clubmoss, seaside centaury, yellow bird's-nest and round-leaved wintergreen, most of which can be seen in the central section covered by *Ainsdale and Birkdale Sandhills*.

In all one third of the Lancashire coast is now protected in 12 nature reserves and will be further enhanced when local authority plans for a coastal footpath are implemented.

Inland, the Lancashire landscape contains as much variety as the coast. There are three principal regions: the lowland sands and marls on the west side; the Coal Measures of the crescent around Manchester with upland moors and valley woods leading to the Pennines; and the limestone of the rocky hills in the north reaching over 2000 ft on Leck Fell—a wedge of Lancashire in the Yorkshire Craven District. Each region is represented by fine, distinctive reserves.

Mere Sands Wood locates itself—situated on the Bunter sandstone on the plain a few miles inland from Southport it is a series of meres excavated from the sand which are attractive to birds, plants and people.

Healey Dell would be a dingle in Shropshire—a wet wooded valley with a bubbling stream in the bottom serving to remind the visitor of the type of vegetation which once covered hill and dell in what then became an industrial hell, but is now being revived with a laudable list of Country Parks and Local Nature Reserves as local authorities change dereliction into delectation.

Warton Crag rises like a buffer at the north end of the county and seems to say 'stop a while'. The Silverdale woods and limestone pavement, Gait Barrows NNR, and the fresh and salt water marshes round *Leighton Moss* combine to make this beautiful area one of the top ten localities for wild flowers and birds in Britain—a compelling inducement for visiting naturalists to change their status and become residents.

- Lancashire Trust for Nature Conservation (LTNC), Cuerden Park Wildlife Centre, Shady Lane, Bamber Bridge, Preston PR5 6AU. 0772 324129.

Ainsdale and Birkdale Sandhills

Map 108 SD29-12- 670 acres (271 ha)
3 miles south-west of Southport on the Lancashire coast: reached via coast road to crossroads north of Pontin's and turning down Shore Road, Ainsdale to coast where there is parking on the beach or at the Ainsdale Lido. SSSI, LNR. Sand dunes, dune slacks, scrub.

Access   AYR on foot from CP at SD295129 onto well-marked paths which visitors are asked to keep to.

Information   Leaflet from TI Office in Southport: many reserve signs and information boards at entrances and *en route*.

History   The reserve consists of high dune ridges, dune valleys, and slacks which are often filled with water in winter. These latter contain many rare and local plants and animals including our rarest amphibian, the natterjack toad. Their 'singing' on spring and summer evenings is such that they are known locally as 'Southport Nightingales'. Some areas are now overgrown by sea buckthorn which was originally introduced to stabilize the sand but has spread rapidly to shade out other species.

What to See   In the damper slacks are carpets of early marsh-orchid, marsh helleborine and grass-of-Parnassus whilst in drier areas round-leaved wintergreen and dune helleborine occur. The dune ridges carry many colourful species such as ploughman's spikenard, hound's-tongue, heath dog-violet and Portland spurge. These flowers attract butterflies in large numbers such as common blue, grayling, gatekeeper and small copper. The buckthorn scrub provides food for fieldfare, redwing and redpoll in winter and nesting sites for willow warbler, whitethroat, reed bunting and redpoll.

T near the Lido and to the south along the beach.

Cuerden Valley Park

9

Map 102 SD56-23- 650 acres (263 ha)
4 miles south of Preston leaving M6 at Exits 28 or 29 and making for junction of A49 Preston to Wigan road with B5256 to Clayton Green: ½ mile along B5256 turn left into Shady Lane for entrance to Visitor Centre and LTNC HQ on right. Woodland, meadows, marsh, lake, river.

Access   AYR on foot from CP at SD562236 onto network of good paths through extensive parkland. A nature reserve area may be visited with a permit from LTNC HQ in CP.

Information   Trail guide from Visitor Centre.

History   Cuerden Park is a large area of delightful open space which follows the valley of the River Lostock as it flows north to meet the River Ribble at Preston. The Park surrounds the early nineteenth century building of Cuerden Hall designed by Lewis Wyatt 1816–19.

What to See   The big spreading parkland oaks are interspersed with areas of meadowland managed for hay which harbour yellow-rattle, adder's-tongue and a large population of common spotted-orchid. The well-wooded areas attract long-tailed tits, a variety of warblers, nuthatch, treecreeper and great spotted woodpecker. The river holds the only known Lancashire population of the banded demoiselle, *Agrion splendens*: kingfisher feed here whilst heron feed in the lake.

T[D] in Trust HQ. Refreshments at Sue Ryder Home, Cuerden Hall.
Wheelchairs have good access onto paths.

Healey Dell

Map 109 SD87-15- 173 acres (70 ha)
2 miles north-west of Rochdale off A671 to Whitworth, turning west at junction of Whitworth Road and Market Street by sign for Reserve. LNR. Sessile oak wood, heather moor, stream.

Access   AYR on foot from CP at SD880159 onto well-marked nature trail.

History   This south-facing damp valley on the Coal Measures has ancient oak/birch woods on the west side, but the east side has been planted with sycamore. There are open spaces of heath with heather, bilberry and bracken. Below the wood a disused railway, which crosses the stream by a viaduct, was built using limestone gravel as ballast on which several unexpected lime-loving plants now grow.

What to See   Damp woodland has lady fern, hart's-tongue and lemon-scented fern, marsh-marigold, marsh violet, water avens and ragged-Robin whilst both southern and northern marsh-orchids and a range of hybrids occur. Woodland birds include blackcap, garden warbler, woodcock and tawny owl whilst kestrel, snipe, redpoll, twite, pied and grey wagtails also occur to be joined by siskin and waxwing in winter.

Leighton Moss

11

Map 97 SD47-75- 321 acres (130 ha)
2 miles north-west of Carnforth on minor road from Yealand Redmayne to Silverdale, to CP nearly opposite Silverdale station. SSSI and Ramsar site. Freshwater marsh, reed-beds, willow and alder carr.

Access   AYR daily (except Tues) 9 a.m.–9 p.m. (or dusk if earlier) but public hide on causeway to the north-east of the entrance is always open. Good paths lead to four other hides.

Information   Leaflet and permit to visit restricted areas from RSPB Visitor Centre in CP, which also has comprehensive displays.

History   The reserve is situated in a small wooded valley flanked by the limestone hills of Silverdale and Wharton Crag. The valley floor is lined with marine clay and deposits of peat have built up in the undrained area which, with several small springs, has given rise to a complex of reed-beds, shallow pools (meres) and wet woods. Islands have been created in the meres as additional breeding areas.

What to See   The 200 acres of reed-beds have become the only breeding site for bittern in the north of Britain, with up to 13 pairs. Other species breeding here include bearded tit, reed warbler and water rail. Ducks which breed here in numbers are mallard, teal and shoveler, with smaller populations of pochard, tufted duck, gadwall and occasional garganey. Of the waders lapwing, redshank and snipe are abundant, oystercatcher less so. Buzzard and sparrowhawk breed, osprey and marsh harrier are regular visitors on passage. There is a brilliant display of water plants with many sedges and marsh-orchids, and an abundance of insect life with over 300 species of moth recorded and many dragonflies. There are red squirrels in the woods and occasional otter in the water.

T[D] and shop in CP.

Wheelchairs have access to a hide overlooking mere and reed-bed.

Mere Sands Wood

Map 108 SD44-15- 105 acres (42 ha)
6½ miles south-east of Southport on B5246 ½ mile west of Rufford. SSSI. Lakes, heath, broad-leaved and coniferous woodland.

Access   AYR on foot from CP on the north side at SD448160 onto way-marked trail of 1 or 2 miles with four hides and an observation platform.

Information   Trail leaflet from Visitor Centre in CP: warden on site.

History   A wood planted in the nineteenth century stands on what was once the shore of a large lake. When the lake was drained alternating layers of peat and sand were exposed on its shore which are of such geological interest that the area is an SSSI. The sand also interested quarry companies and extraction took place from 1974–82. Under a planning agreement this was done so as to leave the best areas of woodland and develop marsh and heathland and shallow-edged lakes.

What to See   Trees around the margin include birch, beech, rowan, oak and alder whilst the water has yellow iris, greater spearwort and water-plantain. Amongst the breeding waterfowl are tufted duck, mallard, gadwall, shelduck and ruddy duck, great-crested and little grebes: in winter they are joined by teal, goldeneye and pochard with occasional pintail and shoveler. Woodland birds include tawny owl, treecreeper, willow warbler and blackcap. Mistle thrush and fieldfare feed on rowan berries in winter when kingfisher may come to feed on stickleback and gudgeon. Red squirrel inhabit a small stand of Scots pine.

T in CP.

Wheelchairs have good access including hide near CP.

Ribble Marshes

Map 102 SD3-2- 5688 acres (2302 ha)
South shore of Ribble estuary between Southport and Preston. NNR and Ramsar site. Sand banks, mud flats, salt marsh, grazing marshes.

Access   AYR on footpaths and sea wall (except for salt marsh study area opposite Old Hollow Farm, the NCC warden's house, and Hesketh Out Marsh) from parking space opposite Crossens Pumping Station at SD377207. Best viewing on a rising tide in winter. There is a 5-mile walk ending on road at Hundred End at SD415226.

Information   Reserve signs at entrances.

History   The south shore of the Ribble has one of the longest continuous areas of salt marsh in Britain with reclaimed marsh behind it which is now grazed by sheep and cattle to create the best conditions to attract wintering birds. However some areas are fenced to allow marshland plants to flourish.

What to See   The estuary holds over 100,000 waders in winter including 70,000 knot, 20,000 dunlin, 10,000 oystercatcher with bar-tailed godwit, curlew, ringed plover and redshank. Wildfowl include 10,000 or more pink-footed geese, 15,000 wigeon and teal, 4000 pintail and some Bewick's swan, with common and velvet scoter, goldeneye and red-breasted merganser off shore. Autumn migration brings many sea-birds such as kittiwake, little gull and skuas. Black-headed gull, redshank and common tern nest in large numbers. The salt marshes include sea aster, thrift, sea arrowgrass, Danish scurvygrass and annual sea-blite whilst there are meadows full of southern marsh-orchids in June.

Seaforth Docks   14

Map 108 SJ31-97- 100 acres (40 ha)
1 mile north-west of Bootle off the A565 Crosby Road South through the entrance into the Free Port of Liverpool. SSSI. Sea-birds, saltwater and freshwater pools.

Access   AYR (except 25 and 26 December and 1 January) open 8 a.m.–sunset on foot from CP on Front at SJ315970 to path through reserve to hide overlooking freshwater pool.

Information   Leaflet and Bird Report from Warden at Reserve Office by CP: there is a small Interpretative Centre.

History   There are two large pools and overgrown rubble mounds on a site reclaimed in 1961 from a beach and derelict sand dunes: dumping continued until 1981. There are now habitats ranging from marshy beds of bulrushes and dry sandy areas to saltwater and freshwater pools.

What to See   The main importance is as a roost and feeding place for sea-birds, particularly little gulls, up to 400 of which can be seen together here in April. Other gulls recorded are Mediterranean, glaucous, and Iceland gulls. The spring migration brings large numbers of wheatear, whinchat, redstart, willow warbler, yellow wagtail, little ringed plover and common tern. Southern marsh-orchid and hemlock have invaded the marsh whilst the 16 species of butterflies include clouded yellow, painted lady and small copper.

Warton Crag   15

Map 97 SD49-72- 202 acres (82 ha)
1 mile north of Carnforth in Crag Road, Warton to CP immediately behind the Black Bull Hotel. SSSI, LNR. Limestone cliffs, scree, grassland, pavement, scrub, woodland.

Access   AYR on foot from CP at SD495725 onto a circular way-marked trail of 1 mile on rough paths.

Information   Notice board near entrance: leaflet from LTNC.

History   One of the best examples of Carboniferous limestone grassland in Lancashire at the south end of a ridge which ends in a series of terraces above Warton. There are also areas of limestone pavement at the top and of ash/hazel woodland. There are fine views over Morecambe Bay, the Pennines and the Forest of Bowland to the south-east.

What to See   The flowering plants include spring cinquefoil, spring sandwort, common thyme, horseshoe vetch and common rock-rose. They attract a long list of butterflies amongst which are high brown fritillary, common blue, orange-tip, wall and meadow brown. Birds of the area include many common warblers, tits, great spotted woodpecker and tawny owl whilst goldfinch and redpoll visit in autumn. The squirrels are red.

T and refreshments at Black Bull Hotel.

The Isle of Man

The Isle of Man, twice the size of the Isle of Wight, lies in the middle of the Irish Sea, separated from mainland Britain by 16 miles to its nearest point in Galloway, and by over 30 miles from the Irish coast in County Down. It has been separated from Great Britain for over 8000 years and may never have been connected to Ireland.

Separation before European species had completed the crossing of the mainland is the reason for the absence of species common in England such as snakes, toads, voles and moles, whilst plants such as white dead-nettle and dog's mercury only occur as recent introductions.

Although the island rises to over 2000 ft this is not high enough to produce a significant mountain flora and fauna: the only plants to qualify might be dwarf willow, cowberry and parsley fern. The geology is dominated by Manx Slates of the Cambrian period which cover three-quarters of the island, giving rise to siliceous soils suitable for a few, frequently repeated, acid-loving plants.

In the Neolithic period there was considerable tree cover but most had been cleared by the Middle Ages so that familiar woodland plants and birds are often absent; there are, for example, no resident woodpeckers or bullfinches. For this reason many of the best woodlands are plantations and several have been made into nature reserves because of the relatively large number of woodland birds they hold: good examples are *Cooil Dharry* and Ballamoar on the west side of the island.

The finest natural wildlife habitats in Man are undoubtedly on the coast with superb cliff scenery, particularly in the south-west and on the east side which contrasts with the flat, sandy beaches and dunes over most of the northern quarter.

The cliffs between Peel and Port Erin are particularly fine but those further south, round *Spanish Head*, are more accessible. Here are some of the best sea-bird colonies in Britain including thousands of auks, kittiwake and fulmar. The Calf of Man, across The Sound, is a bird sanctuary protected by its remoteness which is especially exciting during the spring and autumn migrations and for the small population of breeding Manx shearwater. Amongst the sand and shingle of *The Ayres* in the north-west it is the ground-nesting and ground-feeding birds which form the major attraction—four species of tern in the most southerly major tern colony on the west side of Britain, with the addition of numerous waders passing through in spring and autumn.

Between The Ayres and the central uplands there are some areas of wetland which are also of ancient origin and represent relics of vegetation which may have survived through the Ice Age. These are known locally as curraghs. The most extensive is *Ballaugh Curragh*; this is being developed into a major National Nature Reserve and lies west of Ramsey: another, Greeba Curragh, is in the valley between Douglas and Peel.

There is open access to much of this island, notably in the central hills: for those who wish to enjoy wildlife in peace and solitude the Isle of Man is one of the best places to visit in the British Isles.

- Manx Nature Conservation Trust (MNCT), Ballamoar House, Ballaugh. 0624 897611.
- Manx Museum and National Trust, Douglas. 0624 75522.

The Ayres 16

Map 95 NX43-03- 96 acres (39 ha)
5 miles north-west of Ramsey via Ballaghennie road leading north from A10 from Bride to Jurby 1 mile west of Bride. PNNR. Dunes, shingle ridge, maritime heath.

Access   AYR on foot from CP at MNCT Visitor Centre at NX438039, Blue Point NX395025, Rue point NX415027, Point of Ayre NX468047 etc.

Information   Nature trail leaflet from Manx Museum and Visitor Centre: open Easter–September Thurs, Sat and Sun 2–5 p.m.

History   Ayre is a Norse term for a shingle ridge: there are many ridges here, several now underlying the unusual lichen covered heathland which has developed on the inland side of the area. On the shore are extensive, marram-dominated dunes with fixed dunes behind them.

What to See   The mixed dunes are rich in wild flowers especially crane's-bill, stork's-bill, forget-me-not, bird's-foot-trefoil, mouse-ear, cat's-ear, pyramidal and early-purple orchids. Arctic, little, common and Sandwich terns nest nearby with shoveler, black-headed gull, mute swan and tufted duck in wetter places. In winter there are numerous divers off shore and snow bunting and golden plover are regular visitors.

Wheelchairs have limited access from the Visitor Centre, Rue Point and Point of Ayre: latter has good views of sea birds feeding off shore.

Ballaugh Curragh 　　　　　　　　　　　17

Map 95 SC36-95- 750 acres (300 ha)
2 miles north-east of Ballaugh village north of A3. NNR. Marsh, reed-bed, willow carr, open water.

Access　　AYR on foot from CP off A3 at SC367941 and from limited parking space at Killane Bridge at SC365955 onto good paths including 'board walk' nature trail.

Information　　Leaflets and guides from CP and Manx Museum.

History　　Probably the site of the pre-glacial Lake Andreas which may have remained a wetland continuously throughout the post-glacial. Formerly kept open by peat digging, hay cutting and grazing, the area is now overgrown with tall willow.

What to See　　The more interesting plants include bogbean, bog-myrtle, Royal fern, round-leaved sundew and several species of marsh-orchid. The area was formerly rich in molluscs but populations have been affected by agricultural run-off though the duck mussel was recently refound. A long list of dragonflies and damselflies includes the common hawker, common darter, large red, blue-tailed and common blue damselflies. Redpoll, grasshopper and sedge warblers are amongst the breeding birds whilst it is a major hen harrier roost in winter.

　T[D]. Refreshments.

　Wheelchairs have good access.

Cooil Dharry 　　　　　　　　　　　　18

Map 95 SC31-90- 17 acres (7 ha)
¼ mile south-west of Kirkmichael on A3. Wooded glen.

Access　　AYR on foot from CP space opposite Glen Wyllin entrance at SC315901.

Information　　Nothing on site.

History　　A mile long stretch of wooded valley planted with mixed deciduous trees and rhododendrons in nineteenth century when an artificial lake was also created. The main trees are holm and turkey oak, beech, lime, maple, and sweet chestnut. There are fascinating geological features including steep ridges forming promontaries overlooking the glen.

What to See　　The ground flora includes spring woodland flowers, giant hogweed and yellow iris whilst 35 species of birds have been recorded breeding here including tree creeper, coal tit and chiffchaff.

Spanish Head, the Chasms and the Sound 　　19

Map 95 SC18-66- 378 acres (153 ha)
The south-west corner of the island. Coastal cliffs, sea birds, acid heath.

Access   AYR on foot on coast path from CP at end of A31 to Calf of Man at SC173667 or from SC191668 via lane from Cregneash village.

Information   Numerous printed accounts from Manx Museum.

History   Cliffs of Manx Slates from the Cambrian period rise to over 250 ft and run east for nearly 3 miles backed by unspoilt open heathland. These link via small fields with the Cregneash Folk Museum, which was the first of its kind in Britain: open early May–late September Weekdays 10 a.m.–1 p.m., 2–5 p.m., Sun 2–5 p.m.

What to See   Cliffs with plants like rock samphire, rock sea-spurrey and hemp-agrimony are the breeding ground for large numbers of shag, razorbill, guillemot, puffin, kittiwake, fulmar, raven and chough and attract numerous solitary wasps. The heath and cliff grassland are often a blaze of colour from spring squill in May to western gorse, heather and bell heather in autumn.

T at Cregneash Museum.

Wheelchairs have views of sea birds fom CP at end of A31.

NORTH-EAST

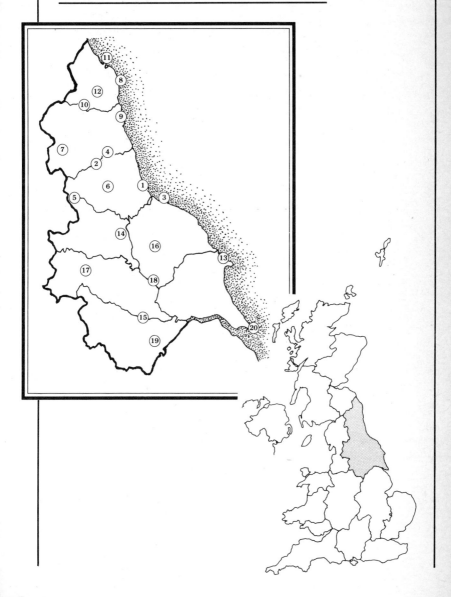

Durham and Cleveland

The counties of Durham and the more recent Cleveland have suffered more than most from exploitation and industrialization. The mouths of the three great rivers which cross the area, the Tyne, the Wear and the Tees, have all been suffocated by the expansion of Newcastle, Sunderland or Middlesbrough, and very little of the coast remains undeveloped. Immediately inland the great wedge of the Magnesian limestone plateau is mostly used for farming but also bears the scars of centuries of quarrying. Further inland, especially on the low-lying middle stretches of the River Wear, are the coal measures, where the ravages of deep mining in the past and of more recent open-cast mining has often left a bleak and cruel landscape. Even the Pennines, which form the western boundary rising to over 2400 ft on the Cumbria border, have not escaped—their natural beauty harmed by the creation of concrete dams to hold water for cooling the heated activity below.

Yet these ravages are superficial: above, between and below this seeming chaos are some of the most beautiful and important wildlife areas in Britain. *Upper Teesdale*, despite the intrusion of Cow Green reservoir, is still one of the most treasured areas for wildlife in the kingdom—a relict of our arctic past accompanied by the crashing splendours of High Force, England's highest waterfall, and Cauldron Snout, where the Tees tumbles over the hard intrusive basalt of the Whin Sill. Upper Weardale is less spectacular but carries one of the highest roads in England to over 2200 ft. Further north the building of a reservoir in the Derwent valley has brought its compensations and the nature reserve at the west end of *Derwent Reservoir* is attractive to birds and birdwatchers alike.

In their middle stretches these boisterous Pennine rivers have cut deeply into the rocks and, though many valley sides have been mined, and their woods felled for fuel in the past, new growth has hidden the scars and clear water, fit for dipper and kingfisher, slips past groves of oak and ash. A complex of valley woods and grassland can now be enjoyed in the Derwent valley, centred on *Thornley Wood* where the Woodland Centre is a starting point for exploration only a few miles from the centre of Newcastle.

The Wear at Durham meanders under cliffs crowned by the most inspiring of Norman cathedrals, and is equally attractive. Higher up the river, at *Witton-le-Wear*, gravel extraction, natural scenery and the imagination of the Durham Wildlife Trust have combined to create a wildlife sanctuary rich in birds, insects and flowers tucked into a quiet corner of the county.

There are still deep ravines hidden below the Magnesian limestone plateau. These are known as the Denes, with steep, often nearly vertical, wooded slopes which are havens of wildlife and lungs for people of places like Peterlee, which has Hawthorn Dene to the north and the most celebrated of all, *Castle Eden Dene*, to the south. Even further south, in Cleveland, the *Saltburn Gill*, cuts through the Lower Jurassic strata, on its way to the sea. These valleys, combined with a few stretches of unspoilt cliffs, as at Boulby, east of Saltburn, and Marsden, north of Sunderland, are the best that is left for wildlife on this otherwise desolate coast.

- Cleveland Wildlife Trust (CWT), The Old Town Hall, Mandale Road, Thornaby, Stockton-on-Tees TS17 6AW. 0642 608405.
- Durham Wildlife Trust (DWT), 52 Old Elvet, Durham DH1 3HN. 091 386 9797.

Castle Eden Dene

Map 93 NZ43-39- 500 acres (200 ha)
½ mile south of Shotton between A19 and the sea: signposted off A19 on the north side of Dene onto Durham Way for about 1 mile then turning right into Stanhope Close immediately after Oaklands pub to the Visitor Centre. NNR. Wooded valley, coastal cliffs.

Access   AYR on foot from CP at Visitor Centre, Oakerside Dean Lodge, at NZ426393 onto good paths which lead down into the Dene.

Information   Guide books, leaflets and trail guides from the Visitor Centre: open peak hours. If closed, from the Warden's house next door or from TI Offices in Peterlee and Durham City.

History   The finest and best protected of the Denes, the deep incised valleys which run down to the east coast of Durham between Sunderland and Hartlepool. The floor of the valley is 200 ft below the level of the cultivated fields on the plateau above and the steep sides are covered in natural oak, ash and elm woods with frequent additions of yew.

What to See   There are 300 different species of flowering plant and nearly 150 mosses and liverworts, including herb-Paris, lily-of-the-valley, dyer's greenweed, round-leaved wintergreen, crosswort, giant bellflower, cowslip, columbine, wood crane's-bill and bird's-nest, fly and early-purple orchids. There is a long list of woodland birds of which chiffchaff, garden, willow and grasshopper warblers, cuckoo, lesser whitethroat and whitethroat, pied and spotted flycatchers, redstart and tree pipit arrive in summer to join great spotted woodpecker, nuthatch, treecreeper, tree sparrow, tawny owl, woodcock and five tits resident here. On cliffs at the Dene's mouth are common rock-rose, bloody crane's-bill and carline thistle where northern brown argus butterflies may be seen in June and July.

Derwent Reservoir

Map 87 NZ01-52- 274 acres (111 ha)
5 miles west of Consett on the border between Durham and Northumberland, on B6278 1 mile west of A68 from the crossroads at Carterway Heads. Open water, heathland, wildfowl and waders.

Access   AYR:

1. to the nature reserve at the west end where birds can be viewed from lanes at NY985519 or 991524.
2. from Pow Hill Country Park on the south side at NZ010573 where there is a hide up steps opposite the toilet.
3. from roads round reservoir and across the dam which are reached via the Water Company offices on the B6278 on east side of bridge over the River Derwent.

Information   Leaflet on reservoir as a whole, map and birdlist from Water Company offices: further details from Pow Hill Country Park.

History   The reservoir was completed in 1966 to provide water for the area between Tyne and Tees. The west end has been established as a reserve from which sailing is excluded, which has become attractive to wildfowl and where numbers have not declined after flooding as frequently happens in reservoirs. Pow Hill is a small area (45 acres) of moorland dominated by heather and bracken.

What to See   Since it was flooded over 150 species of bird have been recorded with, in winter, up to 600 duck at any one time, mainly mallard, teal, wigeon and tufted duck but with small numbers of shoveler, pochard, goldeneye, goosander, smew and common scoter. Residents include heron, great crested grebe, coot and sparrowhawk whilst there are good numbers of waders in autumn such as common sandpiper, dunlin and oystercatcher.

T[D] at Millshield. Picnic site on the north shore at NZ013532.

Wheelchairs have good viewing from lanes at the west end.

Saltburn Gill   3

Map 94 NZ67-20- 52 acres (21 ha)

At the east end of Saltburn between the A174 Saltburn to Brotton road and the minor road to Skelton. SSSI. Deciduous woodland, gorse, bracken, stream.

Access   AYR on foot from CP at the Boating Lake, Saltburn at NZ667216. Turn in off Skelton road and park by white wooden bridge. Cross the bridge and, through a gap in the wall, the Skelton road into a pony field. Cross the Saltburn Gill, turn right and follow path to reserve entrance which starts walk of 1½ miles on good path.

Information   Notice boards near entrance: leaflet from CWT.

History   The gill was cut through the glacial clays, shales and sandstones of the Lower Jurassic period. It is a steep-sided coastal dene of which the eastern slopes are covered in deciduous woodland—one of the few remaining areas of this kind in Cleveland. There are also slopes of bracken and steep, gorse covered banks above the woodland at the southern end.

What to See   A rich ground flora under oak, wych elm, ash and willow includes early-purple orchid, bluebell, goldilocks buttercup, wood anemone and ramsons: the rare Dutch rush also occurs. This mixture of woodland and bracken supports a good number of warblers and tits, great spotted woodpecker, tawny owl and woodcock: grey wagtail are frequent by the stream.

Thornley Wood   4

Map 88 NZ17-60-90 acres (36 ha)
1½ miles south of Blaydon in Derwent Valley on A694 to Rowlands Gill signposted to Woodlands Centre. Part of Derwent Walk Country Park. Sessile oak and coniferous woodland, meadows, pond, streams.

Access   AYR on foot from CP at Woodlands Centre at NZ178604 onto good way-marked paths of duration varying from ½–1½ hours.

Information   Nature trail guides to this and other parts of Country Park from Woodlands Centre: open Mon–Fri 12 noon–2 p.m., W/Es and BHs noon–5 p.m.

History   These ancient woodlands are situated in a steep sided dene cutting through the Coal Measures and running down into the Derwent valley: they are dominated by sessile oak, birch, ash and wych elm with hazel and holly in the understorey. An old waggon track runs along the south edge of the wood: it was used to carry coal from the Thornley and Garesfield pits further west down to the Derwent: it closed in 1960.

What to See   A rich ground flora contains bluebell, greater stitchwort, primrose and ramsons in spring followed by cow-wheat, wood sage and bilberry with marsh woundwort, ragged-Robin, betony and meadowsweet in damper areas. Woodland birds include whitethroat, willow warbler, woodcock and sparrowhawk with goldcrest and coal tit in the planted conifers and dipper and kingfisher by the stream. Clearings attract butterflies whilst a pond supports frogs, southern hawker dragonfly and large red damselfly. Red squirrel feed on beech nuts or the cones of Norway spruce whilst badger and roe deer are present.
T[D] at Woodlands Centre.

Upper Teesdale   5

Map 92 NY8-2- 8650 acres (3500 ha)
6 miles north-west of Middleton in Teesdale, west of B6277. NNR. Upland moorland, limestone grassland, base-rich flushes.

Access   AYR on foot:

1. from CP at High Force Hotel at NY874286 walk ½ mile towards Middleton to the entry to Holwick Head House just before the sign 'No footway for 600 yds' to the reserve entrance on the other side of the sleeper bridge.
2. from council CP at Cow Green at NY817309 which leads onto 1½ miles of Widdybank Fell nature trail and Cauldron Snout waterfall.

Information   Reserve sign at entrances: leaflets and trail guides from Bowlees centre of DWT at NY906281 in old chapel signposted off B6277 ¾ mile west of Newbiggin: open daily Easter–October 10 a.m.–5 p.m., W/Es March, November, December 12.30–4 p.m. (small charge). The Centre has extensive displays on the history and natural history of Upper Teesdale. Widdybank Fell trail guide from dispenser in Council CP.

History   One of the most important botanical sites in Britain with a relict flora of species which have survived here since the Ice Age about 10,000 years ago. Much of the vegetation is extremely fragile and, at this altitude, slow-growing: it is easily damaged so all visitors are asked to keep strictly to the rights of way many of which, including the Pennine Way, cross the reserve. Numerous shafts of former lead and barytes mines persist and the south side of the River Tees is in a military firing range: neither presents a risk to those keeping to the paths.

What to See   Sphagnum moss, heather, cottongrass and matgrass grow on the acid soils over sandstone and shale, whilst the soils on the limestone support, in damp flushes, many rare sedges, common butterwort, bird's-eye primrose, Scottish asphodel and yellow saxifrage whilst drier areas have common rock-rose, mountain pansy, spring gentian, northern bedstraw and moonwort. Typical upland birds which nest here are golden plover, redshank, lapwing, curlew, wheatear, skylark, meadow pipit, dunlin, short-eared owl, merlin and red grouse.

T. Picnic site in CP at Bowlees Centre: T[D] in CP at Cow Green.

Wheelchairs have access to River Tees and view of High Force from path opposite High Force Hotel (small charge) and on track from Cow Green CP.

Witton-le-Wear   6

Map 92 NZ16-31- 84 acres (40 ha)
3 miles north-west of Bishop Auckland via A689 toward Crook turning south at High Grange onto minor road to reserve entrance at Low Barns after ¾ mile. SSSI. Woodland, scrub, grassland, marshes, lakes.

Access   AYR on foot from CP inside entrance gate near farmhouse at NZ160315 onto way-marked nature trail of ¾ mile which has five hides.

Information   Leaflet from laboratory on site open when part-time Warden is about or from DWT. Information boards in buildings.

History   This area of former farmland was worked as a gravel pit until 1964 when it was given to DWT. Much of the centre of the reserve was landscaped and trees such as spruce, pine, larch, oak, rowan, willow and poplar have been planted by the Trust: conifers are sold as Christmas trees to provide income. Natural features include a mature alder wood, small streams and the River Wear which forms the southern boundary.

What to See   Amongst many striking plants are viper's-bugloss, butterbur, wild mignonette, yellow-rattle, bladder campion, whitlowgrass, meadow crane's-bill, marsh-marigold, northern marsh-orchid and hybrids with common spotted-orchid. Garden, grasshopper and willow warblers, great tit, treepipit, tree sparrow, tawny owl, stock dove and great spotted woodpecker breed in the woods whilst coot, mallard, teal, wigeon, pochard and tufted duck are frequent on the lakes in winter with a few goldeneye and goosander and occasional whooper swan. Dipper, heron and kingfisher visit the river where ringed plover, oystercatcher and common sandpiper may be seen feeding on gravel banks. Roe deer also visit the area.

T in laboratory buildings when open or in Witton-le-Wear village.

Wheelchairs have some access on good paths.

Northumberland

Away from its industrialized South-East, Northumberland is one of the least populated, least spoilt counties in England with few towns and villages and a plethora of sites for wildlife of national and international importance.

For the visiting naturalist there are two main centres of attraction—the uplands of the Cheviot and the Pennines to the north and west, and the 40 miles of magnificent and ever-changing coastline which grows in beauty and stature the nearer the Tweed is approached.

In the south, not a dozen miles from Morpeth and still within the influence of the Coal Measures, a 5-mile stretch round *Druridge Bay* is being developed into an outstanding area for birdwatchers, within easy reach of the conurbation around Newcastle, by exploiting the artifacts of industry. Land ravaged by opencast mining and subsidence and now of little use for agriculture, has been landscaped to create pools and marshland and a series of banks to hide watchers from birds.

North of Druridge, Coal Measures give way to Carboniferous limestone which dominates the coast from Alnmouth to Berwick-on-Tweed and through which runs one of Northumberland's most famous geological features—the Whin Sill. This is a doleritic intrusion which forms a great escarpment across the county from Greenhead, near Hadrian's Wall on the Cumbrian border, to the sea round *Craster and Low Newton-by-the-Sea.* Quarrying of the Whin Sill left the tree-covered hollows which are now the Arnold Reserve at Craster from which there are splendid views of Dunstanburgh Castle standing proud on a doleritic crag thrust up by volcanic activity. The castle grounds and cliffs are important breeding areas for sea-birds such as eider duck, kittiwake and fulmar.

The Whin Sill strikes the coast again at Bamburgh: here another rugged castle crowns the cliffs and crags. This is a vantage point from which to survey one of the richest wildlife panoramas in Britain. To the east the Farne Islands provide some of the best opportunities to see large colonies of puffin, guillemot and razorbill at close quarters, with the bonus of sightings of inquisitive grey seal. To the north lies *Lindisfarne*, Holy Island, with a vast expanse of sand dunes and mud flats which attract tens of thousands of waterfowl and make the whole area of international importance.

Only a dozen miles to the south-west the cliffs of volcanic origin on the coast give way to the massive granites of the Cheviot which intrude into the andesite lava of this long extinct volcano. This peat-covered wilderness is one of the magnets of the *Northumberland National Park* which can be approached by any one of a number of valleys which radiate from its awesome dome. Easiest from the east, and with a friendly, inconspicuous Visitor Centre at *Ingram* on the way, is the River Breamish. Perhaps the most attractive of all the valleys gathering water from the Cheviot, Coquetdale, lies a little further to the south. Here there are still a few areas of ancient woodland on the valley sides as at Holystone, which give way rapidly to the black heather moorlands above where red grouse may rise underfoot on a short walk up from the Visitor Centre to the Fell sandstone tors of *Harbottle Crags*.

The best of the ancient woods of Northumberland are further south on the other side of the South Tyne along the River Allen flowing north from the Pennines. Here, at the NWT reserve of *Briarwood Banks* and the adjacent NT property of Allen Banks, it is possible to gain some idea of the riches of the woods of these northern areas before they were cleared.

Despite these losses, so much remains to be enjoyed that Northumberland must have a very special place for all who want the wilderness to themselves.

Briarwood Banks

Map 87 NY79-62- 29 acres (12 ha)
4 miles south-west of Haydon Bridge via A686 towards Alston; turning right at Langley for Plankey to parking space at Plankey Mill. SSSI. Ancient deciduous woodland, scree.

Access AYR on foot across suspension bridge over River Allen from the parking space at NY795623 onto a good path to the reserve which crosses Kingswood Burn. Once inside please keep to the paths.

Information Notice board near entrance: leaflet from TI Offices and National Park Information Centres.

History Part of Staward Woods SSSI purchased from FC in 1988. Bounded by River Allen on the east and Kingswood Burn on the south. One of the best areas of ancient woodland left in the county with many mosses and liverworts otherwise rare on the east side of the Pennines. Ash and wych elm dominate the canopy though sessile oak and birch are more common on the poorer soils and alder fringes the burn. Other trees include yew, holly, planted beech and some old coppiced hazel.

What to See The rich woodland flora includes wood crane's-bill, sanicle, woodruff, ramsons and the rare wood fescue which grows on scree below sandstone crags. Other noteworthy plants which occur are toothwort, oak fern, bird's-nest orchid and broad-leaved helleborine. Amongst rare birds are wood warbler and pied flycatcher whilst roe deer and red squirrel may be seen. Interesting insects include sprawler moth (on alder) and the pale November moth (on elm).

T. Picnic site at Allen Banks, NT reserve on minor road to Ridley off A69 1 mile east of Bardon Mill.

Craster—Low Newton-by-the-Sea   8

Map 75 NU2-2- 2½ miles of coast.
6 miles north-east of Alnwick on east coast of Northumberland east of Embleton.
Part SSSI. Woodland, scrub, sand dunes, pools.

Access   AYR on foot:

1. from NWT Arnold Reserve at Council CP at Craster at NU255197 reached by following the signs to Dunstanburgh Castle.
2. from the road end at Low Newton-by-the-Sea, parking in CP at the top of the hill at NU240249 and turning right up the lane by the notice on the wall 'Footpath to Embleton Dunes and Bird Hides'. This leads behind the Ship Inn and directly to Newton Pool Reserve hides in 10 minutes. There is a 2½-mile coastal walk from Craster to Newton.

Information   From NWT/NT caravan in CP at Craster with leaflets about Arnold Reserve and coastal walk: open daily Spring BH to September, W/Es only Easter to Spring BH and October. Colourful display boards in CP: other boards at access points to coastal walk.

History   The Arnold Reserve is 3 acres of secondary woodland in disused quarries into the Whin Sill. One of the few pieces of woodland on the coast it is important for breeding birds and autumn migrants. Newton Pool lies behind the north end of Embleton Dunes: it is a reed-fringed freshwater lake covering 22 acres which attracts many birds in summer and winter.

What to See   At Arnold bluebell and primrose are followed by foxglove, wood sage, harebell and lesser periwinkle. Summer birds include blackcap, chiffchaff, sedge and willow warblers whilst autumn migrants have included bluethroat and wryneck: lesser redpoll moult here. At Newton Pool there is a large breeding population, up to 800 pairs, of black-headed gull. Other breeding birds are teal, mute swan, little grebe, sedge warbler and reed bunting whilst winter visitors include goldeneye and pochard. Autumn migration brings ruff, water rail, snipe and redshank when short-eared owl may hunt over the marshy margins. Dune flowers on the walk to the Pool include crosswort, bloody crane's-bill and burnet rose with pyramidal orchid in damper areas.

   T by Information Caravan at Craster.

   Wheelchairs have easy access on wooden track to specially adapted hide overlooking Newton Pool.

Druridge Bay   9

Map 81 NZ2-9- 6 miles of coast.
Coast 20 miles north-north-east of Newcastle, between Newbiggin and Amble.
Mainly SSSI. Mud flats, sand dunes, meadows, marshes, reed-beds, pools.

Access   Roads or footpaths run the length of the coast but four main visitor centres have already been developed (see below) and a fifth, with a reed-bed to attract bearded tit and bittern, is to be created at Chevington at NZ26-99-.

Information

1. Hauxley Visitor Centre at the north end of Bay at NU283023: 1 mile south of Amble turn left to Hauxley and Lower Hauxley. Immediately after Hauxley the road bears left but take the firm track straight on which leads to CP and Visitor Centre.
2. Blakemoor Farm Visitor Centre at the south end of the Bay at NZ283941 2½ miles south of Cresswell on the coast road. Turn left to farm buildings just after sign 'Roads liable to flooding'. Information on birds of Cresswell Pond ½ mile further north with CP at NZ282947.
3. Druridge Pools at NZ272970 which are through a gate at the point where the coast road north from Cresswell turns inland: notice boards near entrance give guidance to hides overlooking deep lakes.
4. Druridge Bay Country Park at NU275005 down a road running east from South Broomhill has a lake attractive for wildfowl and wardens to give advice.

History   Druridge Bay is rapidly becoming one of the most important places for birds in North-East England. Until recently much of it had been extensively worked for opencast coal but, as British Coal have restored the land, NWT has created a fascinating range of habitats which include deep water lakes, shallow pools, reed-beds and gravel islands behind a natural coastline of mud flats, brackish lagoons and sand dunes. It will eventually have the largest reed-bed in the North-East.

What to See   Many sea-birds nest or roost near the vantage points including roseate tern and shelduck whilst the lakes in winter attract large flocks of wigeon, teal, tufted duck, scaup and goldeneye with occasional smew and red-breasted merganser. Autumn migration brings ruff, whimbrel, black-tailed godwit, curlew sandpiper and knot whilst turnstone, oystercatcher, ringed plover, snipe and redshank may be seen at any time. The dunes along the bay have bloody crane's-bill, burnet rose, viper's-bugloss, autumn gentian and purple milk-vetch with marsh helleborine and grass-of-Parnassus in dune slacks.

T[D] at Visitor Centres.

Wheelchairs have good access to hides and view points.

Harbottle Crags   10

Map 81 NT92-04- 388 acres (158 ha)
9 miles west of Rothbury in Coquetdale via B6341 to Flotterton onto minor road to Harbottle village: go ¼ mile through village to FC CP on left immediately after isolated house on left. SSSI. Heather moor, sandstone crags, lake.

Access   AYR on foot from CP at NT925048 onto the footpath from the south-east corner which leads uphill through a wicket gate. The army red flag, if flying near the gate, applies to the military range across a fence on the west side—do not cross it.

Information   Trail guide and full reserve guide from Information Hut in CP:
open Spring BH–September W/Es and BHs 2–5 p.m.: also from NWT.

History   These hills, which are below 1000 ft, were formerly covered in
oak/birch woods but a programme of regular burning has allowed heather to
become the dominant cover of a typical grouse moor. The moors lie on the Fell
sandstone of the Carboniferous period dating from around 280 million years ago.
It has been used as a source of mill stones and remains of circular holes about
5 ft across from which they were cut may be found near the Drake Stone, a glacial
relict which bears gouged striations on its surface cut by passing glaciers.

What to See   Wooded cliffs have climbing corydalis and chickweed
wintergreen beneath birch and rowan. The dry moorland is mainly heather but
there are patches of bog-myrtle, bell heather and bilberry with abundant sheep's
sorrel and tormentil and patches of cowberry, crowberry, broad buckler-fern and
hard fern. Wet flushes elsewhere have bog asphodel, round-leaved sundew and
heath spotted-orchid whilst a small lake, Harbottle Lough, has a narrow fringe
of bottle and white sedges. In addition to red grouse the moors have ring ouzel,
meadow pipit, wheatear, whinchat, curlew, redshank and snipe, and occasional
merlin.

Lindisfarne   ⬛11

Map 75 NU1-4- 8100 acres (3278 ha)
10 miles south-east of Berwick on Tweed on the north Northumberland coast
including Holy Island and adjacent intertidal shores. NNR and Ramsar Site. Mud
flats, salt marsh, sand dunes, sea cliffs.

Access   At low water via a causeway from Beal Sands, where there is a CP
at NU080428, to other CPs on the island, but birds on the intertidal areas can
also be viewed from the mainland at points such as Waren Mill on Budle Bay,
NU149345, or Low Moor Point on Fenham Flats, NU096398.

Information   Display boards at Beal Sands CP which also has tide tables with
advice on when you may pass to the island and for how long. Leaflets may also
be available from dispensers on site or from Information Centre in Main Street,
Holy Island village.

History   Large areas of tidal mud flats lie within a circle of sand dunes broken
by a harbour between Ross Links and Holy Island. This is an internationally
important site for wildfowl, one of the few with pale-bellied Brent geese (over
1000) in winter, which also attracts 200 whooper swan, nearly 50,000 other
wildfowl and 30,000 waders. The sand dunes are calcareous and behind a
seaward fringe of marram and sand couch there are extensive slacks. Low cliffs
cut into Boulder clay and the Whin Sill provide nesting sites for sea-birds.

What to See   The salt marshes have thrift, scurvygrass, sea aster, cord-grass
and glasswort: the damper dunes have marsh helleborine, coralroot orchid, early
marsh- and northern marsh-orchids, as well as the rare dune helleborine,

saltmarsh flat-sedge and curved sedge whilst viper's-bugloss, hound's-tongue and an alien from New Zealand, pirri-pirri-bur are associated with the dune meadows. Duck regularly seen on the flats include mallard, wigeon, teal and shelduck with a few pintail and pochard, whilst off shore are eider, scoter, long-tailed duck, red-breasted merganser and a few goldeneye which may be joined by red-throated diver and Slavonian grebe. Waders are abundant: large numbers of dunlin and knot with some bar-tailed godwit, sanderling, purple sandpiper and spotted redshank. Snow bunting can be common. Fulmar, common, little and arctic terns all breed here.

Northumberland National Park— Ingram Visitor Centre   12

Map 81 NU02-16- 280,000 acres (113,110 ha)
3 miles west of Powburn, off A697 Morpeth to Wooller road up the valley of the River Breamish through Ingram village to Visitor Centre down lane to the east end of church. SSSI—National Park with many SSSIs. Heath, moorland, valley woods.

Access   AYR on foot on numerous well-marked paths, one starting from the Visitor Centre in CP at NU020163.

Information   Leaflets, book of walks, with good maps, from Visitor Centre: open daily Easter–September.

History   The most northerly National Park in England stretching from Hadrian's Wall to the Scottish border. Much was once covered in sessile oakwoods with bracken, heath bedstraw and tormentil beneath. Some areas survived, especially in the valleys, but elsewhere the moors have only scattered open birch and heather. In wet valleys alder dominates with bog-myrtle whilst on Cheviot in the north, which rises to 2676 ft, there are extensive blanket bogs with thousands of acres of cottongrass and *Sphagnum* moss. The base-rich Whin Sill crosses the Park and supports a wide range of lime-loving species.

What to See   In the oak woods chickweed wintergreen and, under heather, lesser twayblade occur whilst wet woods may have grass-of-Parnassus and marsh violet. The Cheviot has bogs with dwarf cornel and cloudberry and streams with alpine willowherb, starry saxifrage and hairy stonecrop. Where there are lime-rich rocks roseroot, alpine saw-wort, globeflower, mossy saxifrage and green spleenwort may be found. The woods shelter redstart and pied flycatcher whilst the uplands have golden plover, dunlin, merlin, curlew and short-eared owl with dipper and grey wagtail in the streams.

T at Visitor Centre and at Balby's Wood with T[D] 1 mile west of Ingram.

Yorkshire

Despite the size of England's largest county it falls conveniently into only four main geological and geographical areas. Three are uplands: to the west are the Pennines consisting mainly of Carboniferous rocks; to the north-east the North Yorkshire Moors dominate the horizon underlain by deposits from the Jurassic period; on the east side, south of the Vale of Pickering, Cretaceous rocks form the rounded hills of the Wolds. The largest area is low-lying and runs through the middle of the county from Doncaster in the south to Thirsk and Northallerton in the north—the Vale of York, which embraces the River Ouse and all its tributaries as they gather water from each of the upland areas and deliver it to the River Humber whose tidal waters penetrate nearly 50 miles inland from the open sea at Spurn Head.

Much of the Pennines consists of outcrops of the acid rocks of the Millstone grit. Under the persistently high rainfall this gives rise to large expanses of monotonous peat-bogs dominated by heather and cottongrass. In contrast, wherever the Great Scar limestone comes to the surface, as in the Craven District in the heart of the Yorkshire Dales National Park, there is a rich assemblage of flora and fauna which give rise to some of the loveliest nature reserves and scenery in Britain. Outstanding amongst these is *Grass Wood* with its intimate mixture of native deciduous woodland, screes and limestone grassland.

Across the Vale the North Yorkshire Moors also provides contrasting scenery— between the acid uplands and the well-wooded valleys, with somewhat richer soils, below. The best place to start exploration is amongst the heather at the top of Sutton Bank only 4 miles east of Thirsk where one can quickly reach the Jurassic rock outcrop at Whitestone Cliff within the *Garbutt Wood* reserve taking in, on the way, the superb view of Gormire Lake at its foot.

Whilst inland the gentler Wolds with their softer, mainly calcareous rocks, have been extensively cultivated there is still a magnificent coastline. The most awe-inspiring cliffs in Yorkshire are those at *Bempton* where, at the northern limit of the chalk in Britain, they fall sheer for 400 ft into the sea below providing one of the best sea-bird nesting sites in the country. Further south, where wind and tide have been constantly eroding and rebuilding, is that extraordinary coastal phenomenon, *Spurn Head*: sometimes a spit, sometimes a series of islands, hardly within human power to control.

In contrast all the wildlife areas in the Vale of York and adjacent valleys have been modified by man if not wholly created by him. The south and west of the county is still part of the industrial heartland of the nation with landscapes dominated by coal tips, cooling towers and tall factory chimneys. But, as reclamation and restoration gather pace, new areas for wildlife arise—and this applies especially to bird reserves. So it is that one of the best places to see birds in Yorkshire, only 2 miles from Ferrybridge Power Station, is *Fairburn Ings*, where mining subsidence has produced a series of pools and marshes beside the River Aire. Further north near Catterick gravel extraction beside the River Swale has left a complex of lakes and scrapes at *Bolton-on-Swale* which is now the largest area of open water in Richmondshire and has quickly achieved SSSI status.

Perhaps the reserve where man's influence is most obtrusive, and yet where wildlife continues to flourish with apparent unconcern, is *Potteric Carr* through which high-speed trains hurtle at 125 mph temporarily obscuring views over lakes full of geese, swans and ducks and where little bittern linger in the summer: one of the many examples of BR providing an NR.

Elsewhere more premeditated creativity also produces reserves. For many years the Yorkshire Wildlife Trust has worked with the Local Health Authority to provide improved facilities at *Moorlands*, a hospital 5 miles north of York. Though planted with introduced conifers, rhododendrons and azaleas the bird-life and the sheer abundance of flowers is a constant attraction for visitors right in the centre of this county of roses.

● Yorkshire Wildlife Trust (YWT), 10 Toft Green, York YO1 1JT. 0904 659570.

Bempton Cliffs   13

Map 101 TA 19-74- Narrow strip for 5 miles of cliff.
At end of Cliff Lane 1 mile north of Bempton turning off B1229 Flamborough-Filey road at White Horse Inn. SSSI. Magnificent chalk cliffs with enormous sea-bird colonies May-mid July.

Access   AYR on foot from CP at the lane end at TA197738 to a path which runs the length of the reserve.

Information   Leaflet from RSPB summer warden or Bampton PO.

History   The highest chalk cliffs in Britain dropping sheer into the North Sea 400 ft below and the most southerly sea-bird cliffs on the east coast. They not only provide a niche for tens of thousands of breeding birds but are a vantage point for watching migrant birds and birds at sea.

What to See   In summer up to 80,000 pairs of kittiwake nest as well as fulmar, herring gull, razorbill and puffin. The 650 pairs of gannet are the largest mainland colony in Britain. Manx shearwater, arctic skua, little gull, common, arctic and sandwich terns are amongst the other species most frequently seen in summer. All three divers occur in winter whilst scoters and scaup are frequent off shore. The landscape away from the edge is full of hedges which hold large numbers of migrants in spring and autumn: redstart, wryneck, ring ouzel and pied flycatcher regularly occur with occasional rarities such as yellow-browed warblers.

Wheelchairs have some access to the cliff top.

Bolton-on-Swale Lake
14

Map 99 SE24-98- 27 acres (11 ha)

½ mile east of Catterick on the east side of the River Swale. Leave A1 at roundabouts north or south of Catterick and drive to crossroads north of Catterick Bridge. Turn east on to B6271 towards Bolton-on-Swale. After 1½ miles turn right into Back Lane at footpath sign 'Coast to Coast' which leads to reserve in ½ mile. SSSI. Wintering wildfowl and waders.

Access   AYR. Good views over lake from Back Lane which has ample parking space. A hide on the west side at SE247985 can be reached on foot on a path which leaves Back Lane at sharp bend at SE244991.

Information   Leaflet from YWT.

History   The reserve sits in an area of Pleistocene gravels deposited by glaciers when they retreated 10–15,000 years ago. The lake resulted from gravel workings and is fed by springs. Much of the surrounding land has been returned to agriculture but in one 6-acre field a herb-rich mixture has been sown for the benefit of butterflies and small mammals.

What to See   Wintering wildfowl include large flocks of mallard, wigeon, pochard and coot with teal, shoveler, tufted duck, goldeneye and shelduck in smaller numbers. A good number of whooper swans and grey-lags are joined by occasional white-fronted and pink-footed geese. Amongst waders golden plover and curlew may be numerous with snipe, lapwing and oystercatcher. The latter also breed as have little ringed plover and common sandpiper. Other breeding species include common tern, sand martin, sedge warbler and reed bunting.

Wheelchairs have good viewing from Back Lane.

Fairburn Ings
15

Map 105 SE45-27- 580 acres (275 ha)

Immediately west of A1 at Fairburn signposted from both north and south carriageways. SSSI and LNR. Bird sanctuary for wildfowl and waders.

Access   AYR. Reserve can be viewed from road which runs along the north side for 2½ miles. There are footpaths leading to hides from CPs at the east end (SE470279) and the west end (SE432276). There is also a hide at the Visitor Centre CP 1 mile west of Fairburn village at SE452278.

Information   Leaflet with map and other publications from RSPB Visitor Centre open W/Es and BHs 10 a.m.–5 p.m.

History   The 'Ings' are wet meadows beside the River Aire which forms the southern boundary. However mining subsidence, especially during the last 50 years, has created a series of shallow pools or flashes providing open water over nearly a third of the reserve throughout the year. In addition there are spoil-heaps planted with a mixture of conifers and broad-leaved trees, and some low-lying, abandoned farmland.

What to See The reserve is on a flyway through the Aire Gap across the Pennines. Over 250 species of birds have been recorded of which around 180 are seen every year and 70 breed or have bred. These latter include mallard, teal, shoveler, gadwall, tufted duck and pochard. In winter up to 100 whooper swan arrive joined by goldeneye and goosander with a few shoveler and scaup. Ruff, spotted redshank, greenshank, dunlin and various sandpipers call in during migration. Redpoll and siskin feed in the trees in winter. Amongst mammals water vole and harvest mice are recorded whilst noctule bats catch midges by the river on summer evenings.

T at Visitor Centre.

Wheelchairs have access to a hide.

Garbutt Wood   16

Map 100 SE50-83- 60 acres (24 ha)
4 miles east of Thirsk on A170 near Visitor Centre at the top of Sutton Bank. SSSI. Ancient woodland, scrub, cliff and scree.

Access AYR on foot from south-west corner of Visitor Centre CP at SE515830 following footpath signs to Cleveland Way.

Information Guide to way-marked nature trail to Garbutt Wood from Visitor Centre open: Easter–31 October 11 a.m.–5 p.m., November–Easter (weather permitting) 11 a.m.–4 p.m.

History The east margin of the reserve is marked by the immense 70 ft Whitestone Cliff made of Jurassic sandstone approximately 150 million years old. This was undercut by glaciers during the last Ice Age and frequent rock falls since have created a boulder field below the cliff. The land then falls steeply 200 ft through woodland to the shores of Lake Gormire (which is private land not in the reserve) which was itself formed by a late glacial landslide.

What to See Boulder-strewn, bracken-covered areas with scrub of birch, hazel and sallow give way above the lake to a mixed oak/birch wood with some sycamore. Lime-rich rocks harbour common rock-rose and bloody crane's-bill whilst more acid sites have bilberry, bluebells, foxgloves and wood sage. Roe, red and fallow deer visit the wood which has its resident foxes, badgers and grey squirrels. Birds include great spotted and green woodpecker whilst coots and great-crested grebe may be seen on the lake below.

T[D]. Refreshments at Visitor Centre.

Wheelchairs have some access.

Grass Wood   17

Map 98 SD98-65- 196 acres (80 ha)
1 mile north-west of Grassington on minor road on the east side of the River Wharfe. SSSI. Ash wood on limestone with crags and grassland.

Access   AYR on foot from CP in quarry on the west side of wood at SD984652.

Information   Booklet from YWT.

History   The reserve is situated on the Carboniferous limestone and includes cliffs, screes and limestone pavement sloping south-west down to the River Wharfe. Formerly managed by the FC and planted with conifers which are now being selectively felled to return it to a mixed deciduous woodland. At Far Gregory, in the middle of the wood, there is a Brigantian fort established against Roman invasion, whilst Park Stile at the south-east corner was an Iron Age settlement.

What to See   The trees and shrubs include whitebeam, bird cherry, privet, burnet rose and guelder-rose. The ground flora contains lily-of-the-valley, bloody crane's-bill, mountain melick and woodruff whilst wild thyme carpets the crags along with rock-rose, limestone bedstraw and common milkwort. Treecreepers, nuthatches, four species of tits, woodcock and woodpeckers live and nest in and among the trees, whilst slow-worms and lizards breed amongst the rocks.

Moorlands   18

Map 97 SE57-58- 17 acres (7 ha)
2 miles north-east of Skelton off A19 north-west of York. Planted wood with fine spring and summer flowers.

Access   AYR on foot from cars parked on verges near entrance gate at SD580589.

Information   Leaflet and guide to nature trail from Information Centre on the west side of the reserve.

History   Possibly a remnant of the former Royal Forest of Galtres which covered a wide area of the Vale of York, but heavily planted as an Estate woodland in the nineteenth century and subsequently with an amazing selection of rhododendrons, azaleas, daffodils and narcissi.

What to See   The display of flowers is best in spring and early summer: other plants of interest occur in and around three ponds and include Royal fern, bog-bean and water-plantain. Foxgloves showing a variety of colours flourish in open woodland which has, as breeding birds, marsh tit, goldcrest, spotted flycatcher, and great spotted woodpecker. Willow warbler and chiffchaff are amongst the summer visitors whilst brambling, redwing and fieldfare come in winter. There is a healthy badger sett in the higher part of the wood and roe deer are occasionally seen.

Potteric Carr   19

Map 111 SE59-00- 350 acres (140 ha)
2 miles south-east of Doncaster. Leave M18 at Junction 3 and follow A6182 north

for 1 mile to first roundabout and take third exit 'No through road' to CP on right after 50 yds. SSSI. Marsh, pools, grassland, reed beds.

Access   AYR on foot from CP at west end of reserve at SE598010: access across railway lines only with permit from J. Frankish (0302 536959). Paths lead to hides overlooking pools.

Information   Visitors Guide from YWT.

History   The reserve is in the centre of Potteric Carr, a shallow, wet basin covered in peat, marl and clay 6–12 ft deep now dissected by a network of railway lines, the first dating from the 1840s and the last from 1910, with the exception of a connection to Rossington Colliery to the south in 1931. The mining here brought about subsidence which extended the area of wetland considerably. The first part of the reserve to be created, now Eller's Loop, was leased from British Rail in 1968.

What to See   The marshes and pools harbour marsh-marigold, marsh stitchwort, water-violet, purple-loosestrife and many sedges with, among grasses, purple small-reed. The grassy railway banks support lime-loving species such as ploughman's spikenard, common centaury and yellow-wort. The bird life is extraordinarily rich with 85 known breeding species including gadwall, teal, shoveler, pochard, water rail, sparrowhawk, snipe, woodcock, long-eared owl, kingfisher and willow tit. Bittern, marsh harrier and black tern are regular visitors. Grass snakes and all three species of newt have been recorded.

Spurn Head   `20`

Map 113 TA40-11- 280 acres (112 ha)
30 miles south-east of Hull following A1033 through Hedon following signs for Withensea as far as Patrington, then B1445 to Easington, Kilnsea and reserve entrance. SSSI. Migratory birds and superb sand dunes.

Access   AYR from road which runs through whole reserve to lighthouse at southern tip. CPs at Information Centre at the north end at TA420147 and at the south end at TA402111.

Information   Leaflet from Information Centre open: July–September daily (not Fridays), October–June W/Es and BHs. Also from Humber Bridge Country Park at the north end of bridge west of Hull and from YWT.

History   Spurn has a continuous history of growth and destruction at the hands of the sea. It was first called Spurn Head in 1564 when it looked much as it does today but in 1608 it was washed away and the build up had to begin again. In the 1840s and 50s it was reduced to a string of islands. After restoration this century it is again under threat.

What to See   The dunes hold a fine display of wild flowers—stork's-bill, restharrow, yellow-wort, sea bindweed, sea holly and sea rocket amongst them. Two 'aliens' have recently spread rapidly—sea buckthorn and springbeauty, whilst two other species reach their northern limit here: suffocated clover and curved hard-grass. Migratory birds vary from year to year. Three species of tern pass through in considerable numbers; wheatear, whinchat and flycatchers usually occur in August and September. Waders like dunlin, knot, turnstone and curlew may be seen on the shore from July–April. Brent geese and shelduck winter here but little tern no longer nest due to public pressure.

W A L E S

SOUTH WALES

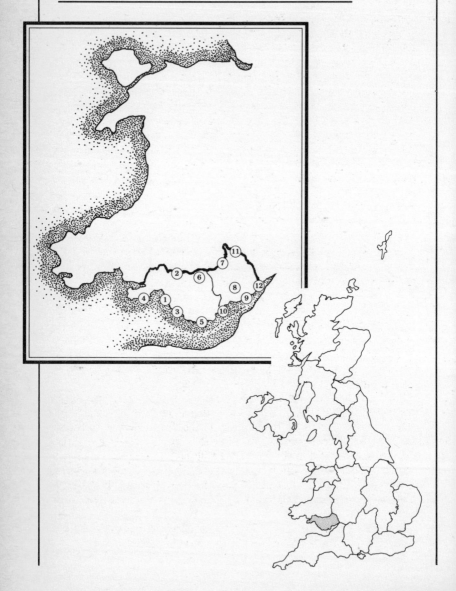

Glamorgan

There are few parts of Britain where industry and wilderness, people and wildlife, are so closely intermingled as in Glamorgan. Though to the casual visitor the valleys seem to be filled with traffic flowing beside frequently polluted rivers, only a short, stiff, climb up a rushing tributary stream to the brim opens up a vista of mountains and moorland which rise to over 2000 ft and include parts of the Brecon Beacons National Park to the north.

This northern half of the county belongs to the uplands of central Wales: the southern half provides a complete contrast, with the fertile and pastoral Vale of Glamorgan between Cardiff and Port Talbot to the east, and the prominent rugged cliffs of the Gower to the west of Swansea.

For both man and wildlife the Carboniferous has been the most important period geologically: its Coal Measures fuelled the industrialization but its mixture of acid and basic, hard and soft rocks, has provided a rich variety of habitats for plants and animals. Nowhere is this better demonstrated than in the valley woods where the fast running streams and rivers have cut their way through the strata. The alternation of hard Millstone Grit and soft shales has produced some spectacular waterfalls surrounded by mosses, liverworts and ferns which flourish in the damp atmosphere created by their spray. Beauty and botany go hand in hand at *Melincourt,* just one of the many falls which line the side of the U-shaped Vale of Neath.

Near Merthyr Tydfil, on the River Taff and its tributaries, it is the alternation of limestone and gritstone which provides the conditions for so many different species and explains why *Taf Fechan* should be one of the best sites for mosses and liverworts in the county.

The Carboniferous limestone forms a ring around the Coal Measures and outcrops again as a ridge which runs across the south of the county from Cardiff to Porthcawl. In the east much is beech-covered with lime-loving shrubs and frequent orchids; in the west, where exposed to the full force of the wind funnelling up the Bristol Channel, the hills are bare and there are areas with fine limestone heaths such as *Ogmore Down,* though even here, in sheltered valleys, pockets of woodland like Coed-y-Bwl support a rich flora.

But it is in the incomparable cliffs and headlands of the Gower Peninsula that the Carboniferous limestone is most majestic and exciting: stretching in an almost unbroken line from the Mumbles to the Worms Head it harbours a tantalizing list of rare flowers such as yellow whitlowgrass, spiked speedwell and goldilocks aster as well as sites for nesting guillemot, razorbill and puffin: with sand dunes, salt marshes, freshwater marshes and sandstone ridges in addition Gower demonstrates almost all the wildlife habitats of the county—and they come together in a remarkable way in *Oxwich Bay* at the very centre of the south coast.

However Gower does not have the monopoly of limestone cliffs in Glamorgan—the Vale is dominated by younger, Jurassic, rocks and from Ogmore to Barry are some of the finest, but least known, cliffs in the kingdom. At their east end they can be enjoyed within the surprising peace of *Porthkerry* Country Park, only a mile from the pleasure domes of Barry, whilst the western stretch from Aberthaw to the dunes of Merthyr Mawr is protected as a Heritage Coast.

Merthyr Mawr is but one example of the enormous sand dunes which the wind and the sea have thrust into the mouth of Swansea bay: enriched by constant supplements of shell sand they provide another range of habitats, wet and dry, fresh and salt, which make the Glamorgan coast so attractive despite the intrusions of power stations, steelworks, oil refineries and seaside towns: nowhere demonstrates the variety or the alternative better than *Kenfig Pool and Dunes* sandwiched between Margam steelworks and Porthcawl.

Perhaps it is the proximity of so many people to places of such delight and importance which has stimulated a response but Glamorgan is better served than most other counties in the facilities provided for the visiting naturalist. Along the coast from west to east are the Reserve Centre at Oxwich, the Kenfig Visitor Centre, the Heritage Coast Centre at Dunraven Park and Porthkerry Country Park, but inland, and most central of all, at the junction of the Vale and the Valleys and only 3 miles north-west of Bridgend, is the Nature Centre of the Glamorgan Wildlife Trust, a starting point for the discovery of all the wonders of this county's wildlife.

- Glamorgan Wildlife Trust (GWT), Nature Centre, Fountain Road, Tondu, Mid Glamorgan CF32 0EH. 0656 724100.

Kenfig Pool and Dunes   ■

Map 170 SS79-81- 1270 acres (515 ha)
5½ miles west of Bridgend between Port Talbot and Porthcawl. Leave A48 at Pyle roundabout taking minor road south-west over railway bridge and through Maudlam village following signs for Kenfig. NNR. Sand dunes, dune slacks, pool, marsh, reed-bed, woodland.

Access   AYR on foot from CP at Reserve Centre at SS800812 on to a footpath to the sea and back, with a hide at the south-west corner of the pool, giving a 3-mile walk.

Information   Booklet and many well-produced leaflets covering all aspects of the natural history from the Visitor Centre in CP; open daily Mon– Fri 8.30 a.m.– 4.30 p.m., W/Es and BHs 2–5 p.m. The Centre also has exhibits and displays about the reserve: there are frequent guided walks.

History   Formerly the property of the aldermen and burgesses of the medieval Borough of Kenfig who had rights of grazing, wildfowling and fishing, it was transferred to Trustees in 1972 and is now managed to protect its exceptional wildlife. The magnificent dunes are made of lime-rich sand and rise to over 50 ft: they are mobile and constantly changing on the seaward side. Inland are stable dunes with extensive, low-lying, wet slacks between them. The 70-acre Kenfig Pool is a freshwater habitat, fed by springs, of great value for birds, amphibians, fish and invertebrates.

What to See   Over 500 flowering plants have been recorded including, on the sea-shore, sea rocket, sea-holly, sea spurge and sea bindweed whilst inland the grassland is coloured by evening-primrose, viper's-bugloss, kidney vetch, restharrow, wild pansy and wild thyme. The slacks have amazing displays of green-winged orchid, marsh-orchids, marsh helleborine and round-leaved wintergreen and the pool contains four species of pondweed and quillwort. Grasshopper, reed and sedge warblers breed round the pool which attracts garganey, teal, mallard, gadwall, shoveler, tufted duck, Bewick's and whooper swans in winter. Birds on passage include curlew, greenshank, redshank, sanderling and whimbrel. Grass snake and common lizard may be seen.

Wheelchairs have some access.

Melincourt

Map 170 SN82-01- 13 acres (5 ha)
5 miles north-east of Neath on B4434 on the south side of the Vale of Neath. SSSI. Waterfall, river gorge, mixed woodland.

Access   AYR on foot from CP at SN822020 on the opposite side of B4434 on to a ¼ mile walk up a gentle path to the waterfall.

Information   Notice board at entrance: reserve leaflet and other details from TI Office in Aberdulais.

History   A most spectacular waterfall which not only inspired Turner to sketch it in 1795 but also the poet, W. Sotherby who in 1793, in 'Melincourt', contrasted the picturesque calm then with the 'sulphurous blasts that dim the noon day sun' which had prevailed at the beginning of the eighteenth century when an ironworks and furnace filled the north rim of the gorge. The scars have now healed and the path leads through a damp oak, ash, birch wood with some alder, beech and small-leaved lime with an understorey of hazel, holly and rowan.

What to See   The damp atmosphere supports 20 species of ferns including Wilson's filmy-fern and a long list of mosses with opposite-leaved golden-saxifrage and enchanter's-nightshade in flushes. The wood is full of bird song: redstart, wood warbler and pied flycatcher nest here whilst dipper and grey wagtail work the Melincourt Brook.

Ogmore Down

Map 170 SS89-76- 65 acres (26 ha)
2½ miles south of Bridgend on B4265 to St Bride's Major. SSSI. Limestone grassland, heath, scrub.

Access   AYR on foot from CP on the west of B4265 just north of quarry at SS896760.

Information   Nothing on site: leaflet with map from GWT.

History   The reserve lies between two quarries cutting into the Carboniferous limestone and includes a plateau and steep south-east facing slopes.The thinner soils of these steep slopes carry a limestone heath which is an intricate mixture of lime-loving and lime-hating plants: the deeper, more acid, soils of the plateau carry gorse and heather. It is one of the largest remaining areas of this kind of vegetation in Western Britain.

What to See   Unusual wild plants include mountain everlasting (rare in Southern Britain), horseshoe vetch and the rare, soft-leaved sedge as well as common rock-rose, common centaury, wild thyme, small scabious, hairy violet and autumn lady's-tresses. Birds nesting amongst the scrub and rough grassland are skylark, stonechat and yellowhammer: kestrel are frequently seen. A special feature of the reserve on summer evenings is the pale light of glow-worms.

Oxwich
4

Map 159 SS50-86- 714 acres (289 ha)
South side of Gower Peninsula at the west end of Oxwich Bay via A4118 and minor road to CP on sands near Oxwich village. NNR. Sand dunes, dune slacks, salt marsh, freshwater marsh, woods.

Access   AYR on foot from CP at Reserve Centre at SO501865 on a series of walks through the major habitats including boardwalks and an observation tower.

Information   Leaflets and numerous guides to trails and different groups of plants and animals from Reserve Centre: there are exhibits and displays and guided walks in summer.

History   Oxwich Bay formerly extended back to the bottom of the hill by which the road descends to the dunes but, about 500 BC, the tide and waves formed a barrier of dunes across the bay behind which a lagoon that had formed was gradually filled with wind-blown sand. This is now an area of marsh with pools, the remains of fish ponds dug in the early nineteenth century.

What to See   The calcium-rich dunes harbour sea bindweed, evening-primrose, yellow-wort, common centaury and the rare dune gentian. In damp dune slacks are marsh helleborine, early and southern marsh-orchids. The paths through Oxwich and Crawley Woods pass beneath a high forest of oak and ash with an understorey of hazel and holly over bluebell, ramsons and hart's-tongue. The woodland birds include blackcap, chiffchaff, spotted flycatcher, willow warbler, goldcrest, nuthatch, tree pipit, redpoll, redstart, redwing, siskin, treecreeper and all three types of woodpeckers, with buzzard, tawny owl and sparrowhawk hunting for prey. Oystercatcher and redshank are common along the shoreline. Reptiles such as grass snake, adder and slow worm may be seen. The list of nearly 30 resident butterflies includes dingy skipper, purple and white-letter hairstreaks, brown argus, small pearl-bordered, silver-washed and dark green fritillaries, speckled wood and grayling.

T[D] at Reserve Centre.
Wheelchairs have some access.

Porthkerry
5

Map 170 ST09-67- 250 acres (91 ha)
1 mile to the west of Barry via A4226 from A48 to Waycock Cross roundabout, straight across down Pontypridd Road to second roundabout in ½ mile, turn right into Park Crescent and right again into Park Road which leads to the park entrance. Part SSSI, LNR, Country Park. Woods, grassland, cliff, shingle, stream, pond.

Access   AYR on foot from CP at east and west ends at ST095673 and 085669 from which numerous nature trails lead through woods and onto the shore.

Information   Leaflets and maps from Golf Hut by CP at west end or from Warden at Nightingale Cottage near the railway bridge: open daily.

History   Only Cliff Wood, east of the beach, is strictly a nature reserve but the park as a whole has a wide range of other habitats including a long shingle beach, high limestone cliffs, a stream which once powered a saw-mill and a pond. Cliff Wood is on Jurassic limestone and is dominated by oak and ash with an understorey of hawthorn, hazel, field maple and yew which has been managed as coppice-with-standards.

What to See   The ground flora of the wood has such interesting plants as purple gromwell, traveller's-joy and wood anemone whilst wild madder and maidenhair fern grow on the cliffs, the latter first discovered here by Edward Llwyd in 1698: sea beet and bulbous foxtail occur on the shore. Woodland birds include green woodpecker, chiffchaff and willow warbler whilst oystercatcher work the shore for shellfish.

T[D]. Refreshments by the west CP.

Wheelchairs have good access to coast and in vicinity of CPs.

Taf Fechan
6

Map 160 SO04-09- 102 acres (41 ha)
2 miles north of Merthyr Tydfil on minor road to east from junction of A470 and A465 at Cefn-coed-y-cymmer which follows the north bank of Taf Fechan for 1 mile to bridge at Pont Sarn: cross bridge and park up lane to left near public house. SSSI, Country Park. Mixed deciduous woodland, stream, springs and flushes, limestone grassland.

Access   AYR on foot from car parking space at SO045097 over a stile near the Blue Pool on to a 3-mile way-marked trail following route of old tramway.

Information   Notice boards on the reserve: leaflet with map from GWT.

History   A river valley with steep sides cutting through the Carboniferous limestone and Millstone grit carrying a mixture of acid and basic grassland, scrub and ancient broad-leaved woodland. One of the richest sites for mosses and liverworts in Glamorgan with over 120 species recorded. The main trees are oak, ash and sycamore with some small-leaved lime, beech and bird cherry with an understorey of field maple, guelder-rose and dogwood and alder beside the stream.

What to See   The river edge carries monkeyflower, marsh-marigold, greater tussock-sedge, water avens and hemlock water-dropwort whilst primrose, betony, wood anemone and goldenrod occur on better drained slopes. Here and there wild columbine may be seen and it is one of the few localities in the county for the limestone fern. Woodland birds include chiffchaff, willow warbler, redstart, long-tailed tit, great spotted woodpecker and buzzard: dipper nest along the stream. Amongst less common butterflies are silver-washed fritillary, ringlet and painted lady.

Gwent

The smallest of the present-day Welsh counties, Gwent, or the old county of Monmouthshire, has as wide a range of habitats as almost any other county in Wales, lacking only the more dramatic sea cliffs and sand dunes.

Much of the north-west is mountainous and falls within the Brecon Beacons National Park: the highest points include the unmistakable Sugarloaf, above Abergavenny, and the Black Mountains on either side of the mysterious Llanthony Valley. Here the Devonian rocks of Old Red sandstone, which give a characteristic red colour to the soil where it is cultivated in the valleys, also shape the free-draining and sheep-grazed grasslands on the hills. On the steep valley sides, if the sheep can be excluded, small woods survive as examples of the natural vegetation before the forest clearance: such an area, *Strawberry Cottage Wood*, stands near the mouth of the Llanthony Valley, its wildlife enriched by the nearness of the Afon Honddu sweeping past on its way to join the Usk.

These valley woods are even richer where the torrent has cut through a series of strata exposing both acid and basic rocks: this has happened at *Cwm Clydach* where a layered cake of Millstone grit, Carboniferous limestone and Old Red sandstone supports a diverse array of woodland types in a small space: it is also one of the most westerly native sites for beech in Britain.

The deep cutting by rivers is at its most extreme in the wondrous valley of the Wye—in the series of incised meanders through which it worms its way along the eastern border between Monmouth and Chepstow. The 700 ft drop from the heights of *Wyndcliff* to the tidal Wye below more than compensates for the absence of cliffs along the shore. The extensive ancient woodlands on the steep slopes contain a remarkable number of plants, especially on the limestone, where there are several rare species of whitebeam as well as wild service-tree and small- and large-leaved lime.

The other great river of Gwent is the Usk which, like the Wye, is swift and clear, excellent for salmon and trout and most attractive to dipper, kingfisher and grey wagtail. Usk and Wye join the Severn Estuary 15 miles apart and behind its shore, between them, is a narrow strip of land, wider in the west, known as the Gwent Levels, mainly less than 25 ft above sea-level and protected from the threat of flooding by sea walls, perhaps since Roman times. Wet fields are separated by deep ditches or reens and represent some of the finest fenland anywhere in Wales: *Magor Marsh* reserve is a splendid example both for its vegetation and for the insects and birds which it shelters within a mile of the sea.

The Severn Estuary itself is an amazing refuge with its dramatic, twice-daily changes in water-level giving food and space which attracts the greatest variety of ducks on the Estuary to this northern shore—particularly to the east of the Usk mouth: it is here at *Peterstone Wentlooge*, especially in Peterstone Pill, that some of the best bird-watching in the county can be enjoyed.

Elsewhere in Gwent areas for large numbers of waterfowl to congregate are few: the west is covered by the steep valleys and rounded hills of the former coalfields and has only occasional barren pools. However, in the lowlands between the Usk and the Wye there are two significant areas—the flood plain of the Usk itself and the relatively recent *Llandegfedd Reservoir* which has become the best stretch of freshwater for birds in the county. That this and other wildlife refuges exist in such close proximity to the great industrial centres of Cardiff, Newport and the Valleys gives them an added importance.

● Gwent Wildlife Trust (GWT), 16 White Swan Court, Church Street, Monmouth NP5 3NY. 0600 5501.

Cwm Clydach   **7**

Map 161 SO21-12- 58 acres (23 ha)
1 mile east of Brynmawr on the south side of A465 at Blackrock. NNR. Mixed deciduous woodland.

Access　　AYR on foot from Clydach Gorge CP at SO215124 through Dan y Coed housing estate or from minor road to Daren Felen. Please keep to the path.

Information　　Leaflet on Clydach Gorge from TI Office in Abergavenny or Merthyr Tydfil: leaflet on Cwm Clydach from NCC.

History　　At the south edge of the Brecon Beacons National Park the River Clydach, tributary of the River Usk, cuts through the northern rim of the South Wales coalfield forming a gorge 2 miles long exposing quartz conglomerates of Old Red sandstone and Carboniferous limestone. The north facing slopes are covered by a wood of beech which is here near the western limit of its distribution in Britain. On well-drained, shallower soils oak and birch are also present in the canopy with an understorey of rowan, hazel, hawthorn and willow. The wood was used to provide charcoal for the furnaces of local ironworks in the eighteenth and nineteenth centuries.

What to See　　Bracken, bilberry, wood-sorrel and hard fern are frequent on the more acid soils with ramsons, shield-ferns, hart's-tongue, wild thyme, early and common dog-violet, yellow bird's-nest, bird's-nest orchid and soft-leaved sedge in the more base-rich areas. Amongst 20 species of breeding birds are green and great spotted woodpecker, nuthatch, treecreeper, and various warblers and tits. Predators include sparrowhawk, kestrel and tawny owl and there are dipper and grey wagtail along the river.

Llandegfedd Reservoir

8

Map 171 ST33-99- 570 acres (230 ha)
2 miles south-east of Pontypool, via A4042 to Newport turning onto minor road at New Inn to CP at south end of reservoir. SSSI. Open water, woodland.

Access   AYR on foot from CP at ST329985 onto a complex of walks round the reservoir which are up to 5 miles long including a hide on the north shore.

Information   Notice boards at entrance: leaflet from Gwent County Council.

History   Since its creation in 1963 the reservoir has become one of the most important sites for wintering wildfowl in South Wales. Apart from a small area in the south-east corner no recreation is allowed from November to February. The shallowest and best part is the north end near the hide, but the south end is often used for roosting.

What to See   Winter waterfowl include large numbers of mallard, pochard and wigeon with smaller numbers of teal and tufted duck as well as great crested grebe, goldeneye, goosander, mute, whooper and Bewick's swans. Terns may be seen on migration.

T. Refreshments in CP.
Wheelchairs have some access to paths.

Magor Marsh

9

Map 171 ST42-86- 60 acres (24 ha)
Immediately south of Magor village on B4245: follow signs for Redwick over railway bridge, turn left at T-junction to reserve entrance 200 yds on right. SSSI. Fen, meadows, ditches, pond, reed-bed, willow carr.

Access   AYR on foot from parking space at ST425869 onto network of often wet paths including a hide at the south-west corner of the pond. It is normally very wet—wellingtons essential.

Information   Nothing on site: trail leaflet from GWT.

History   This reserve is a remnant of the fenland area which formerly occupied the low-lying ground along the Severn estuary and was used for hay and pasture. The fields are drained by a series of ditches or reens. The drier fields are still grazed and others cut for hay. Other habitats include reed and sedge beds, scrub and wet woodland. The reserve is very attractive to breeding wetland birds.

What to See   Plants of particular interest in the reens are frogbit, arrowhead, flowering-rush, lesser water-plantain, lesser water-parsnip, water dock and greater duckweed whilst, in the meadows and fens, are ragged-Robin, bog stitchwort, marsh willowherb, tubular water-dropwort, creeping forget-me-not, marsh valerian, cyperus sedge, mare's-tail and lesser spearwort. Breeding birds include reed, sedge and grasshopper warblers, water rail, reed bunting, redshank, snipe and yellow wagtail though mink have reduced the success of many water birds. A good list of dragonflies includes the ruddy darter, otherwise very rare in Wales.

T. Refreshments at Public House in Magor village.
Wheelchairs have limited access at entrance.

Peterstone Wentlooge   `10`

Map 171 ST26-79- 2½ mile length of coastline
3 miles east of Rumney on the south side of B4239 to St Bride's Wentlooge. SSSI.
Mud flats, salt marsh.

Access   AYR on foot down public footpaths to sea wall from:

1. car parking space on road at Marshfield turn off B4239 at ST273810 which
   leads direct to Peterstone Gout.
2. Six Bells Public House CP in Peterstone at ST269801 (ask permission of
   landlord) following sign 'Footpath, Sea Wall' beside the church then walk east
   along sea wall to Peterstone Gout.

Information   Nothing on site.

History   The most important bird reserve in Gwent with over 170 species of
bird recorded. The salt marshes and mud flats attract large numbers of
waterfowl. The best area is Peterstone Gout north-east of the village where
Peterstone Pill, a large ditch or reen, discharges water into a rectangular basin
which empties through a sluice into the sea: it is only full at high tide and its
muddy shores and the saltings between the pill and the sea are particularly
important.

What to See   Duck present throughout the year include mallard, wigeon,
scaup, pintail, garganey, gadwall, long-tailed duck, common scoter and shoveller
whilst shelduck breed along the shore. Redshank and yellow wagtail also breed
here whilst 4000 dunlin regularly feed on the mud where such rarities as wood
sandpiper, little ringed plover, avocet, ruff and little stint are sometimes seen.
In winter merlin, peregrine and short-eared owl may appear and snow bunting
are occasionally recorded. Maritime plants such as sea-blite, sea aster, sea
plantain and greater sea-spurrey are abundant on the seaward side of the wall.

T. Refreshments at the Six Bells.
Wheelchairs have access to the sea wall for good viewing.

Strawberry Cottage Wood   `11`

Map 161 SO31-21- 16 acres (6 ha)
4 miles north of Abergavenny on road up Llanthony Valley from Llanvihangel
Crucorney over River Honddu from Stanton. SSSI. Mixed ash/oak wood.

Access   AYR on foot from the parking space in lay-by 100 yds up the road to
the Forest Coal Pit from Stanton at SO311212, walking back to the footbridge
across the river then across a field towards a cottage: pass through the gate and
turn left onto a path which climbs up through wood.

Information   Nothing on site: leaflet and map from GWT.

History   The wood covers a west facing Old Red sandstone bluff on the eastern edge of the Brecon Beacons National Park. Dominant trees are sessile and pedunculate oaks and ash with smaller numbers of aspen, yew and birch, a single small-leaved lime and much dead wych elm: shrubs include holly, hazel, rowan and field maple. A small area near the entrance is being coppiced: some of the oaks are very fine.

What to See   The ground flora is not rich because of former grazing pressure but does include nettle-leaved bellflower and southern woodrush. The wood supports many species of birds: pied flycatcher, redstart, wood warbler, great spotted woodpecker, tawny owl and buzzard amongst them.

Wyndcliff Nature Trail   12

Map 162 ST52-97- 200 acres (80 ha)
2 miles north of Chepstow on A466 turning north on a bend on to minor road ½ mile after passing through St Arvans and climbing steep hill to CP at top. FNR, AONB. Ancient woodland.

Access   AYR on foot from CP at ST523972 on to a circular nature trail of ¾ mile which includes the Eagle's Nest with superb views over the Cotswolds and the Mendips.

Information   Leaflet from TI Offices in Tintern or Chepstow.

History   Ancient woodland on limestone with a mixture of high forest and coppice-with-standards. The main trees are oak, ash, beech, wild cherry and wych elm, the latter mostly dead. The shrub layer includes traveller's-joy, spindle and several rare species of whitebeam. Nearly 700 ft below, the tidal Wye meanders in a great entrenched loop round the Lancaut peninsula on the English side.

What to See   These limestone woods have a rich ground flora with rare and local plants such as wild madder, spurge-laurel, herb-Paris, wood spurge, upright spurge, common wintergreen, bird's-nest, mountain melick with fingered and soft-leaved sedges. Birds include five species of tits, goldcrest, nuthatch, treecreeper and heron whilst buzzard may be seen overhead and cormorant fishing in the river below. Butterflies of note are speckled wood, holly blue and silver-washed fritillary.
   T[D] in Tintern.

WEST WALES

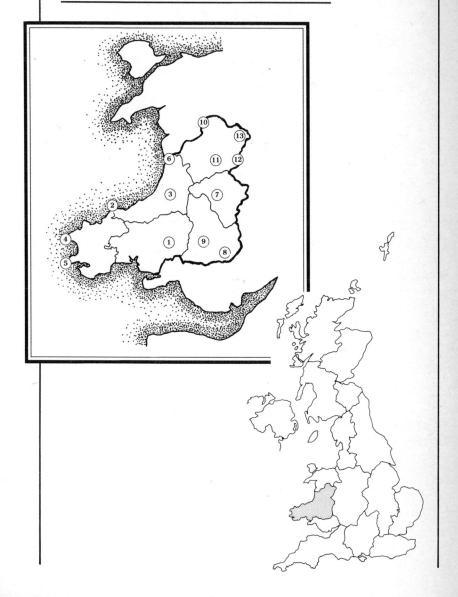

Dyfed

Dyfed, combining the three former counties of Cardiganshire, Carmarthen and Pembrokeshire, is the largest Welsh county and third, after Yorkshire and Devon, in England and Wales. It occupies the whole of the country west of a line from Machynlleth in the north to Llanelli in the south. It is an old landscape with no rocks younger than the Carboniferous and some of the oldest in the world, the pre-Cambrian, forming the rocks on which the tiny cathedral city of St David's has stood firm through the centuries.

There are no other cities, few large towns and only two industrial areas, one old and one new, and both based on fuel. The old is around Llanelli at the western end of the South Wales coalfield, the new around Milford Haven, that finest of natural harbours, now a haven for oil tankers, terminals, refineries and an oil-fired power station.

Though these two areas intrude upon the coast, elsewhere it is one of the major glories of the county embracing every kind of scenery. The coastline is so precious that 168 miles are given special protection within the Pembrokeshire Coast National Park. The coastal footpath starts near Cardigan and one gets a taste of the infinite variety of its scenery whilst walking through the *Cemaes Head* reserve of the Dyfed Wildlife Trust—wildflowers underfoot, sea birds, chough and peregrine in the air and grey seals bobbing like buoys in the ocean below.

Further along the coast, around the St David's and Marloes peninsulas, there is the added attraction of the islands out to sea: Skokholm, distant Grassholm, Ramsey and *Skomer*; collectively forming one of the most important sea-bird refuges in Europe. Nearest, largest and most easily visited is *Skomer* which is not only a bird island, with endearing puffins on sentry duty watching you arrive at the gangway, but also a microcosm of all the lowland coastal habitats.

Near St David's, only a short distance inland from the path and filling the centre of the peninsula, are a series of wet, acidic commons, including *Dowrog Common*, which hold wonderful examples of oceanic vegetation, with a group of plants confined to this western fringe of Europe such as yellow centaury, wavy St John's-wort and pale dog-violet.

Away from the coast Dyfed is still a rural county with upland areas reaching 2468 ft on Plynlimon in the north-east—source of the Severn and the Wye. But there have been changes—once extensive heather moors have largely disappeared under reclamation schemes and conifers and it is only through the most intensive efforts of keen naturalists for over 80 years that Dyfed can still claim to be the land of that majestic bird, the red kite. Though there may be only 70 pairs they range widely in search of carrion and there is a good chance of seeing them especially when visiting that magnificent raised bog of *Cors Caron* in the Teifi valley just north of Tregaron. There are few examples of raised bogs in Britain which are so intact and it is undoubtedly a site of world importance. Yet such places are, by their very nature, so fragile that they can only be viewed from raised boardwalks. A similar area with similar constraints, Cors Fochno or Borth Bog, lies on the south side of the Dyfi estuary which, together with the nearby sand dunes of Ynyslas and the woods in the valleys at *Ynys-hir*, form a natural area of beauty and variety unparalleled in Wales.

Most of the broad-leaved woods which remain in Dyfed are on steep valley slopes as at Ynys-hir. They often harbour species like small-leaved lime and wild service-tree, which are indicators of ancient woodland. There are fine examples above the broad valley of the Afon Teifi near Llandeilo where the *Castle Woods* overlook flood meadows and contribute to another unspoilt, and historic, landscape including a deer park and the romantic ruins of Dynefwr Castle, once the stronghold of the ruling Princes of South Wales.

● Dyfed Wildlife Trust (DWT), 7 Market Street, Haverfordwest SA61 1NF. 0437 5462.

Castle Woods

Map 159 SN62-22- 70 acres (28 ha)
¼ mile west of Llandeilo between A40 and River Tywi. SSSI. Ancient woodland, quarry, clearings.

Access   AYR on foot from CP on A40 at north end of Llandeilo on south side of fire station at SN626225 to entrance across road 80 yds towards town through iron gates of Penlan Park: keep right of bandstand on hill then follow badger footprint signs to old church.

Information   Leaflet from Information Centre in Llandyfeisant Church in hollow at end of first stretch of woodland at SN621221: open W/Es and BHs Easter–September; occasional guided walks during this period. There is a summer warden to help visitors.

History   The woods are adjacent to Dynefwr Deer Park, a fine example of old parkland with open woodland and small copses containing a herd of fallow and a few red deer. The castle consists of an impressive circular keep of a type rare in Wales well preserved by the Dinefwr family during the eighteenth and nineteenth centuries. It is now being renovated and will then be open to the public on a regular basis.

What to See   The woods, mainly on the steep south facing limestone slopes, have large sections which are ancient primary woodland otherwise rare in this part of Wales, with ash, wych elm, oak, beech, wild cherry, spindle, hazel and holly over a rich ground flora including early dog-violet and toothwort. Lichens are noteworthy especially on old parkland trees. There are active badger setts, foxes are frequent and otters inhabit the River Tywi below. There is a long list of woodland birds: all three woodpeckers, many tits, nuthatch and treecreeper. Buzzard, sparrowhawk and raven are often seen whilst the wet meadows by the Tywi attract wildfowl in winter including, occasionally, a flock of Siberian white-fronted geese.

Cemaes Head

■2

Map 145 SN13-50- 40 acres (16 ha)

4 miles north-west of Cardigan via B4546 through St Dogmael's to Poppit Sands and then via minor 'No Through Road' for 1¼ miles to CP. Sea cliffs, maritime grassland, geological formations.

Access   AYR on foot from CP at SN136494 along the way-marked Pembrokeshire Coast Path which passes through the reserve. There is no access off the path without a permit from DWT.

Information   Leaflets about this and other sections of the path from all TI Offices, nearest Cardigan and Newport, and NT shops etc.

History   Cemaes Head is at the northern end of the Pembrokeshire Coast Path which starts at St Dogmael's and continues for 168 miles to Amroth which is to the east of Tenby. The whole path is one of the most beautiful walks in Britain, especially in late spring when the drifts of yellow, blue, white and pink make it one of the wild flower wonders of the world. The path is a magnificent viewing platform for birds of sea and cliff and also makes its way through woods and thickets which give shelter to smaller birds: in all over 150 different birds have been seen on, or from, the path. The cliffs also present a series of geological exposures in which the earth's history, from the pre-Cambrian to the Carboniferous, can be examined.

What to See   At Cemaes wild flowers which contribute to the spring display include thrift, spring squill, heather and bell heather whilst western gorse is a feature of the autumn. Chough breed on the cliffs with fulmar and shag whilst peregrine, raven, kestrel, wheatear and stonechat will be seen in the air: in the sea below grey seals are frequent with porpoises and dolphins off shore.

Cors Caron

■3

Map 147 SN68-63- 1956 acres (792 ha)

2 miles north of Tregaron on the west side of B4343. NNR. Raised bog.

Access   AYR from CP on B4343 at SN693630 onto a 1 mile walk along an old railway track crossing part of the bog and finishing at an observation tower.

Information   Leaflets and guides from dispenser 50 yds up track from CP.

History   A classical raised bog which has developed in the valley of the River Teifi since the last glaciation through a series beginning with a shallow lake and passing via a flood-plain marsh to this acid peat-bog. The centre of the bog is both the highest and the wettest of bogs with a mosaic of humps of heather and hollows of *Sphagnum* moss.

What to See   Where the trail crosses the bog a boardwalk gives access to a point from which the active wet area of the bog can be seen with plants such as cottongrass, beak-sedge, bogbean, marsh willowherb, marsh cinquefoil and sundews: pools contain *Sphagnum* and broad-leaved pondweed. From the tower wildfowl and waders may be seen including breeding teal: in winter whooper swan are regular visitors. Red kite and buzzard are frequently seen over the reserve: watch out for adders on the path on sunny days.

Wheelchairs have access along track once lifted up from CP.

Dowrog Common

Map 157 SM77-26- 200 acres (81 ha)
1½ miles north-east of St David's on the north side of A487 to Fishguard. SSSI. Lowland heath, wetland, pools.

Access   AYR on foot from CP at the north end at SM772274 which can be reached on a made-up road from both A487 and from a minor road to the north.

Information   Nothing on site: leaflet from DWT.

History   The most important of the 32 St David's commons which provide a wide range of acid heath and wetland habitats around the city. Formerly owned by the University of Wales but now owned by the NT and leased to DWT. Management includes grazing by cattle in summer and horses in winter with controlled burning of small plots to maintain diverse areas of heath.

What to See   350 species of wild flowers include such rare plants of western heath as yellow centaury, pale dog-violet, wavy St John's-wort and pale butterwort whilst the pools contain three-lobed crowfoot, pillwort, floating water-plantain and lesser bladderwort. These pools attract 14 species of dragonfly including small red damselfly, rare elsewhere in Dyfed. Rare butterflies occur, notably green hairstreak and marsh fritillary. Buzzard, kestrel, sparrowhawk and water rail breed on the reserve whilst whooper and Bewick's swans, hen harrier, merlin and several species of duck are winter visitors.

Wheelchairs have good access on minor road crossing the reserve.

Skomer Island

5

Map 157 SM72-09- 721 acres (292 ha)
2 miles off the coast on the south side of St Bride's Bay. NNR. Sea-bird cliffs, heath grassland, marshes.

Access   By boat from Martin's Haven, a small beach on the north side of the Marloes peninsula at SM761091, March–September daily (not Mon except BHs) weather permitting. A landing fee is payable on arrival. There is a 4 mile path round the island.

Information   Booklets at Information Centre, Lockley Lodge, Martin's Haven, open March–September or from DWT. There is a small Information Centre in old farm buildings in the middle of the island.

History   Inhabited from Bronze and Iron Age times Skomer was farmed until 1949. It was bought by NCC in 1959 with help from DWT. Rabbits were first recorded on Skomer in 1325 and may have been introduced even earlier by the Normans: they are now an important ecological factor: sea birds nest in their burrows and they control scrub and tall grasses.

What to See   Contains one of the finest sea bird colonies in Europe with nesting fulmar, shag, kittiwake, razorbill, puffin, guillemot and three large gulls. There is also an immense colony (about 100,000) of manx shearwater nesting in burrows. Buzzard, short-eared owl, raven and chough are regularly seen. An endemic race of vole, related to the bank vole, lives in the bracken whilst grey seal abound off shore and breed on the island in the autumn and the common porpoise is frequently seen off shore playing in the tide races. The seas around have been declared a Marine Nature Reserve. The wild flowers in May and June, with sheets of bluebell, campion and thrift, are an amazing sight.

   T at Information Centre on Skomer.

Ynys-hir   6

Map 135 SN68-95-1079 acres (437 ha)

7 miles south-west of Machynlleth on the south shore of Dyfi estuary signposted off A487 at Eglwysfach opposite Mill and then down the track for 1 mile. SSSI, Ramsar Site. Salt marsh, freshwater marsh, reed-bed, peat bog, moorland, woodland.

Access   AYR on foot from CP at SN682963 onto the nature trail leading to four hides with views over the estuary and wader scrape. (Charge to non-RSPB members.)

Information   Leaflets and guides from Information Centre in CP: open daily 9 a.m.–9 p.m. (or sunset when earlier).

History   The area round the Dyfi estuary is one of the richest habitats in Wales with not only the salt marsh and sands which attract thousands of sea-birds and waders but, on the south side, there is Dyfi NNR covering over 5000 acres which includes Borth Bog and the extensive dunes of Ynyslas whilst there are oakwoods in the RSPB reserve and along the north shore. Though Ynys-hir is primarily a bird reserve and one of the richest in terms of species in Britain it is also a haven for flowers, mammals, dragonflies and butterflies.

What to See   Over winter, October–early April, there is a small flock of Greenland white-front geese, joined in February/March by some Bewick's swan. There are usually small numbers of pintail, goldeneye and red-breasted merganser with wigeon, teal and shelduck in much larger numbers. The spring brings many waders and gulls including occasional Mediterranean and ring-billed, whilst the autumn passage includes black-tailed godwit and spotted redshank. Heron begin nesting in February and are followed by a large number of woodland birds such as pied flycatcher, coal tit, nuthatch, treecreeper, kestrel, tawny and barn owls, all three types of woodpecker, buzzard, kestrel and sparrowhawk. Dipper and common sandpiper are seen by the streams and red kite may fly over in spring and summer. Dormice and polecats inhabit the woods whilst silver-washed and small pearl-bordered fritillaries, green and purple hairstreaks, speckled wood and holly blue fly in the clearings.

   T in CP. Refreshments in Eglwysfach.

Powys

Powys is the heart of Wales and, though it lacks a coastline except for a fragment where it touches the sea at the head of the Dyfi Estuary, it is an area of great variety with wonderful examples of all the main habitats to be found in the Principality ranging from the high, peat-clad mountains of the Berwyns in the north and the Brecon Beacons in the south to the valleys of the Severn, the Wye and the Usk which become broad and fertile along the eastern border.

Nowhere can this variety be better appreciated and enjoyed than in the Brecon Beacons National Park with its contrasting areas of Carboniferous limestone along its southern boundary and the Old Red sandstone in the north. The limestone cliffs of *Craig-y-Cilau* are some of the finest and, botanically, most important in Britain and they have the additional interest of having the entrance to one of our largest underground caves. The sandstone also outcrops in crags, as at Craig Cerrig-gleisiad, south-west of Brecon, which can be seen from the many walks which lead off from the Mountain Centre over the surrounding heath and bog, one of the nearest taking in the commons around Mynydd Illtud and the BWT reserve of *Daudraeth Illtud*.

Much of the north of Powys lies on acidic Silurian shales producing a landscape of rounded, peat-covered hills and thousands of acres of moorland and acid grassland where sheep are more numerous than people. Whilst these often barren lands provide territories for hen harrier and red kite the major interest for plants and insects lies in hollows with boggy pools and flushes. This is the setting of *Llyn Mawr* off the road from Newtown to Machynlleth and one of the few upland lakes where riches in terms of nutrient run-off have not yet destroyed the wildlife riches.

To the east the monotony is relieved by volcanic intrusions which have brought hard, igneous rocks to the surface. Most characteristic is Breidden, on the gateway road into Wales from Shrewsbury to Welshpool, with rocky ledges carrying spiked speedwell, sticky catchfly and rock cinquefoil. Less prominent, but easier to climb is *Roundton Hill* tucked behind Corndon on the English side of Offa's Dyke, which deserves to be visited annually for rare annuals in the spring and at any time for its peace and seclusion.

Hills, and hollows artificially filled by man, have combined to create one of the outstanding areas for wildlife in mid-Wales. *Lake Vyrnwy,* where wooded valleys surround the 100-year old reservoir that replaced the small stream once there, now attracts ducks and gulls in large numbers.

The best remaining ancient woods are found in the valleys and several are linear Wildlife Trust reserves. Brecon has Pwll-y-Wrach near Talgarth north-east of Brecon whilst Radnor has *Bailey Einon* close to their headquarters in Llandrindod Wells—both with rushing streams for dipper and kingfisher.

Stiller waters are found in the *Shropshire Union Canal* which, although essentially English, puts its 'arms' into Wales in numerous places, the Montgomery Arm being one of the longest and, botanically, most exciting with extensive patches of floating water-plantain and clear water full of rare pondweeds and water-starworts. These can be seen easily from the towpath at numerous points near the A483, notably at *Wern Clay-Pits* which, with its picnic tables in the shade and gliding swans, is one of the best places to begin to appreciate the wildlife of this relatively unexplored county.

- Brecknock Wildlife Trust (BWT), Lion House, 7 Lion Street, Brecon LD3 7AY. 0874 5708.
- Montgomeryshire Wildlife Trust (MWT), 8 Severn Square, Newtown SY16 2AG. 0686 624751.
- Radnorshire Wildlife Trust (RWT), 1 Gwalia Annexe, Ithon Road, LLandrindod Wells LD1 6AS. 0597 3298.

Bailey Einon   7

Map 147 SO08-61- 11 acres (5 ha)
1½ miles east of Landrindod Wells via Cefnllys Lane to CP at Shaky Bridge over River Eithon. Oak/ash ancient woodland, stream.

Access   AYR on foot from CP at SO083612 onto a 1¼-mile way-marked trail which may be muddy. A second trail continues from the reserve to Alpine Bridge (8 miles).

Information   Leaflet from dispenser at entrance or from TI Office in Llandrindod Wells or RWT.

History   Fine example of a Welsh lowland woodland with standards of oak and ash with an understorey of hazel and field maple and willows and alder in wetter areas. Part is being managed as coppice-with-standards on a 24-year rotation.

What to See   Ground flora is mainly bluebell, primrose, dog's mercury, wood-sorrel and early-purple orchid. Woodland birds include pied flycatcher, redstart, green and great spotted woodpecker, nuthatch, willow warbler and buzzard. Purple hairstreak and speckled wood butterflies are features and the river attracts water birds and insects as well as sustaining populations of otter.

Craig-y-Cilau   8

Map 161 SO18-15- 157 acres (63 ha)
2 miles south-west of Crickhowell, on the north facing escarpment of Mynydd Llangatwg via Usk Bridge and minor road to Beauford to parking space immediately after cattle grid in 1 mile. NNR. Limestone cliffs, wooded rocky slopes, screes, acid moorland, caves.

Access   AYR on foot from parking space at SO186169 along rough track to base of cliffs. Rock faces and screes can be dangerous.

Information   Nothing on site: leaflet from NCC.

History   North and east facing cliffs of Carboniferous limestone with a capping of Millstone grit on the plateau above. Below the cliffs quartz conglomerates of

Old Red sandstone are largely hidden below boulders and scree from the limestone above. A small raised bog, Waen Ddu, has developed in a hollow in the conglomerates near the north end. In the centre of the reserve is the entrance to the Agen Allwedd cave system at least 12 miles long, one of the largest single-entrance caves in Britain.

What to See   Four endemic species of whitebeam grow on the cliffs with yew, wych elm, small and large-leaved lime and it is probably the most westerly native locality for beech in Britain. Other notable plants are mountain melick, angular solomon's-seal, hutchinsia, alpine enchanter's-nightshade, mossy saxifrage and limestone fern. About 50 bird species breed on the reserve such as buzzard, sparrowhawk, kestrel and tawny owl, raven, ring ouzel, wheatear and whinchat on the cliffs or in the open with tits, redstart, warblers, flycatchers and tree pipit in the scrub woodland. There is a colony of lesser horseshoe bat in the cave.

Daudraeth Illtud   9

Map 160 SN96-25- 150 acres (61 ha)
5 miles south-west of Brecon off A470 at Libanus following the signposts to Mountain Centre. Birch scrub, wet moorland, pools.

Access   AYR on foot from Mountain Centre CP at SN976262 on well marked trail of 2½ miles. One wet area, Traeth Bach, is very dangerous and should not be visited.

Information   Trail leaflet from Mountain Centre: open daily (except 25 December). Centre also has A/V displays and exhibitions on the National Park.

History   A large area of common belonging to the Lord of the Manor which is mainly wetland and includes two peaty areas, Traeth Mawr and Traeth Bach, as well as Blaencamlais Pool to the north at SN959264. Traeth Mawr is a mosaic of peaty tussocks and pools. Drier, heathery parts are being invaded by downy birch.

What to See   Heather and bilberry heath in the dry areas give way to purple moor-grass, mat-grass and heath rush with flea, bottle and greater tussock-sedges, great fen-sedge in wet areas and shoreweed and lesser marshwort on the margins of pools. Snipe, redshank, reed bunting, teal and heron are frequently seen and a large flock of lapwing is usually present. On sunny days green hair-streak may be seen on the wing and common lizard basking amongst the heather.
   T[D]. Refreshments at Mountain Centre.
   Wheelchairs have access on good tracks from Mountain Centre.

Lake Vyrnwy   10

Map 125 SH9-2- 17,500 acres (7090 ha)
7 miles west of Llanfyllin on B4393 north of Llanwddyn. SSSI. Flooded valley, woodland, moorland, grassland.

Access   AYR from viewing points on roads and footpaths around the lake: there is a public hide on the north-east side at SJ000215.

Information   Leaflets and trail guides from Visitor Centre 100 yds down minor road at the west end of the dam on the other side from Llanwddyn: open Easter, Whitsun–October 11 a.m.–6 p.m.

History   A flooded valley at the south-west end of the Berwyns surrounded by conifers and screened by trees from the road. There are areas of moorland and old meadows as well as upland streams and valley bogs. The steep-sided banks are not ideal for water-birds but the stony edge of the lake provides nesting and feeding sites for a few waders. At an altitude of nearly 800 ft it is too cold in winter for many resident birds.

What to See   Wild flowers around the lake include Welsh poppy, goldenrod, English stonecrop, climbing corydalis, petty whin, ivy-leaved bellflower, globeflower, starry saxifrage and lesser twayblade whilst several unusual ferns occur such as beech, oak and parsley ferns. Breeding 'water' birds such as mallard, teal, great crested grebe, goosander, common sandpiper, grey wagtail, dipper and kingfisher occur with pochard, tufted duck, wigeon and whooper swan in winter. 6000 black-headed gulls roost here before flying to other nesting sites. The woodland breeding-bird list has siskin, redpoll, green and great spotted woodpecker, spotted flycatcher, redstart, wood warbler, tree pipit and whinchat. Over 24 species of butterfly are known and there are good populations of polecat, badger and red squirrel.

T[D]. Shop at Visitor Centre.

Wheelchairs have good viewing from roads and paths.

Llanymynech Rocks

See under Shropshire

Llyn Mawr   ▪11

Map 136 SO00-97- 30 acres (12 ha)
7 miles north-west of Newtown via A470 and turning north onto a minor road 2 miles west of Caersws, passing through Bwlch-y-Garreg to the parking space on the roadside just before the bungalow on the left. Lake, marsh, willow carr, acid moorland.

Access   AYR on foot from the parking space at SO011970.

Information   Nothing on site: leaflet from TI Office in Newtown or MWT.

History   The lake lies in a narrow basin with hill ridges to the north and south at an altitude of 1280 ft. It is surrounded by marshland and wet heath with, in one place, an area of wet woodland dominated by willow, birch and rowan. The drier slopes leading down to the shore are covered in acid grassland, bracken and gorse.

What to See   Wetland plants include bogbean, quillwort, shoreweed, bog asphodel, lousewort, common sundew, common butterwort, northern and early marsh-orchids, bog asphodel, marsh cinquefoil, cranberry and cross-leaved heath. Amongst breeding birds are black-headed gull, teal, tufted duck, great crested grebe, snipe, curlew, stonechat, whinchat and reed bunting: pochard, wigeon, goldeneye, goosander and whooper swan are winter visitors. Birds of prey which may be seen hunting over the reserve are buzzard, kestrel and merlin.

Roundton Hill   12

Map 137 SO29-94- 87 acres (35 ha)
1 mile north-east of Church Stoke on the A489 Newtown to Craven Arms road 12 miles east of Newtown via minor road to Old Church Stoke turning left and then immediately right in village opposite Old Oak Inn: after bend to right turn right down shady lane to gate at entrance to reserve and CP across the stream. SSSI. Crags, acid grassland, marsh, stream, scrub.

Access   AYR on foot from CP at SO295947 onto a network of paths.

Information   Notice board in CP: leaflet from dispenser in CP, from Old Oak Inn, TI Offices or from MWT.

History   The hill, which really is a 'round ton', is of volcanic origin made up of very hard, erosion-resistant, igneous rocks. It rises to 1214 ft and, from the top, there are wonderful views over South Shropshire to the east and over Montgomery town to the Severn valley and the mountains of mid-Wales beyond.

What to See   Dry, rocky crags are covered by annuals in spring such as shepherd's-cress, upright chickweed and lesser chickweed. Later mountain pansy colours the short grassland of the steep slopes whilst yellow rock stonecrop and navelwort adorn the screes and rocks. The stream at the bottom is lined with monkeyflower, water mint and meadowsweet. Over 100 species of mosses and lichens have been recorded. Buzzard and raven may be seen overhead whilst wheatear nest in old rabbit burrows. Other breeding birds are redstart and tawny owl.

Shropshire Union Canal–Wern Clay Pits   13

Map 126 SJ25-14- 5 acres (2 ha)
5 miles north of Welshpool off B4392 from Arddleen to Guilsfield turning onto minor road ½ mile south of Arddleen across bridge over canal and turning immediately right to CP in ½ mile before another bridge (Red Bridge). SSSI. Open water, canal banks, marsh, hedgerows.

Access   AYR on foot from CP at SJ251141.

Information   Notice board in CP: leaflet on whole of Montgomery Arm of canal from Rednal to Newtown from TI Offices in Newtown, Welshpool etc.

History   The Montgomery Arm runs north to south for 35 miles along the Welsh-English border. Built between 1792 and 1821 to bring limestone from Llanymynech Hill (see Shropshire, p. 161) to wharves in the Upper Severn valley where it was burnt in kilns to make lime for agriculture. The canal fell into disrepair and was closed in 1944.

What to See   The clear water holds a large number of submerged aquatic plants, including 10 different pondweeds, and floating plants such as frogbit and greater duckweed. There are also interesting emergent species : flowering-rush, sweet-flag and water dock. The area supports a large number of dragonflies, such as brown and southern hawkers, and damselflies including the nationally rare white-legged damselfly. Heron and kingfisher feed in the canal whilst whinchat, blackcap, whitethroat and spotted flycatcher breed in nearby hedges.

NORTH WALES

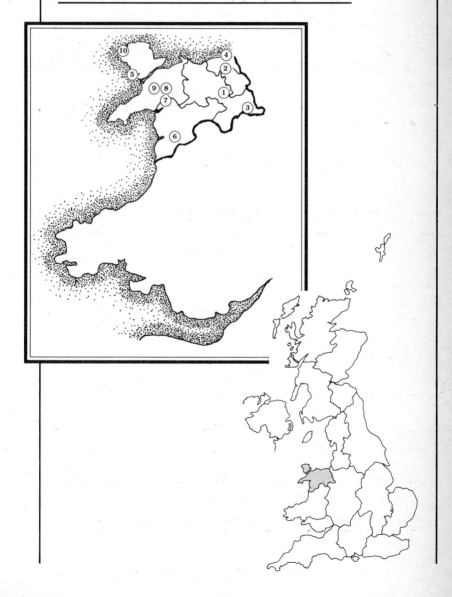

Clwyd

Clwyd is a modern Welsh county formed from the fusion of Flint and Denbighshire, with a piece of Merioneth, which takes its name from the river which flows through the Vale of Clwyd past Ruthin, Denbigh and St Asaph's to the sea at Rhyl.

Clwyd is also a border county and along its eastern side it is hard to distinguish it from England immediately—there is no feeling, driving west across the River Dee, of entering a new country. The Triassic sandstones of the Cheshire Plain extend into Wales beyond the river and place names like Holt, Hope and Hawarden do not have a Celtic flavour.

Further west the landscape is more convincingly Welsh. The Coal Measures formed in the Carboniferous period run north from the Shropshire border to form the western shore of the Dee estuary and, in the heather-covered hills rising to 1600 ft amidst a scattering of pit-head winding gear, there is a feeling of the valleys proper.

The rest of the county is predominantly rural and mostly upland where, traditionally, sheep are being raised on the mountains, which rise to over 2700 ft in the Berwyns, and stock are grazed in the valleys. Here there are still many areas where wildlife survives despite the many thousands of acres lost to afforestation.

The richest habitats for both plants and animals are found on the two parallel outcrops of Carboniferous limestone which run north to south on either side of the Vale of Clwyd. The upper slopes are still unploughed and grazed by sheep whilst, in the valleys, fragments of woodland remain. They range from the spectacular cliffs of Eglwyseg Mountain, above the beautiful Vale of Llangollen, to the smaller, but very varied, *Cilygroeslwyd* reserve near Ruthin with its mixture of ash and yew woods and areas of limestone pavement and dry grassland.

Streams flowing over, and through, the limestone become very rich in calcium which is precipitated when the streams enter waterlogged hollows and spread out in damp areas so that water is removed by evaporation. This is the origin of the white, crystalline, tufa which can be seen at *Ddol Uchaf*, a few miles inland from Holywell, where the Afon Pantgwyn is flowing from the limestone on the east side of the Vale.

Streams over the sandstone should have less to precipitate. It is perhaps significant that one which carries water through the Park of the great house of Erddig should be called the Black Brook; it receives effluent from a nearby coal washing plant at Hafod Colliery. But it also runs through the picturesque *Hafod Wood*, an unexpected wildlife bonus for visitors to Erddig.

Other visitors are not a bonus to the wildlife of Clwyd. Most of the coast of the Dee estuary has been lost to coal mining and other industries but, on the north coast—which still retains extensive sand dune systems—chalets, caravans and holiday camps have left little which is undeveloped. Only the *Point of Air*, at the mouth of the Dee, is relatively free and even here the future for little tern trying to nest on the beach must be in doubt. But the sand banks, salt marshes and mud flats are left to the birds and the seals emphasizing that there is a wealth of wildlife to enjoy in Clwyd—if you know where to look.

● North Wales Wildlife Trust (NWWT), 376 High Street, Bangor, Gwynedd LL57 1YE. 0248 351541.

Cilgroeslwyd Wood   1

Map 116 SJ12-55- 10 acres (4 ha)
1½ miles south of Ruthin west of A494 to Bala. SSSI. Ash/yew woods on limestone, scrub, open grassland, limestone pavement.

Access   AYR on foot, from the parking space in the lane leading to Llanfair Dyffryn Clwyd just beyond Eyarth Bridge at SJ126553, back across A494 to a stile in an iron fence; go left along a path through woodland to the reserve entrance over a stone wall and wire fence, onto way-marked paths.

Information   Nature trail leaflet from dispenser at entrance or NWWT.

History   A variety of woodland types on the Carboniferous limestone in the Vale of Clwyd including yew wood, ash wood, mixed ash/yew, and oak with coppiced ash, wych elm and hazel. There is little ground flora beneath the yew but elsewhere there are carpets of wild flowers.

What to See   Lime-loving shrubs include spindle and traveller's-joy whilst amongst the more interesting flowers are stinking hellebore, greater butterfly and bird's-nest orchids, herb-Paris, rock-rose and, unusually, both giant and nettle-leaved bellflower. Woodland birds include green and great spotted woodpeckers, coal and long-tailed tits, nuthatch, goldcrest and tawny owl: hawfinch, woodcock and tawny owl nest here. Polecat and badger have been seen on the reserve and an interesting insect recorded is the oak bush-cricket.

Ddol Uchaf   2

Map 116 SJ14-71- 9 acres (4 ha)
4 miles to the south-west of Holywell just north of A451 Mold to St Asaph road at Ddol, 1 mile east of Afonwen and ¾ mile west of Ysceifiog. SSSI. Marl pit, woodland, lime-rich grassland, pools.

Access   AYR on foot from the parking space on a wide verge behind Ddol Chapel at SJ141712 to two access points:

1. at north-east corner by Interpretative Centre.
2. at SJ140714 on the west side onto a circular path which can be slippery after rain.

Information   Leaflet from Interpretative Centre: open third Sunday each month (except winter) 10 a.m.–4 p.m.: otherwise leaflet from NWWT.

History The reserve is in a disused and much disturbed pit last worked for
marl and tufa (a form of fossil-rich limestone) in 1945: it is crossed by a stream,
the Afon Pantgwyn. There are many habitats in a small space including a mixed
sycamore wood, willow carr, blackthorn scrub, areas of tall-herb, open lime-rich
grassland, and bare marl banks with sparse vegetation. The name in English
means 'upper meadow'.

What to See Plants in the drier areas are cowslip, yellow-wort, ploughman's-
spikenard, wild basil and kidney vetch whilst damper areas have marsh-orchids,
hemp-agrimony, meadowsweet, mare's-tail, common spike-rush and grass-of-
Parnassus. The rather dark woodland has only dog's mercury, ground-ivy and
wood avens. The reserve is specially rich in molluscs with 36 species recorded,
whilst over 40, mainly woodland, birds have been listed such as nuthatch, tits,
woodpeckers and magpie with dipper in the stream. A rare, small, pinkish
woodlouse, *Androniscus dentiger*, is also found.

T at Interpretative Centre.

Wheelchairs have only limited access.

Hafod Wood

3

Map 117 SJ32-47- 19 acres (8 ha)

1½ miles to the south of Wrexham via A493 road to Ruabon turning south into
a narrow lane where National Trust is signposted at SJ323493: after 1 mile enter
Erddig Estate at Plas Grono Lodge onto a one-way estate road to the parking
space on the left over the first cattle grid. SSSI. Mixed deciduous and coniferous
woodland, marsh, stream.

Access AYR on foot for 200 yds further along the road across a stream to the
entrance on the right at SJ324477, down some steep steps to a stile which leads
to good paths, including 150 yds of board-walk.

Information Nothing on site: leaflet from NWWT (and from Erddig).

History A narrow strip of mixed woodland extending to about ½ mile on both
sides of the Black Brook and varying in width from 50–200 yds. The board-walk
leads to an area of fen which can be seen without damaging it. The main native
trees are ash and alder and there is one tree of true black poplar. The understorey
has guelder-rose and red currant whilst sycamore, bird cherry and beech have
been planted.

What to See Interesting plants include wild daffodil, wood spurge, bottle
sedge, hemlock water-dropwort, giant horsetail, greater chickweed and large
bitter-cress. Amongst breeding birds are coal and marsh tits, great and lesser
spotted woodpeckers, blackcap, spotted flycatcher, tawny owl, mallard and
kestrel. Dipper, kingfisher, green woodpecker, grey wagtail and woodcock are
also present. Water voles live along the banks of the stream which has minnows
and trout.

T[D] in main yard at Erddig. Refreshments, picnic site.

Wheelchairs have limited access to reserve and house.

Point of Air

4

SJ11-83- 450 acres (182 ha)
3 miles to the east of Prestatyn at the north-west tip of Dee Estuary off A548
at turning into Station Road, Talacre at SJ114834. SSSI, Ramsar site. Saltmarsh,
sand flats, sand dunes, willow scrub, migrating waders, wintering duck.

Access   AYR on foot from the parking space at the end of Station Road near
the holiday camp at SJ122845 to a path through the dunes.

Information   Leaflet 'Bird Watching in Clwyd' from RSPB, c/o 51 Brighton
Road, Rhyl LL18 3HL or from RSPB warden in summertime.

History   This is the west side of the internationally important Dee Estuary
which attracts many wildfowl and waders in winter though it is somewhat
disturbed in summer. Up to 20,000 birds may be seen from the Point at any one
time with nearly 1000 ducks and geese on the reserve. Sea watching to the north
from near the disused lighthouse can also be rewarding. Here too are substantial
sand dunes with a good range of plants such as sea-holly.

What to See   Wildfowl include teal, wigeon, shoveler, pintail, mallard,
goldeneye, shelduck, scaup, common scoter and red-breasted merganser along
with red-throated diver, great crested grebe, guillemot and razorbill: skuas and
terns fly past and, in autumn, there are hundreds of martins and swallows on
passage. Regular visiting waders are bar-tailed godwit, knot and oystercatcher
whilst snow bunting and shorelark may arrive in winter. Grey seals may be seen;
they haul out onto the West Hoyle Bank 1 mile north-east of the Point.

Gwynedd

Can there be any county in England or Wales as rich and diverse as Gwynedd?
A combination of the three former Welsh counties of Anglesey, Caernarvonshire
and Merionethshire, it covers almost 1 million acres and is comparable in size
with Essex and Hampshire but incomparable with any other county in its range
of topography, geology and wildlife.

There is almost alpine scenery in the rugged peaks and crags of the mountains
whilst at their feet lie lakes where glaciers first cut and then dammed deep
valleys radiating from their summits. In complete contrast there are, to the west,
the mostly low-lying, sea-girt lands of the Lleyn Peninsula and the Isle of
Anglesey. Their coastlines and those of the mainland, stretching from the hard
headland of the Great Orme in the north to the softer sands of Aberdovey in the
south, add further to Gwyndd's fascination.

This fascination is enhanced by, as well as being partly dependent upon, the
extraordinary range of rock formations on which the county rests. They vary
from some of the oldest in the world, from the pre-Cambrian, which are over
3000 million years old and form the greater part of Anglesey, to some of the
youngest. Some are almost pure silica producing mineral-deficient, acid soils

whilst others, such as the limestones or some volcanic rocks, give rise to soils which are base rich.

Half of the county lies within the Snowdonia National Park and this suggests the importance of this landscape, its variety of habitats, and the need to manage the area both to protect it and provide facilities for millions of visitors to enjoy it—amongst those facilities is a bewildering choice of nature reserves.

Four of the most important reserves in Gwynedd are in the National Park and are National Nature Reserves, and three represent the finest of the arctic-alpine vegetation of Wales. For botanists the outstanding place must be Twll Du, the Devil's Kitchen, in *Cwm Idwal* with a collection of plants, many of which are here at their southern limit in Britain and one of which, the Snowdon lily, is known only from North Wales and has its main headquarters in Cwm Idwal, having disappeared from the summit of Snowdon many years ago.

Snowdon, inevitably, just because at 3559 ft it is the highest mountain in England and Wales and has a train to the top, has been overused but, away from the summit and away from the line, the grandeur is undiminished and the unscalable cliffs and crags are still the haunts of chough and raven.

More remote and without a railway, but with equally dramatic scenery, *Cader Idris* broods above Barmouth and Dolgellau. Though it does not reach 3000 ft, the north face is so steep, shady and sheep-free that several alpine plants persist.

Though Cader is wooded on its lower slopes the majority of hills are grazed and regeneration is poor. It is the absence of grazing and the natural regeneration which has occurred since it was fenced by the NCC in the late 1960s, which now makes *Coedydd Maentwrog* such an important reserve and of NNR quality. Although Newborough Warren on the west coast of Anglesey is also an NNR, because it is one of the most exciting sand dune systems in Britain, almost all the area near the road has been planted with Corsican pine and it is a long walk through them to reach the coastline. *Aberffraw Dunes* present no such problem: ease of parking, immediate access to the dunes and a Visitor Centre nearby, open on summer afternoons. This makes the reserve one of those which ask to be seen. At *South Stack Cliffs* on Holy Island AONB could either stand for Area of Outstanding Natural Beauty or for Area of Outstanding National Birds—no doubt the RSPB, who manage it, would opt for the latter. But this, like many other reserves seems to be outstanding for more than one reason, which goes some way to explaining why this area is likely to continue to be one of the best loved and most visited parts of Britain.

- North Wales Wildlife Trust (NWWT), 376 High Street, Bangor LL57 1YE. 0248 351541.

Aberffraw Dunes 5

Map 114 SH35-68- 445 acres (180 ha)
South-east of Aberffraw village off A4080 on the west coast of Anglesey. SSSI. Sand dunes, dune slacks.

Access   AYR on foot from the parking space near the old bridge over Afon Ffraw at SH356689 onto roads and paths crossing the dunes to the sea.

Information   Guides and maps from a Visitor Centre, Llys Llewelyn, in the village across the river: open daily June–September 2–5 p.m. There are also displays about birds, marine life, wild flowers and archaeology.

History   A fine dune system built of sand with a high proportion of broken shells and therefore rich in the calcium needed for many of its plant species. The dunes now occupy the site of a large estuary which has been filled up so that Aberffraw, the mouth of the River Ffraw, is now 1½ miles inland.

What to See   Foredunes covered with marram with frequent sea and Portland spurge give way to short rabbit-grazed turf full of other sand-binding species like sand sedge and common restharrow. More stable areas have lady's-bedstraw, common thyme, kidney vetch, field gentian, bee orchid and wild pansy, food plant of the dark green fritillary. The winter-wet dune slacks have large areas of creeping willow as well as good colonies of early and northern marsh-orchids. Birds are abundant but restricted to those of the open country: skylark, meadow pipit, oystercatcher and lapwing.

  T across the bridge in the village. Refreshments and shop in the Visitor Centre. Wheelchairs have easy access on the roads across the dunes.

Cader Idris

Maps 124 & 125 SH71-13- 1062 acres (430 ha)
2½ miles south of Dolgellau. NNR. Mountain cliffs, alpine plants, woods, lakes.

Access   AYR on foot from:

1. CP at Minffordd at junction of A487 and B4405 at SH732116 which leads to Llyn Cau.
2. Ty'n-y-Ceunant at SH699152 by Foxes' Path to summit which is also starting point for a zig-zag track known in Welsh as Llwybr Cam Rhedynen.

Information   Nothing on site: there are guided walks from CP at Minffordd on Thursdays at end July and in August.

History   Precipices on the northern side towards Dolgellau are made of a hard, crystalline, igneous rock called granophyre, rare elsewhere in Snowdonia: other rocks include volcanic lavas and metamorphosed slate formerly mined above Arthog. The last glaciation gouged out the cwm with Llyn y Gadair on the north face leaving only a narrow summit ridge between it and the fearsome cliffs of the cwm around Llyn Cau to the south.

What to See   On narrow bands of north-facing calcareous rocks mountain sorrel, mossy and purple saxifrages, globeflower, spring sandwort and Welsh poppy occur along with ferns such as green and forked spleenworts and alpine woodsia. Much rarer are moss campion, alpine meadow-rue and alpine saw-wort. Raven and ring ouzel nest on the crags whilst wheatear and meadow pipit are common amongst the rocks below. The broad-leaved woods on the northern side of Talyllyn Pass are rich in mosses and lichens.

Coedydd Maentwrog   7

Map 124 SH66-41- 169 acres (69 ha)
3 miles west of Ffestiniog and 1 mile north of Maentwrog in the Vale of Ffestiniog
on A496. NNR. Sessile oak woods, stream.

Access   AYR on foot:

1. to the western section from CP opposite Llyn Mair on B4410 Maentwrog to
   Beddgelert road at SH652413.
2. to the eastern section from parking space near Oakley Arms on A496 down
   the lane to the east to the gate at SH664411 or up the hill to the west on B4410
   for 50 yds to gate at SH660410.

Information   Nature trail leaflet to western section (Coed Llyn Mair) from
dispenser in CP or from Tan-y-Bwlch railway station shop.

History   Formerly part of the Tan-y-Bwlch estate of the Oakley family who
were owners of the slate quarries at Blaenau Ffestiniog. Their management of
the wood was enlightened and felled trees were replaced by native oak so that
introduced trees are few. Bought in 1965 by the National Trust with financial
help from NWWT the area has been leased to NCC and became an NNR in 1966.
The first task was to fence the wood to exclude sheep which were preventing
natural regeneration.

What to See   Ancient sessile oakwood on acid, Cambrian, sedimentary rocks
receiving an annual rainfall of over 70 inches. There are a number of 200-year
old oaks which are covered in mosses and lichens whilst the polypody fern grows
thickly on their branches. Ground flora includes common cow-wheat, primrose
and bluebell with carpets of mosses and many different ferns. Resident birds
include four species of tit, great spotted and green woodpeckers, nuthatch and
treecreeper: they are joined in summer by pied flycatcher, redstart and wood
warbler. Buzzards wheel overhead and badgers have a sett in the wood.
     T and refreshments at the Oakley Arms.

Cwm Idwal   8

Map 115 SH64-59-983 acres (398 ha)
5 miles south of Bethesda at head of Nant Ffrancon off A5. NNR. Mountain cliffs,
scree, lake.

Access   AYR on foot from CP at Ogwen Cottage at SH648603 onto the path
to Llyn Idwal in ½ mile.

Information   Nature trail guide from National Park Visitor Centres: nearest
in Betws-y-Coed and Llanberis. The trail is over 2 miles long. There are guided
walks from CP on Thursdays at the end of July and in August.

History   The spectacular north-facing cwm with a corrie lake in its bottom
1200 ft above sea level forms one of the finest nature reserves in North Wales,
important for its rocks and soils, its dependent plants and animals, the evidence

of past glaciation and the history of the landscape. The steep cliffs have a dark central cleft, Twll Du (Devil's Kitchen), which marks the bottom of the great rock fold of the Snowdon syncline, whilst the damp ledges are crowded with arctic-alpine plants which have survived here since the ice retreated.

What to See   Wild flowers on the cliffs include purple, mossy and starry saxifrages, alpine meadow-rue, moss campion, globeflower, oak fern, roseroot, mountain-sorrel, green spleenwort and northern bedstraw whilst Llyn Idwal holds quillwort, water lobelia, floating water-plantain, awlwort and pillwort. Raven and ring ousel nest on the crags, common sandpiper on the lake margin. Heron and cormorants fish for minnow and brown trout whilst chough forage in the grassland. Winter brings visiting whooper swan, goldeneye and pochard if the lake is not frozen.

Snowdon   9

Map 115 SH6-5- 4142 acres (1677 ha)
4½ miles south-east of Llanberis. NNR. Mountain cliffs, scree, moorland, cwms, corrie lakes.

Access   On foot from several CPs on roads around the peak including from:

1. Rhyd Ddu on the west side at SH571526.
2. Llanberis via the side road (signposted) south of Mountain Railway station at SH581594.
3. Pen-y-pas on the east side at SH647557.

    The access points are joined by Sherpa bus so one may go up and down by different routes. The Mountain Railway operates from Llanberis mid-March–mid-October: book early in day of travel in holiday season.

Information   Leaflets and guides giving details of walks from National Park Visitor Centres: nearest are Llanberis and Betws-y-Coed. A nature trail guide to the Miners' Track from Pen-y-pas is produced by NCC.

History   Some of the oldest rocks in the world have been crushed, folded and weathered into a geologist's paradise. Over the last million years, glaciers gouged great hollow cwms at the heads of the valleys, dammed the valley bottoms with debris behind which lakes have formed, and left hanging valleys high up from which waterfalls tumble down immense cliffs. The rocks have yielded slate, copper and even gold and the mountain is littered with the debris of old mines and ruined buildings.

What to See   Much of the mountain is open, acid, sheep-grazed moorland of mat-grass, deergrass, cottongrass, purple moor-grass, tormentil, heath bedstraw, heather and bilberry. Higher up cowberry, fir and alpine clubmoss occur whilst damp, sheltered cliffs commonly hold wild thyme, moss campion, roseroot, starry and mossy saxifrage, spring sandwort, mountain sorrel and holly fern. Screes are covered with parsley fern. Overhead raven croak whilst wheatear and meadow pipit flit between the rocks and dipper and grey wagtail work the streams. Some of the lakes were poisoned by copper mining but others hold minnow and brown trout.

T at CPs at Rhyd Ddu and Pen-y-pas.

South Stack Cliffs

10

Map 114 SH20-82- 780 acres (316 ha)
2 miles west of Holyhead in the north-west corner of Holy Island signposted to left after passing harbour going north in Holyhead. SSSI. Area of Outstanding Natural Beauty. Sea cliffs, heath grassland.

Access   AYR on foot from CPs at SH210819 onto a network of paths. There is also access to the Ranges on Penrhosfeilw Common 1½ miles south from CP at SH215804.

Information   A Visitor Centre in Ellen's Tower at SH205822 overlooks the main sea-bird colonies and has displays, leaflets, TV close-ups of cliff-face. Open daily: Easter–mid-September 11 a.m.–5 p.m.

History   The area has been occupied since the Bronze Age with hut circles adjacent to the reserve dating from 1500 BC. There is a hillfort, Caer y Twr, on the summit of Holyhead Mountain enclosing 17 acres with a drystone wall. The South Stack lighthouse dates from 1808. South Stack is a classic site for studying the folding in rocks of the pre-Cambrian period.

What to See   In May and June nine species of sea-bird are breeding on the dramatic 400 ft cliffs including guillemot, puffin, razorbill, kittiwake and fulmar. Several species of land bird also breed on the cliffs: peregrine, raven and chough can be seen here all year round. In spring and early summer the cliffs are a blaze of colour with spring squill, thrift and kidney vetch. Amongst rarities are field fleawort and spotted rock-rose.

T in CP. Refreshments.

SCOTLAND

SOUTH-WEST
SCOTLAND

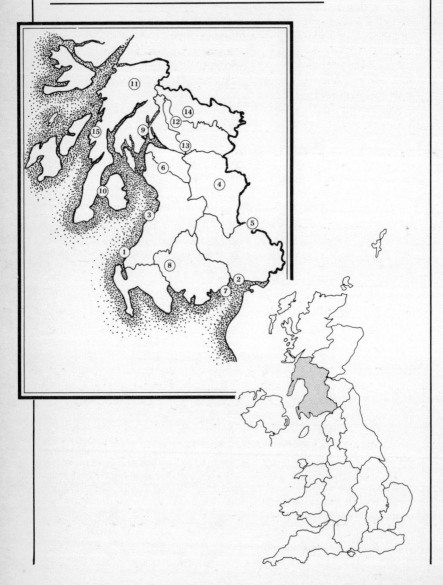

South-West Scotland

Those who would enjoy the wildlife of Scotland without the long and often tedious wind behind a string of caravans through narrow glens, should turn off the A74 soon after passing the clutter of Gretna and explore the enormous variety of this region—highlands without hassle.

The 'highlands' rise to the east of the A74 a few miles from the comfortable breadth of Moffat's main street where the statue of a ram symbolizes that the past prosperity of these uplands rested on sheep. Ironic then that their principal feature should be a *Grey Mare's Tail*, a waterfall of over 200 ft tumbling from the finest hanging valley in southern Scotland. This is a true glacial landscape with U-shaped valleys and corrie lakes like Loch Skeen surrounded by formidable cliffs clothed in arctic-alpine plants.

Waterfalls never fail to attract and those at the *Falls of Clyde* are no exception, adding an extra dimension to the remarkably preserved village of New Lanark, especially when the river is in spate or water is deliberately released from the hydro-electric scheme above. But, for the naturalist, it is the deciduous woods which flank the gorge which excite attention with their spring blaze of bluebell and anemone, for such woods are rare away from water, and the spruce platoons of conifers which march across the rounded hills roundabout are no substitute.

Alien plantations now cover 30 per cent of Dumfries and Galloway so it is a relief to find that a large block of ancient broad-leaved wood does still survive, the *Wood of Cree*, up river from Newton Stewart, where flycatchers still fly and dippers still dip—though the threat of further conifers and potential acidification of the streams with consequent loss of aquatic invertebrates on which the dippers depend, exists even here.

Other fragments of ancient woodland have survived on coastal cliffs especially where raised beaches have distanced them from the sea: such is the narrow strip above the shore on the *Southwick Coast*, but one of the biggest areas is the 300 acres enclosed within *Culzean Country Park* which, though almost entirely planted, has aquired a woodland ground flora and attracted a long list of breeding birds increased by its fascinating shoreline and sandstone and volcanic cliffs. There are few more inspiring places in Britain than Culzean with its Robert Adam remodelled castle and exquisite farm buildings defying the ocean and looking out to the granite eminence of Ailsa Craig. Granite which, pounded and rounded and flattened, has been washed down the coast to form the shingle spits of *Ballantrae* where, if you take a turn along the beach you may take in two—little and arctic—which nest there, or three if it's a Sandwich year.

The whole coast from the Forth of Clyde to the Solway is a haven for sea-birds in summer—gannets on Ailsa Craig, auks breeding on cliffs and eider, shoveler, common scoter and shelduck on the shore, but it is the winter which is of greater importance. The north side of the Solway has the largest area of unreclaimed salt marsh in Britain: from November to February there is nowhere to compare with *Caerlaverock* for geese—pinkfeet, barnacles and greylags in thousands and as many as 24 different waders in one season. This National Nature Reserve is at the heart of their area but they spread to the west shore of the Nith and along the Merse Sands to the *Southwick Coast*.

So, ardent birdwatchers turn left at Gretna and take the coast road through Annan. But even those who stick to the A74 and stay in Glasgow can see birds with ease—at Possil Marsh within the city limits—or at *Lochwinnoch* a few miles the other side of Paisley: and even if you have avoided all hassle and arrived by train, a quick change of platform at Central Station and you can be watching great crested grebe courting from the observation tower at Lochwinnoch in 30 minutes—except on Sundays when BR observes the Sabbath.

● Scottish Wildlife Trust (SWT), 25 Johnston Terrace, Edinburgh EH1 2NH. 031 226 4602.

Ballantrae

1

Map 76 NX08-82- 55 acres (22 ha)
South end of Ballantrae village. SSSI. Shingle spit, lagoons, breeding terns.

Access   On foot from CP by the pool on the sea front 100 yds west of the church down Shellknowe. No access to the shingle spit when terns are breeding from May–mid-August.

Information   Leaflet from TI Offices in Girvan and Stranraer: warden during breeding season.

History   South of Ballantrae the mouth of the River Stinchar is turned south by a narrow shingle spit which consists of flat grey stones which originated from the granite mass of Ailsa Craig 10 miles north-west out to sea. The reserve includes this shingle ridge, tidal mudflats, brackish lagoons and grassland. The spit is unstable and is breached by storms from time to time so that plants have difficulty in colonizing the area.

What to See   The most important feature is the colony of breeding terns. Little, sandwich and arctic have all been successful recently, but common have not bred since 1982. The little tern colony, though small, is the largest and most permanent on the Clyde coast and of national importance, but very liable to disturbance. Other birds present include mute swan, little ringed plover, oystercatcher, shelduck and red-breasted merganser whilst common sandpiper, redshank, dunlin and turnstone may be seen on the shore: eider and gannet are often visible out to sea. Plants on the shingle include sea campion, sea sandwort, thrift, sea mayweed, scurvygrass, sea plantain and the decreasing oysterplant near its southern limit in Britain. On the landward side meadow crane's-bill, bird's-foot trefoil and naturalized Japanese rose occur.

T in CP.

Wheelchairs have view of reserve from CP and some access to track on east side.

Caerlaverock and East Park ▪2

Map 85 NY05-65- 12,587 acres (5501 ha)
On the northern shore of Solway Firth 15 miles west of Annan, 8 miles south-east
of Dumfries taking turning off B725 at Bankend for Caerlaverock Castle which
is on the Solway Heritage Trail: after 1 mile turn left at the sign for Blackshaw
to the NCC office in Holland Farm Road or Wildfowl and Wetland Trust at East
Park at the road end. NNR, Biosphere Reserve. Foreshore, saltmarsh.

Access   To NCC reserve restricted to parties by agreement: contact NCC
Warden, second house on left in Holland Farm Road at NY042659: tel. 038777
275. To WWT reserve parties are accepted daily at 11 a.m. and 2 p.m. during
the season from 16 September–30 April: parties of 20 or more should book in
advance: tel. 038777 200.

Information   NCC leaflet from Warden's office: WWT leaflet from Visitor
Centre at East Park at NY051657.

History   Declared an NNR in 1957 with agreement from local landowners and,
covering a 6-mile stretch of coast between River Nith and Lochar Water, it is one
of the largest areas of unreclaimed saltmarsh in Britain. Dominated by red fescue
and dotted with sea aster it provides grazing for cattle in summer and large
numbers of geese and other wildfowl in winter, as well as being a feeding ground
for passing waders.

What to See   The best time for visiting is from November onwards when up
to 8500 barnacle geese will have arrived from Spitzbergen and some 500
pinkfeet, which reach 3000 by January/February, should be present. Whooper
swan numbers are highest in November: Bewick's come a little later and may
number 70 or more, the largest regular gathering in Scotland. Oystercatcher,
pintail, wigeon, teal and mallard all occur in large numbers. This is the most
northerly site in Britain for the natterjack toad. They breed in shallow, unshaded
pools fringing the saltmarsh. The croaking chorus of the males can be heard a
mile away on warm, still nights.
   T[D] at Visitor Centre.
   Wheelchairs have a fine view of waders at high tide from the west side of River
Nith at Carsethorn at NX990600.

Culzean Country Park ▪3

Map 70 NS23-10- 566 acres (229 ha)
4 miles west of Maybole and 12 miles south-west of Ayr on A719. SSSI. Woodland,
rocky shore, sand dunes, ponds, geology.

Access   AYR 9 a.m.–sunset on foot from CP near shore north of Culzean
Castle at NS236105 to a network of six well-marked walks for 1–3 hours from
easy to strenuous (charge to non-members of NTS or NT).

Information   Leaflets and guides from Visitor Centre in CP in beautifully
restored farm buildings designed by Robert Adam : open daily April–October

10.30 a.m.–5.30 p.m. The Centre also has exhibitions and an A/V display. Notice boards give up-to-date wildlife details and there are frequent guided walks.

History   Culzean was Scotland's first Country Park, established in 1969. It includes 300 acres of mixed, planted woodlands with rides, glades and narrow glens, and 3 miles of coastline with dramatic cliffs. Those to the south, on which Culzean Castle stands, are volcanic and made of sheets of lava from the Devonian whilst those to the north, from which the Castle and other buildings were constructed, are of Old Red sandstone. The cliff tops here support a relict heathland which is a mixture of acid and salt tolerant species.

What to See   Woodland wild flowers include bluebell, ramsons, spotted-orchids and foxgloves and the long list of birds includes breeding sparrowhawk, kestrel, woodcock, cuckoo, tawny owl, great spotted woodpecker, whitethroat, blackcap, chiffchaff, garden, willow and wood warblers, pied and spotted flycatchers, four tits, treecreeper, jay, siskin and redpoll. Other breeding species are shelduck in rabbit burrows, oystercatcher, fulmar, tufted duck, ringed plover and rock pipit. Winter visitors include great northern diver, Slavonian grebe, eider and long-tailed ducks, scoter and smew. The shore is a fascinating mixture of rock pools, sandy shore and cliffs, and a fine place to look for green, pink and red agates amongst the pebbles.

T[D]. Refreshments, shop at Visitor Centre.

Wheelchairs have excellent access along fine paths.

Falls of Clyde   4

Map NS88-41- 165 acres (67 ha)
1 mile south of Lanark following Thistle signs for New Lanark to CP above the historic village of New Lanark. SSSI. Ancient gorge, woodland.

Access   AYR on foot to Visitor Centre for the reserve at the south end of village close to the Falls, which are visible and audible, from which pleasant riverside walks lead off.

Information   Leaflets and guides from the Visitor Centre: open daily Easter–mid-October 11 a.m.–5 p.m., otherwise W/Es 1–5 p.m. (except January). Parties should book in advance: 0555 65262. The Centre also has exhibits on the area and an A/V display. There are frequent guided walks.

History   The model village of New Lanark was begun about 1785 and managed from 1800 by Robert Owen, founder of the Co-operative movement. It became one of the world's largest cotton mill complexes. The whole is now being restored for present-day use.

What to See   The nature trail leads through deciduous woodland beside the Clyde, which includes birch, oak, rowan, hazel and Scots pine, to a viewpoint overlooking Corra Linn, a spectacular waterfall which drops 70 ft into a pool surrounded by cliffs. The spot was painted by Turner and visited by the poets

Wordsworth and Coleridge. A rich flora includes wood vetch, common cow-wheat and purple saxifrage. Dipper and kingfisher may be seen on the river whilst other breeding birds include great spotted woodpecker and spotted flycatcher. Red squirrel, badger, mink and roe deer live in the reserve.

T[D] in the main New Lanark Visitor Centre.

Wheelchairs have access to village and view of Falls.

Grey Mare's Tail

Map 79 NT18-14- 2511 acres (1016 ha)

10 miles north-east of Moffat on A708 along the Moffat Water. SSSI. Cliffs, upland flushes, loch, waterfall.

Access   AYR on foot from CP at NT187145 onto paths and slopes which can be slippery.

Information   Leaflet and guides from Information Point in CP: there is a summer warden.

History   The finest area for mountain vegetation in Southern Scotland with classic U-shaped valleys, corries and a hanging valley down which crashes a 200 ft waterfall, the Grey Mare's Tail, one of the biggest in Britain. The Silurian shales and Greywackes are sometimes base-rich and there are areas of relict oak wood with a good list of wild flowers. The outstanding feature, however, is the north and north-east facing cliffs, strongly calcareous in places, which carry a rich assemblage of montane and submontane plants. Above the waterfall lies Loch Skeen, once the nesting place of the sea eagle but now taken over by the common gull, though still the haunt of peregrine and raven.

What to See   The most important plants are oblong woodsia, holly fern, alpine saxifrage, pyramidal bugle, alpine mouse-ear, downy willow and black alpine-sedge. An Arctic-alpine moth, *Anarta melanopa*, is near its southern limit here and there is a large herd of feral goats which graze the plants on all but the steeper slopes.

Lochwinnoch

Map 63 NS35-58- 580 acres (235 ha)

8 miles south-west of Paisley via A737 towards Dalry: turn right at roundabout for Lochwinnoch onto A760 which crosses the reserve: well signposted to CP. SSSI. Open water, marsh, scrub, woodland.

Access   AYR 9 a.m.–9 p.m. or sunset on foot from CP at NS355583 onto nature trail with two hides (charge for non-RSPB members). Can be reached by train from Glasgow Central (not Sundays).

Information   Leaflets and guides from Visitor Centre in CP which also has exhibits and an A/V display, with an observation tower overlooking pools and meadows: open daily (except Christmas and New Year BHs) 10 a.m.–5.15 p.m. There are frequent guided walks.

History   The reserve is divided into the Aird Meadow to the north and the more extensive Barr Loch to the south. Early in the nineteenth century the meadow and loch were drained during the summer so that crops were grown and livestock grazed. But the system was abandoned in the 1950s and it has since reverted to marsh and scrub and extensive reed-beds. The area now attracts over 60 species of breeding birds amongst which the great crested grebe, with up to 11 breeding pairs, are a notable feature. The woodland consists of alder, ash, beech, lime, oak and rowan with a shrub layer of hawthorn, rhododendron and dog-rose.

What to See   Breeding water birds include little grebe, mallard, tufted duck, teal, shoveler and mute swan whilst sedge, willow, grasshopper and garden warblers and blackcap also breed here attracting cuckoos to their nests. The list of migrant birds has whimbrel, spotted redshank, greenshank and ruff and in winter the Centre is surrounded by redwing and fieldfare with wigeon, greylag geese, pochard, goldeneye, goosander and whooper swan on the pools. Colourful plants include yellow water-lily and bogbean in the water, marsh-marigold, marsh cinquefoil and purple-loosestrife round the margin, with wood crane's-bill, greater butterfly and bird's-nest orchids and broad-leaved helleborine in the wood.

T[D] Shop, refreshments at W/Es, picnic site at Visitor Centre.
Wheelchairs have access to hides.

Southwick Coast 7

Map 84 NX91-56- 40 acres (16 ha)
5 miles south-east of Dalbeattie on the A710 beyond Sandyhills between the road and the sea. SSSI. Wooded cliffs, fen, salt marsh.

Access   AYR on foot from CP near the east end of the reserve at the turning to Nether Clifton at NX913562.

Information   Leaflet from TI Offices in Dalbeattie and Dumfries or from SWT.

History   The cliffs are made of volcanic rocks and were formed after the last glaciation when the sea level was higher—now they are separated from the sea by the Southwick and Preston Merses. A natural rock arch, the Needles Eye, passed through on the path from the CP and a stack, Lot's Wife, were also formed by the sea. The narrow oakwood along the shore, Heughwood, appears to be undisturbed and includes some ancient woodland indicators. The Merse attracts vast numbers of wildfowl in winter.

What to See   The woodland contains holly, hazel and early-purple orchid whilst the marsh below has sea club-rush, sea lavender and beds of reeds. In winter the shore attracts barnacle geese, greylag and pinkfeet which spill over from the internationally significant Solway populations which can be seen at Caerlaverock (q.v.). The Merse is also a breeding area for lapwing, redshank, dunlin and oystercatcher.

Wood of Cree

Map 83 NX38-70- 590 acres (239 ha)
4 miles north of Newton Stewart on the east side of River Cree via minor road
from the east end of bridge: well signposted over two bridges, then cattle grid
to parking space on the west side of road. SSSI. Sessile oakwood, marshes,
streams, moorland.

Access   AYR on foot from parking space at NX382708 onto 1-mile long forest
walk.

Information   Notice board at entrance: Warden at Gairland, Old Edinburgh
Road, Minigaff, Newton Stewart DG8 6PL. 0671 2861.

History   There are historical references to a wood here in the thirteenth
century and the reserve is part of the largest remaining ancient woodland in
Southern Scotland. It was clear-felled in 1875 but has regenerated into an
overgrown coppice of sessile and hybrid oak with ash, birch, hazel, rowan and
willow. On the west side of the road are marshy meadows beside the River Cree,
a fine salmon river.

What to See   Woodland wild flowers include bluebell, primrose, ramsons,
common cow-wheat, woodrush and bilberry whilst the damp meadows have
purple-loosestrife, yellow iris, sneezewort, marsh bedstraw and meadowsweet.
Amongst the birds are grasshopper, wood and garden warblers, redstart, tree
pipit, spotted and pied flycatchers and willow tit, the last two rare in Scotland.
Tawny owl, buzzard and sparrowhawk occasionally nest: dipper, grey wagtail
and goosander work the streams and the river. Purple hairstreak and Scotch
argus fly in the clearings where damselflies and dragonflies are abundant.

West Central

It would be very hard indeed to find another part of Britain which would attract
so many superlatives as the West Central area. It has, in Loch Lomond, the
largest freshwater lake in Britain; in Flanders Moss, the largest raised valley bog
in Britain and, in Taynish, one of the largest remaining areas of native oakwoods
in Scotland. In addition it is penetrated in the south and west by long fingers
of the sea bringing damp, warm, frost-preventing Atlantic air miles inland: it
is 35 miles from the open sea at Ardlamont Point to the head of Loch Fyne at
Clachan and yet, only four miles away, Ben Ime, rising to over 3300 ft, carries
an arctic-alpine flora so that the region can also demonstrate one of the most
rapid changes of climate anywhere in Britain.

Ben Ime is at the north end of the *Argyll Forest Park*, one of the two
magnificent Parks which give access to such a large part of this region. The other
is the *Queen Elizabeth Forest Park* which includes, in the Trossachs and Loch
Ard, some of the most beautiful Highland scenery in easy reach of Glasgow and
Edinburgh. It holds too the high cliffs on Ben Lomond which, with Ben Ledi and
Ben Vorlich, form the major peaks across the southern Highlands.

Ben Lomond is but one of the features of the east side of *Loch Lomond* which, on its shore line and on its islands towards the south-east corner, has some of the least exploited woodlands, showing a greater variety, than anywhere else in the Highlands: the Highland Boundary Fault crosses the Loch and juxtaposes acid sandstones with base-rich limestones to give a wide range of soils.

A very similar juxtaposition, which brings about similar variety, can be seen in *Glen Nant* on the way to Oban. Here is an example of a wood which has been exploited for hundreds of years for timber and, in the eighteenth and nineteenth centuries, to supply charcoal for iron smelting on Loch Fyne and Loch Etive: the old stools of coppiced oak can still be seen and, had they not been of economic importance, these woods would probably have disappeared long ago.

Perhaps even finer than Glen Nant is *Taynish*, lapped on both sides by the Atlantic on the remote west coast of Kintyre: the trees here are festooned with lichens, the woodland floor is a maze of boulders covered in luxuriant mosses whilst on the shore is the additional bonus of frequent sightings of otters and seals.

But to see seals, both common and grey, and other large sea mammals like dolphins, porpoises and whales there can be few better places than the Scottish Wildlife Trust reserve of *Carradale Point*, another 30 miles further south on the east side of Kintyre overlooking the hills of Arran—with Goat Fell in front of you and a goat smell behind you, because Carradale harbours an unusual herd of white, wild goats.

But not all the best places to enjoy wildlife are so far afield. Ever since the early nineteenth century Glasgow naturalists have been taking the short journey to *Possil Marsh*, only 3 miles north of the city centre. According to Sir William Hooker, Professor of Botany at the University 1820–41, 'Every Glasgow naturalist is baptised in Possil Marsh.' A wonderful example, on the doorstep, of the rich variety of wildlife which awaits the naturalist who goes on to probe more widely into this extraordinary region.

- Scottish Wildlife Trust (SWT), 25 Johnston Terrace, Edinburgh EH1 2NH. 031 226 4602.

Argyll Forest Park   9

Maps 56 and 63 NS18 and 19, NN10- 20,100 square miles (21,500 ha)
Between Loch Fyne and Loch Long. Forest Park. Moorland, corries, woodland, sea lochs.

Access   AYR from many points on A83, A815, B828 and B839 which pass through it. Details from Forest Offices at Ardgartan on A83 at NN272034; Glenbranter on A815 at NS112977; and Kilmun on the north side of Holy Loch at NS160825.

Information   Guides and trail leaflets from Forest Offices.

History   The first Forest Park in Britain, set up in 1935, and a demonstration of the coordination of forestry with tourism and natural history. Less than half the land is afforested, with the upper limit of planting at about 1350 ft. Above this lies moorland with many peaks over 2000 ft and some over 3000 ft where arctic and alpine plants are not uncommon on north and east facing corries. Elsewhere semi-natural oakwood survives, especially on loch shores and in gullies in the glens, with a mixture of ash, birch, hazel and alder. No part of the Park is more than 4 miles from the sea: it is mild and damp and extremely rich in ferns, mosses, liverworts and lichens. The sea lochs have dense beds of seaweeds sheltering large numbers of sea creatures attractive to birds, seals and even basking sharks.

What to See   Arctic and alpine flowers include alpine lady's-mantle, alpine meadow-rue, moss campion, dwarf willow, alpine lady-fern, alpine saw-wort, holly fern, globeflower, purple saxifrage and roseroot. Woods are full of bluebell, wood anemone, dog-violet and primrose in spring. Moorland birds include buzzard, raven, red grouse, curlew, twite, skylark and stonechat with occasional golden eagle. Lower down, in the woods, there are wood, willow and garden warblers, chiffchaff, blackcap, long-tailed, great, blue and coal tits. Otters feed in the rivers and sea lochs and golden-ringed dragonflies hawk over the bogs.

T at Forest Offices.

Wheelchairs have excellent views of woods and sea lochs.

Carradale Point   10

Map 69 NR81-37- 173 acres (70 ha)
1 mile south of Carradale on the east side of Mull of Kintyre opposite the middle of Arran. Coastal grassland, low cliffs, feral goats.

Access   AYR on foot from:
1. Port Righ at the road end at NR816378.
2. track on the right 100 yds before bend on the road into Port Righ which leads to CP at NR 815376 and the path to the north-west corner of the reserve onto a 3-mile circular walk.

Information   Nothing on site: leaflet from TI Offices at Tarbert or Campbeltown.

History   A small, hilly promontary reaching 133 ft covered in grass, heather and bracken with marshes and ditches and fine views over Kilbrannan Sound to the Arran hills. This is the best place on the west coast of Scotland for seeing large marine mammals. The area became a reserve at the instigation of author, Naomi Mitchison, particularly to try to protect an unusual herd of white feral goats which have grazed here for over a hundred years. Nearly destroyed by shooting in the late 1970s the herd is slowly being rebuilt.

What to See   The large mammals which may be seen include common porpoise, white-beaked dolphin, bottle-nosed and killer whales: both common and grey seals bask on rocks off shore. Sika, fallow and roe deer all graze on the point, one of the few places in Scotland where all three are together, whilst otters work the shoreline and frequent caves on the east side. Gannet are frequent off shore with red-breasted merganser, red-throated diver and eider. Kestrel, buzzard and golden eagle may be seen overhead whilst slow worm, common lizard and adder must be avoided underfoot.

Glen Nant

11

Map 55 NN01-28- 500 acres (200 ha)
3 miles south of Taynuilt on both sides of B845. NNR. Deciduous woodland.

Access   AYR on foot from FC CP on the west side of valley at NN014280 onto way-marked nature trail of 1¼–2 hours.

Information   The nature trail is self-guiding with numerous marked instructive posts: the leaflet available from FC is not essential.

History   These woods were formerly the source of charcoal for the Bonawe Iron Furnace and the signs are still apparent: stumps of coppiced oaks and levelled circles where charcoal was made. The Glen is a narrow ravine in volcanic lavas of Old Red sandstone age with some glacial drift which combine to produce a wide range of soils. Ash and hazel are dominant on calcareous rocks with an understorey of hawthorn, blackthorn and guelder-rose whilst sessile oak and birch with rowan, holly and bird cherry are present on acid soils: ferns, lichens, mosses and liverworts are particularly abundant.

What to See   Lime-loving herbs of the woodland floor include primrose, ramsons and wild strawberry: elsewhere there are small quantities of mountain melick, globeflower and bird's-nest orchid. The presence of Wilson's filmy-fern and hay-scented buckler-fern represents a strong Atlantic element. Breeding birds include great spotted woodpecker, redstart and wood warbler. Roe deer are common and cause considerable damage to young trees.

Loch Lomond

12

Map 64 NS41-90- 1057 acres (428 ha)
At Balmaha 4 miles west of Drymen on B837 in the south-east corner of Loch Lomond.

Access   By boat to Inchcailloch, an island opposite the pier at Balmaha at NS418909. Boats run regularly from the boat yard (small charge).

Information   There is a leaflet to the 2½-mile nature trail round Inchcailloch from the boat-yard or the village shop in Balmaha. Other information on Loch Lomond from TI Office in Library in Drymen in the south-west corner of the charming little square; open daily (not Weds and Sun).

History   Loch Lomond is the largest freshwater lake in Britain and the reserve includes sections of its beautiful wooded shores as well as the five islands of Inchcailloch, Torrinch, Creinch, Clairinsh and Aber Isle. A fine example of sessile oakwood can be seen on Inchcailloch with alder and ash in damper areas and

Scots pine on drier rocks with willow, broom, gorse, bog-myrtle and guelder-rose on the Loch shore. The islands lie along the line of the Highland Boundary Fault which occurs at the junction of the Old Red sandstone and the Dolomite Fault Rock which is rich in lime and affects the flora. The islands shelter the south-east corner of the loch which attracts wildfowl in winter.

What to See   The lime-rich soil supports dog's mercury, woodruff and sanicle whereas the acid soils have heather, bilberry and honeysuckle: in wetter areas yellow iris and ramsons occur whilst tutsan, globeflower, columbine and whorled caraway may be found along the islands' shores. On the mainland is the only British locality of the rare Scottish dock. Greylag geese and whooper swan winter here with a small number of Greenland white-fronts. A few whooper stay to breed with some shoveler and shelduck: in dry years a large number of waders stop to feed on the muddy shores during migration. The oaks support large numbers of caterpillars which attract many woodland birds such as garden, willow and wood warblers, tree pipit, redstart and great spotted woodpecker.

T[D]. Refreshments in Balmaha.

Possil Marsh   13

Map 64 NS58-70- 69 acres (28 ha)
3 miles north of Queen Street Station, Glasgow between A879 to Milngavie and Forth and Clyde Canal. SSSI. Bird Sanctuary. Loch, marsh, dry grassland, scrub.

Access   AYR on foot from the parking space at Lambhill Bridge at the south end of reserve at NS584695.

Information   Nothing on site: leaflet from SWT.

History   A fragment of once-extensive system of lochs and marshes which covered much of west-central Scotland. Most were drained in the late nineteenth and early twentieth centuries: Possil Marsh survived because it was needed to help control the level of the adjacent canal. But, being so near to Glasgow, it suffered from human interference and, to protect the birds of the loch, it was acquired and declared a nature reserve in 1930 and given as a gift to SWT in 1982.

What to See   Over 150 species of birds recorded include breeding reed bunting, little grebe, tufted duck and moorhen: great crested grebe, redshank and water rail are less frequent visitors whilst many migrants stop in spring and winter. The loch is surrounded by a fringe of bulrush with marsh cinquefoil, bottle sedge, greater spearwort, mare's-tail and the rare tufted loosestrife in the swampy margin. Large numbers of invertebrates have been recorded over the years by generations of Glasgow naturalists.

Queen Elizabeth Forest Park, David Marshall Lodge

14

Map 57 NN52-01- 200 square miles
½ mile north of Aberfoyle on A821 to Trossachs. SSSI, part NNR, Forest Park, Moorland, corries, woodland, lochs.

Access   AYR on foot from CP below Visitor Centre at NN520015 onto good network of well-marked paths and nature trails.

Information   Leaflets and guides from Visitor Centre; open daily April– October. The trails have excellent, durable, informative signs *en route*. There is an impressive wall map of the area in the Centre. Other details of area from TI Office in Aberfoyle.

History   The Park includes the well-wooded eastern shore of Loch Lomond, Scotland's favourite mountain, Ben Lomond and, in the Trossachs, some of the most romantic scenery in the Highlands. The woodlands round Aberfoyle are a mixture of native oak, birch and juniper and introduced conifers. The trail from David Marshall Lodge leads through the forest to a waterfall passing abundant slate quarries and climbing to a viewpoint above Loch Achray. The lochs and lochans attract small numbers of duck in winter.

What to See   Areas of natural oakwood have bluebell, dog's mercury and wood-sorrel: elsewhere bilberry, heather and wavy hair-grass predominate whilst boggy ground has cross-leaved heath and bog-myrtle, with globeflower and lesser clubmoss along stream sides. Woodland birds include pied flycatcher, wood warbler, redstart, woodcock, tawny and short-eared owls, siskin, redpoll, crossbill, green and great spotted woodpecker with goldcrest in the conifers. Dipper and grey wagtail work along the streams whilst little grebe, goosander, goldeneye and pochard live on the lochs where heron fish in the shallows. Otter and water vole are also occasionally seen along the shores whilst red squirrel feed in the pines amongst which the roe deer roam.

T[D]. Refreshments at the Lodge.
Wheelchairs can be driven to the Lodge for superb views.

Taynish

15

Map 55 NR73-84- 914 acres (370 ha)
10 miles south-west of Lochgilphead on a minor road to the east of B8025 which turns off immediately south of Tayvallich village. NNR. Oakwoods, bogs, heath, marine life.

Access   AYR on foot from road which ends for unauthorized vehicles near the south end of Lochan Taynish at NR735852 onto track which leads through reserve. Please keep to path and keep dogs on a lead.

Information   Nothing on site: leaflet from NCC.

History   This peninsula has one of the most extensive oakwoods left in Scotland. It consists of a system of north-east/south-west ridges and hollows which result in a great range of soils supporting three main types of woodland: sessile oakwood on block scree and well-drained slopes; mixed deciduous woods with ash, wych elm, alder and hazel on the lower slopes near sea-level; and birch wood on the upper and exposed slopes. Waterlogged hollows have rich fen communities and Lochan Taynish a swamp of bottle sedge. The area has a remarkable moss and liverwort list with several Mediterranean/Atlantic species at or near their northern limit.

What to See   Woodland wildflowers include wood-sorrel, bugle, climbing corydalis and enchanter's-nightshade with Tonbridge and Wilson's filmy-ferns, hay-scented buckler-fern and oak fern locally frequent. Heath-spotted and northern marsh-orchids grow in open areas where Scotch argus butterflies are abundant in August. Herons feed on the shore of Linne Mhuirich on the west side of the peninsula where wigeon are attracted to the beds of eelgrass in winter. Common seal and otter frequent the unpolluted water.

SOUTH-EAST
SCOTLAND

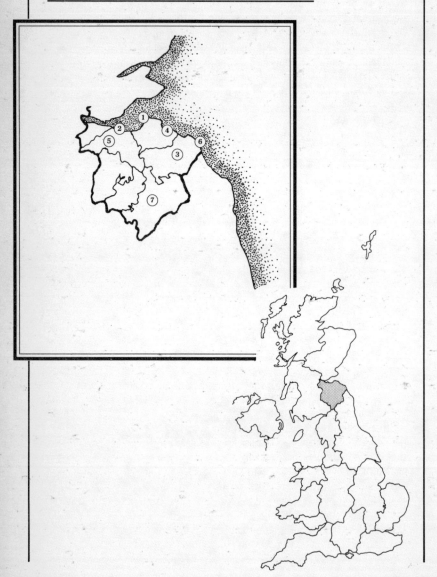

Borders and Lothian

The well-advised traveller to Scotland for the first time will take the A68 up Redesdale to Carter Bar where, suddenly, at the top of the crest you enter another land and the Scottish Borders lie below, sun-flecked and green, an endless succession of hummocky hills and valleys. The road down the other side soon picks up a tributary of the River Tweed as it descends into the valley of this great salmon river which provides some of the most fertile agricultural land in the region.

The northern tributaries of the Tweed come from the Lammermuirs which, with the Moorfoots and the Pentlands, form a ring of hills round the south side of Lothian with Edinburgh at its heart. Keeping to the A68 the 'Carter Bar experience' can be repeated as the descent from the Lammermuirs begins at Soutra Mains. From here the eye can take in the coastal plain from Auld Reekie to Dunbar, the sweep of the Firth of Forth beyond, half the width of Scotland, and the series of volcanic plugs which are the outstanding, and upstanding, features of the landscape: Castle Rock and Arthur's Seat in Edinburgh, North Berwick Law, which is not a coal tip, on the coast, and the Bass Rock off it.

It is within this varied framework, but particularly along the superb 80 mile coastline, that some of the best, but least known, habitats for wildlife in Scotland are to be found.

Those bare hills, covered today in a mixture of grassland and heather managed for red grouse, were once covered in woods of birch and juniper: most have been lost and, of the very few fragments which remain today, the best are sessile oakwoods in the steep valleys, especially in the tributaries of the Tweed, such as *Whitlaw Wood* on the outskirts of Hawick, and in the deep, narrow gorges which run from the Lammermuirs to the sea, such as Woodhall Dean inland from Dunbar.

Elsewhere the woods are of planted origin. Some of the more recent conifer plantations have been created sympathetically with wide rides and clearings but cannot yet compare with the old policy woodlands planted several centuries ago around the great estates and in their parks such as the Hirsel and Bowhill: some, including those around *Duns Castle*, on the north edge of the Merse, are now valuable nature reserves.

Other losses in the uplands, for which there is no substitute, have followed the draining and cutting of the raised bogs and valley bogs which built up over thousands of years: the handful which remain must be protected, not only from exploitation but from the more insidious threat of eutrophication and spraying from adjacent farms. Several bogs are now in the care of the Scottish Wildlife Trust, notably Gordon Moss, and the *Red Moss of Balerno* in the Pentlands less than 10 miles from Edinburgh.

The Old Red sandstone and Carboniferous grits which underlie much of the region rarely carry sites rich in wild flowers and the base-rich volcanic basalts often seem like oases in a botanical desert—none more so than *St Abb's Head* where the grassy slopes down to the sea are bright with primrose, rock-rose, thyme and thrift in spring and early summer. Important as these are locally they cannot compare with the international significance of those superb cliffs which are the breeding site for over 60,000 sea-birds.

From here the coast stretches 80 miles to Bo'ness embracing on the way every kind of maritime habitat including a marine nature reserve at St Abb's and the gannetry on Bass Rock which is the wildlife spectacular of the region. The shoreline of the Forth is famous for its wintering ducks, geese and waders, particularly in East Lothian where *Aberlady Bay* and the *John Muir Country Park*, formerly known as Tyninghame, give exceptional opportunities to watch sea-birds and birds at sea within half an hour's drive of the centre of Edinburgh.

Even closer, beneath the crags of one of the most famous habitats in Scotland, Arthur's Seat, with its rare flowers and ferns, birds can be watched before breakfast or during the lunch hour on *Duddingston Loch*, an SWT reserve within the city.

There is wildlife to enjoy almost everywhere in this region, even when visiting SWT's offices on the slopes of Castle Rock in Edinburgh which is a blaze of yellow wallflowers in spring.

- Scottish Wildlife Trust (SWT), 25 Johnston Terrace, Edinburgh EH1 2NH. 031 226 4602.

Aberlady Bay   1

Map 66 NT46-80- 1439 acres (582 ha)
1 mile north of Aberlady on A198 East Lothian Coast road. LNR. Mud flats, salt marsh, freshwater marsh, grassland, scrub, sand dunes, lime-rich grassland.

Access   AYR on foot from:

1. CP on bend of A198 east of Aberlady at NT471805 across a flimsy footbridge visible from road.
2. CP on Gullane Links at NT465831.

Information   Notice board at entrance east of Aberlady with up-to-date bird news.

History   The first site in Britain to be declared a Local Nature reserve on 16 July 1952, which gave a measure of protection from wildfowlers who now operate under a permit system, so that it has become the most valuable site for dabbling ducks on the south side of the Firth of Forth: it also attracts a large number of pinkfeet. The area is of great botanical interest: there are grey dunes carrying large numbers of mosses and lichens, large areas are dominated by dense thickets of sea buckthorn and others with extensive dune slacks and pools.

What to See   On the shore prickly saltwort, lymegrass and rush-leaved fescue occur whilst the dunes have purple milk-vetch, wild thyme and hairy violet: features of the slacks are grass-of-Parnassus and early and northern marsh-orchids. The pools hold fen pondweed, greater bladderwort, bog pimpernel and marsh stitchwort whilst Scots lovage may be seen on the rocks. In winter up to 15,000 pinkfeet roost here at night with a small flock of whooper swan. Waders include grey plover, bar-tailed godwit and knot whilst purple sandpiper and turnstone feed on the rocky shore. There are many interesting ducks in the bay: long-tailed, common and velvet scoters, red-breasted merganser and eider, the latter nesting in large numbers in the dunes. Divers especially red-throated, are common whilst this is the best place in Britain to see red-necked grebes. Merlin and peregrine may be seen hunting. Harvest mice reach their northern limit in Britain here.

T at CP east of Aberlady.

Wheelchairs have limited access from Gullane Links CP: good viewing from Longniddry.

Duddingston Loch and Bawsinch 2

Map 66 NT28-72- 65 acres (26 ha)
On the south-east side of Arthur's Seat, Edinburgh in Old Church Lane, Duddingston. SSSI. Wildfowl loch, reed-bed, ponds, goose-green.

Access   AYR viewing over the reserve from CP on the north shore at NT283726. Key available for access to hide from Holyrood Park Visitor Centre in Holyrood Road near the Palace. Gate is in Duddingston Road West on the east side of the reserve.

Information   Leaflet from Holyrood Park Visitor Centre: open daily June–September noon–4 p.m., May W/Es 10 a.m.–5 p.m.

History   The loch and woodland were presented to the nation in 1923 and designated as a bird sanctuary in 1925. Bawsinch, a former market garden, was purchased by SWT in 1971 after planning permission to build houses had been refused. New habitats, including ponds, scrub, woods and grassland, have been created. Trees planted are mainly oak, aspen, birch, hazel, alder, ash, wild and bird cherry, and willow but there are some Scots pine, rowan, juniper and larch. There is a complete collection of native trees.

What to See   A large flock of over 200 greylag geese are descendents of 13 released here in 1961. Other breeding waterfowl are great crested grebe, tufted duck, mute swan and mallard. There is a heronry, a large population of coot as well as many sedge warbler in the reed-bed. In winter pochard, teal, shoveler and goldeneye may be seen. Pochard have declined in recent years—they fed at night at sewage outfalls in the Firth of Forth and roosted here by day—but new sewage works have reduced the food source.

Duns Castle 3

Map 74 NT77-54- 190 acres (77 ha)
On north side of Duns town between Duns Castle and B6365. Mixed planted woods, artificial lochs.

Access   AYR on foot to:

1. south end through gateway at top of Castle Street through Castle grounds for 10 minutes on good track keeping right after memorial to John Duns Scotus.
2. north end via B6365 from Duns to bottom of hill, with sign to Duns Castle, to CP in 50 yds at NT783560 from which way-marked path leads to hide on west side of lake.

Information   Notice board near entrance: leaflet from SWT.

History   The reserve is contained within a former glacial drainage channel between Duns Law to the east and Hare Law to the west. A mire once covered the area but this was excavated in the eighteenth century to create the two lochs, Hen Poo, covering 18 acres, to the south and the much smaller Mill Dam to the north.

The surrounding land was then planted with native and introduced hardwoods principally beech, ash and oak. Mill Dam was used to power the estate sawmill and the woods have been intensively managed for timber for 200 years. There are rides and glades attractive to butterflies.

What to See   Water plants around Hen Poo include yellow water-lily, greater spearwort, sweet-flag, bogbean and bulrush. The woods have ramsons, wood crane's-bill, water avens, purple toothwort, naturalized near the Castle, common twayblade and common wintergreen. Nesting birds are green and great spotted woodpecker, pied flycatcher, redstart, chiffchaff, marsh tit and four other species of tits, mallard and mute swan whilst pochard, goosander and tufted duck are present in winter. The long list of mammals includes roe deer, badger, red squirrel, water shrew and occasional otter.

T. Refreshments in Duns town.

Wheelchairs have easy access on good track from Castle Street entrance.

John Muir Country Park   4

Map 66 NT6-7- 1667 acres (675 ha)
Lothian Coast north of the A1 immediately west of Dunbar including Belhaven Bay; Tyne Sands and Dunbar Castle. Sand spits, mud flats, sand dunes, woods, cliffs.

Access   AYR on foot from four CPs from west to east:

1. Tyninghame Links via turning to east off A198 between Whitekirk and Tyninghame at NT628810.
2. Linkfield via turning to north off road to Dunbar ½ mile after leaving A1 just before West Barnes village sign at NT650783.
3. Belhaven at west end of Shore Road at NT662786.
4. Dunbar close to Castle ruins and the harbour at NT678791.

Information   Leaflets from TI Office, Main Street, Dunbar: notice boards on access roads and on site.

History   The Park takes its name from John Muir, born in Dunbar in 1838, who was taken to America in 1849 and became a founder of the National Park System there. This Park was established and named after him in 1976 when it was the first of its kind in Scotland. The heart of the Park is the estuary of the River Tyne of which the west end is partially enclosed by two sand spits, Sandy Hurst and Spine Island: this provides a haven for waders, especially in winter, whilst buckthorn scrub gives cover for smaller birds.

What to See   The mud flats have eelgrass and glasswort with saltmarsh-grass and sea-milkwort in the marshes. There are volcanic rocks with bloody crane's-bill and cliffs at Dunbar with meadow saxifrage. Shelduck, mallard, redshank, ringed plover, kittiwake and eider duck breed in the Park whilst turnstone, purple sandpiper, wigeon, teal, goldeneye, bar-tailed godwit, knot, dunlin, oystercatcher and about 80 mute and whooper swans are regular winter visitors. Great, arctic and pomarine skua are often seen offshore in autumn with gannet from Bass Rock ever present.

T[D] at Linkfield and Belhaven CPs.

Wheelchairs have good access.

Red Moss of Balerno   `5`

Map 65 NT16-64- 57 acres (23 ha)
1½ miles south of Balerno west of minor road to Bavelaw Castle just after Marchbank Hotel. SSSI. Raised bog, birch wood.

Access   AYR on foot from parking space on west side of road at NT164636 to east side of reserve. Please do not walk on the bog surface which is easily damaged and dangerous.

Information   Nothing on site: leaflet from SWT.

History   One of only four raised bogs surviving in the Lothians. It is 20 ft deep in places with a domed top covered in heather, cottongrass and six species of *Sphagnum*: the lower margin is fringed with rowan, birch, Scots pine and willow. It was set aside in the seventeenth century as a source of peat and *Sphagnum*, the latter as a dressing for wounds. To maintain the water level so that active growth can continue the drainage channels have been dammed.

What to See   The 'Moss' has bog asphodel, round-leaved sundew, ragged-Robin, lesser spearwort, marsh ragwort, cuckooflower and heath spotted-orchid. The marginal thicket attracts breeding redpoll, willow warbler and tree pipit whilst hen harrier and short-eared owl may quarter the reserve: snipe display over the heather in spring. Common lizard, frog and toad live here and roe deer come to graze.

St Abb's Head   `6`

Map 67 NT91-69- 192 acres (77 ha)
On coast off B6438 1 mile north-east of Coldingham from which there are

signposts. NNR. Sea cliffs, freshwater, coastal grassland, marine nature reserve.

Access   AYR on foot from:

1. Main CP on road from Coldingham to St Abb's village at NT912674 to path which leads to reserve after ⅓ mile.
2. CP at Harelaw Hill at NT913692 via road from main CP.

Information   Leaflets from fine small Visitor Centre down steps from main CP: open daily April–September 10 a.m.–5 p.m. Leaflets also from TI Office in Eyemouth Museum.

History   Magnificent coastal scenery with sheer cliffs of volcanic basalt which drop nearly 300 ft to narrow shingle beaches, flanked by softer, more acid, sedimentary rocks which form sloping cliffs. The soils vary from acid to basic and carry a wide range of plants. These cliffs also provide nesting sites for up to 60,000 sea birds from April to late July which are most easily seen on cliffs and stacks to the north-west of the lighthouse. There is also good sea watching, especially in autumn, whilst small birds settle in the shelter of the scrub round the artificial Mire Loch on the route to the cliffs.

What to See   Wild flowers include early-purple orchid, cowslip, primrose, purple milk-vetch, rock-rose, common thyme, thrift, spring sandwort, with heath milkwort and tormentil on more acid sites and Scots lovage on steep grassy banks. The majority of nesting birds are kittiwake and guillemot with razorbill, shag and fulmar in smaller numbers and occasional puffin. There is a good list of butterflies such as northern brown argus, grayling, small copper and common blue.

T[D] Refreshments (good cakes) at Visitor Centre: open daily June – September, W/Es April, May and October.

Wheelchairs have access from CP at Harelaw Hill.

Whitlaw Wood

7

Map 79 NT50-13- 22 acres (9 ha)
1 mile south of Hawick on south side of B6399. SSSI. Ancient broad-leaved woodland, herb-rich meadow.

Access   AYR on foot from the parking space at NT495139 on Haggis Ha' Brae, a continuation of Rosebank Road going south-west from Hawick, along the track to the entrance in 500 yds.

Information   Nothing on site.

History   The wood is on Silurian shales and Greywackes, base-rich in places, on a north facing slope above the Slitrig Water where it turns north to join the River Teviot. The dominant trees are ash and elm with some beech, hazel, wild cherry, oak, rowan and blackthorn: much hazel coppice is present which was last cut in the 1950s. Many of the elms have been killed by Dutch elm disease but have been left as habitats for birds, mosses and ferns. There is a small herb-rich meadow in the wood which helps to swell the plant list to over 120 species.

What to See   The ground flora contains primrose, woodruff, goldilocks buttercup, wood vetch, wood-sedge, sanicle, early-purple and bird's-nest orchids whilst wet flushes have wild angelica and meadowsweet. Woodland birds include woodcock, great spotted woodpecker and sparrowhawk whilst dipper and grey wagtail feed along the river.

NORTH
SCOTLAND

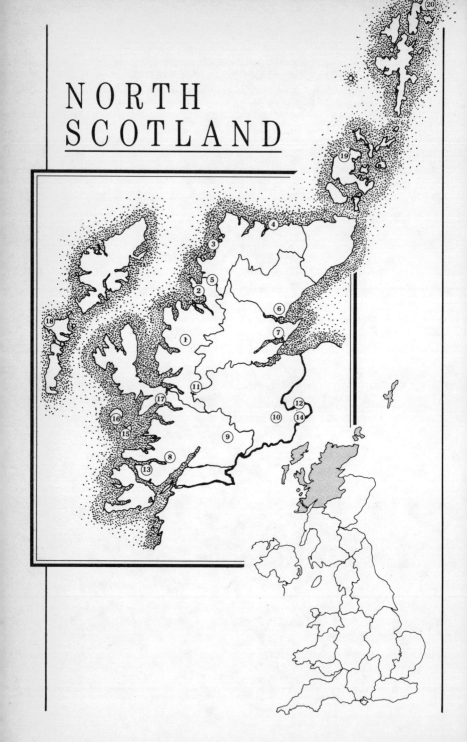

Highland North

Scotland north of Inverness contains some of the remotest and most haunting landscapes in Britain. Whereas further south there are deep glens where the traveller feels penned in by mountains, in the north individual mountains like Stac Pollaidh, Cul Mor, Cul Beag and Ben Hope can be recognized from a distance by their distinctive shapes. In between is space—in the north-west this is space for the most part without people, except in villages and small towns, almost all on the coast.

Stac Pollaidh, Cul Mor and Cul Beag all fall within the *Inverpolly* National Nature Reserve, the second largest, after Cairngorm, in Britain: it is without roads except round the perimeter and, with a rough and difficult terrain which deters most walkers, it is one of a small and diminishing number of real wildernesses left in this country where nature is largely undisturbed. It is joined, on its south side, to the Scottish Wildlife Trust Reserve of *Ben More Coigach* and, together, they cover nearly 64 square miles on the west coast north of Ullapool.

The shape of these mountains is distinct because their outlines are bare of trees and many slopes are rock fields with sparse vegetation of any kind. But, here and there, are occasional fragments of woodland. At Inverpolly and Coigach, on the acid rocks of the Lewissian Gneiss and Torridonean sandstone, birch is normally the dominant tree which regenerates, especially on islands in lochs which the abundant red deer cannot reach. But, in some areas further south, relics of the old Caledonian pine forest persist, notably on the slopes above Loch Maree where one of the finest is safeguarded within the boundaries of the *Beinn Eighe* National Nature Reserve, the first to be established in Britain, over 40 years ago.

Though most of the riches in the north are on acid rocks there is a narrow band of Durness limestone which runs up the western side from Kishorn, north of Skye, to reach the north coast east of Cape Wrath, and on it pine gives way to ash—most importantly in the Rassal Ashwood NNR where about 30 acres of limestone pavement is covered by the most northerly ashwood in Britain.

Trees are less restricted on the east side of this region and, on the low-lying coastal strip and up the straths which run down to it, there are large areas of plantations of mainly native trees, some over 200 years old, which have now developed a strong woodland ground flora. Fine examples can now be seen around *Loch Fleet* with Balblair Woods on its north shore and the fine alder woods of The Mound inland.

More controversial tree planting has been taking place further north where large parts of the continuous blanket bog of the 'Flow Country' of Sutherland and Caithness have been drained and covered with totally alien conifers destroying a habitat of world importance in the process.

Loch Fleet has one of the few areas of sand dunes on this coast where several plant species, like purple milk-vetch, are near their northern limit in Britain. Elsewhere along this coastline the land falls sheer into the sea in a series of superb stretches of cliff: in the north and east the Old Red sandstone of Caithness including, most famously, John O'Groats and, in the north west, the Torridonean sandstone of Sutherland which weathers into ledges which hold large numbers of breeding guillemot, kittiwake and fulmar, with black guillemot on rocks below and puffins in the turf above the cliffs.

In between the sandstones lie the Moine schists, which form a wedge over 30 miles wide through the region and dominate the coast between Strathy Point and Whiten Head. In the middle of this stretch, at *Invernaver*, is one of the most remarkable areas for plants in the British Isles, known to botanists as Bettyhill, the nearby village. Lime-rich sands blown over the schists by the northerly gales of centuries have allowed a fascinating mixture of lime-hating and lime-loving species to grow side-by-side whilst, at the same time, the cool summers of this exposed coast brings many mountain plants down to sea-level with sheets of mountain avens, bearberry and mountain cranberry just behind the beach.

One of the most remarkable places for birds is the small island of *Handa*, just a few hundred yards off the west Sutherland coast, where the cries of 100,000 nesting sea-birds in summer almost drown the crashing of the waves 300ft below.

The most remarkable area for birds in the region in winter, is Cromarty Firth: behind its narrow mouth this deep Firth opens out into sheltered areas of mud flats and sand banks which attract wildfowl and waders in vast numbers particularly into *Nigg and Udale Bays*. Since the 1960s this shelter has also attracted industrialists and the growth of chemical factories, a now defunct aluminium smelter and oil-rig maintenance yards has brought considerable human influence into a region which is otherwise still so little affected by man.

● Scottish Wildlife Trust (SWT), Northern Office, Pitgaveny House Flat, Elgin, Moray IV30 2PQ. 0343 548105.

Beinn Eighe   1

Map 19 NG97-60- 11,752 acres (4758 ha)
2 miles north-west of Kinlochewe, west of the A832 between Achnasheen and Gairloch. NNR, Biosphere Reserve. Pine forest, bog, moorland, mountain.

Access   AYR on foot from CP on the east side of road at NH002650 to two nature trails:

1. 1 mile long, rising to 300 ft takes 1 hour.
2. 4 miles long, rising to 1800 ft takes 4–5 hours of often stiff walking over rocky ground for which strong shoes are essential.

Information   Trail guides from dispenser in CP. Other publications and a historical display on crofting at the Aultroy Visitor Centre, 1 mile towards Kinlochewe on the west side of road: open Mon–Fri 9 a.m.–12noon, 1–5 p.m. Leaflets also from Filling Station in Kinlochewe.

History   This was the first NNR in Britain selected particularly for the native pine woods which cover the lower east end and south flanks of this rugged mountain area. The lower ground is often too wet for tree growth and develops into open, boggy areas: one of these, visible from the higher nature trail, is called Tansley Bog and was named after the pioneer British ecologist, Sir Arthur Tansley, who was the first chairman of the Nature Conservancy, as the first government conservation organization was called when set up in 1949. The high ground above 1000 ft is a good example of mountains and moorlands of the northern Highlands and rises to 3309 ft. The reserve also has great geological interest with rocks containing some of the oldest fossils in Scotland.

What to See   Some of the ancient pines, known as granny pines, are over 350 years old. They and their offspring provide shade for common wintergreen, chickweed wintergreen, creeping lady's-tresses, globeflower and moonwort. Above the tree-line patches of dwarf juniper, dwarf cornel, trailing azalea, bearberry and crowberry are frequent whilst base-rich ledges hold moss campion, alpine saw-wort, sibbaldia and northern rock-cress. There is a breeding population of 3-400 pairs of crossbill which feed on the pine cones, whilst great spotted woodpecker, redstart, long-tailed tit and dipper may be seen in the lower areas: above, ptarmigan, red grouse, buzzard, raven and golden eagle are more likely. Amongst mammals red deer and mountain hare are often seen but pine marten, wild cat and fox are more elusive.

Ben More Coigach   ▨2

Map 15 NC09-04- 14,694 acres (5949 ha)
6 miles north-west of Ullapool, but only accessible via Achiltibuie by taking the A835 Lochinver road and turning left at Drumrunie. Part SSSI. Rocky shore, marsh, moorland, oak scrub, birch wood, small islands.

Access   AYR on foot from the road through the west side of the estate at Achvraie near the south end at NC045056.

Information   Leaflet from Polbain Stores, north of Achiltibuie. Further information from TI Office in Ullapool. The local SWT representative leads guided walks and gives evening lectures which are advertised locally.

History   Ben More Coigach dominates the sky-line north of Ullapool and behind it lies the small township of Achiltibuie. Many people displaced by the Highland clearances settled here and the land is still managed as crofts. The crofters who remain help to plan the management of the Coigach estate with SWT.

What to See   The main botanical interest lies in the woodlands: oak scrub on the shore at the south end of the reserve near Culnacraig and birch woods, especially on the east side along the shores of Loch Lurgainn. There is a restricted flora of alpine plants on the crags and summits of the three main mountains, Ben More, 2438 ft, Sgurr an Fhidhleir (The Fiddler), 2285 ft, and the twin peaks of Beinn an Eoinn. Large numbers of red deer roam the reserve whilst pine marten, otter, badger and wild cat also occur. Red grouse and ptarmigan feed on the heather whilst barnacle geese visit the shore-line meadows in winter.

Handa

▮3

Map 9 NC13-48- 895 acres (363 ha)

2½ miles north-west of Scourie via A894 and minor road to Tarbet. SSSI. Sea-bird cliffs, moorland, bogs, lochs, sandy bays, plantation.

Access   1 April–10 September daily (except Sundays) by boat from Tarbet (from 10 a.m.) at NC163488 to a 3-hour walk round the island. Please keep to the paths.

Information   Leaflet from RSPB summer Warden: shelter and display on landing quay.

History   Sandstone cliffs rising to 300 ft have ledges which are ideal nesting sites for over 100,000 sea-birds. Away from the coast are submaritime grasslands with a number of small lochs and bogs which attract nesting skuas and waders. There is also a small plantation of pines which shelters small birds in winter when the island also provides a refuge for a small flock of barnacle geese.

What to See   The nesting sea-birds are guillemot, black guillemot, razorbill, kittiwake, fulmar, puffin and shag. On the moors red-throated diver, great and arctic skua, snipe, golden plover, stonechat and wheatear nest. On the rocky shore there are nesting sites for oystercatcher, ringed plover, rock pipit and common tern. Offshore divers, shearwaters and gannets are often present: here too are grey seal, porpoise, common dolphin and killer whale. Cliff-top turf holds thrift and sea campion whilst the moorland has heath-spotted and northern-marsh orchids, pale butterwort and bog asphodel: other plants of interest are Royal fern and Scots lovage.

Invernaver

▮4

Map 10 NC69-61- 1363 acres (552 ha)

1 mile west of Bettyhill north of A836 between the mouths of the Borgie and Naver Rivers on the north coast of Sutherland. NNR. Sand dunes, raised beach, upland grassland, moorland, lochans.

Access   AYR on foot:

1. from the small group of houses signposted 'Invernaver' on the west bank of the River Naver at NC708600.
2. via a wooden bridge over the Borgie River at NC681612 having taken minor road to Skerray, parking on right after 1½ miles.

Information   A short account under 'Torrisdale Bay' in *Tongue and Farr* by J.A.Johnston from local shops.

History   One of the most important botanical sites in Scotland. Strong northerly and north-west winds blow a mixture of fluvio-glacial and shell sand inland creating sand dunes over 100 ft high and enriching with lime what would otherwise be acid soils on the ridge of Druim Chuibhe, ½ mile inland, to a height of 360 ft. There is thus a remarkable mixture of lime and acid loving species as well as lowland and montane species—arctic and alpine species grow here at sea-level.

What to See   The lime-rich dunes and grassland supports montane species like crowberry, bearberry, mountain avens, moss campion, yellow saxifrage, creeping willow and prostrate juniper alongside thrift and sea campion. Amongst other local species are Scottish primrose, dark-red helleborine and purple oxytropis. Birchwood by the River Naver attracts sparrowhawk and woodcock: buzzards may be seen overhead whilst snipe and greenshank breed on the moorland at the south end.

Inverpolly   5

Map 15 NC1-1- 26,817 acres (10,857 ha)
10 miles north of Ullapool, west of A835 Ullapool to Elphin road and 6 miles south-east of Lochinver. NNR. Mountain, moorland, bogs, woodland, lochs.

Access   AYR on foot from numerous points but contact Wardens on Elphin 234 or Lochinver 204 before entering from 1 September–21 October. The ascent of Stac Pollaidh begins at the CP on the south side at NC110095 onto well-marked path to lowest point on ridge: 4 hours return walk.

Information   Nature trail and other leaflets from kiosk at Visitor Centre at Knockan Cliff on A835 at NC188090 on east side of reserve. Centre is open May–September, Mon–Fri 10 a.m.–6 p.m.

History   This is the second largest nature reserve in Britain but only 15 acres around Knochan Cliff are owned by NCC, the rest are parts of three large estates. It includes the sandstone peaks of Cul Mor, Cul Beag and Stac Pollaidh (Polly) as well as Loch Sionascaig with birch covered islands, an undulating plateau of gneiss and sea shore.

What to See   Amongst the 360 plant species recorded are alpine lady's-mantle, yellow saxifrage, plentiful on scree slopes, holly and brittle bladder-ferns: birch woodland contains lemon-scented and Wilson's filmy-fern. On wet heath sundews and butterworts flourish in the cottongrass and bog myrtle. The long list of birds includes ring ouzel, greenshank and stonechat on the moorland, wood warbler, spotted flycatcher and long-eared owl in the woodland, red-breasted merganser and goosander on the lochs and barnacle geese on islands in winter. Otter fish along loch shores: pine marten and wild cat also occur with up to 500 red deer .

Wheelchairs have access and good views over reserve from Visitor Centre and over freshwater and sea lochs from narrow and scenic roads along the south and west boundaries.

Loch Fleet   6

Map 21 NH78-96- 2873 acres (1163 ha)
4 miles north of Dornoch, east of A9 and including Balblair Woods on the north-

east side and Ferry Links and Coul Links north and south of the mouth of the Loch. SSSI. Mud flats, sand dunes, coastal heath, dunes, pine woods.

Access   AYR:

1. Loch Fleet: can be viewed from public roads on the east, west and south sides.
2. Balblair Woods can be entered at a reserve sign at NH815975 1½ miles down the road from Golspie which goes left just before Golspie station.
3. Ferry Links at the end of the road from Golspie from CP at NH805959. Permits are required from SWT to visit other parts of the reserve.

Information   Notice boards at Ferry Links CP and at Skelbo on the south shore at NH795952. Leaflets from TI Offices in Bonar Bridge and Dornoch which also have details of guided walks.

History   At one time the River Fleet entered the sea in a large bay surrounded by cliffs but, as the sea-level fell, shingle spits and sand dunes built up on the north and south sides of the bay leaving only a narrow channel at Little Ferry: this encloses a basin which becomes a large area of mud flats at low water which are most attractive to wading birds. Balblair Wood and the wood at Ferry Links were possibly planted early in the twentieth century but natural regeneration of Scots pine is now occurring and typical species of native pine woods are present.

What to See   The combination of so many habitats provides a wide range of plants and animals. The pine woods have one-flowered wintergreen, creeping lady's-tresses and lesser twayblade whilst capercaillie, crossbill, redstart and siskin breed there. The sand dunes of the links are a colourful sight with purple milk-vetch and autumn gentian whilst the Loch margin has a narrow band of saltmarsh containing sea-milkwort and sea centaury along the shore. Shelduck, redshank and oystercatcher feed on the mud flats in summer and waders feed on mussel beds along the river course. Winter brings wigeon, teal, goldeneye, common scoter and long-tailed duck. Common seal haul out on the sandbanks and can be watched from the shore.

Wheelchairs have excellent views from roads round the Loch and access to dunes at Ferry Links.

Nigg and Udale Bays   7

Map 21 NH76 and 77- 1581 acres (640 ha)
South and east of Invergordon on the north and south sides of the Cromarty Firth towards the seaward end. NNR. Mud flats, sand banks.

Access   AYR good viewing from roads on the north and south shores e.g.:

1. at a lay-by ½ mile south-west of Barbaraville at NH745719.
2. west of Nigg at NH796720.

Information   Nothing on site.

History   Cromarty Firth is by far the most important site in north-east Scotland for wintering wildfowl and waders and for passage migrants in spring and autumn, despite the growth of industry, especially that related to the offshore oil along the north side of the Firth: it could be renamed 'Rig' Bay.

What to See   In winter the growth of eelgrass attracts hundreds of whooper and mute swans: there is also the largest flock of pintail in North Scotland as well as thousands of wigeon, and smaller numbers of teal, scaup, goldeneye, red-breasted merganser and shelduck. The mud is a feeding ground for large numbers of waders including oystercatcher, curlew, dunlin, knot and redshank. Also, 2–3000 pink-footed geese are regularly seen and in autumn a large part of the East Ross greylag population roosts in the Firth.

Wheelchairs have good views from the roads on the north and south sides.

Highland South

This region is the heart of the Highlands: a huge plateau straddling the Great Glen which runs from Inverness near the head of the Moray Firth to Fort William and is carried towards the Atlantic in this submerged coastline as Loch Linnhe. In the west it contains the highest mountain in the British Isles in Ben Nevis only four miles south-east of Fort William and in the east it has one of the largest areas of upland wilderness in Britain—the Cairngorms south of Aviemore. The region has 36 peaks over 3000 ft.

Glaciers have cut deep U-shaped valleys and dammed their mouths to produce, in Loch Ness, Loch Morar and Loch Sheil some of the biggest freshwater lochs in Britain. The action of the ice can be observed nowhere better than in the remarkable 'parallel roads' of *Glen Roy* where the valley sides have been cut into a series of benches. Water and ice have worked together to produce waterfalls which drop hundreds of feet into foaming pools. One of the highest in Britain is the *Falls of Glomach* which has a single fall of 300 ft then another of 50 ft. The Gaelic name Glomach means forbidding, an apt description for this fearsome phenomenon in wild country north of *Kintail* and Glen Shiel.

High rainfall and melting snow can create rapid flooding. The Spey in spate has left a magnificent mixture of lochs and marshes which are attractive to nesting ducks and wintering geese and where there is always the possibility of an osprey dropping in: the RSPB *Insh Marshes* are a fertile example.

But for a more certain and fascinating view of ospreys it is necessary to go a further 15 miles north to the other side of Aviemore through the 'Osprey Village' of Boat of Garten to *Loch Garten* in the Abernethy Forest. When the first pair chose to return to nest in Britain in the 1950s they could hardly have found a more convenient place, within five miles of the main road to Inverness where 90,000 visitors a year can come to peer and marvel. The way to the hide is through ancient Caledonian pine forest which is the natural woodland of this colder, drier more continental side of the Highlands providing a habitat for plants and animals which are rare or absent elsewhere in Britain: creeping lady's-tresses, coralroot orchid, twinflower, and several species of wintergreen with pine marten and wild cat on the ground and crossbill and crested tit in the trees.

Some of the finest pine forest starts just across the Spey from Aviemore in *Rothiemurchus Forest* which covers some 2000 acres and reaches up to almost 1500 ft on the north slopes of the Cairngorms.

On the warmer, wetter, western side of the Highlands where sea-lochs penetrate deep inland and headlands are exposed to frequent gales the tree-line is much lower—rarely above 750 ft, and pine gives way to sessile oakwoods with trees covered in abundant mosses, liverworts, lichens and ferns. This impression of almost tropical luxuriance can be well appreciated when walking through *Ariundle* by Loch Sunart, especially if it is raining or has rained recently.

As the tree-line comes down then so do the alpine flowers. Those who want the thrill of alpine lady's-mantle and moss campion after climbing less than 1000 ft would appreciate those basalt-capped, flat-topped friendly twins, Beinn Iadain and Beinn na h-Uamha, which make up the *Rahoy Hills*. But these windswept summits at 1500 ft with golden eagles riding the wind are high enough to give the feel of the wilderness all around and the indelible beauty of sun-flecked green mountains and deep blue sea.

● Scottish Wildlife Trust (SWT), Northern Office, Pitgaveny House Flat, Elgin, Moray IV30 2PQ. 0343 548105.

Ariundle 8

Map 49 NM82-63- 173 acres (70 ha)
1 mile north-east of Strontian in Strontian Glen on the north side of river on a track which carries straight on where the minor road to Pollack turns left away from the river. NNR. Ancient oakwood.

Access AYR on foot from CP up the track at NM822632 to the entrance to the reserve in ½ mile and then on the 1½-mile walk through the wood and back on a good track.

Information Leaflet from Information Caravan in Strontian, local hotels or NCC.

History An ancient Highland oakwood, a remnant of the series which once stretched from Devon to Sutherland along the west side of Britain. Continuous woodland cover for thousands of years has encouraged the growth of around 250 species of mosses, liverworts and lichens which only grow in this type of mild, humid and unpolluted area. The survival of the woodland depended in part on its use from the late eighteenth century as a source of charcoal for an iron furnace at Bonawe on Loch Etive (see p.258) which closed in 1876. The oaks were then managed on a 20-year coppice cycle and relicts remain in the wood, notably charcoal-burners' hearths, stone walls and an abandoned croft house.

What to See Delightful in spring when the woodland floor is covered in lesser celandines, wood anemones, dog-violets and primroses. Later open areas have common cow-wheat and grass-of-Parnassus. The birds include great spotted woodpecker, buzzard and tawny owl all the year which are joined in summer by numerous warblers, tree pipit and redstart. Signs at least may be seen of pine marten, wild cat, otter and roe deer and, in sunny weather, butterflies including Scotch argus, small pearl-bordered fritillary and green hairstreak are flying.

Wheelchairs, if stoutly manned, have some access up track through wood.

Glen Roy   9

Map 41 NN31-89- 2885 acres (1168 ha)
3 miles north of Roybridge on the west side of River Roy taking the minor road off A86. NNR. Geological features from the Ice Age.

Access   AYR on foot from road through reserve: there is a CP and viewpoint at the south end at NN297854.

Information   Leaflet from TI Office in Fort William and Spean Bridge Tourist Caravan, or from NCC.

History   The Glen contains some of the most spectacular glacial landforms in Britain. The 'Parallel Roads of Glen Roy' are a remarkable example of the effect of the Ice Ages on the Scottish landscape. These 'Roads' are a series of benches along the side of the Glen formed by a large lake dammed by ice which cut the benches as the level of the lake rose and fell over 10,000 years ago.

What to See   Over 120 flowering plants and ferns have been recorded including purple and yellow saxifrages, alpine lady's-mantle and several species of clubmosses. Hunting birds to be looked for are buzzard, kestrel, merlin, peregrine and golden eagle with ring ouzel, golden plover and red grouse on higher ground and oystercatcher, common sandpiper, red-breasted merganser and occasional goosander by the river. Red deer are frequently seen.

Wheelchairs have good access to the viewpoint and from road through reserve.

Insh Marshes   10

Map 35 NH78-00- 2105 acres (852 ha)
1½ miles south of Kingussie near Ruthven Barracks in Spey valley on the south side of A9 with entrance on B970. SSSI. Woodland, wet meadows, marsh, open water.

Access   AYR on foot from small CP at NN775998 to two hides with magnificent views overlooking the marshes and to paths through the reserve: open daily 9 a.m.–9 p.m. or sunset when earlier.

Information   Leaflet from RSPB Warden.

History   The broad, marshy plain of the River Spey is over a mile wide here and liable to flooding: numerous attempts have been made in the past to drain the marshes for agriculture and many ditches were dug and banks created, but to no avail. The valley bottom is now a tangle of willow carr, reed-beds, ditches, marshes and open water with some birch and juniper scrub on higher, drier ground.

What to See   Good numbers of duck such as shoveler, goosander, goldeneye and red-breasted merganser breed on the reserve along with many waders including occasional wood sandpiper. Spotted flycatcher, buzzard and sparrowhawk also breed here whilst water rail and spotted crake may be heard. In winter, floods attract greylag in large numbers and up to 300 whooper swan. Hen harrier roost in winter and marsh harrier sometimes come in spring: osprey and peregrine are regularly seen.

Wheelchairs have views over reserve from B5192 on the north side and from B970 on the south side. Views over Loch Insh, where ospreys fish, from Boat House cafe at the east end.

Kintail and Falls of Glomach   11

Map 25 NG91 and NH02- 15,000 acres (6073 ha)
18 miles east of Kyle of Lochalsh on the east side of Glen Shiel, south of Shiel Bridge on the A87. Part SSSI. Grassy mountains, lochs, waterfalls, streams.

Access   AYR on foot from CP at the Countryside Centre at Morvich at NG961211 where details of routes in the mountains are available.

Information   Booklets and leaflets from Countryside Centre at Morvich or from Lochalsh Garden Kiosk at Balmacara, 3 miles east of Kyle of Lochalsh at NG804281. There are ½ day ranger-led walks from Morvich on Mon, Weds and Fri in July and August.

History   The main part of Kintail is the Five Sisters, a chain of five peaks of about 3000 ft with the highest, Sgurr Fhuaran (3505 ft), in the centre. They are some of the steepest grass-sloped mountains in Scotland. Behind, across Glen Lichd, lies the massive 7-mile block of Ben Attow and, north of this, the dramatic 300 ft Falls of Glomach.

What to See   Herds of red deer and wild goat roam the mountains whilst there are roe deer lower down: fox, badger, wild cat and pine marten are also frequent. The north and east faces of the higher peaks contain a rich array of alpine plants including five species of saxifrage, alpine meadow-rue and sibbaldia whilst the streams and wet flushes support pale butterwort, long-leaved sundew and both species of butterfly-orchid: the high tops are covered in dwarf cudweed, mountain azalea, dwarf willow and alpine clubmoss.

T at Morvich.

Loch Garten   12

Map 36 NH97-18- 2915 acres (1192 ha)
2 miles east of Boat of Garten on River Spey between A95 and B970. Well signposted from A95 during osprey breeding season. SSSI, Bird Sanctuary. Pine woods, lochs, moorland.

Access   On foot from CP at NH978184 to the Visitor Centre and hide: open daily from mid-April–August, whilst osprey are breeding and feeding their young, 10 a.m.–8.30 p.m. There are also tracks through the woods round Loch Garten which are open to visitors.

Information A comprehensive exhibition about ospreys at the hide where there is a Warden to answer questions and a close-up TV of the nest. Leaflets and guides available with guided walks on Weds and Fri.

History The osprey became extinct as a breeding bird in Britain early in the twentieth century because it was extensively shot. However recolonization by one pair at Loch Garten in the early 1950s has been followed by such success that there are now 50 breeding pairs in Scotland and around 75 young are raised annually: over 50 young osprey have been raised at Loch Garten alone in the last 40 years.

What to See The view of adult and young osprey from the hide is magical but there is much more. The reserve is a fine example of ancient scots pine forest where crested tit nest in rotten stumps, crossbill feed on pine cones and blackcock display in a 'lek' on the moors. Over 50 species nest on the reserve including goldcrest, golden plover, dunlin and sparrowhawk. The low scrub of heather, cowberry and juniper below the pines has an exciting flora such as chickweed wintergreen, creeping lady's-tresses and lesser twayblade. There are small lochs full of white water-lily, water lobelia and greater bladderwort.

Shop at Visitor Centre.

Wheelchairs have access to hide: cars may be driven to it by arrangement.

Rahoy Hills █ 13 █

Map 49 NM65-53- 4357 acres (1764 ha)
4 miles north of Lochaline on the north side of the Sound of Mull. SSSI. Mountains, lochs, ancient oakwood.

Access There are guided walks and open days at various times during the summer. Details from the Information Office, Estate Yard, Ardtornish at NM703473 which should be visited for advice before entering the reserve.

Information Leaflet from Information Office which also has an exhibition about the reserve.

History The reserve embraces the two basalt capped mountains of Beinn Iadain and Beinn na h-Uamha (the last three letters are silent). The basalt, which was deposited by a volcano centred on Mull, weathers to a mineral rich soil which is in great contrast to the greensand which outcrops on the lower slopes. There is an extensive oakwood on the southern side of the reserve above Loch Arienas which was coppiced for charcoal in the past but is now being managed to exclude sheep and deer from some areas to encourage regeneration.

What to See Mountain plants grow here at low altitudes: three species of saxifrage, mountain avens, moss campion, holly fern and Norwegian sandwort begin to appear at around 1000 ft. The extensive blanket bog has flushes containing bog-rush, long-leaved sundew and the rare bog orchid. Red-throated diver and greenshank breed in the area whilst golden eagle may be seen around the summits. Scotch argus butterflies are frequent in August.

Rothiemurchus ▪ 14

NH90- 21,736 acres (8,800 ha)
1 mile south-east of Aviemore on B970 between River Spey and the Cairngorm mountains to the south-east. Part NNR. Ancient pine woods, lochs, moorland.

Access Most of year on many paths for walkers but there are restrictions when deer are being culled in September and October or when they are calving in May and June. Details and advice from the two Visitor Centres on the B970 at Inverdruie at NH903108 or at Loch an Eilein at NH898083.

Information Displays at the Inverdruie Visitor Centre give an insight into the facilities and the plants and animals to be seen as well as details of guided wildlife walks which leave the Loch an Eilein Centre at 9.30 a.m. daily (except Tues or Thurs). Booking in advance advisable.

History The estate contains 2000 acres of some of the finest remaining Caledonian pine forest—part of a landscape which demonstrates integrated management for raising stock, farming deer, fishing, recreation and wildlife conservation. Some of the pines are 250 years old. There is a picturesque late-fourteenth-century castle on an island in Loch an Eilein to the south of which, at Loch Gamhna, Iron Age relics have been found.

What to See On walks through the pine woods common, intermediate, serrated and one-flowered wintergreens, creeping lady's-tresses, lesser twayblade and chickweed wintergreen may be seen amongst the heather, bilberry and cowberry. Red squirrel and crossbill feed on the pine cones: other birds include coal tit, crested tit and treecreeper. The lochs have brown trout, pike and eels which provide meals for otter, heron and osprey. Scotch argus and dark green fritillary butterflies are frequent.

T at Loch an Eilein.

Wheelchairs have access to both Visitor Centres and have good views from roads over lochs and River Spey.

Islands

To enjoy wildlife at its most wild, in a landscape of unmatched beauty, take the road to the Isles—the 400 or so islands off the west and north coasts of Scotland: the Hebrides, Orkney and Shetland.

Most of these islands are remote, difficult to reach except in a small boat in favourable weather, and battered by gales one day in five. Only 10 per cent are now inhabited and, where crofters have given up and emigrated to the mainland or another continent, wildlife has taken over. The last family left the Monach

Isles, off the west coast of the Outer Hebrides, in 1950; now, in the absence of human interference, 2000 grey seal pups are born there every autumn and a large flock of barnacle geese from the east coast of Greenland spends the winter there.

Lack of interference has been one of the main attractions of islands and stacks for nesting sea-birds: another is the natural ledges formed by the old, hard pre-Cambrian rocks, but the third is the abundance of fish in the seas around, enriched by the waters of the Gulf stream. Many of these nesting sites are recognized as of international importance: St Kilda with nearly 60,000 pairs has the largest gannetry in the world: *Rhum* with 130,000 pairs, has the largest colony of Manx shearwater in Britain: Hermaness, at the north tip of Shetland, has tens of thousands of puffin in a total of over 100,000 auks, gulls and petrels.

The remoteness and richness of the sea means that these islands and the waters around them have become the main refuge for the otter in Britain. The early riser who sits by the shore will surely soon see the head and tell-tale wake breaking the water's surface: and now, for the later risers who wish to watch in comfort, there is the hide at the Otter Haven at *Kylerhea* on Skye.

With the help of the wind and the waves the riches of the sea are brought ashore. The millions of sea shells, pounded into small fragments by the Atlantic, are carried hundreds of yards inland by the wind so that, along most of the west coast of the Outer Hebrides and in some areas in the Inner Hebrides, this lime-rich 'shell-sand' has changed what would otherwise have been acid heath, bogs and lochs into grassland full of wild flowers, the machair, base-rich fens and pools full of aquatic plants and animals. These riches attract large numbers of breeding birds because they provide nesting sites and plentiful food, especially when given the added protection of a nature reserve and summer wardens like the RSPB reserve at *Balranald* on North Uist.

Though the wind helps to enrich the soil it inhibits the growth of trees and, in most of the Outer Hebrides, Orkney and Shetland, they grow only in sheltered valleys and, even where there are woods, they are low and scrubby, mainly of hazel. In the Inner Hebrides there are small areas with proper woods and woodland flowers and birds. On *Eigg*, though hazel predominates, it is mixed with willow, rowan, hawthorn and blackthorn and, on Skye, there is ashwood at Tokavaig on Durness limestone and oakwood on the Torridonian sandstone.

Elsewhere it is not only the wind which inhibits the growth of trees but the nature of the soil. At the *Keen of Hamar*, on the island of Unst, the most northerly inhabited island in Britain, there is one of the few deposits of serpentine in this country: this rock contains elements, such as nickel and chromium, toxic to plant life which only a handful of species can tolerate. This is the exception to the general rule that these islands have life abundantly.

It is this very abundance, combined with lack of disturbance over vast areas, which means that these hundreds of uninhabited islands act as nature reserves, whether they have been declared or not, and can support the larger predators at the top of the food chain.

Even when they had been almost lost elsewhere in Britain, at the beginning of the twentieth century, hen harrier survived in Orkney on the moors north-west of Kirkwall. Now they are additionally protected in the reserves at *Birsay* and *Cottasgarth* and the re-establishment of this species as a breeding bird throughout the British Isles gathers pace as threats from gamekeepers and egg-collectors diminish.

It is to be hoped that, as the human population of the islands continues to decline, wildlife will go on expanding and the surplus will first invade, and then be sustained by, the adjacent mainland. For this reason the 'Isles' must be recognized as one of the greatest reserves of nature in these British Isles.

● Scottish Wildlife Trust (SWT), Northern Office, Pitgaveny House Flat, Elgin, Moray IV30 2PQ. 0343 548105.

Inner Hebrides—Eigg   15

Map 39 NM4-8- 3750 acres (1518 ha)
10 miles west of Arisaig off the west coast of Inverness-shire. SSSI. Upland moorland, cliffs, scrub woodland, bogs, lochs.

Access   AYR by ferry from Arisaig or Mallaig and then on foot from the pier at the south-east corner of the island at NM485837.

Information   Leaflet from TI Office in Mallaig or from SWT summer Warden which gives details of six walks from 2–4 hours duration. Guided walks for long-stay visitors.

History   Eigg is a mountainous island with an elevated plateau ridge fringed by craggy, basalt cliffs divided in the middle by a col with a road over it, connecting crofts near the pier with others round the Bay of Lairg in the north-west. Three areas have been established as nature reserves: two protect the plateau ridge and cliffs in the north-east and south-west whilst the third, and smallest, lies to the west of the road and includes willow and hazel scrub and the largest extent of bog on the island. Two wooded ravines cut through the stepped basalt descending to a deep pool, the Giant's Footstep, which has floating islands of sphagnum moss.

What to See   Plants of interest include least willow, moonwort, Wilson's filmy-fern, grass-of-Parnassus, moss campion, Norwegian sandwort, mountain avens, bog orchid and small-white orchid: woods have bluebell, wood anemone and wood-sorrel. Amongst 68 species of breeding bird are red-throated diver, red-breasted merganser, oystercatcher, sandpiper, golden plover, snipe, heron, long-eared and short-eared owls, raven, golden eagle and corncrake whilst sea-birds include black guillemot, shag and Manx shearwater, and there are spotted flycatcher and treecreeper in the woods.

Inner Hebrides—Rhum   16

Map 39 NM3-9- 26,461 acres (10,794 ha)
15 miles west of Mallaig off the coast of Inverness-shire. NNR, Biosphere Reserve. Mountains, moorland, cliffs, lochs, bogs, sand dunes, machair.

Access   AYR by ferry from Arisaig and Mallaig and then on foot from pier in harbour on the east coast at NM406991 on well-marked trails.

Information   Nature trail and reserve leaflets from Kinloch Castle at NM402995 or Post Office.

History   Within this one reserve are almost all the major habitats of the Highlands and islands. The 30-mile coast has rocky shores, sand dunes, and small areas of salt marsh which are backed by maritime grassland, heath and species-rich machair. Above, craggy volcanic mountains rise to 2500 ft with areas of basic and ultra-basic rocks and cliffs which have a rich montane flora, and acid rocks covered by wet heath and blanket bog and flushes with fen-like vegetation. The bird and insect fauna is extensive and the whole island is widely used as an outdoor laboratory where wild populations of red deer and feral goats are studied and where the reintroduction of the sea eagle began in 1975.

What to See   Montane plants include pyramidal bugle, wood bitter-vetch, mountain avens, alpine saxifrage and Norwegian sandwort. Amongst sea-birds regularly seen are eider duck, red-breasted merganser, red-throated diver and heron whilst kittiwake, fulmar, puffin and Manx shearwater breed on cliffs and in burrows. Woods have wood and willow warblers, tits, treecreeper, goldcrest and woodcock, and in the mountains are golden eagle, golden plover, peregrine, merlin and raven: corncrake may still be heard in summer. There are numerous butterflies including speckled wood, dark green and small pearl-bordered fritillaries, green hairstreak, large heath, common blue and grayling.

Inner Hebrides—Kylerhea, Skye   17

Map 33 NG78-22- 2 miles of the shore.
4 miles south-east of Kyleakin via A850 to Broadford turning onto minor road to Kylerhea after 4 miles. Rocky shore.

Access   AYR on foot from CP at NG788215 north of the ferry pier ½ mile to hide: open Easter–October 8 a.m.–dusk. Please do not approach the shore elsewhere and make no noise. Leave dogs in the car.

Information   Leaflet at hide or from TI Offices in Broadford and Kyle of Lochalsh: notice boards on the path.

History   The site has been developed to give good opportunities to watch otters: there are suitable places for their holts among the tumbled rocks and there is a plentiful supply of fish in the narrow Kyle which separates Skye from the mainland. The best time to see otters is early in the day. With assistance from the Vincent Wildlife Trust surveys were carried out in 1987 and the Otter Haven and hide were opened in July 1988.

What to See   Birds of the area which should be seen are cormorant, red-breasted merganser, heron, black guillemot, osprey, golden eagle, sea eagle, peregrine, buzzard, raven, stonechat and whinchat with waders such as oystercatcher, turnstone, dunlin, sanderling and ringed plover. Grey seals are frequent in the Kyle.

Picnic site at CP.

Outer Hebrides—Balranald, North Uist   18

Map 18 NF70-70- 1625 acres (658 ha)
3 miles north-west of Bayhead off A865 on the west coast via minor road to Hougharry and reception cottage at Goular. SSSI. Sand dunes, machair, pools, marshes.

Access   AYR on foot from reception cottage at NF706707.

Information   Leaflet from summer Warden at reception cottage, which also has a display on the reserve.

History   Along this Atlantic coastline lime-rich shell-sand is blown inland over the acid grass and peat to create a fertile, herb-rich grassland, the machair. Pools and marshland are also affected and the shallow Loch nam Feithean in the middle of the reserve, has a rich invertebrate flora with abundant submerged and emergent vegetation as well as a fringing margin of fen. There are sandy beaches on the coast and dunes interspersed with rocky headlands. This wide range of habitats attracts over 50 species of nesting birds and provides winter food and shelter for many more.

What to See   The machair grassland changes colour with the seasons: yellow with buttercups, red with poppies, or orange with corn marigold and white with daisies on the paths. In and around the Loch are mare's-tail, marsh-marigold, marsh lousewort, ragged-Robin, yellow iris and abundant water-milfoil. Gadwall, tufted duck, wigeon, mallard, shoveler, shelduck, corncrake, snipe and redshank regularly raise their young in this wetland as well as, occasionally, do red-necked phalarope and red-breasted merganser. Lapwing, ringed plover, dunlin, arctic and little terns breed in the machair, dunes and sandy beaches. Winter brings pintail, scaup, geese and whooper swan whilst off shore gannet, shearwaters and skuas are frequently seen. Otter live along the shore line and around the lochs attracted by brown trout of over 4lb in weight.

Orkney—Birsay Moors and Cottasgarth   19

Map 6 HY31 and 32- 5780 acres (2340 ha)
SSSI. Moorland, flushes, lochs, willow scrub.

1. Birsay: 7 miles north of Finstown via A966, turning left onto minor road after 7 miles at Evie, ½ mile north-west of B90957 turn to hide near wind generators.
2. Cottasgarth: 3½ miles north-east of Finstown via A966, turning left onto minor road after 3 miles and then, after ¾ mile, along track to right leading to car parking and hide.

Access

1. on foot from car parking at HY346261 on Burgar Hill to hide overlooking Lowrie's Water.
2. on foot from CP at HY370194 to hide. Please do not walk on the moors.

Information   Guide to all the Orkney RSPB reserves from summer warden here.

History   Gently rolling, sub-montane moorland, which was once widespread in Orkney, ranging from dry heath and grassland through wet heath and blanket bog to slightly enriched flushes where willow scrub may flourish.

The moors are famous for their birds of prey and are still most important for hen harrier which, early in the twentieth century, were found only in Orkney and the Outer Hebrides. This is the sole locality in Britain where kestrel nest on the ground.

What to See   The most important other birds are merlin, short-eared owl, golden plover, stonechat, great and arctic skuas, greylag geese and whimbrel with red-throated diver on the lochs. Amongst more interesting plants are alpine meadow-rue and black bog-rush in lime-rich flushes: common valerian and water avens by rocky streams and occasional moonwort, common and lesser twayblades.

Shetland—Keen of Hamar   20

Map 1 HP64-09-74 acres (30 ha)
1½ miles north-east of Baltasound, Unst. NNR. Serpentine vegetation.

Access   AYR on foot from parking space on bend in A968 at HP635097.

Information   Nothing on site.

History   This famous botanical site is on one of the few major outcrops of serpentine rocks in Britain and is a complete contrast with the Lizard Peninsula at the southern tip of the country. Two kinds of vegetation occur here: closed heath with short heather, numerous grasses and small herbs and few, or no, montane plants: and an open, stony community on serpentine debris with a large number of montane species most of which belong to the Pink family.

What to See   The montane species include moss campion, northern rock-cress, Norwegian sandwort and Shetland mouse-ear whilst, in the closed heathland there is mountain everlasting, field gentian, alpine meadow-rue, spring squill and lesser clubmoss.

EAST SCOTLAND

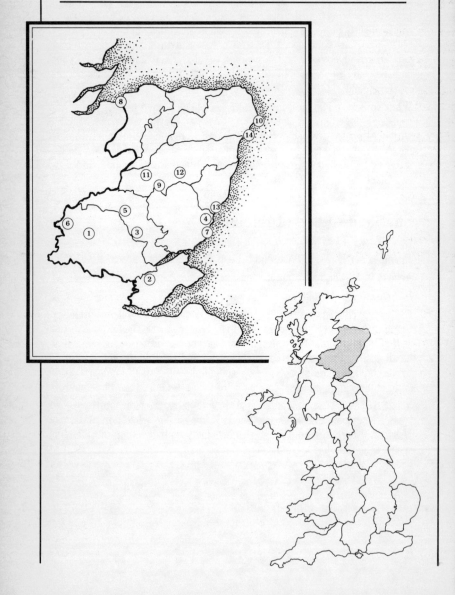

Fife and Tayside

A region centred on the river which flows from Loch Tay, at the foot of the Breadalbane Mountains, through Aberfeldy and Perth to its mouth in the Firth 'where small fishes sport and play in the silvery Tay' to adapt William Mcgonagall, the 'poet' who made it and its ill-fated bridge so famous.

For botanists, *Ben Lawers* is the most celebrated, most important, mountain for arctic and alpine plants in Britain and, though Caenlochan on the Aberdeen-Angus border also has high claims, Lawers sets the standard by which all others are compared.

Though Ben Lawers is of great national importance for its flora the site of greatest international importance lies further west near the Argyll border. Each mile further west in this area the rainfall rises by an inch and, on *Rannoch Moor*, it is very wet indeed—nearly 100 ins compared with 55 ins on Ben Lawers. These conditions have contributed to the creation of a vast desolate bog which is not only one of the finest areas of its kind in Europe but the site of 30 per cent of the north-west European population of the Rannoch rush.

Though at about 1000 ft and well below the tree-line the only 'woody' plants here are bog-myrtle and dwarf birch but, eight miles east, on the south side of Loch Rannoch there are remains of Caledonian pine woods which once covered much of the central highlands in the *Black Wood of Rannoch*.

Lower down, in Strath Tay or Glen Garry which joins it near Pitlochry, the pine woods give way to deciduous woods of sessile oak, ash, wych elm and alder. Some of the finest and least spoilt line the narrow *Pass of Killiecrankie* despite some invasion by those woodland weeds, sycamore and rhododendron.

There are also deciduous trees fringing the *Loch of the Lowes* but here the originally introduced pines form the all important nesting site for the pair of osprey which, since 1969, have been supporting the fund-raising efforts of the Scottish Wildlife Trust by choosing a site so close to the A9 to Inverness.

But for accessibility there is no comparison with *Loch Leven* which is overlooked, for three miles between Exits 5 and 6, by the M90. However, such public gaze has done nothing to detract from its importance for having the largest breeding population of duck in Britain or for acting as a kind of distribution centre for wintering geese which arrive here *en masse* in autumn before setting off for various other feeding grounds in Scotland. This also used to be the site for a flock of 500 non-breeding, moulting mute swan but, when many aquatic plants were killed by algal blooms and shooting came under control at *Montrose Basin*, the swans changed their allegiances and are now to be enjoyed 50 miles to the north-east. Having had a basinful at Loch Leven they now fill the basin at Montrose.

The whole coast of this region is rich in wildlife: the estuaries of the Tay and the north side of the Firth of Forth; a series of sand dune systems, or links, which spell out such golf-club names as St Andrew's and Carnoustie and the National Nature Reserve of Tentsmuir; and the rose-red cliffs older than 350 million years at *Seaton Cliffs* east of Arbroath, the glory of the Angus coast, where many plants and sea-birds mingle in a riot of colour and sound.

● Scottish Wildlife Trust (SWT), 25 Johnston Terrace, Edinburgh EH1 2NH. 031 226 4602.

Ben Lawers

Map 57 NN63-41- 9816 acres (3140 ha)
North of A827 between Killin and Aberfeldy on north side of Loch Tay. The turn to the Visitor Centre near Lochan na Lairige is signposted from the A827. This mountain road is steep and one-track, unsuitable for coaches. NNR. Mountain, moorland, cliffs, flushes, lochs.

Access   AYR on foot from CP at Visitor Centre at NN609380 which leads to a 1½ hour nature trail and on to the mountain top, but there are restrictions from 12 August–15 February.

Information   Leaflet and guides from Visitor Centre: open daily Easter–September 10 a.m.–5 p.m. The Centre has a display on the area. Guided walks are frequently given.

History   Perhaps the best known mountain to botanists in Britain: long celebrated for its superb arctic-alpine flora including species which occur hardly anywhere else in the country. These plants are associated with lime-rich schists on steep slopes at high altitudes which are constantly eroding to produce an unusual habitat: most of the rocks between the Visitor Centre and the summit are of this kind.

What to See   Amongst the ferns to be found are holly fern, green spleenwort and alpine woodsia whilst arctic and alpine flowers include rock whitlowgrass, mountain sandwort, alpine mouse-ear, sibbaldia, alpine cinquefoil, alpine and drooping saxifrages, mountain willow, alpine gentian, alpine forget-me-not and alpine fleabane. Birds of the upland which may be seen are golden eagle, buzzard, peregrine, merlin, ptarmigan, dotterel and raven. Red deer, roe deer and mountain hares are frequent and of the butterflies small pearl-bordered fritillary and mountain ringlet are noteworthy.
    T[D] at Visitor Centre.

Loch Leven

Map 58 NO14-01- 4404 acres (1783 ha)
10 miles to the north of Dunfermline on the east side of M90 via Exit 5 to access points off B996 on the west side and B9097 on the south side. NNR, Ramsar Site. Open water, islands, reed-beds, birch wood, heather moor, wintering geese, breeding duck.

Access   AYR to:

1. Kirkgate Park, 400 yds east of Kinross town off B996 at NO125018.
2. Findatie, at south-east corner of Loch off B9097 2½ miles east of M90 at NT174994.
3. Vane Farm, on south side on B9097 2 miles east of M90 at NT160990, RSPB Visitor Centre with hide, and nature trail to top of 824 ft hill overlooking Loch (small charge for non-RSPB members).

Information   Leaflets and trail guides from RSPB Visitor Centre: open daily 10 a.m.–5 p.m. except January–March, W/Es only 10 a.m.–4 p.m.

History   This mainly shallow loch, 40 per cent under 10 ft, attracts large numbers of wintering geese and holds the largest concentration of breeding duck in Britain: it is of European importance. The shallow water and surrounding farmland provide feeding areas for wildfowl and the islands in the Loch give shelter where ducks raise their young, the majority on St Serf's Island near the south end. Though the area of marshland was greatly reduced when the water level was lowered in the middle of the nineteenth century the wetter fields are still breeding areas for a number of waders. Run-off from the surrounding agricultural land has contributed to periodic algal blooms which have reduced aquatic pondweeds and stoneworts.

What to See   Pinkfeet, up to 14,000, peak in early autumn when they arrive from Iceland, and again in March. Greylag arrive later and may reach 2500 but stay longer whilst barnacle, Brent, Canada and white-fronted and snow geese may also be seen along with some whooper swan. Breeding ducks are mainly mallard, tufted, shelduck, gadwall, wigeon, teal and shoveler. The surrounding moorland has red grouse and the birch woods redpoll and tree pipit. Breeding waders include curlew, redshank and snipe whilst dunlin, greenshank and ruff may be seen on passage

T[D]. Shop at Visitor Centre.

Wheelchairs have good viewing.

Loch of the Lowes and Loch of Craiglush   **3**

Map 53 NO04-43- 333 acres (135 ha)
2 miles east of Dunkeld turning right off A923 road to Blairgowrie onto minor road to reserve entrance at the west end of Loch of the Lowes. SSSI. Open water, marsh, woodland, breeding osprey.

Access   AYR on foot from CP at NO040434 to Visitor Centre and hide: hide is always open.

Information   Leaflets, guides and up-to-date news about wildlife on the reserve from Visitor Centre: open daily April–September: April 10 a.m.–5 p.m.; May–June 10 a.m.–6 p.m.; July–mid-August 10 a.m.–7 p.m.; mid-August– September 10 a.m.–5 p.m. There is a small aquarium and an A/V display.

History   These beautifully sited lochs are at the junction of the Highlands and lowlands and nestle amongst rugged hills. Most of the reserve is water, much of it shallow, and the water plants are characteristic of nutrient-poor water. The narrow strip of woodland along the shore is a mixture of conifers and broad leaves including Scots pine, juniper, ash, oak, birch and cherry.

What to See   Ospreys, which first came to the Loch of the Lowes in 1969, return regularly about the end of March nesting in an old pine which can be watched from the hide. Other birds which feed on the Loch are mallard, coot, tufted duck, goldeneye, goosander and great crested grebe: greylag and Canada geese join them in winter. Other birds of note are sparrowhawk, buzzard, grasshopper and wood warblers, woodcock, green and great spotted woodpeckers, treecreeper, redpoll, siskin, crossbill, tree pipit, redstart and spotted flycatcher. Water plants include water lobelia, quillwort, shoreweed, bogbean, yellow water-lily (the 'Lowes') and amphibious bistort.

T[D] in Dunkeld.

Wheelchairs have access to the hide.

Montrose Basin
4

Map 54 NO69-57- 2500 acres (1012 ha)
Inland from Montrose. SSSI, LNR. Mud flats, reed-beds, wintering wildfowl.

Access   AYR on foot:

1. from CP on north-west side of the Basin at Mains of Dun off A935 at NO669591 onto the track to two hides.
2. from CP at the south-east corner on south side of the bridge over main outlet on A92 at NO710570.
3. from CP at the north-east corner on A935 at NO710590 to the hide 500 yds to the south.

Information   Leaflet from TI Office in Montrose: Warden Naturalist may be available.

History   The finest enclosed river basin on the east coast of Scotland and unpolluted. Mud flats and creeks covered in eelgrass and glasswort provide feeding grounds for thousands of waders and wildfowl at the mouth of the South Esk River, best viewed at high tide when birds gather at west end of the Basin which fills and empties twice a day. The months from August to February are the most productive with up to 12,000 pinkfeet and 2000 greylags roosting in the Basin after feeding on nearby farmland by day. Different species of wildfowl and waders peak at different seasons. There has been a dramatic increase in pinkfeet since the reserve was created in 1981—from 200 to over 9000.

What to See   There are curlew in August and March, redshank in September and March, oystercatcher in October and November, knot in January, dunlin in February whilst some redshank and oystercatcher stay to breed in the area. The Basin is of national importance for moulting and wintering mute swan and has regular visits from mallard, teal, wigeon, eider, shelduck, pintail, red-breasted merganser, goldeneye and tufted duck. Cormorant, common and arctic terns may also be seen whilst sedge warbler breed in the reed-bed.

T in Montrose.

Pass of Killiecrankie

■ 5

Map 43 NN91-62- 54 acres (22 ha)
3 miles to the north-west of Pitlochry on the old road on the west side of the A9. SSSI. Sessile oakwood, heather moorland.

Access   AYR on foot from NTS Visitor Centre CP at NN917626 onto paths through the Pass. These link to the Linn of Tummel trail to the south-west.

Information   Leaflets on the history and natural history of the Pass from Visitor Centre: open daily 27 June–17 September 9.30 a.m.–6 p.m. There are frequent guided walks and talks.

History   The site of a famous victory by the Scottish Catholic supporters of James II over the English Protestant forces of William and Mary in 1689. The gorge is also the site of a fine lowland sessile oakwood which rises from the rocky bed of the River Garry to heather moorland nearly 1000 ft above. The exposures of metamorphic rock in the gorge are of considerable geological importance. Trees include birch, ash, wych elm and alder with a hazel understorey and some whitebeam and guelder-rose.

What to See   The ground flora of the oakwood includes bird's-nest orchid, giant bellflower, melancholy thistle, lily-of-the-valley, stone bramble and wood vetch whilst redstart, spotted flycatcher, green and great spotted woodpeckers and wood warbler breed here. Higher up among the birches and on the jagged cliffs buzzard, kestrel, raven and redpoll may be seen and curlew breed on the moorland.

T in Pitlochry.

Wheelchairs have access to Visitor Centre and views up the Pass from road bridge across it.

Rannoch Moor

■ 6

Map 42 NN41-54- 3645 acres (1499 ha)
6 miles west of the west end of Loch Rannoch, south of Rannoch Station. NNR. Moorland, bogs, lochs.

Access   AYR on foot from Rannoch Station at NN422578.

Information   Nothing on site.

History   The reserve is part of an extensive tract of moorland at over 1000 ft which covers over 90 square miles between the Breadalbane Mountains and those of Glencoe, full of peaty depressions and small lochs. Blanket bog over the slopes gives way to more base-rich mires in the valleys. A notable feature of the Moor is the presence of Rannoch-rush in its only remaining British locality which represents 30 per cent of the north-west European population.

What to See   Characteristic plants of the blanket bog are bog-myrtle, great sundew, dwarf birch and purple moor-grass with many species of *Sphagnum* moss whilst the valley mires have several rare sedges, and three species of bladderwort. Greenshank breed here as well as other moorland birds. The insects are all too numerous but include two local Scottish dragonflies, the blue aeschna and the northern emerald.

Seaton Cliffs, Arbroath   **7**

Map 54 NO66-41- 27 acres (11 ha)
¾ mile east of Arbroath at the end of the promenade. SSSI. Sandstone cliffs, wooded glen, sea-birds.

Access   AYR on foot from the parking space at the east end of Arbroath promenade at NO648409 onto a 3-mile nature trail on a well-defined path. Please keep to the path, the cliffs are dangerous.

Information   Trail guide from TI Office in Arbroath or SWT.

History   These cliffs of Old Red sandstone form a great red wall to the east of Arbroath. The rock is relatively soft and erosion by the sea continues. The line of the cliffs is broken by some gentler slopes which are covered by luxuriant vegetation whilst at the east end a small valley, Seaton Den, is clothed in thick woodland. The rock is quite rich in minerals and supports a number of lime-loving species whilst many woodland flowers grow in the open grassland in sheltered places. Occasional springs create marshy hollows which add further variety.

What to See   Unusual plants include clustered bellflower, carline thistle, wood vetch, early-purple orchid, northern marsh-orchid, wild liquorice, bloody crane's-bill, purple milk-vetch, greater knapweed and sweet-briar. Few birds nest on the cliffs but there are fulmar, rock dove, house martin (in their original habitat) and herring gull whilst in summer arctic tern, eider, gannet, cormorant, shag, puffin, guillemot, razorbill and kittiwake may be seen 'fishing' off shore. The butterflies include common blue, small heath and meadow brown: banded snails are very abundant.

    T. Refreshments in Arbroath.

Grampian

Grampian is the part of mainland Britain with wildlife and climate most clearly related to Scandinavia: hard, ice-moulded mountains, extensive native pine and birch woods, with dry, often hot summers but chill, bitter winters when temperatures occasionally drop below −20°C. Its glories are its granite mountains, a coastline of infinite variety and its pure rivers with the best water to make whisky, of which the Dee, also one of the finest salmon rivers in Scotland, is the most famous.

    Deeside not only has a string of castles—Balmoral, Braemar, Crathes—but a string of nature reserves which reflect its wildlife riches. The most extraordinary,

Morrone Birkwood, is only a mile from Braemar, on the south side of the Dee. To step into the light shade of its downy birches and walk between its stunted junipers is like stepping into a sub-alpine wood in Norway, an experience which cannot be repeated anywhere else in Britain. *Dinnet Oakwood*, lower down the Dee on the south side east of Ballater, is less surprising though it is one of the few remaining mixed sessile and pedunculate oakwoods left in North-East Scotland.

The most widespread, and successful, woodland in Deeside is a mixture of pine and birch. Where grazing is absent it can spread rapidly, as it has done on the *Muir of Dinnet* across the Dee from the oakwood, where it hides some of the remarkable glacial landforms for which the Muir is famous.

Where grazing is intense woodland is curbed and can only grow in enclosures. This can be seen at *Glen Muick*, one of the best places to enjoy the sight of red deer at relatively low altitudes because they are fed around the visitor centre there. However, in summer, they ascend to the alpine zone to avoid the flies and it is only the sheer, inaccessible granite cliffs of mountains like *Lochnagar* which give the alpine plants a refuge beyond the reach of the jaws of the stags and hinds.

Equally impressive granite cliffs also occur on the coast—at *Longhaven*, about 20 miles north of Aberdeen, where they provide a refuge not so much for plants as for birds—23,000 pairs of sea-birds. A refuge only saved from the jaws of bulldozers in the late 1970s by the efforts of the Scottish Wildlife Trust and the North-East Mountain Trust, which effectively opposed proposals to quarry the cliffs away.

Further south, around 20 miles the other side of Aberdeen, pink granite cliffs have given way to Old Red sandstone at *St Cyrus*: the nesting sea-birds are fewer but the wild flowers are wonderful, many reaching their northern limit in Britain on these south-facing slopes or in the somewhat lime-rich sand dunes which stretch south for two miles to the mouth of the River North Esk.

The dunes of the *Sands of Forvie*, midway between Aberdeen and Peterhead, are a complete contrast. Here the wind blown sand which forms the 60 ft dunes is lime-deficient and the heathland vegetation which has developed, with dominant heather and crowberry, is not rich in species—the riches are the birds. Sometimes known as the eider duck capital of Britain it attracts 6000 of these most attractive sea-birds to nest every spring and, by June, fluffy ducklings are everywhere in the dunes and on the heath.

The dunes at *Culbin* were once as fine but here the hinterland has been planted with pines, many exotic, and only the coastal strip with its sand bars out to sea remains unaltered—but it is still a superb reserve for sea-birds at all seasons of the year and the abundant crested tit and Scottish crossbill in the trees are there as a reminder that this is a very special part of Britain.

● Scottish Wildlife Trust (SWT), Northern Office, Pitgaveny House Flat, Elgin, Moray IV30 2PQ. 0343 548105.

Culbin Sands   8

Map 27 NH90-57- 2069 acres (862 ha)
1 mile east of Nairn at Kingsteps, on minor road past golf course. SSSI. Sand
banks, mud flats, salt marsh, shingle bars, dune slacks, lochs.

Access   AYR on foot from:

1. the west end from the parking space at the end of the track on the left at
   Kingsteps at NH901573.
2. the south side from FC CP at Cloddymoss, 2 miles north of Brodie Castle at
   NH983599.

Information   From small Visitor Centre at Cloddymoss.

History   The largest sand dune system in Britain much planted with Corsican
and Scots pine over its 6-mile length. The sand is lime-poor and, in the small
areas which remain unplanted, are many plants which reach their northern limit
in Britain here. The vegetation varies from open dunes to dwarf shrub and pine
wood whilst, in wet hollows, there are marshes and scrub with alder, birch and
willow. There is a well-marked shingle beach along the shore and, off shore, a
shingle spit which encloses a large area of sand banks, mud flats and salt marsh.
The whole area is specially important for wintering duck and waders.

What to See   Rare wild flowers include lesser twayblade, creeping lady's-
tresses, greater butterfly-orchid, coralroot orchid, chickweed wintergreen,
Scots lovage, one-flowered and intermediate wintergreens. Amongst breeding
birds are eider duck, redshank, oystercatcher, ringed plover, common and arctic
terns along the shore with buzzard, sparrowhawk, capercaillie, long-eared owl,
crested tit, siskin and Scottish crossbill in the woodland. Passage migrants
include whimbrel, curlew sandpiper, greenshank and spotted redshank whilst
in winter all three types of divers are regular off shore with common and velvet
scoter, long-tailed duck, red-breasted merganser and black guillemot. Greylag
and whooper swan feed on land whilst the flats and salt marsh attract up to 1000
bar-tailed godwit and 2000 oystercatcher: some knot, dunlin, little ringed plover
and curlew are present most of the year.

Glen Muick and Lochnagar   9

Map 44 NO25-85- 6348 acres (2570 ha)
10 miles south-west of Ballater off B976 at end of minor road to CP at Spittal
of Glenmuick. SSSI. Moorland, lochs, mountain cliffs, red deer.

Access   AYR on foot from CP at NO308851 on paths to and around Loch Muick
which are easy going, or to the summit of Lochnagar at 3786 ft which is a rough,
tough climb.

Information   Reserve leaflet and other details from Visitor Centre at CP:
open most of summer season, especially W/Es.

History   Lochnagar is a granite mountain with dramatic northern corries with alternating buttresses and gullies which shoot loose stones onto scree slopes below but with a fine collection of alpine plants on inaccessible ledges. Pine and birchwood once flourished on the lower slopes below 2000 ft where hogs were probably raised, as Glen Muick in English means 'sows' valley'. The area is now part of a working estate which demonstrates farming, stalking and conservation living together. It is one of the best places in the Highlands to see red deer and they often graze near the Visitor Centre. The uplands are covered with montane heathland with lichens predominant on exposed summits.

What to See Plants of interest are alpine blue-sow-thistle, highland cudweed, highland saxifrage, mountain azalea, alpine speedwell, alpine mouse-ear, downy willow and alpine foxtail. Birds likely to be seen are snipe, redshank, common sandpiper, red grouse, golden eagle, merlin, hen harrier and peregrine with ptarmigan and dunlin breeding high up. Mountain hare and stoat are frequent whilst large day-flying moths such as northern eggar and emperor also occur: common lizard and adder may be seen on the paths.

Longhaven Cliffs
10

Map 30 NK11-39- 150 acres (60 ha)
4 miles south of Peterhead via A952 turning south onto track at NK113400, ½ mile after the road leaves coast, to CP at entrance to quarry. SSSI. Coastal cliffs, sea-birds, cliff-top plants.

Access AYR on foot from CP at NK114395 200 yds from cliff edge. Please take care: the cliff path can be dangerous.

Information Nothing on site: leaflet from SWT.

History Granite cliffs rise 200 ft from the sea which have been weathered into inlets, caves, arches and stacks. The attractive pinky-red granite has been used for years in Peterhead for road-metal and building and is still being quarried. The ledges provide nesting sites for about 20,000 pairs of nine species of sea-birds whilst less severe slopes harbour a wide variety of colourful plants. The cliff edge has patches of stunted heath.

What to See Breeding birds include herring, great and lesser black-backed gulls, kittiwake, guillemot, puffin, razorbill, shag and fulmar. The cliff slopes are bright in spring with bluebell, sea and red campions, thrift, violets, primrose, marsh marigold and lesser celandine whilst there are patches of burnet rose, Scots lovage, and roseroot. The cliff-top heath is made up of such plants as crowberry, devil's-bit scabious, bell-heather and grass-of-Parnassus.

Morrone Birkwood
11

Map 43 NO13-90- 556 acres (225 ha)
On the west side of Braemar ½ mile west of bridge over Clunie Water to CP at top of Chapel Brae. NNR. Birch/juniper wood, blanket bog, mountain moorland.

Access   AYR on foot from CP at NO143911 onto a way-marked path.

Information   Notice board on site: leaflet from TI Office in Braemar.

History   The best example in Britain of a subalpine wood on basic soils where, on a north-facing slope, downy birch stands over a dense understorey of low, heavily grazed, juniper. The rock is Dalridian schist which is calcareous with bands of limestone. There are many wet hollows and flushes in open areas which harbour several montane species: there is also a limestone knoll with species-rich grassland and small wooded crags. All these contribute to a list of over 280 species of flowering plants and ferns and there is a rich moss, liverwort and lichen flora. The nearest similar vegetation is found in Norway.

What to See   Wild flowers of the woodland floor include species characteristic of pine woods such as wintergreens and twinflower as well as lime-loving herbs like alpine cinquefoil, northern bedstraw and alpine bistort which are protected from grazing by the juniper. Flushes have Scottish asphodel and yellow saxifrage whilst the crags have holly fern, wood vetch and small white-orchid.

Muir of Dinnet
12

Map 37 NO43-99- 3495 acres (1415 ha)
5 miles north-east of Ballater on both sides of the A97 from Cambus o'May to Tarland. NNR. Bogs, moorland, woodland, lochs, glacial features.

Access   AYR on foot from CP at Visitor Centre at Burn o'Vat on A97 at NO429997 on a way-marked trail.

Information   Notice boards at entrance; trail leaflet and reserve guide from Visitor Centre: open Weds–Suns, May–September 10 a.m.–5.30 p.m.

History   A site of great variety of interest because of the glacial features formed towards the end of the Ice Age including deep channels cut by streams running under the ice, gravel morraines and kettle holes. Two lochs, Davan and Kinord, were formed by the melting ice and there is a gigantic pot-hole, the Vat. The lower hills and gravel are covered with heather and bearberry moor which is being rapidly colonized by pine and birch. An older wood at New Kinord, between the lochs, is mixed, with aspen, ash, hazel and blackthorn. The lochs are relatively alkaline and support a rich aquatic flora and fauna with a fringing reed-swamp with some club-rush backed by birch wood: there are also valley bogs at Ordie Moss.

What to See   The heather moorland is rich in species such as wild thyme, petty whin, lesser twayblade and intermediate wintergreen: the bogs have numerous sedges, bog-myrtle and willow carr whilst the margins of the lochs have poor fen with bog asphodel, cross-leaved heath and purple moor-grass. The lochs themselves are white and yellow with water-lilies in summer and bright with bogbean in spring. Amongst 76 species of breeding birds are goosander, black-headed gull, willow warbler, redpoll, woodcock and black grouse whilst greylag and pink-footed geese and whooper swan are regular winter visitors.

Otter may be seen from the northern shore of Loch Davan as well as frequent red and roe deer.

St Cyrus   13

Map 45 NO74-64- 227 acres (92 ha)
6 miles north-east of Montrose via A92 on coast between River North Esk mouth and Milton Ness. NNR. Foreshore, sand dunes, cliffs, mud flats.

Access   AYR on foot from CP at Visitor Centre 1 mile south-west of St Cyrus in old salmon bothy at NO742635, except in tern-breeding season when access is restricted.

Information   Notice boards on site: leaflets from Visitor Centre: open Weds–Sun, May–September 10 a.m.–5.30 p.m.

History   On the reserve there are base-rich Old Red sandstone cliffs and steep slopes which rise to 200 ft and are south facing. They have a rich flora and fauna and a number of species reach their northern limit in Britain here including wild liquorice, Nottingham catchfly and clustered bellflower. South of the cliffs there is a dune system of moderately lime-rich sand but, following a sand-blow in 1967, an area of salt marsh has almost disappeared.

What to See   Dune plants of interest include maiden pink, marjoram, great mullein, viper's-bugloss, carline thistle and henbane with annuals such as spring vetch and common cornsalad. Amongst 47 species of breeding bird are little tern at the south end of the reserve, grasshopper warbler, stonechat, whitethroat and yellowhammer in gorse scrub, whilst eider duck breed in the dunes. Fulmar and herring gull nest on the cliffs but many more sea-birds are seen on migration—skuas and sheerwaters in particular. Otter work the River North Esk and grey seal are seen offshore. Amongst butterflies are small blue, small copper and grayling.

Sands of Forvie and Ythan Estuary   14

Map 38 NK02-27- 2403 acres (973 ha)
4 miles south-east of Ellon on the coast via A975 which passes through the reserve. NNR. Sand dunes, dune slacks, heath, cliff, salt marsh, mud flats, lochs.

Access   AYR:

1. Ythan estuary can be seen from numerous parking places on A975.
2. on foot from CP at the west end of Waterside Bridge at NK001269 along track going north up the River Ythan.
3. on foot from CP at the east end of Waterside Bridge along the track going south and east to ruins of old Forvie Church: also down river to hide overlooking ternary—other paths here may be closed when terns are breeding.

4. on foot from CP at Forvie Visitor Centre at Kirktown of Slains at NK033291 via B9003 to Collieston, to the track which leads through the reserve. Please keep to paths.

Information   Leaflet from Forvie Visitor Centre: open daily 9 a.m.–5.30 p.m.

History   One of the largest and least disturbed sand dune systems in Britain which, with the adjacent estuary, attracts large numbers of terns, waders and wildfowl: it has the largest breeding colony of eider duck in Britain. The sand is lime-deficient and is colonized by heath species such as crowberry and heather whilst there are wet hollows dominated by willows and sedges. There are sea cliffs of andalusite schists at the north end of the reserve rising to 130 ft, small areas of salt marsh in the Ythan estuary and three freshwater lochs. This range of habitats makes this a most exciting area.

What to See   Plants of interest are creeping lady's-tresses, stag's-horn clubmoss, wild pansy, thrift, kidney vetch, cowslip, primrose and grass-of-Parnassus with lousewort, marsh-marigold and bogbean in wet slacks. Nesting birds include common, arctic, little and Sandwich terns with black-headed gull at the south end, and small numbers of fulmar, kittiwake and razorbill on the cliffs to the north. Whooper swan, greylag and pink-footed geese feed in the estuary in winter whilst duck in large numbers, including some long-tailed, common and velvet scoter, goldeneye and red-breasted merganser, appear off shore: eider numbers build to 6000 by February. Waders include greenshank and ruff with occasional other species. Small pearl-bordered and dark green fritillaries are abundant in the summer when emperor moth and their huge caterpillars are common amongst the heather.

NORTHERN IRELAND

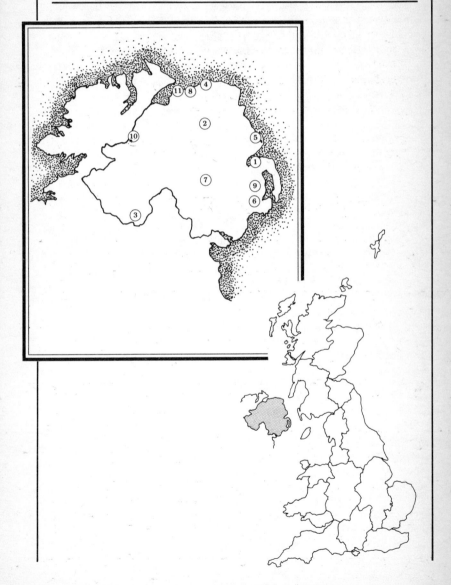

Northern Ireland

The plants and animals of Ireland as a whole lack many species common in Britain which failed to make the crossing before the water rose and closed the route: notable examples are trees such as small-leaved lime and field maple and, of course, amongst the vertebrates common toad, grass snake and adder. There are compensations—a group of species with affinities with the Mediterranean and North America which do not occur in Britain, but most of these are found in the south and west of Ireland, in the Republic, and only one or two, such as blue-eyed-grass around Lough Erne, are found in Northern Ireland.

But what it may lack in species the North certainly makes up in sheer variety and abundance of habitat. Though modern agriculture and the growth of an increasingly industrial society have reduced the abundance of small fields and hedgerows which are a feature of the countryside, mangled roadside verges, thrown motorways across the landscape and exploited much of the once abundant peat, the natural shape of the coastline, the rugged mountains and the myriad of lakes, both large and small, are resistant to change and have endured to be enjoyed. Fortunately Northern Ireland has long been one of the leading areas in the United Kingdom in the provision of public access and information to visitors about its natural treasures: information centres and guide books abound.

The star turn on the coast is the *Giant's Causeway*, a World Heritage Site: but this is but a fraction of the enchanting history and natural history of the north Antrim coast which provides a succession of majestic bays, bold headlands and high cliffs with air and sea, sea-birds and seals. The cliffs continue down the east side of Antrim where the plateau of basalt over chalk drops dramatically into the sea—even as far south as the *Isle of Muck* where auks and other sea-birds can be watched across a narrow strait.

Further west, on either side of the mouth of the River Bann cliffs give way to long, sandy strands like *Portstewart*, backed by golden dunes which embrace low-lying, damp marshy 'slacks' where grass-of-Parnassus flowers amongst the creeping willow. Taller willows are joined by alder and ash in more sheltered streamside locations to form damp, fen-like woodlands which are a feature of *The Umbra* and other dunes around Magilligan.

But the finest dunes in the Province are in Down—around the charming village of Dundrum and beneath the misty splendour of the Mourne Mountains. *Murlough* has sand—and so much more—mud flats, heath and even woodland, though the pines here were planted only 30 years ago.

Ancient woodland is one of the natural habitats which has suffered most from the hands of man—cut for fire in a land where fossil fuel is scarce. The best has survived in places where access was difficult, such as the oak woods on the islands in Lough Erne around *Crom*. Other woodland remains in narrow glens with clear streams and bobbing dippers such as *Strabane Glen* near the Donegal border in the west or *Crawfordsburn* on the Bangor road from Belfast in the east.

Even secondary woodland, when it was planted several hundred years ago, can acquire a 'characteristic' flora and fauna which justifies its selection as a nature reserve. Hence the inclusion of *Creighton's Wood*, in the Bann valley north of Lough Neagh. Once this also included an area of peat bog but the majority has now been cut over and destroyed. South of the Lough, almost up to its southern shore, an area which has been protected is *Peatlands Park*—one of the best places to appreciate the importance of peat in the economy and of the need to protect the remaining fragments of a heritage which is also of world importance, but sadly less resilient than the Giant's Causeway.

Freshwaters and estuaries are threatened throughout the British Isles—Lough Neagh more than most—since its catchment occupies nearly half the land area of Northern Ireland. It is currently the only Ramsar site in Northern Ireland. Strangford Lough, in County Down, is also threatened—by tourism, pollution and development proposals. However the National Trust and other conservation organizations are working together to protect this, one of our most important estuaries. There are many opportunities to enjoy this rich and varied area—one of the most accessible, which provides an excellent introduction, is at *Quoile Pondage* only a mile or so north-east of Downpatrick.

- Ulster Wildlife Trust (UWT), Ulster Wildlife Centre, New Line, Crossgar, County Down BT30 9EP. 0396 830282.
- National Trust (NT), Rowallane, Saintfield, County Down BT24 7LH. 0238 510721.
- DOE(NI), Countryside and Wildlife Branch, Calvert House, 23 Castle Place, Belfast BT1 IFY. 0232 230560.

Crawfordsburn Country Park, County Down ◼1

Map 15 J46-82- 300 acres (120 ha)
9 miles north-east of Belfast north of Crawfordsburn village via minor road off B20 to Bangor. Country Park: wooded glen, cliffs, rocky and sandy shores.

Access   AYR on foot from CPs on the ring road through the Park onto a network of paths and walks: also from Helen's Bay or Crawfordsburn Station at edge of the Park.

Information   Leaflet and guides from Countryside Centre at J465821: open daily 11 a.m.–dusk.

History   Once an estate part of which was owned by a Scotsman, William Crawford, who gave his name to the stream which runs for a mile through the bottom of the wooded glen from a delightful waterfall to the sea with the remains of a water mill on its banks. This sheltered area contrasts with the exposed coast with headlands and cliffs of Silurian rocks and Boulder clay encircling sandy beaches.

What to See   The rich coastal flora includes rock sea-spurrey, spring squill, common stork's-bill and sea rocket whilst the woods harbour wood anemone, primrose and many species of ferns, mosses and liverworts. Dipper occur along the stream and, amongst butterflies, small copper, red admiral, speckled wood and meadow brown may be seen.

Creighton's Wood, County Londonderry   2

Map 8 C92-11- 79 acres (32 ha)
1 mile south of Kilrea off B75 to Maghera taking lane signposted Kilrea Golf Course. Woodland, scrub, peat bog, marsh, open water.

Access   AYR on foot from CP at end of lane by Golf Club House at C927113. Non-members of UWT need permit in advance.

Information   Leaflet from UWT.

History   The woodland dates from the seventeenth century, reputedly planted by a certain Creighton Hutchinson. Hazel is coppiced and some of the cut rods are used to make skeaghs (eel traps) for fishing in the nearby River Bann. The bog is part of an extensive area of peat drained and cut for fuel for many centuries. Many large oaks were felled during the Second World War but there is still a small area dominated by sessile oak.

What to See   Interesting woodland plants are sanicle, pignut, wood-sorrel, wood anemone, wood brome and wood-sedge whilst the bog holds bog-myrtle, round-leaved sundew, cottongrass, bogbean, bilberry and marsh violet. Amongst the birds sparrowhawk, treecreeper, curlew, snipe and meadow pipit are notable whilst badger, hedgehog and wood mouse also occur. There is a wide variety of butterflies such as small copper, orange tip, green hairstreak, common blue and large heath, and several species of damselflies and dragonflies.

T. at Club house.

Crom Castle Estate, County Fermanagh   3

Map 27 H36-24- 1350 acres (547 ha)
4 miles west of Newtownbutler at end of minor road. Oak woods, meadows, reed-beds, open water.

Access   1 April–30 September 2–6 p.m. on foot from CP at H361247.

Information   Leaflets and guides from visitor reception caravan in CP.

History   This estate lies on the shore of Upper Lough Erne amongst the drowned, drumlin landscape which forms a maze of wooded islands, bays and open water. Though 200 acres of old oak woods were felled in the late 1950s and replaced with conifers these are now being removed and new stands of oak planted: several oaks are over 400 years old and are particularly important for their lichens.

What to See   These rich woods contain wood anemone, dog-violet, wood-sedge and sanicle whilst the marshes and open water hold cowbane, marsh pea, marsh fern and frogbit. Birds include sedge, wood and garden warblers whilst butterflies such as purple hairstreak and silver-washed fritillary may be seen.

T[D] near CP. Picnic site.

Wheelchairs have access to some good paths.

Giant's Causeway, County Antrim   4

Map 5 C94-44- 175 acres (71 ha)
2 miles north of Bushmills on B146 Causeway to Dunseverick road. World Heritage Site, NNR. Volcanic rock formations, rocky coast.

Access   AYR on foot from CP at Causeway Head at C942439 onto choice of four coast walks of 1½–5 miles.

Information   Leaflets and guides from Visitor Centre near CP: open daily mid-March–end June, September and October 10 a.m.–5.30 p.m.; July and August 10 a.m.–7 p.m.

History   The Causeway resulted from volcanic activity in the Tertiary period about 60 million years ago. It is formed of approximately 40,000 symmetrical, polygonal basalt columns which jut out of the sea, the result of even cooling through the lava. Waves have cut the Causeway into 3 distinct parts called Grand, Middle and Little. Legend has it was built by the Irish giant Finn MacCool as a stepping stone to Scotland where similar columns occur on the island of Staffa, off Mull, in Fingal's Cave.

What to See   Splendid cliffs produce such plants as sea spleenwort, thyme broomrape, hare's-foot clover, spring squill, spring sandwort and frog orchid whilst oysterplant occurs on the beach below. Fulmar and rock dove nest whilst gannet, guillemot, razorbill, oystercatcher, shag and cormorant may be seen in the air and grey seal in the water. Port na Brock, east of Bengore, is named after the badgers which still live here.

T[D] at Visitor Centre Shop. Refreshments.

Wheelchairs have some access.

Isle of Muck, County Antrim   5

Map 9 D46-02- 14 acres (6 ha)
⅓ mile east of Portmuck Castle off north-east coast of Island Magee, 3 miles due east of Larne harbour. ASI. Nesting sea-birds.

Access   None, except to members of UWT with permits but sea-bird colonies can be viewed from Coast Guard Station at Portmuck.

Information   Nothing on site.

History   This rocky basalt island is long and thin—½ mile long by approximately 100 yds wide with almost sheer cliffs for ⅔ of its perimeter on the south and east sides rising to nearly 100 ft. The plateau top and less steep north and west slopes have some vegetation including elderberry bushes, but have been much degraded by the gull colony.

What to See Guillemot, black guillemot, razorbill, kittiwake, fulmar and shag all breed on the cliffs whilst puffin, greater black-backed and herring gulls have colonies on the plateau. Blackbird and shelduck have also been reported.

Murlough, County Down 6

Map 29 J40-34- 697 acres (282 ha)
2 miles north-west of Newcastle on the south side of A2 to Dundrum. NNR. Sand dunes, mud flats, heath, woods.

Access AYR on foot from CP at J396340 onto network of paths.

Information Leaflets and guides from Nature Centre at CP: open daily June–mid-September 10 a.m.–5 p.m., with guided walks Sun 3 p.m.

History One of only three large sand dune systems in Northern Ireland it has been inhabited by man since Stone Age times. Rabbits were introduced, probably by the Normans, and the dunes were managed as a warren for centuries, The crash of the rabbit population in the 1950s, following myxomatosis, led to the invasion of the dunes by trees and shrubs, notably sea buckthorn which was originally planted: at about this time 1000 Corsican pines were planted near the south end of the reserve where they dominate the landscape.

What to See Pyramidal orchid and burnet rose are a feature of the stable dunes whilst heather, bell heather and many lichens cover the heath inland which also holds shepherd's cress, blue fleabane, bird's-foot and viper's-bugloss. The air is full of birds: in summer four species of tern and six species of gull are regularly seen with occasional skuas, gannet, fulmar, cormorant and shag whilst shelduck, red-breasted merganser, heron, kingfisher, reed bunting, stonechat and whitethroat breed in the area. Winter brings common scoter, velvet scoter and long-tailed duck and various divers and auks.

Picnic site in CP.

Peatlands Park, County Armagh 7

Map 19 H90-60- 625 acres (250 ha)
7 miles north-west of Portadown immediately north of Junction 13, the Loughgall exit, on the M1 motorway from which it is signposted. Part NNR. Bogs, woodland, lakes.

Access AYR on foot from CP at entrance at H901600: a narrow gauge railway, with three stops, begins nearby.

Information Leaflets and guides from Visitor Centre near CP: open daily (except Christmas Day) 2–8 p.m. or dusk, if earlier. The Centre has exhibition of history and natural history of peatland: guided walks, bog garden.

History An area of parkland planted with pine and rhododendron and used for hunting, shooting and some turf cutting until it was acquired by the Irish

Peat Development Company in 1901. Peat was cut commercially until the late 1960s and extracted through 10 miles of narrow gauge railway. Now half the area is occupied by two NNRs, Annagarriff and Mullenakill, the former the site of a lake drained in 1938. Both have areas of oak/birch woodland with hazel and yew.

What to See   Interesting plants include marsh clubmoss, bog-rosemary, round-leaved sundew, alder buckthorn, cottongrass, Royal fern, greater spearwort and cranberry whilst many species of butterflies occur such as wood white, orange tip, small copper, common blue, speckled wood, wall and large heath. Badger, hare, red and grey squirrels occur and newts and lizards may be seen. Waterfowl nesting in the area include mallard, teal and tufted duck.
   T[D] in CP.
   Wheelchairs have access to good tracks and railway.

Portstewart Strand, County Londonderry   8

Map 4 C80-36- 106 acres (43 ha)
1 mile south-west of Portstewart. ASI. Sand dunes, saltmarsh.

Access   AYR on foot from car parking space on the Strand.

Information   NT Visitor Information: open daily June–August 11 a.m.–6 p.m.

History   Traditionally a place for picnics and bathing attracting over 1000 cars daily which threatened the irreversible erosion of these impressive dunes. However, with excellent wardens, path creation and the banning of motorbikes by NT their future is secured and much is now protected especially at the west end distant from the road where there is a small area of saltmarsh beside the River Bann.

What to See   Interesting sand dune plants include burnet rose, Scots lovage, smooth cat's-ear, yellow bartsia and bee orchid whilst the rare dwarf spike-rush forms large colonies in sandy mud near the River Bann mouth.
   T[D] at Portstewart end. Shop. Refreshments.
   Wheelchairs have good access to beach and seaward end of dunes.

Quoile Pondage, County Down   9

Map 21 J49-47- 490 acres (198 ha)
1½ miles north-east of Downpatrick via A25 towards Strangford. NNR. Scrub woodland, reed-beds, marsh, open water.

Access   AYR on foot from CP at Quoile Castle at J487471.

Information   Leaflet and nature trail guide from Visitor Centre in CP. The Centre has a display on the history and wildlife of Strangford Lough.

History   A tidal barrage was built on the Quoile Estuary 1 mile down river from Downpatrick in 1745 and a second 1½ miles further down in 1957. The area between has since changed from being a tidal estuary to a freshwater lake and marsh with ash, oak, birch, broom and hawthorn scrub on the upper shore.

What to See   Several species of willow and their hybrids occur which are host to a rich insect fauna. Many woodland and wetland birds occur including 12 species of duck, golden plover, knot, dunlin and bar-tailed godwit in winter and breeding heron, cormorant and great crested grebe in summer. Fox, stoat, badger and otter are sometimes seen.

T[D] at Visitor Centre and at Quoile Quay to the south. Picnic site. Wheelchairs have access to reserve from CP.

Strabane Glen, County Tyrone   10

Map 12 H35-98- 27 acres (11 ha)
1 mile east of Strabane. Wooded glen, clearings, cliffs.

Access   AYR on foot from parking space on B49 at H356998 via farm track through two gates onto path along the bottom of the glen.

Information   Maps and other information from UWT.

History   This steep-sided valley with prominent cliffs and a bottom strewn with glacial boulders is ¾ mile long: much is covered in hazel, wych elm, ash, birch, rowan and scrub oak but there is a clearing in the middle, the site of an old hunting lodge. Lundy's Cave is supposed to have been used by Captain Lundy when fleeing from the siege of Londonderry in 1689.

What to See   On the valley floor yellow iris, marsh-marigold, bog stitchwort, wavy bittercress and greater tussock-sedge occur whilst the woodland holds foxglove, devil's-bit scabious, trailing St John's-wort, wood-sorrel and bugle with polypody and navelwort on the rocks. The crags are the nesting site of birds of prey, such as peregrine, and raven and a good list of mammals includes badger, stoat, red squirrel, mink, wood mouse and pygmy shrew.

The Umbra   11

Map 4 C72-35- 74 acres (30 ha)
1 mile west of Downhill on north side of A2 from Coleraine to Limavady immediately west of level-crossing. ASI. Sand dunes, dune slacks, damp woodland.

Access   AYR on foot from parking space at C724355 through two gates next to a small cottage onto footpath.

Information   Leaflet from UWT.

History   Part of the largest area of unspoilt dunes in Northern Ireland. Near the sea they are dominated by sand couch and marram and are constantly shifting but, further back, they become stable and covered with mosses and lichens with abundant blackthorn and burnet rose. Hollow 'slacks', which have standing water in winter, hold many marshland species. Along the southern edge a damp woodland of alder, ash and willow has developed.

What to See   A unique feature is the extensive area of Corsican heath in the dune slacks, originally planted but now spreading. With it grow grass-of-Parnassus, adder's-tongue and marsh helleborine. Several other orchids occur including early marsh-orchid, bee, pyramidal, fragrant and frog. Prominent birds include buzzard, cuckoo and jay with fulmar nesting on cliffs: rabbits abound but fox, badger and mink also occur.

GLOSSARY

Acid rock—rock which breaks down to produce acid soil

Acid soil—soil where the pH is usually under 5.0

Acidification—process of water passing through the soil removing nutrients and lowering pH

Ancient woodland—woods which have covered a site continuously since AD 1700 or earlier

Basic rock—rock which breaks down to produce a basic soil

Basic soil—soil where the pH is usually above 7.0 with plentiful calcium, magnesium, potassium and/or sodium

Brachiopod—a marine animal with two shells called lamp shells: remains are frequent in rocks from the Cambrian period onwards

Calcareous—soil or rock in which the most abundant base is calcium

Clay—Boulder—clay of glacial origin often containing nitrates and phosphates
—Kimmeridge—clay of Upper Jurassic period, younger than Oxford
—London—clay of Eocene period
—Oxford—clay of upper Jurassic period older than Kimmeridge
—Wealden—clay of Cretaceous period

Coppice-with-standards—woodland which is generally coppiced but leaves a number of trees to grow for timber

Coppiced—trees or shrubs cut off near ground level every few years and growing again from a stool

Deciduous—of leaves which fall in the autumn

Epiphyte—plant growing on another plant for support but not for food

Eutrophication—enrichment of a water body by input of organic material or inflow of water containing nitrates and phosphates

Flush—area of boggy vegetation where water seeps out of a hillside

Glaciation—grinding of rocks and the movement of material by sheets of ice in glaciers which grow when winter snowfall exceeds summer melt

Igneous—rocks formed from the solidification of molten material breaking through the earth's crust

Marl pit—hole in the ground from which marl, a lime-rich mudstone, has been excavated

Oolite (oolitic)—limestone made of tiny eggs from the middle Jurassic period

Pedunculate—of flowers or fruits, having a stalk attaching them to the stem

Polyzoan—small, colonial marine animal feeding by tentacles and sheathed in a gelatinous, horny or lime-rich case

Post-glacial clay—clay left by glaciers over the land surface when they have melted and retreated

Rocks—Cambrian—505–570 million years old
—Carboniferous—286–360 million years old
—Cretaceous—65–144 million years old

—Eocene—38–65 million years old
—Jurassic—144–213 million years old
—Ordovician—438–505 million years old
—Pre-Cambrian—over 570 million years old
—Triassic—213–248 million years old

Salt marsh—low-lying vegetation by the sea subject to periodic inundation by salt water

Scree—loose rock on a mountain slope

Sessile—without a stalk

Shingle bar—narrow strip of shingle built up by waves at right angles to their direction

Spoil heap—pile of rock or other waste material in a quarry

Tufa—a usually lime-rich sedimentary rock formed by evaporation from aqueous solution

USEFUL BOOKS

British Wildflowers. Franklyn Perring and Max Walters. Macmillan.
Butterflies and Day-flying Moths of Britain and Europe. Michael Chinery. Collins.
Butterflies of the British Isles. J.A. Thomas. Hamlyn.
Excursion Flora of the British Isles. A.R. Clapham, T.G. Tutin and E.F. Warburg. Cambridge.
RSPB Guide to British Birds. David Saunders. Hamlyn.
The Age of the Earth and *Britain Before Man.* Geological Museum, London.
The Birds of Britain and Europe. Hermann Heinzel, R.S.R. Fitter and John Parslow. Collins.
The Dragonflies of Great Britain and Ireland. Cyril O. Hammond. Harley.
The Macmillan Field Guide to Bird Identification. Alan Harris, Laurel Tucker and Keith Vinicombe. Macmillan.
The Mammals of Britain and Europe. Gordon Corbet and Denys Ovenden. Collins.

OTHER
ORGANIZATIONS

FORESTRY COMMISSION (FC), 231 Corstorphine Road, Edinburgh EH12 7AT. 031 334 0303.

LONDON WILDLIFE TRUST, 80 York Way, London N1 9AG. 071 278 6612/3.

NATURE CONSERVANCY COUNCIL (NCC), Northminster House, Peterborough PE1 1UA. 0733 340345.

NCC regional offices:

England

East Anglia 60 Bracondale, Norwich NR1 2BE. 0603 620558.

East Midlands Northminster House, Peterborough PE1 1UA. 0733 340345.

North-East Archbold House, Archbold Terrace, Newcastle-upon-Tyne NE1 1EG. 091 2816316/7.

North-West Blackwell, Bowness-on-Windermere, Windermere LA23 3JR. 096 62 5286.

South Foxhold House, Thornford Road, Crookham Common, Newbury RG15 8EL. 063 523 8881.

South-East Zealds, Church Street, Wye, Ashford TN25 5BW. 0233 812525.

South-West Roughmoor, Bishop's Hull, Taunton TA1 5AA. 0823 283211.

West-Midlands Attingham Park, Shrewsbury SY4 4TW. 074 377 611.

Scotland

North-East Wynne-Edwards House, 17 Rubislaw Terrace, Aberdeen AB1 1XE. 0224 642863.

North-West Fraser Darling House, 9 Culduthel Road, Inverness IV2 4AG. 0463 239431.

South-East Research Park (Avenue 1), Riccarton, Edinburgh EH14 4AP. 031 449 4933.

South-West The Castle, Loch Lomond Park, Balloch G83 8LX. 0389 58511.

Wales

Dyfed-Powys Plas Gogerddan, Aberystwyth SY23 3EE. 0970 828551.

North Plas Penrhos, Ffordd Penrhos, Bangor LL57 2LQ. 0248 370444.

South 43 The Parade, Roath, Cardiff CF2 3UH. 0222 485111.

NATIONAL TRUST (NT), 36 Queen Anne's Gate, London SW1H 9AS. 071 222 9251.

NT regional offices:

England

Cornwall Lanhydrock, Bodmin PL30 4DE. 0208 74281/4.

Devon Killerton House, Broadclyst, Exeter EX5 3LE. 0392 74287.

Wessex Stourton, Warminster BA12 6QD. 0747 840224.

Southern Polesden Lacey, Dorking RH5 6BD. 0372 53401.

Kent and East Sussex Estate Office, Scotney Castle, Lamberhurst, Tunbridge Wells TN3 8JN. 0892 890651.

East Anglia Blickling, Norwich NR11 6NF. 0263 733471.

Thames and Chilterns Hughenden Manor, High Wycombe HP14 4LA. 0494 28051.

Severn Mythe End House, Tewkesbury GL20 6EB. 0684 850051.

Mercia Attingham Park, Shrewsbury SY4 4TP. 074 377 343.

East Midlands Clumber Park Stableyard, Worksop S80 3BE. 0909 486411.

Yorkshire Goddards, 27 Tadcaster Road, Dringhouses, York YO2 2QG. 0904 702021.

North-West Rothay Holme, Rothay Road, Ambleside LA22 0EJ. 05394 33883.

Northumbria Scot's Gap, Morpeth NE61 4EG. 067 074 691.

Wales

South The King's Head, Bridge Street, Llandeilo SA19 6BN. 0558 822800.

North Trinity Square, Llandudno LL30 2DE. 0492 860123.

Northern Ireland Rowallane, Saintfield BT24 7LH. 0238 510721.

NATIONAL TRUST FOR SCOTLAND, 5 Charlotte Square, Edinburgh EH2 4DU. 031 226 6922.

ROYAL SOCIETY FOR NATURE CONSERVATION (RSNC), The Green, Witham Park, Lincoln LN5 7JR. 0522 544400

ROYAL SOCIETY FOR THE PROTECTION OF BIRDS (RSPB), The Lodge, Sandy SG19 2DL. 0767 680551.

RSPB regional offices:

Scotland

17 Regent Terrace, Edinburgh EH7 5BN. 031 556 5624.

Wales

Frolic Street, Newtown SY16 1AP. 0686 26678.

URBAN WILDLIFE TRUST (Birmingham), Unit 213, Jubilee Trade Centre, 130 Pershore Street, Birmingham B5 6ND. 021 666 7474.

WILDFOWL AND WETLANDS TRUST, Slimbridge, Gloucester GL2 7BT. 045389 333.

WOODLAND TRUST, Autumn Park, Dysart Road, Grantham NG31 6LL. 0476 74297.

INDEX